HF335389

ENDURE

The Diaries of Charles Walter Stetson

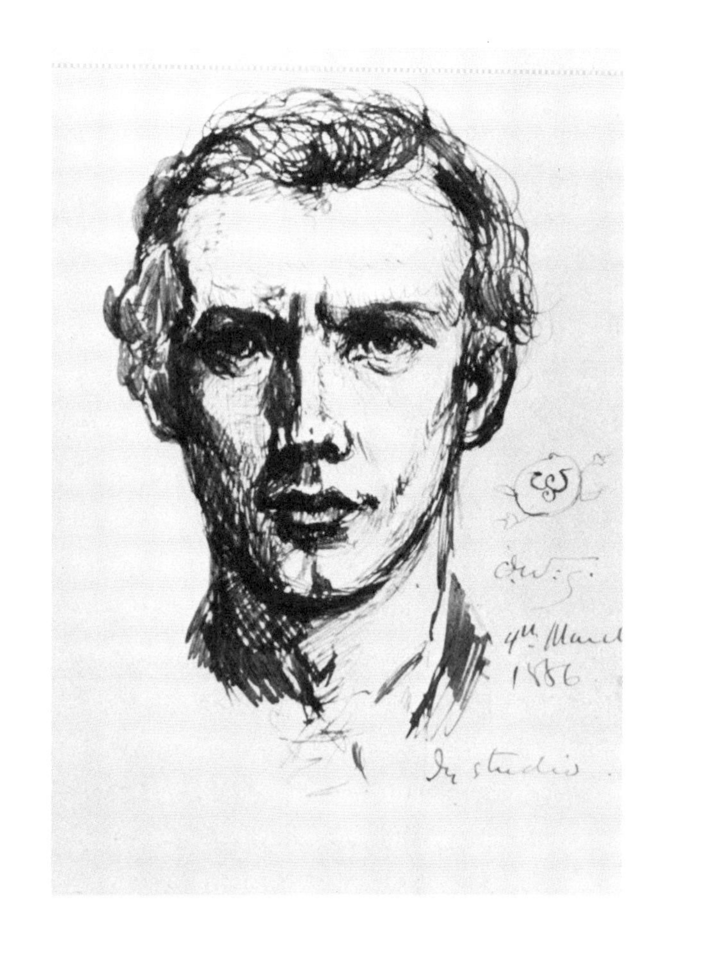

4th March
1886.
In studio.

ENDURE

The Diaries of Charles Walter Stetson

Edited by Mary Armfield Hill

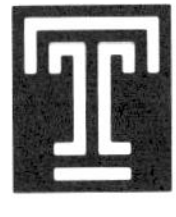

TEMPLE UNIVERSITY PRESS
Philadelphia

FRONTISPIECE: Self-portrait of Charles Walter Stetson, 1886, ink on paper (8⅛ × 5¼ inches). From the David Goodale Collection, Santa Cruz, Cal.

Temple University Press, Philadelphia 19122
© 1985 by Temple University. All rights reserved
Published 1985
Printed in the United States of America

Library of Congress Cataloging in Publication Data

Stetson, Charles Walter, 1858–1911.
    Endure: the diaries of Charles Walter Stetson.

    Includes paraphrased conversations and direct quotations from letters of Charlotte Perkins Gilman.
    Bibliography: p.
    Includes index.
    1. Stetson, Charles Walter, 1858–1911.   2. Painters—United States—Biography.   I. Hill, Mary Armfield.   II. Gilman, Charlotte Perkins, 1860–1935.   III. Title.
ND237.S7A2   1985   759.13 [B]   84-23963
ISBN 0-87722-373-4

In Memory of
DAVID GOODALE
and
SARA PRATHER ARMFIELD HILL

CONTENTS

Illustrations   xi
Preface   xiii
Introduction   xvii

CHAPTER I

. . . time healed the wounds
August 1883   3

CHAPTER II

. . . how blest in friends
October 6 – December 29, 1881   7

CHAPTER III

. . . a new heaven on earth
January 1 – February 6, 1882   23

CHAPTER IV

. . . it is hell to live thus
February 8 – March 21, 1882   43

CHAPTER V

. . . of tender love and selfish struggle
March 22 – August 12, 1882   61

CHAPTER VI

. . . something mighty stirring
August 14 – October 9, 1882   85

CHAPTER VII

. . . spirits plot and counterplot
October 11, 1882–January 19, 1883   109

CHAPTER VIII

. . . the sickness of hope deferred
January 27–April 2, 1883   131

CHAPTER IX

. . . how I cling to Art
April 4–April 25, 1883   157

CHAPTER X

. . . the binding promise
April 26–June 16, 1883   175

CHAPTER XI

. . . the curse of poverty
June 18–July 28, 1883   199

CHAPTER XII

. . . etchings and exhibitions
July 30, 1883–March 13, 1884   217

CHAPTER XIII

. . . petty exactions of a domestic sort
August 18, 1884–September 8, 1885   257

CHAPTER XIV

. . . and she shall someday preach
September 10, 1885–October 27, 1886   287

CHAPTER XV

. . . spasms of horror
November 18, 1886–July 20, 1887   317

CHAPTER XVI

. . . to her I say God speed
August 4, 1887–June 15, 1888   345

Index   367

ILLUSTRATIONS

Self-portrait of Charles Walter Stetson — frontispiece
Charlotte Perkins (Stetson) Gilman — 31
A Country [?] *Justice of the Peace* — 87
Drawing of unidentified faces — 103

FOLLOWING PAGE 180:

Susanna and the Elders
May Dance
Fog Coming at Sunset, Baddeck, Cape Breton
Charlotte Perkins (Stetson) Gilman
Charles Walter Stetson, 1885
Charles Walter Stetson, ca. 1900
Katharine Beecher Stetson (Chamberlin)
Grace Ellery Channing (Stetson)
Rebecca Steere Stetson (mother of Charles Walter Stetson)
Joshua Augustus Stetson (father of Charles Walter Stetson)
Diary page, July 30, 1888
After the Bath
Katharine with Pomegranates

Katharine — 278
Drawing of Katharine in high chair — 294
Drawing of Fleur de Lys Building, Thomas Street,
    Providence, R.I. — 296
Lullaby — 326
Drawing of unidentified faces — 336

PREFACE

THIS BOOK owes its existence to my dear friend, the late David Goodale, who not only enthusiastically encouraged me to publish the Stetson diaries, but also generously shared his scholar's trove of Stetson data: the "Opera" Book, the Grace Channing letters, numerous personally transcribed letters, sketchbooks, photographs of Stetson paintings, and scrapbooks of Stetson articles and reviews. Equally important, David shared his passion for this project, and my deepest regret is that he did not live to see it in published form.

The publication of these diaries was possible also because of the kind support and permission of Dorothy and Walter Chamberlin, granddaughter and grandson of Walter Stetson and Charlotte Gilman. Each time I made a trip to Pasadena, Dorothy Chamberlin generously helped me to work through an additional collection of letters, sketchbooks, paintings, and photographs that she and Walter Chamberlin jointly own.

Charles Eldredge, Director of the National Museum of American Art at the Smithsonian, facilitated this project in a number of ways. His superb biographical and artistic study, *Charles Walter Stetson: Color and Fantasy*, was enormously helpful, as was his generosity in sharing his rich collection of Stetson slides and documents, answering my endless questions, and also offering corrective suggestions on the manuscript itself. Without his expertise and sustained interest it would have been difficult to proceed.

Another enthusiastic supporter of this project was Marian Bowater, who recently purchased and restored a large number of Stetson paintings for the Bowater Gallery in Los Angeles. She generously supplied color transparencies for a number of the illustrations in this volume, shared some invaluable Stetson information, and also assisted through the sheer force of her love for Stetson art.

I wish also to thank the staff at the Arthur and Elizabeth Schlesinger Library on the History of Women in America for their efficient and generous help in answering questions and in locating materials from their unusual and rich collection of Charlotte Perkins Gilman papers. Quotations from the Gilman diaries and the reproduction of the Gilman photograph are made with their kind permission.

I am grateful also for the permission given by the Rhode Island Historical Society to quote from Walter Stetson's Art Club Lectures and from the letters of Charlotte Perkins to Martha Luther.

For permission to publish the color illustrations of Stetson paintings in this volume, I would like to thank the following: Marian Bowater of the Bowater Art Gallery, Los Angeles, for *Susanna and the Elders*; Julia C. Goodale of Santa Cruz, California, for *Katharine with Pomegranates*; Joseph K. Ott of Providence, Rhode Island, for *Fog Coming at Sunset*; Dr. and Mrs. Rodney E. Sanneman, Burbank, California, for *May Dance*; the National Museum of American Art, Washington, D.C., for *After the Bath*; and the Topeka Public Library for *In Grief*.

I have received financial and professional assistance from a number of sources. A grant (primarily for work on Charlotte Gilman) from the National Endowment for the Humanities (1980–81) was helpful on this project, as was a fellowship (1981–82) from the National Humanities Center, Research Triangle Park, North Carolina. I am thankful particularly for the almost idyllic environment at the Humanities Center. The superb research facilities, the first-rate secretarial staff, the constantly stimulating dialogue with scholars and friends—all made for a memorable and special year. I am particularly grateful for the advice and support of William Banks, William Chafe, John Clark, John Hope Franklin, Vincent Franklin, Harvey Gross, Paul Murphy, and Anna Nardo. A number of members of the staff were also very helpful, especially Kent Mullikin, Rebecca Sutton, Alan Tuttle, Karen Carroll, Madeline Moyer, and Jan Paxton.

Needless to say, I owe much to many people unnamed here; but those whom I thank most directly must in no sense, of course, bear responsibility for any mistakes of the final work.

Bucknell University also generously offered support for this project. I am grateful for a sabbatical leave in 1981–82, a summer research grant in 1983, and also additional funding for typing and proofreading assistance. I want also to express my appreciation to the numerous Bucknell friends and colleagues who so generously supported me, though not all can be listed here. For a close reading of my introductory essays, I especially thank Katherine Warner, Vice President Frances D. Fergusson, Professor Mark Neuman of the History Department, Professors Gerald Eager and James H. Turnure of the Art Department, and Mary Ann Wingate of the Bucknell Writing Center.

To Professor Gerald Cooke of Bucknell University, collaborator and supportive friend, I would like to offer a very special word of thanks. At every stage of the manuscript's progression—from the initial meetings with David Goodale, to the first exciting readings of the diaries, through the years of painstaking research, editing, and writing—he has been helpful beyond measure.

Also, the Bucknell librarians, most especially Sharon A. Malecki and Nancy S. Weyant, answered countless questions and tracked down numerous details. Ruth Snyder, Secretary of the History Department, cheerfully gave many hours to proofreading and editing tasks. And Bucknell students repeatedly supported this project as well. Michele Yenser and Gretchen Scales helped to find obscure citations; other students volunteered their proofreading skills; and still others, privately as well as in the classroom, cheered my spirits and inspired my growth.

My friend Mary Stitely deserves a special thank-you. Not only did she undertake the painstaking task of transcribing and typing the original diaries, but she also helped immensely in countless other ways, and made even tedious tasks seem fun.

I am enormously grateful for the first-rate work of the entire staff at Temple University Press. Most particularly I would like to thank David Bartlett, Jennifer French, and Doris Braendel for their efficiency and thoroughness, their endless patience, and their genuine interest in fostering the progress of the manuscript in every way. Without their encouragement, their solicitude, their top-quality advice, I could never have finished, nor even started, this book.

Lastly I would like to thank members of my family. Despite the real inconveniences and painful disruptions this book has sometimes caused, David and Noelle Porter have been cheerful and loving in ways I will appreciate and remember always. To my parents also, I express my heartfelt thanks: to my father, Thomas E. Hill, for his affection, his encouragement, his example as scholar and human being; and to my mother, the late Sara Prather Armfield Hill, who will always be a central inspiration in my life.

A word about editing procedures. Although my first priority was always to remain loyal to the style and flavor of the diaries, I nonetheless have made some changes. Most important, I have condensed the text by approximately one half. I have focused on those sections that discuss Stetson's art, his reading, his community, and his relationship with Charlotte, and I have omitted material which seemed less important or repetitious.[1] Moreover, I have made occasional minor changes in spelling and punctuation. Rather than use the offensive "sic," I have corrected the rare misspellings and added punctuation where it seemed to enhance readability. Although the dates and chronological headings are of course entirely Stetson's, the chapter divisions and chapter titles (either quotes or paraphrases from the diaries) are my own.

There are two volumes of Stetson's diaries. The first is dated October 6, 1881, to October 27, 1886, and measures $8\frac{1}{4} \times 13\frac{3}{4}$ inches. The second is dated November 18, 1886, to November 2, 1888, and measures $7\frac{1}{2} \times 4\frac{3}{4}$ inches.

In addition to Stetson's diaries, the late David Goodale's collection in-

---

[1] Hopefully, the original diaries will soon be publicly available for research.

cluded four sets of materials, referred to in the notes under the following headings:

GEC to EBK—Grace Ellery Channing (Stetson)'s letters to Dr. Edward Balch Knight, reflecting upon the Stetson diaries. They are identified in my notes by page number as well as by date, since Grace Channing (hoping eventually to publish them herself) collected them into a looseleaf notebook and numbered the pages consecutively.

Stetson Scrapbooks—a voluminous series of articles, clippings, and letters originally collected by Walter Stetson, Grace Channing, and Katharine Stetson Chamberlin, and later organized and preserved in a set of scrapbooks by David Goodale. My citations include all information Goodale (or Stetson and his heirs) provided as to the original source; in some cases only Goodale's transcribed version is available.

Stetson "Opera" Book—a notebook covering the years 1879–1911 and containing records for hundreds of his paintings, sketches, and watercolors. It lists titles, dates, exhibitions, sales, personal reflections, and in many cases the reactions and opinions of his family and friends.

Sketchbooks—small but impressive sketchbooks (11½ × 20 inches) containing a number of informal studies, some of which he later used in major paintings. I had access to only four of these sketchbooks. Others remain in the collections of Julia Goodale and Walter and Dorothy Chamberlin.

The following abbreviations are also used in the book:

A. E. Club—Ann Eliza Club

AESL—Arthur and Elizabeth Schlesinger Library on the History of Women in America, Radcliffe College, Cambridge, Mass.

CAP—Charlotte Anna Perkins (1860–1884)

CPG—Charlotte Perkins Gilman (1900–1935)

CPS—Charlotte Perkins Stetson (1884–1900)

CWS—Charles Walter Stetson

EBK—Edward Balch Knight

GEC—Grace Ellery Channing (Stetson)

PAC—Providence Art Club

RIHS—Rhode Island Historical Society

INTRODUCTION

IN 1912, a large memorial exhibit of the paintings of Charles Walter Stetson began an extended American tour. "Truly remarkable," said a Boston critic. "Never, perhaps, has a one-man exhibition made a more sumptuous and imposing appearance," said a Washington reviewer. Or, as Lena McCauley of Chicago put it, "few pictures convey such majesty and sublimity of feeling." Artist Sydney Burleigh likewise praised the paintings. They were powerfully "original," he wrote, "stamped with [Stetson's] personality, and marked by that distinction which comes from a strong artistic temperament working by its own methods to achieve its own end."[1]

According to most contemporary critics, Stetson's greatest strength lay in the range and vision of his color. "So far as I have seen," wrote Lydia Coonley Ward, "there is to-day in the world of Art no color comparable to his in splendor and beauty." Or, as the editor for the Boston *Evening Transcript* put it, "It is a bold statement, but scarcely a challengeable one that there is no other American painter now living who is Stetson's superior as a colorist." Through color, he wanted to express "love in life," not because it is "indispensable," but because "it imparts to living its supremest interest, its heavenliest hope, its most enduring recommendation." "What is an artist but a lover?" Stetson queried. "And what am I but both?"[2]

Unfortunately, however, it was Stetson's fate to experience a grim and debilitating love. His choice, romantic and unwise, was the beautiful, bright, vivacious Charlotte Anna Perkins. She seemed perfect to him—so energetic, so earnestly ambitious, so rebelliously unlike other women that he knew. But that precisely was the problem, for she was so rebellious she rejected what he thought were ideal women's roles. At first her rebellion was self-

---

[1] John Nutting, "Stetson Memorial Exhibit," *Boston Advertiser*, March 17, 1913, Stetson Scrapbook; "Review of Stetson Memorial Exhibition," *Washington Evening Star*, Feb. 8, 1913, part 2, Stetson Scrapbook; Lena M. McCauley, "Art and Artists," *Chicago Evening Post*, March 19, 1914, Stetson Scrapbook; [George W. Whitaker and Sydney R. Burleigh], "An Appreciation of the Late Charles Walter Stetson," *Providence Sunday Journal*, July 23, 1911, p. 10.

[2] L[ydia] A[very] C[oonley] W[ard], "Charles Walter Stetson: An Appreciation," 1912, Stetson Scrapbook; "The Fine Arts: Mr. Stetson's Pictures in Chicago," reprinted from the *Chicago Record-Herald* in the *Boston Evening Transcript*, March 14, 1902, p. 8; Diaries, April 21, 1883.

destructive. It manifested itself in agonizing ambivalence, suicidal depressions, hysteria, and "madness." But when finally she translated rage into constructive action, Charlotte Anna Perkins emerged as Charlotte Perkins Gilman, the "Marx and Veblen" of the women's movement, though also an exasperatingly complicated human being. According to one critic, she was "the leading intellectual in the women's movement during the first two decades of the twentieth century." Suffragist organizer Carrie Chapman Catt called her the "most original and challenging mind which the movement produced." *Women and Economics* (1898), one of her major works, would be translated into at least six languages, go through more than half a dozen printings, and serve as a bible for suffragists and feminists for years.[3]

But all that was the achievement of Charlotte Gilman in her later years, after her divorce from Walter Stetson, after the tale this diary tells. In this volume (covering the years 1881–1888), we see Charlotte Perkins at a different stage, agonizing through courtship, marriage, and motherhood, with Walter patiently trying to endure. And although Gilman later would document the story more professionally and analytically—in her impressive fiction (most particularly "The Yellow Wall-paper"), in her hard-hitting poetry ("it was written to drive nails with"), and also in some pathbreaking full-length books—Walter's diaries have a special interest because they describe it in the raw.[4]

Admittedly, it was my interest in Charlotte Gilman's life and work that first led me to Walter Stetson. When writing my biography of Gilman, I never came to know him fully, though I read his letters in scattered manuscript collections, interviewed his daughter Katharine Stetson Chamberlin and his granddaughter Dorothy Chamberlin, and talked with relatives and friends. But I had never read his diaries. The beginning of my friendship with the late David Goodale marked the turning point. Art lover, Whitman scholar, close friend of the Stetson family, Goodale had acquired the Stetson diaries in the mid-1960s and for a number of years had planned to write a Stetson biography himself. In 1980, however, his health was failing, his progress was painfully slow, and he decided to offer his Stetson materials to me: not only the diaries, but also photograph albums, early sketchbooks, family letters, and scrapbooks of Stetson essays and reviews. Without question, my commitment to this project was inspired first by David Goodale: by his affection, generosity, and confidence, by his intellectual rigor and excitement, by his passion for the world of literature and art.

While David Goodale served as an early and enthusiastic collector and admirer, recently Stetson has again attracted national attention. In 1982,

---

[3] Andrew Sinclair, *The Emancipation of American Women* (New York: Harper and Row, 1965), p. 272; Alice Rossi, ed., *The Feminist Papers: From Adams to de Beauvoir* (New York: Bantam, 1978; 1st pub., 1973), p. 568; Mary Gray Peck, *Carrie Chapman Catt: A Biography* (New York: H. W. Wilson, 1944), p. 454.

[4] "The Yellow Wallpaper" was first published in 1892 as "The Yellow Wall-paper." An interview with CPS, quoted in the *Topeka State Journal*, June 18, 1896.

there was a travelling exhibit of Stetson's paintings (sponsored by the Spencer Museum of Art, the University of Kansas, and the National Endowment for the Arts). Charles Eldredge, Director of the National Museum of American Art, prepared an unusually detailed exhibition biography and catalogue. And in the early 1980s Marian Bowater, of the Bowater Art Gallery in Los Angeles, purchased and restored a large collection of Stetson works. I hope that the publication of these diaries will not only augment his artistic reputation, but also, through his private musings, reveal him as a fascinating and impressive human being.

Of course Stetson never dreamed his diary would be published. It is so totally his private work—his "comfort," his "refuge," his "old friend," or, as he also wrote, a "system of drainage or sewage for this microcosm," his "anodyne for over excited organs." It is "my one place of outpouring that replies nothing." "God pity whoever reads and misjudges."[5]

Although Stetson kept his diary as a tool for private living—trying to clarify his focus, to control his feelings, to claim importance for himself—along the way he became a master in the nineteenth-century art of diary-writing. Articulate, well-read, eloquent, he was perceptive, keenly attuned to dramatic fluctuations of feeling in himself and others, and also remarkably generous in sharing his perceptions. Many diary entries are depressing, to be sure. Creating a persona or alter ego, Walter sometimes tried to control or even stamp out "inappropriate emotions," or used self-flagellating tactics to mold himself according to "manly," "noble" ideals. He was determined to be earnest and hard-working, to be patient, loving, and forgiving always, to "endure" despite the cost. But what is remarkable is that he would succeed so grandly, not in crushing out troublesome emotions, but in sustaining energy and drive. "God is leading me," he wrote. "The spirit that pervades all is developing my soul. I have every reason to believe that in the end I shall be a master."[6]

Born in Tiverton Four Corners, Rhode Island, on March 25, 1858, Walter Stetson never knew a happy home. Uprooted constantly, his family faced agonizing economic worries, repeated illnesses, and an atmosphere of "crushed ambition" and cheerless defeat.

For one thing, his mother, Rebecca Steere Stetson, was habitually ailing. She had a "naturally sensitive" and "affectionate bright nature." She was

---

[5] Quotations in the diaries are taken from April 27, 1886; Oct. 9, 1885; June 16, 1883; April 27, 1886; April 16, 1883.

[6] Diaries, Nov. 15, 1881.

"wonderfully patient and good," but she was also "warped and embittered by poverty and dark struggle." As far back as Walter could remember, she grimly and "calmly" accepted "woman's lot," always "doing the same things, seeing the same things, and I know not but thinking the same things from year's end to year's end."[7]

Although Stetson's drive and confidence by no means came directly from his parents, perhaps their misery inspired him, or their disappointments left him straining for opportunities they missed. His father, the Reverend Joshua Stetson, had been a Freewill Baptist minister during the Civil War years; then he briefly studied medicine; and by the time the family moved to Providence (in his mid-fifties) he was developing and selling herbal cures and patent medicines. But never quite successfully. He was a man of "eminently good parts," in Walter's view. He could have had an "honorable large place" as a "powerful and famous" preacher. Or, had he been where art was cared for, he might have been a painter. But since he had almost no encouragement or opportunity, his talents were "overgrown with . . . weeds" instead, and with family cares and worries. He was "trodden down by what he *could* not throw off," Walter wrote; "his feeling of duty to his children silenced all that he wanted for himself." Besides, his father was so "impractical." He had "beautiful sentiments" and "unusual brains," but "because of his ideality," his "fear of hurting someone," his generosity and "lack of business ability," "he accomplished nothing."

No wonder Stetson admired his father and yet resisted his example. Stetson, Sr., was so "eminently Christian," so "pitiful," "so patient." "My heart aches for him," Walter wrote, but "I am wondering if my life is to be a counterpart or likeness" of his. "Crushed ambitions," "dwarfed acquirements," family burdens and incessant debts—"God No! If I grow maddened Hell shall revisit earth once more—I shall grow mad if my end is not accomplished."[8]

Yet the young Stetson had no money, not even enough for food, much less for paint, canvas, or models, or leisure time to learn his craft. And he had virtually no formal schooling either, nor art school training, nor drawing lessons. Yet by age 19 he had started painting to sell. Stark necessity compelled him. No wonder lack of money was at first his diary's most persistent theme. "Money! I hate it," he wrote resentfully, the "shame" of trafficking in art, groveling to sell a painting, begging for loans. He did not dream, of course, that paintings even of these early years would later hang in the Smithsonian and other significant collections. What he resented, and what for the moment mattered more, was that the city of Providence—one of the richest of its size in the country—cared more for industry and profit than it

---

[7] Diary quotations about Rebecca Steere Stetson are from Jan. 19, 1887; Feb. 12, 1883; Feb. 2, 1882.

[8] Diary quotations about the Reverend Joshua Stetson are from May 13, 1882; Jan. 18, 1885; Aug. 14, 1882; May 13, 1882; Feb. 12, 1883; Sept. 9, 1885; Jan. 19, 1887.

did for art. Even "Raphael would be unknown" in "this stupid little town," he quipped.

Here people are calves and wolves & sheep. They have no love of art, no feeling for it, no knowledge of it, and even do not take interest enough in it to persecute one. It is a damnable place for a fellow like me, that's sure. And here are men too with hundreds of thousands who might almost be Lorenzo de Medici, and by demand inspire us anew and keep us up to a high enthusiasm, make this city famous and beautiful, and get glory to God and themselves. They are too content with their dinners and cotton. And I doubt if it will ever be much different. It comes of the blood.[9]

Although Stetson hated businessmen's scrambling for profit, he nonetheless usually respected and admired wealth. Moreover, he didn't like reformers, especially "moral meddlers" in matters of "political economy" or "affairs of state." He enjoyed discussing aesthetic questions, or reflecting on the work of literary giants—Shakespeare, Milton, Dante Gabriel Rossetti. But he had little patience for the kind of dead-end questions political reformers raise: why some have wealth to spare while others scrape along in poverty, why some have rich cultural exposure while others have to work before they have a chance to learn. Such questions have no answers, Stetson argued. One endures, regardless.

Actually, in his more despairing moods, Stetson tried to shape some answers for himself, and not all of them stressed patience and submission. Occasionally he attributed inequalities to unpredictable and higher powers, to an accident of fate, to God's design. But far more frequently, he felt that failure or success was personally deserved. One must be a "Man," he thought, hard working and nobly earnest, as though good men were necessarily rewarded, and as though he really thought Horatio Alger myths were true. It wouldn't be the first time, of course, that political perspectives had shaped a personality and character; the American Dream, the work-ethic promises, seem so beautifully attractive for the economically successful, and so cruelly crushing for those who fail. No wonder Stetson took himself so seriously, fearing idleness, fearing failure, fearing joy. And no wonder too that he was prematurely middle-aged. If, as one art critic observed, he was "born a young old master," he was also born a young old man. "Ah, to have boyhood's bounding spirit and wide golden visions of a near future! And I am but twenty-five! I—twenty five and feeling so aged that I must cry for past spirit."[10]

While Stetson's duty-oriented ethic repeatedly inspired some heavyhearted grimness, it had its compensations, especially since he actually assumed that he was on the winning side. In fact, he seemed to use his agonies and burdens as a proof of manhood. That led to arrogance at times, to isolation, occasionally to a grim intolerance for the "uninspired." It also helped

---

[9] Diaries, July 21, Oct. 27, 1883; Jan. 14, 1887; July 10, 1883.

[10] "Art Modernity," *Philadelphia Record*, Jan. 5, 1913, Stetson Scrapbook; Diaries, Aug. 8, 1883.

solidify determination and sustain his drive. For whether by choice or temperament, Stetson remained startlingly ambitious to untangle life's complexities, to see clearly, to love fully, to thrust his vision into art. Isolated and aloof though he sometimes was, he tried to be an artist according to his own ideal. "The real artist," he wrote, "is a soul of fire in a form of marble. *Within must be intensest passion, without, profoundest calm,—the result of will. This alone makes creation possible.*"[11]

Very likely it was this kind of push for soul-soaring Emersonian intensity that helped produce the special genius, the "range of color vision," the "majesty and sublimity of feeling" that art critics so often praised. Stetson's work was a "reflection of a superhuman soul," said one reviewer; he "saw life steadily and saw it whole."[12]

Not that Stetson always had enjoyed such glowing affirmations. In fact at the time we come to know him through the diaries, he was quite familiar with barbs and hostile quips as well. One reviewer said his early work was "kittenish." Another called it "artistic gush." Still another felt that his "original feeling for color" might merit "favorable mention" if "done in stained glass," but on canvas was "not even decorative." Even well-intentioned critics were often seriously discouraging. Stetson's paintings were "too good" to sell, said one particularly polite and gentle one; buyers preferred "incident and anecdote" to quality.[13]

Whatever the fairness of such comments, Stetson's early work did have a major problem: his colors were "sensuous" but he couldn't draw. Both friends and critics warned him of the problem, of his "careless and often faulty" techniques. But how could he find time and money for further study?

[U]nder my circumstances, I must make the semblance at least of pictures, or I shall die of utter poverty. If I spend my time at simple studies of head & arms & legs & breasts and hands, and feet and bellies and thighs and backs and shoulders and hair and eyes & the rest who will pay the bills?

"It is more than true that I cannot draw," he continued.

. . . But how am I to get out of the mire? They tell me I'm in up to my neck and stand on the shore and cry unto me to get out. No rope is thrown—or else it is one of sand.

. . . How to buckle down to the drudgery as long as I have my living to get I don't see: and no one who is questioned can tell me. They all say: get the money & go abroad, and do nothing but draw for a year or so. Who tells me how to get the money?[14]

---

[11] CWS, "The Price of a Picture," A. E. Club Lectures, Club Papers no. 118, June 19, 1890, p. 2, RIHS.

[12] W[ard], "Charles Walter Stetson: An Appreciation"; McCauley, "Art and Artists."

[13] Diaries, Dec. 11, Nov. 18, 1881; Sept. 12, 1883; Sept. 25, 1882.

[14] Unidentified clipping, *New York Times*, Feb. 25, 1888, Stetson Scrapbook; Diaries, March 16, 1883; Nov. 25, 1882.

Again and again the diaries expose the intense frustrations Stetson faced—no money, no models, no chance to follow the obviously apt advice. Yet surprisingly the diaries show a mounting pride: "If I could draw—America would have an artist, I know."[15] For one thing, he was getting some public confirmation even in his early twenties. Several of his paintings were accepted at major eastern exhibitions: at the Boston Museum of Fine Arts, the Boston Art Club, the Pennsylvania Academy of the Fine Arts, the Philadelphia Society of Artists, the American Art Association. Also some wealthy and influential patrons began offering support—lending money, buying paintings, sending monetary gifts. It never was enough for uninterrupted study, or models, or European travel. But at least occasionally he had enough to pay the bills.

Undoubtedly the most important early patrons were the extraordinarily warm and friendly Mr. and Mrs. George B. Cresson. Repeatedly they appear in Stetson's diaries, giving him money, inviting him to Philadelphia and Nova Scotia, introducing him to financially well-placed friends—to mill-owner William B. Weeden, for instance, who loaned him money for a studio. Also, Isaac Comstock Bates (of the Comstock Packing Firm) became a "guardian friend" who bought hundreds of Stetson works. And finally there was the professional and financial support of art collector and industrialist Beriah Wall. In 1884, Wall commissioned Stetson to make etched copies of some modern French masters (Daubigny, Decamps, Corot, Couture) for a catalogue of his private collection.[16]

Although Stetson felt that Providence, Rhode Island had decided disadvantages for artists—obviously it couldn't compete with Paris or Rome—in fact it had some striking benefits. It was surrounded by natural beauty; Boston and New York were easily accessible; and most important it boasted a thriving artist colony. Stetson and other struggling artists worked together almost daily, painting from nature, or from casts, or from each other, copying borrowed paintings, criticizing one another's work, debating the ideas of Ruskin or Rossetti until the small hours of the night. To be sure he did not have the contacts or professional exposure he might have had in larger cities; but he didn't have his ego crushed by giants either, or his originality curbed by standard practices, or his flexibility discouraged by deadly drills. Young, inexperienced, lacking formal training, he became a founding member of the Providence Art Club, was repeatedly elected to its executive committee, and was also regularly asked to arrange annual exhibitions and one-man shows.

Local legend has it that George Whitaker was "dean" of the art community in Providence. Originally encouraged by George Inness, he had

---

[15] Diaries, March 8, 1882.

[16] Mrs. Cresson was the daughter of the prominent American sculptor Daniel Chester French. Diaries, Sept. 22, 1885. The Museum of Fine Arts, Boston, has a set of etchings Stetson did of the Beriah Wall collection.

studied in France and was impressed particularly with the Barbizon painters of Fontainebleau. Subsequently Whitaker became a founding member of the Providence Art Club, one of the first oil painting teachers at the Rhode Island School of Design, and also one of Stetson's closest hiking and sketching friends.

Another of Stetson's colleagues and confidants, and another founding member of the Art Club, was Afro-American artist Edward Bannister, bronze medal winner at the 1876 Philadelphia Centennial.[17] Still another was landscape artist Sydney Burleigh. Not only (in Stetson's view) was Burleigh "one of the very best of water colorists of the country," but he was also a leading sponsor of the pioneering Art Workers Guild.[18] Burleigh designed the artistically impressive Fleur de Lys studio building in Providence, and became Stetson's co-worker on a number of other innovative projects in the decorative arts. Lithographs and etching, pen and ink drawing, cloth dyeing, wood burning and carving, marble cutting and tapestry work—such variety typified the art community in Providence. No wonder Stetson was so often praised for his flexibility and variety of artistic techniques. At one time or another he was familiar with them all.

On October 6, 1881, Stetson started working on these diaries: reflecting on artistic aspirations, on colleagues' efforts, on books in vogue. And only three months later, on January 14, 1882, he began to emphasize another theme as well, his evolving love for Charlotte Anna Perkins. Later she would be Charlotte Perkins Gilman, best-selling author, pungent lecturer, flamboyant wit. But for now, she was Walter's choice as the embodiment of feminine ideals. The incongruities are striking: a charismatic national celebrity linked to a man who didn't like reformers; a "radical feminist" committed to an artist whose images of womanhood conformed exactly to those she later would condemn. Why this tragic combination? And from what mistaken motives did these vastly different personalities converge?

In some respects, Charlotte Anna Perkins and Charles Walter Stetson had a lot in common. Both were hard-working and ambitious. Both were self-educated and well-read. And because both also came from miserably unhappy families, they lacked sufficient tenderness in childhood, assumed adult responsibilities at an unusually early age, and thus very likely turned to one another with unhealthy if complementary needs. In any case, Walter sensed, and it was no doubt true, that in Charlotte he had met a woman very

---

[17]The National Museum of American Art at the Smithsonian owns a number of works by Edward Bannister. Many are included in the 1985 exhibition *Sharing Traditions: Five Black Artists in Nineteenth-Century America*, sponsored by the National Museum of American Art.

[18]CWS, "The Studio: Sydney Richmond Burleigh," unidentified clipping from the Providence press, ca. 1892, Stetson Scrapbook.

like himself. "Were you made a man you were not much different from Charles Stetson." [19]

Charlotte *was*, of course, in some respects "masculine" according to the conventions of the time. And no wonder. She was born into a family for whom conventional sex-role expectations didn't fit. She was a Beecher. Whereas most nineteenth-century women were taught "true womanhood" ideals—to be pious and pure in self-sacrificing service to their families—Charlotte was taught, by example anyway, to be a self-assertive reformer instead. Among her relatives, calmness and conformity were the exception, innovative eccentricity the norm. Harriet Beecher Stowe, best-selling novelist, was Charlotte's great aunt, as were nationally known suffragist crusader Isabella Beecher Hooker and authoritative writer Catherine Beecher. Thus Charlotte's female models were fiery abolitionists when women were expected to be peaceful; physical fitness enthusiasts when they were supposed to faint; and prolific public writers when most women occupied themselves at home.

Charlotte's parents were clearly less successful than her famed Beecher aunts and uncles, but they were no less eccentric by the standards of the times. Charlotte's father, Frederick Beecher Perkins, was a drifter. He loved brandishing ideas, but hated formal schooling. He attended Yale, but never graduated. He studied law, but never practiced it. Finally, he tried teaching for a while, then wrote some essays and short stories glorifying home and family life. Yet, when problems with his own wife and children mounted— unpaid debts, crying dying babies, endless domestic chores—he insisted on his "right" to leave. For women he preached self-sacrifice and duty, but for himself he proclaimed an "instinct" to be free. [20]

Charlotte's mother, Mary Westcott Perkins, was thus a rebel by default. Forced to raise two children by herself, to move from relative to relative, to worry about money, about her future, about contemporaries' scorn, she was understandably cheerless, hard-working, and stern. No wonder Charlotte's childhood years were ones of deprivation, discipline, and coldness. She was never cuddled or loved enough by her busy disapproving mother, probably because Mary, like Walter's parents, was so miserably depressed herself.

Although Mary Perkins faced her troubles with unbending toughness, her daughter—to judge from early diaries and letters (1876–1880)—energetically resisted her mother's heavy-hearted style. She learned to "fight fire

---

[19] Diaries, Jan. 29, 1882.

[20] Frederick Beecher Perkins' attitudes are apparent in his own writings. See, for example, Frederick Beecher Perkins, "Childhood: A Study," in *Devil Puzzlers, and Other Studies* (New York: G. P. Putnam's Sons, 1877), pp. 136–140. Frederick and Mary Perkins had two children who survived infancy, Thomas Adie Perkins (b. May 9, 1859) and Charlotte Anna Perkins (b. July 3, 1860). Thomas Henry Perkins was born on March 15, 1858, and died in April that same year. Julia de Wolf Perkins was born January 29, 1866, and died the following September.

For discussion of Charlotte's relationship with her mother, see CPG, *The Living of Charlotte Perkins Gilman: An Autobiography* (New York: Harper & Row, 1975; 1st pub., 1935), pp. 51–69. See also Mary A. Hill, *Charlotte Perkins Gilman: The Making of a Radical Feminist, 1860–1896* (Philadelphia: Temple University Press, 1980).

with fire," "to seek perfection in everything," to become so competent, in fact, so independent and precocious, that she removed herself even further from the cuddling and protective love she craved.

Moreover, since her father was distant and her brother unsupportive, Charlotte sometimes felt compelled to give her mother both financial and emotional support. Having studied briefly at the Rhode Island School of Design, she painted advertisements and greeting cards to sell occasionally, and gave art lessons to younger women. She ran a small day school for "young scholars" with her mother, to say nothing of helping Mary with domestic work. Despite recurrent mother/daughter warfare, Charlotte often felt responsible for Mary, and pitied rather than respected her. The pressures were painful, to be sure—an adolescent taking on adult responsibilities— but the experience confirmed a sense of self-sufficiency that in later years she was reluctant to surrender.

In some respects, the harsh realities of Charlotte's family situation were very like her future husband's. But there were fundamental differences, particularly in the style of their response: whereas Walter tended to absorb misery and grimness into the very structure of his personality, Charlotte usually managed to ward them off with humor and *joie de vivre*. "Have taken a fancy to work hard and be very smart," she wrote. "Let us call good reading solid food; novels candy, poetry fruit—and nonsense the peanuts of life." Also she enjoyed calls and callers, delighted in the local sleigh-ride parties, romped flirtatiously up and down the hills of Providence with "kissing cousins" and perspicacious friends.[21]

Whereas Walter was a loner, easily intimidated by the prominent and wealthy, Charlotte, while remaining economically impoverished, was perfectly comfortable with the upper middle class. One of her closest friends was Grace Channing, granddaughter of the famed Transcendentalist and Unitarian clergyman William Ellery Channing. (Grace would later be Stetson's second wife.) Another was Ada Blake, daughter of Brown University physics professor Eli Whitney Blake. And a third was the "gentle, lovely, intellectual" Martha Luther. In the spring of 1881, Charlotte and Martha entered a "compact of mutual understanding." They agreed never to "'put on' any pretense of feeling," never to allow "the slightest falsehood or deceit," and then—just before Martha left Providence for the summer holidays— they gave each other "lovely little red bracelets with gold across," to be worn as a "badge, ornament, bond of amour." For the next few months Charlotte wrote her almost daily, sometimes ten-, fifteen-, twenty-page letters at a time. "Can't you cuddle me a little? My pet! Fancy me strong and unassailable to all the world beside, and then coming down and truckling to you like a half-fed amiable kitten!"[22]

---

[21] CAP, Diaries, March 26, 1887, AESL.

[22] CPG, *Living*, p. 48; CPG, unpublished autobiography, ca. 1920, p. 54, AESL; CAP, Diaries, May 14, 1881, AESL; CAP to Martha Luther, Aug. 1, 1881, RIHS.

To Charlotte, as to so many nineteenth-century women, there was a basic equality in female friendships that relationships with men so often lacked. Hugging, kissing, commiserating, sleeping unashamedly in one another's beds, they enjoyed what Carroll Smith-Rosenberg has called a "Female World of Love and Ritual," an essential source of "integrity and dignity which grew out of women's shared experiences and mutual affection." Or, as Charlotte put it, "The freedom of it! The deliciousness! The utter absence of 'how will he take it?'! Never again will I admit that women are incapable of friendship." In fact, to compare the letters Charlotte wrote to Martha with later ones to Walter, the differences are striking. The Martha letters have a cheerful energy, an openness, a consistent confidence which in retrospect seem understandable: for, with Martha, Charlotte didn't have to compromise ambition, blunt her "masculine" assertiveness, or assume the burdens of a nineteenth-century wife.[23]

The close phase of their relationship ended in the winter of 1881 when Martha became engaged to Charles A. Lane. Charlotte later said that the pain of losing Martha was the longest-lasting, the deepest she had ever known. Her diary entry at the year's end reads:

A year of steady work. A quiet year and a hard one. . . . A year in which I knew the sweetness of a perfect friendship and have lost it forever. . . . Most of all I have learned what pain is, [and] have learned the need of human sympathy by the unfilled want of it. . . .[24]

In facing her burdens, Charlotte tried turning to her standard sources of support: her self-improvement projects, her physical fitness programs, her reading. In the past, she had experienced occasional depressions, to be sure. But almost always she had managed to control them, rarely thinking, as Walter did, that suffering was God's way of testing, or misery the road to strength. By the winter of 1881, however, her mood fundamentally had changed: she had lost her confidence that ambition was compatible with happiness.

In part it was because both Charlotte Perkins and Walter Stetson were so miserably unhappy—both trying to cope with insecurities and disappointments, both needing friendship and support—that at this juncture their two unhappy lives converged. In early January 1882, just after they first had met, Walter already felt the magnetic force of love. She is "original," "eccentric," and "unconventional," he exclaimed, and also "moral, intellectual and beautiful." "She has a form like a young Greek & a face also resembling a cameo. She is an athlete—strong, vivacious, with plenty of bounding blood. She is an indefatigable worker—but I shall see some of her." A week later, Charlotte also recorded her reaction, but with more reserve. "Mr. Stetson calls. We are left alone, and have a nice talk. I introduce myself as fully as

---

[23] Carroll Smith-Rosenberg, "The Female World of Love and Ritual: Relations Between Women in Nineteenth-Century America," *Signs* 1, no. 1 (Autumn 1975), pp. 9–10; CAP to Martha Luther, Aug. 13, 1881, RIHS.

[24] CAP, Diaries, Dec. 31, 1881, AESL.

possible, and he does the same. We shake hands on it, and are in a fair way to be good friends." [25]

Walter Stetson's diaries were fundamentally shaped by his relationship with Charlotte. They begin only months before he first met her, and they end roughly at the time of separation. Walter the artist, Charlotte the writer and reformer, both struggled with their work commitments and their inordinately ambitious private goals. They worked so conscientiously toward ideal family images, Walter hoping to succeed as the protector and provider, Charlotte as the proper wife. It was almost as though they applied "work ethic" determination to their most intimate relationships, so energetically did they embrace the elevated, romantic imagery common to their generation, so keenly did both aspire to "Victorian" masculine and feminine ideals. If only people were rewarded for their good intentions, surely they would have been a prize-winning pair.

From the very outset, however, Walter was more passionate and eager, Charlotte more doubtful and restrained. Only seventeen days after their first meeting she recorded in her diary, "I have this day been asked the one great question in a woman's life and have refused." Two days later she wrote "An Anchor to Windward."

This is for me to hold to if, as I fore-fear, the force of passion should at any time cloud my reason, and prevent or benumb my will.

Now that my head is cool and clear, now before I give myself in any sense to another; let me write down my Reasons for living single.

In the first place I am fonder of freedom than anything else. . . .

I like to have my own unaided will in all my surroundings—in *dress, habits, diet, hours, behavior, speech,* and *thought.* . . .

I like to be *able* and *free* to help any and everyone, as I never could be if my time and thoughts were taken up by that extended self—a family.

If I were bound to a few I should grow so fond of them, and so busied with them that I should have no room for the thousand and one helpful works which the world needs. . . .

I am cool, fearless, and strong; and have powers which can do good service in proper circumstances if I can only trust in them and coming opportunity. . . .

For reasons many and good, reasons of slow growth and careful consideration, more reasons than I now can remember; I decide to *Live*—Alone.

God help me! [26]

Charlotte's independent outlook, which spelled trouble from the start, reappeared sporadically for years: through courtship, then marriage and motherhood, until finally it led to separation and divorce. But at least she never kept her reservations secret. She told Walter bluntly, in letters as well

---

[25] Diaries, Jan. 14, 1882; CAP, Diaries, Jan. 22, 1882, AESL.

[26] CAP, Diaries, Jan. 29 and Jan. 31, 1882, AESL.

as face to face, that she thought herself too self-directing and ambitious to be capable of marriage. At times Walter seemed to hear her, to respect her ambitions, to accept her right to choose. But gradually he began formulating ways to change her mind. From his point of view, she was "burdened" by "unnatural" and utterly unnecessary conflicts. "Yielding and rebellious," she suffered from that "curious, passionate mixture . . . of tender love and selfish struggle."[27]

It was almost as though Walter used the diaries to claim Charlotte, and also to control her. Clearly he meant that she should read them. For by describing his perspectives, by copying her letters and then drafting a response, he could guide her thinking, correct "indelicate" behavior, even direct her to the "proper" books to read. And another motive was emerging half-consciously as well: to preserve a written record of her progress toward his goal. "If our love letters could be printed verbatim, and side by side," he wrote, "there would be a novel of great truth and philosophical worth. It would give the exact relation of the whole minded of both sexes. I would not be at all surprised to know that Malloch's philosophical novels were actual experiences of someone—either himself or another."[28]

Although the diaries, with Charlotte's copied letters interspersed, provide a fiction-like portrait of a remarkable relationship, they by no means do so according to Walter's intent. He hoped, of course, that they would show the truth and beauty of the friendship. But they show some glaring blind spots as well: his anti-woman bias, his sexual double standard, his failure to tolerate in Charlotte attitudes he assumed were essential for himself. In fact, the diaries show a full-scale battle—Walter trying to impose standard lessons of Victorian morality, Charlotte resisting with every ounce of strength.

Take the issue of combining work successfully with marriage: Walter knew perfectly well, for himself, that love and work were both central to his happiness. But what if someday he were forced to choose? Impossible, he wrote. "I feel my whole essence tremble" at the "unwise economy" of a man sacrificing either. A woman's needs, however, were different. Surely "anything that takes woman away from the beautifying and sanctifying of home and the bearing of children must be sin," he wrote. "Every one knows that I believe in the utmost freedom for women but that freedom is false which makes them rebel against the ties of love and home." Charlotte's ambitions thus reflected such a "deep selfishness," he decided, that he must "stop her on her road for fame and 'freedom' . . . [and] show her what a miserable mess of pottage she was exchanging for her birthright."[29]

Moreover, Stetson showed his double-standard expectations on matters of love and sexuality. From his perspective, men necessarily were the mentors and protectors, while women naturally were inexperienced and pure.

---

[27] Diaries, March 22, 1882.

[28] Diaries, May 20, 1882.

[29] Diaries, July 21, March 28, March 22, April 9, and March 28, 1883.

He didn't want Charlotte to attend the Museum of Anatomy in Providence, "that vile show of monstrosities and sin." Nor did he think it appropriate for women to be "contaminated" by male physicians: "I shuddered to think of any physician (male) using an instrument of any sort in my love's holy place." And finally, he did not want her reading freely or finding information for herself. He wanted to be perfectly sure she read about the "holiness" of sexual relations, and not, he insisted, about "the odor of its perspiration, the action of its phallus, the hairiness of sweating breasts"—or any other "delicacies" such as one would find in Whitman's *Leaves of Grass*.[30]

Whatever the nature of Stetson's sexual prejudices or preferences, he was strikingly blunt about the importance of human sexuality itself, and about the force of his own needs: "much of my energy is consumed in trying to subdue the desires thereof—most innocent and sweet desires, in themselves, but most inconvenient and embarrassing when a mate is lacking." Unfortunately, however, someone in the Stetson family—was it Charlotte? or Katharine? or Grace?—felt that Stetson was too blunt. For whatever the reasons, whether because of disapproval, or respect for loved ones' privacy, or simply shock that "Victorians" weren't as tight-laced as is sometimes assumed, the diaries' anonymous censor took pen and ink and repeatedly deleted the "offending" passages, sometimes even taking scissors and cutting entire pages out.[31]

It would be such an irony—this deleting, this crossing out and cutting up of Stetson's diaries—if a loved one deemed them too earthy, too sexually explicit, and thus degrading to human sexuality and love. Instead Walter was trying so earnestly to celebrate and glorify the "soul delight" and "god-like joy" of sex. It did not occur to him that by idealizing women he might be objectifying and thus denigrating them. From his point of view he worshipped Woman as the model of perfection, "the shape of the soul's form," destined "to lead man back to the dignity so sadly lost." Never mind some nagging personal confusions—that Charlotte didn't fit the image, or that nude models for his paintings usually were "damsels of the demi-monde." He still viewed Woman as man's central inspiration: to impel his genius, to love, honor, and serve him in his life and work. "Wherefore should man be so needy of woman?" he wrote. "Is not Art enough? Is not gold enough? Is not sight enough? But what is sight, or gold, or Art when love is not?" In actuality, Stetson's goal was to secure Love and Woman both, to express not only "the loveliness of womanhood & the purity of the sexual relation," but also to solidify the bond between his love life and his art. The secret of "great painters," he wrote, is their "association with beautiful women."[32]

---

[30] Diaries, June 25, July 14, and June 23, 1883.

[31] Diaries, April 5, 1883. Obviously I cannot be sure of the contents of deleted sections, but the context suggests they are similar to other diary reflections, though more vivid and explicit.

[32] Diaries, April 12, 1882; CWS, "The Nude in Art," A. E. Club Lectures, Club Papers no. 19, Feb. 19, 1886, p. 7, RIHS; Diaries, Aug. 19, 1882; April 23, March 24, and March 22, 1883.

Although Stetson, like most artists, or rather like most human beings, might have wanted us to talk about the uniqueness of his aspirations, art historians typically invoke discussion of "context" and "influence" as well. They remind us that Stetson's work should be compared to that of George Fuller, for instance, or Thomas Dewing, George Inness, and James MacNeill Whistler; or to certain German artists; or to the French painters of the Barbizon school; or perhaps even to the French Impressionists. In short, Stetson was very much a product of his times. He admired his predecessors and contemporaries, studied their paintings at current exhibitions, and learned from their techniques and perspectives. And equally important, he shared many of their interests and concerns. As art historian Charles Eldredge put it, "Stetson's art reflects a general *gestalt* as much as specific borrowing," thus providing "a useful gauge of tastes which prevailed" during the last third of the nineteenth century.[33]

According to contemporary critics, Stetson was a Tonalist or Symbolist painter, whose goal was "to heighten the experience of nature," to paint "softly contoured landscapes and figure studies [which] evoke a mood of reverie, nostalgia and unfulfilled longing." Symbolists generally did not care for sharp, brightly sunlit settings; they preferred more delicate and intimate hues, the half-light of dusk or dawn, or the "clearing mist after rain or snow had bleached out sharp contrasts." Also, like Whistler, many were fascinated with nocturnal scenes and lunar imagery; often they combined their meditative landscapes with religious figure painting, with pagan processions and bacchic dances, with nymphs and naiads, with maenads, centaurs, and satyrs. This choice of classical allegory, of primitive fancy that focuses on man's mysterious relationship with nature, was especially typical of contemporary German painters, of Arnold Böcklin, Anselm von Feuerbach, and Hans von Marées. But according to reviewers, some Americans, and Stetson was among them, also did it well. Many "have tried to conjure up the pagan past of Greece and Rome," wrote Charles De Kay of the New York *Times*, "but not one hits the mark as this obscure painter from Rhode Island." A reviewer for the Chicago *Evening Post* describes the Stetson style:

The fancy is carried to the depths of the forest, the dancers to music float in graceful processions and are part of the woodland spirit. Or an ancient retreat lies before us, the red-cloaked recluses haunt the silence, above bend the whispering trees and over all the azure sky arches in indefinite dome, its scant reflection in the pool, a counterpart of pigmy man in comparison with the mystery of life.[34]

---

[33] Charles Eldredge, *Charles Walter Stetson: Color and Fantasy* (Lawrence, Kan.: Spencer Museum, 1982), p. 105.

[34] Wanda M. Corn, *The Color of Mood: American Tonalism, 1880–1910* (San Francisco: M. H. De Young Memorial Museum and California Palace of the Legion of Honor, 1972), pp. 12, 1–2; Charles De Kay, "Three American Painters," *New York Times*, Dec. 12, 1890; McCauley, "Art and Artists."

Typical landscapes of the Tonalists were similar to those of the French Barbizon painters working near the forest of Fontainebleau: Corot, Jean François Millet, Troyon, and Daubigny. Stetson studied them closely. He admired immensely their rebellion against classical conventions, their success in uncovering the casual beauty of the local rural countryside, their view of nature as a private, purely personal experience.

For the Tonalists' goal was not simply to portray "objects of reality." Rather, as one reviewer put it, they wanted to provide "plausible, absorbing experiences of purer and more perfect states of existence," a "vision for the senses of the soul." "What do you mean by 'reality in Art?'" Stetson queried. "Reality in Art lies only in what moves us & can become part of us." It "consists not in what you see and handle, but in what has power to move your soul, so that you feel, having left the picture, that you have truly seen something new." Thus, Tonalists "distilled" the facts they saw, historian Wanda Corn explains. After eliminating the "distracting" ones, they exaggerated those that best heightened and communicated experience, thus creating "a picture of the sea or the mountain seen in a better, finer way" than the viewer can see it for herself.[35]

Through color Stetson expressed his romantic goals most successfully. Like painters generally, the colorist was not merely "copying nature." Rather, he was the "poet" expressing "an emotion of the soul," offering "visible symbols of an invisible reality." He hoped to awaken "tender responses, revive memories of the dusk and the dew, of the light after rain, of the lingering glow of sunset on the eastern trees and hills—of the swift and splendid majesty of breaking storm clouds—or the parting of the darkness at dawn."[36]

More than any other aspect of his paintings, reviewers enthusiastically acclaimed the "sumptuousness," the "purity" and "luxury," of Stetson's color schemes. As his second wife, Grace Channing Stetson, later put it, his paintings were always "filled with color," "the most beautiful hues being given to such things as are loveliest and most precious, until color has become the type of Love and the symbol of Life—Life, sensuous, joyous, wholesome, and fruitful, which changes the gray of death to the bud and blossom of Spring." One reviewer pushed the matter even further. Lena McCauley of the Chicago *Evening Post* claimed that Stetson was "the first of

---

[35] McCauley, "Art and Artists"; Corn, *The Color of Mood*, p. 7; McCauley, "Art and Artists"; CWS to Walter S. Heineman, Viareggio, Italy, July 19, 1903 (original letter first transcribed by Katharine Stetson Chamberlin and then by David Goodale), Stetson Scrapbook; Corn, *The Color of Mood*, p. 5.

[36] CWS to GEC, ca. 1892 (original letter first transcribed by Katharine Stetson Chamberlin and then by David Goodale), Stetson Scrapbook; Grace Ellery Channing-Stetson, *Catalogue of the Memorial Exhibition of Works by the Late Charles Walter Stetson* (Washington, D.C.: Corcoran Gallery of Art, 1913); CWS, "An Artist's Criticism" (review of Eugene L. Smyth exhibition), *The Telegram* (Providence), Stetson Scrapbook.

American impressionists," a bit ironical since in point of fact Stetson didn't like the work of Impressionists at all.[37]

Although Stetson himself used an increasingly bright palette, as a Tonalist he thought Impressionists' theory was "too scientific and analytic," and their paintings "too objective," "gaudy," and "crude." Most Symbolist painters were not interested in optical effects or scientific statements, but rather in the "expressive potential of nature's colors," in the beautiful, the sublime, the silent miracle of nature itself. More subjective and poetic, they offered "ethereal and mysterious symbols of the artist's private musings" in paintings that suggest the "remoteness and interior quality of dreams."[38]

It is sometimes argued that the Tonalists' preference for the "rarified private pleasures of mind and memory" reflected a widely shared alienation from the commercialism, materialism and technological "progress" of their time. Despite his bias against reform, Stetson might even be considered a turn-of-the-century reformer of sorts, hating the greed and profit-scrambling of the Gilded Age, celebrating instead "the quietude of silent days and moonlit nights." Moreover, like many of his Providence associates, he felt alienated from much contemporary or recent art, from the panoramic and grandiose dramas of the Hudson River School, for instance, or from the "wide-angled," "awe-inspiring" vista painting extolling American expansiveness and greatness.

Stetson and his colleagues felt more negative about America's economic and technological success. Highly sensitive and idealistic, they found it threatening to their sense of truth and poetry, and thus turned to art as their refuge and escape. They wanted distance from the public, "from the hard edges of industrialization and the visual pollution of an urbanizing cityscape." And they wanted also a creative means of expressing their disturbing sense of loss.[39]

Tonalists may have been reformers; but they were by no means activists, nor democrats, nor standard-bearers for the common man. In fact, occasionally they argued that the "masses" were "incapable of understanding" art and beauty, while at the same time claiming "divinely granted powers" for themselves. The politically oriented would no doubt criticize them for their romantic obfuscation, their escape from urban industrial realities, their elitist celebration of artistic pleasures usually unavailable to the common man. And some would find fault also with their view of women's needs. Their worship of female nudes was so ironical and often so destructive. For the

---

[37] GEC, *Catalogue*; McCauley, "Art and Artists." For sample enthusiastic reviews of Stetson's color see also Nutting, "Stetson Memorial Exhibit," and "The Fine Arts: Mr. Stetson's Pictures in Chicago," p. 8.

[38] Corn, *The Color of Mood*, p. 8; Eldredge, *Charles Walter Stetson*, p. 53.

[39] For this brief summary of the major characteristics of the Tonalists, I have drawn primarily from the work of Wanda Corn, *The Color of Mood*, pp. 1–22.

women in their paintings rarely possessed vitality or character. Primarily, to put it bluntly, they had seductive charm and sex appeal. Likewise, women in Stetson's landscapes almost always were idealized—"depersonalized, inactive," transformed with "veils of atmosphere." Charles Eldredge notes that "a graceful somnambulent or ritualistic dancer, generally female, usually nude," would wander through the Stetson "dreamscapes"; or two females would be paired "against atmospheric foliage"; or several "diminutive yet significant" women would "disrobe and pose evocatively in the foreground . . . stilled in a moment of poetic reverie." As another viewer tells us less politely, figures are almost always "dissolved in the same murky penumbra as the ponds and fields."[40]

In art, as in love and life, Stetson was the idealist *par excellence*. Viewing women as models of perfection and art the means to find one's God, he preferred image to reality, the conceptual to the perceptual, the "purer and more perfect states of existence" to the tangles of daily life. Stetson wanted to enjoy his "quietude," his "mind and memory" pleasures, his "silent days and moonlit nights." But tragically, he married Charlotte Perkins Gilman instead. Later to become one of America's most dynamic and charismatic women's movement leaders, she was hardly the patient or peaceful type. For a time, she tried conforming to the standard "True Womanhood" ideals. It very nearly killed her. But in her later years she reversed her efforts, and began to attack vigorously the very notions of wife, home, and motherhood that Stetson and his generation so passionately cherished. At the time, most women did not even recognize their problems: a lack of economic independence, a frequent anger and frustration with full-time domestic chores, a tendency toward self-hatred psychologically and sexually. Yet Charlotte Gilman integrated these problems into an impressive feminist philosophy; and each she presented with a clip and style and drama that had a broad appeal.

---

[40] Eldredge, *Charles Walter Stetson*, p. 102; Corn, *The Color of Mood*, p. 2. See the illustration of *Susanna and the Elders* reproduced in this volume. Stetson's treatment of the biblical story of Susanna and the Elders is standard. The two Elders have returned to Joachim's garden to seduce Joachim's wife, Susanna. As art historian Mary Garrard has pointed out, male artists too infrequently have portrayed Susanna as terrified or even frightened by the Elders' advance (potential rape?); instead she is sexually available, even seductive. Garrard writes, "Few artistic themes have offered so satisfying an opportunity for legitimized voyeurism as Susanna and the Elders." It provided "an opportunity to display the female nude," and had the "added advantage that the nude's erotic appeal could be heightened by the presence of two lecherous old men. . . . It is a remarkable testament to the indomitable male ego that a biblical theme holding forth an exemplum of female chastity should have become in painting a celebration of sexual opportunity." Mary D. Garrard, "Artemisia and Susanna," *Feminism and Art History: Questioning the Litany* (New York: Harper & Row, 1982), pp. 149–50.

For instance, on women's economic dependence, she wrote:

We have not as a class awakened to the fact that we have no money of our own.

[W]hatever the economic value of the domestic industry of women is, they do not get it. The women who do the most work get the least money, and the women who have the most money do the least work.

Or on women's domestic service:

If each man did for himself the work he expects of his woman, there would be no wealth in the world; only millions and millions of poor tired men, sweeping, dusting, scrubbing, cleaning, serving, mending, cooking, washing, ironing—and dying for lack of food.

Or on the female personality:

Of women especially have been required the convenient virtues of a subject class: obedience, patience, endurance, contentment, humility, resignation, temperance, prudence, industry, kindness, cheerfulness, modesty, gratitude, thrift, and unselfishness.

Or on "love" as woman's first priority:

We have been told so long that
   "Love is of a man's life a thing apart,
   Tis woman's whole existence,"
That we have believed it. . . . Our whole existence was carefully limited to this field; we were dressed and educated to grace it; we were bloomed out into a brief and glorious career while under inspection and selection before our final surrender, and then we pursued the rest of our lives with varying devotion and satisfaction in this one department of life.[41]

Charlotte had learned some facts of life the hard way. that romantic goals can be poisonous and sometimes fatal, that purportedly respectful ideals too often map out things a woman should and shouldn't do, like earning money, or having a job, or establishing some independence. As in Stetson's painting of the ideal nude, she was to be an object of adoration: beautiful, innocent, and pure, but also starkly prone and passive, impotent, utterly bored with pedestal life. By romanticizing and idealizing women, Stetson was defining them according to his own fantasies rather than according to their interests and needs.

Almost instinctively, Charlotte seemed to recognize the problem long before it came to pass: that "ideal" marriage required capitulation, and she

---

[41] CPG, "Her Own Money: Is a Wife Entitled to the Money She Earns?" *Mother's Magazine* 7 (Feb. 1912), p. 7; CPG, *Women and Economics: A Study of the Economic Relation Between Men and Women as a Factor in Social Evolution* (New York: Harper and Row rept., 1966), pp. 14–15; CPG, "How Home Conditions React Upon the Family," *American Journal of Sociology* 14 (March 1909), p. 598; CPG, *His Religion and Hers: A Study of the Faith of Our Fathers and the Work of Our Mothers* (New York: Century, 1923), p. 134; CPG, "Love Stories and Life Stories," *Woman's Journal* 35 (May 7, 1904), p. 146.

wasn't of the capitulating kind. Repeatedly she warned him, as much "as I love you I love WORK better, & I cannot make the two compatible."[42]

Walter's diaries, peppered with Charlotte's letters, stand as a blow-by-blow account of Charlotte's struggle for survival and Stetson's maneuvers for control. At times he thought she simply was too "selfish" to be thoughtful, too "daring and independent" to consider his "wants and needs." But at other times, he was ecstatically pleased with his results: "Ah! how different from the triumphant conqueror's look of some time ago!" he wrote. "O how that spirit is broken. The false pride is melting before love rapidly." "She wants to be treated more as a child now than a woman."[43]

Unfortunately, the more child-like Charlotte felt with Walter, the more hatred she directed toward herself. "There is no limit to her self-denunciation," Stetson wrote just months before their marriage; "a great spasm of self-abnegation seems to have come over her. She talked of dying until my heart ached." Yet her psychological deterioration continued, as did their wedding plans. The result was Charlotte's descent into madness, "spasms of horror," and "hysteria," which "The Yellow Wall-paper" grimly and starkly describes.[44]

As readers follow Stetson's daily trials with Charlotte, they almost certainly will sympathize with him. They will respect his helpfulness and patience; very likely they will sometimes see Charlotte as the shrew. But also surely they will see Walter's culpability in the equation: his double-standard expectations, his reactions to her illness, his benevolent but condescending and controlling style. For however helpful, patient, generous, kind, and loving Walter clearly was, he nonetheless assumed that Charlotte's breakdown resulted from unnatural inclinations, from her "old ambitious 'freedom'-loving nature rising in rebellion against the 'weakness' of tenderness and love." In retrospect, the double standard seems so obvious. Walter was acutely aware of his own professional frustrations, yet starkly oblivious to reasons for the anger in his wife. It was wrong to be "wasting" his "energy" on household tasks, he wrote, or to misuse the "power" he needed for his art: "Oh how I long to do my work, and how heavy a burden I bear that gnaws so that I cannot do it!" "If it seems to last very long I must hire help . . . for I cannot afford, nor would it be right for me, to give up all my time and strength to such things." Yet when Charlotte expressed parallel frustrations, Stetson decided she must be mad. She was afraid "that her whole usefulness & real life was crushed out of her by marriage and the care of the baby," he wrote. Her "fierce rebellion at the existing state of things" must be symptomatic of her "brain disease."

It calls for tremendous patience and tact. She still rushes in her mind from all our sweet life to try to go out into the world to rid it at one fell swoop of all evil, pain

---

[42] Quotation from an undated letter, CAP to CWS, Diaries, March 22, 1882.

[43] Diaries, March 21, May 20, 1882; and Jan. 19, 1883.

[44] Diaries, Dec. 3, 1883.

and the like. Strange and terrible how such ideas can take possession of one's brain. She forgets that she could do good right at hand, even in our family. Of what account is that to her! She would convert the world.[45]

Without question, Charlotte was impossible at times. And Walter heroically tried to fill the model husband role. He arranged for a maid, sent for her mother, and did many of the household chores himself. Always he was conscientious; in fact, too much so at times, probing for helpful clues in literature and art and poetry, eagerly absorbing the message—rooted in the very subconsciousness of the culture itself—that would so complicate his life. For Walter as well as Charlotte was a victim of destructive sex-based images. His tormented sense of loyalty and guilt and duty, his conscientious response to three generations' needs, his struggle for professional success, to say nothing of his fatherly concern for Charlotte, all resulted from his misdirected efforts to live according to the standard nineteenth-century tenets for the ideal male. Even his weaknesses—his selfishness, arrogance, and self-serving faith—fit comfortably with the Victorian image of the proper husband-father. And while in retrospect these may seem offensive, their sources often lie outside the private man himself, beyond his own control. In any case, Stetson deserves our admiration. Despite all the gnawing problems in his marriage, all the assaults on his ego, all the costs to his career, he still kept faith in Art and Love. "Years ago," he wrote,

my mind was full of pictures which I did not hesitate to try to paint. But now if ideas come as they will at times, I say—How can I? Every cent I get now has to pay bills and must be spent to distract Charlotte from her brooding. I cannot hire models. I cannot buy any of the accessories that I need. I am become in duty bound a mere supporter of a family."[46]

In the fall of 1888, Charlotte and Walter separated. Charlotte left for California with their daughter Katharine, and Walter stayed in Providence to continue with his work. In early December 1888, after holding an auction to sell his paintings (some 101 watercolors and oils), Stetson joined Charlotte in Pasadena to attempt a reconciliation, but by early 1890 it was clear that they would be divorced.

Out of all this agony, however, there was one strangely pleasant, almost bizarre development: Walter's growing affection for Grace Channing, Charlotte's closest confidante for years. Grace and Charlotte had written short stories and drafted plays together. It was to Grace's home in Pasadena that Charlotte first fled the trials of motherhood and marriage in the winter of 1885–86. In the summer of 1888, Grace again served as Charlotte's main support by dismantling the Stetson household, tackling practical responsibili-

---

[45] Diaries, Nov. 26, 1883; Jan. 25, 1885; Oct. 3, 1887; Jan. 25, and Aug. 24, 1885.

[46] Diaries, Aug. 6, 1887.

ties, and responding to emotional needs. Grace must have been a remarkably sensitive and tactful person, for despite the tensions, she managed not only to remain the confidante of both Stetsons, but also to win Charlotte's blessing after deciding to be Walter's second wife. Walter Stetson married Grace Channing on June 11, 1896; four years later, on June 11, 1900, Charlotte Stetson married Houghton Gilman, providing in each case a relatively happy ending to this complicated tale.

What is particularly striking about this triangular relationship is that it continued to be warm despite some powerfully disruptive tensions: from delays and complications in the divorce proceedings, from the scandal reporters tried to cause, from financial responsibilities for their daughter Katharine and where Kate would finally live. There were some inevitable resentments, as will shortly be apparent. But for the most part, they worked them through with remarkable good will. Katharine lived alternately and amicably with both parents, and Grace and Charlotte—sharing a husband and a child—remained life-long friends. After Walter died, on July 20, 1911, Grace and Charlotte became close New York neighbors. And in 1935, when Charlotte was dying of cancer, Grace came to California to share her last few months of life.

Several books could and should be written on the intervening decades. An art historian should trace Walter's professional development. A biographer or two should probe the women's lives.[47] And perhaps a novelist could try to see the story whole. By contrast, however, and with regrets, I only briefly summarize.

From 1890 through 1894 Walter lived in Providence. After his marriage to Grace, he returned to California, this time staying long enough to have Californians claim him as a "native" artist, and also to complete some major works. Stetson's paintings of California flowers are particularly impressive: "At their best," Charles Eldredge writes, "they demonstrate a power of composition and delicacy of execution equal to almost anything of the type being produced in America at the time."[48]

Although Walter loved the skies, gardens, colors, and sumptuous growth of California, only when he later moved to Italy did he find his "natural place." "It was no wonder he loved Rome," Grace Channing wrote, "seeing that he had been painting her all his life." He loved the landscape—"the emerald meadows set with gay figures, the clustered trees, the temples, the fountains and carved seats of stone he had created in his New England attic." And even more he loved the "subtler beauty" and the "spiritual message" Rome conveyed. He was "the heir of his intense Puritan forefathers," Grace continued, "intensely religious," but "merely" more "pagan" in his views.[49]

---

[47] The papers of Grace Ellery Channing-Stetson have recently been purchased by the Arthur and Elizabeth Schlesinger Library at Radcliffe College, and are now available for research.

[48] Eldredge, *Charles Walter Stetson*, p. 58.

[49] GEC, *Catalogue*, pp. 11–24.

Perhaps the two most significant artistic developments in Stetson's "Roman years" were the intensification of his colors to "even more startling . . . combinations," and the changes in choice of theme. Whereas earlier he had focused on grief and suffering, "as the shadow deepened about his own life," Grace wrote, he turned to themes of "health" and "joy." Despite a painful and protracted illness, the pictures of his later years express "serenity and a large repose."[50]

Also, Grace Channing noted, Walter became increasingly withdrawn in Rome, though not because he ever felt unwelcomed. Friends and even strangers came "by the score" to see him at his studio, Grace insisted. "Cordially" and repeatedly he was invited to show his work in Italian exhibitions. Nonetheless, he preferred to be alone, perhaps because his health was failing, or possibly because he suffered from growing deafness in his later years. More likely, Grace acknowledged, he wanted an "excuse for the detached life he loved."[51] In Rome he finally found his peace and solitude. He delighted in the extended visits of his daughter Katharine, and enjoyed the companionship of a few devoted friends, of artist Elihu Vedder particularly. Most important, he finally achieved his life-long goal: a peaceful and satisfying integration of his Art with Love. In Grace Channing he had found a woman who could not only love him fully, but also, without self-sacrifice, respect his commitment to his art. Grace wrote proudly:

Art, for him, was not a profession—but a vocation; not a large prepossession, nor a more or less absorbing occupation, not even the chief business of his life; it *was* life,—his reason for being here, the justification of his existence, and to it he gave the whole of life.[52]

The first attempt to edit and annotate Walter's diaries was begun years ago, in May 1912, by Grace Channing-Stetson. She started the project rather casually, almost accidentally, less than a year after Walter's death. As she was reading the diaries, she began sharing her reactions in a series of letters to a mutual friend, Dr. E. B. Knight—family physician, art patron, and Stetson's confidant for years. Knight was "woven all through" the diaries, Grace told him, and by describing them and quoting them, she wanted to give him a "foretaste" of what she hoped to publish later as a book. "There is so much that is inspiring and of profound interest," she wrote, "not because you and I loved him, but because he was a wonderful human being and because destiny . . . moulded all his days in strange and unusual ways." "Will it not make a

---

[50] Eldredge, *Charles Walter Stetson*, p. 86; GEC, *Catalogue*, pp. 20–25.

[51] Grace wrote: "Three of [Stetson's] canvases were hanging by invitation on the walls of [the Italian] central palace in the International exhibition of 1910, at the time of his death," GEC, *Catalogue*, p. 25. Walter's extended stay in Rome, and also his personal withdrawal, must account in part for the eclipse his reputation suffered in the years following his death.

[52] GEC, *Catalogue*, p. 23.

book for everybody—can you not see already the *human* quality in it—which only very rare souls are ever able to transmit, for themselves?" "But it is *he*—what he *was* that makes the book so great a human document."[53]

As Grace wrote these letters, she was preparing a travelling exhibition of Walter's paintings, collecting and sorting through his major works, and also, of course, mourning deeply. Her sympathetic, respectful, and at times eulogistic response to the diaries is understandable and moving. But what of her reactions to her late husband's love for Charlotte Gilman? What of her thoughts about this national celebrity and long-time friend? Grace must have felt some powerfully conflicting loyalties as she read of Walter's passion, or of the traumas that earlier she had witnessed from Charlotte's side. Clearly she respected Charlotte's public efforts, her theoretical achievements, her long-term fight for women's rights. And certainly she felt Charlotte was among her closest friends. But she felt some deep ambivalence as well, which, despite disclaimers, could not be disguised.

As she reviewed the written record, Grace tried hard to be sympathetic and supportive. Here were "two such wonderful young people" entering "a new heaven on earth," she wrote. "He had found out that she was both 'wonderful and good,'—and she can't have discovered less; they had begun that 'perfect friendship' of which each had dreamed, and which was to mould all their lives—and that of others." In fact, Grace continued:

No one who loves him ought to be able to help loving Charlotte. At the very moment when he so needed a companion and inspiration—she was both to him. He had never known a woman so fine and so capable of nobility and understanding, and through all the ups and downs of the years that followed, before their marriage, which were alternate heaven and hell to him, as she decided she could not live without him or could not live with him (and she changed her mind constantly) yet she remained to him steadily a flame of purity, and however faultful or capricious, was never anything but noble, honest and right-meaning. It is impossible to guess—even though she martyrised him,—what she may have saved him from of worse, with that sensitive imagination, his great need of loving *something*, and only the barren field of Providence (the city) to draw from. She furnished to him constantly a noble ideal and a steadfast purpose, just when both were so necessary to him; and if she very nearly killed him by inches afterwards, still that was not her fault.[54]

Grace's account of this ill-fated friendship is sometimes eulogistic, but also it is often factually sound. Charlotte *was* "faultful" and "capricious." Also, as Grace rightly claims, Charlotte rarely understood the pain that women's freedom sometimes causes men. But still it seems to me that Grace also had her blind spots. For to argue that Charlotte "threw" away "an earthly paradise," an "ideal love" and marriage, sounds a bit too much like Walter's point of view; or alternately, like a posthumous celebration of her own marital success; but in either case not in accordance with the "hysteria"

---

[53] GEC to EBK, May 16, 1912, p. 49; May 19, 1912, p. 66–67; May 16, 1912, pp. 49–50.
[54] GEC to EBK, May 23, 1912, pp. 77–78.

or "madness" Charlotte actually experienced, or with the "love" relationship "The Yellow Wall-paper" describes. It was almost as though Grace had forgotten some fundamental differences in situation. She had been a journalist, a novelist, a professional—all before she married Walter. Equally important, she had learned from first-marriage mistakes. It seems more than likely that Grace managed successfully to hold her own with Walter, to love him without threatening either her career or her identity. But then again perhaps she felt some undercurrents of insecurity herself, for in my view her disclaimers seem a bit too repetitious, and her pity condescending:

Of all the people in this world,—I pity Charlotte most! She had—actually *had* in her very hands, heaven on earth, and threw it away. With youth, beauty, an ideal love who had already made an almost story-book success (the first Boston exhibition was over)—a perfect child, —what had all the world to offer her or any woman more. I love Charlotte very much, and I blame her not at all—as he never blamed her—but I look at her now, when she comes here, still beautiful and full of her own work and interests, and I pity her from the depths of my soul. She was fairly *within* an earthly paradise—once. She was not in the least to blame—not in the very least; but she nearly killed him. And the miracle is that she did not kill his art. That however was indestructible; in the worst of times it still flamed on. The strangest thing is that Charlotte has gone through life with a conviction that *she* was nearly wrecked by that marriage, and without even a passing suspicion that he suffered in any way whatever from it! This is fact.[55]

Although Grace Channing never managed to complete her editing-annotating project, she did leave a fascinating set of letters in the care of E. B. Knight. Respectfully saved by Walter's daughter Katharine, and later by her dear friend David Goodale, they offer a personal perspective on many diary entries. Typically Grace would copy lengthy passages and write comments in response, providing in the process some of the rich data quoted in the footnotes of this book. Fortunately, she also wrote several letters introducing Knight to Walter's diaries. Clearly she was not writing them for publication; perhaps she would have felt them to be overwrought. But in my view they certainly deserve inclusion, for they not only give a special flavor to the diaries, but also provide a very personal foreword for a very personal book.

623 West 136th St.
April 2, 1912.

Dear Friend:

    . . . I have had such a wonderful experience. I have been reading [Walter's] journals—the sealed journals, not to be opened till after his death. . . . What shall I say of them!—I have read all the great self-revelations of famous men, but I never have read anything so wonderful as these. I can't and mustn't say these things to others, but I may say them to you;—sometimes he seems to me the most marvellous being I ever heard of. No wonder he could write letters! From earliest youth he had trained himself to keep these records; they are marvels of literary skill, but they are

---

[55] GEC to EBK, May 6, 1912, p. 32.

infinitely more than that, they are the records, so simply made, of what was surely one of the rarest souls that ever lived. . . . What a life! As I have relived, year by year, his early struggles, his youth and his vivid manhood, I no longer wonder that he could not live longer,—I wonder that we kept him so long as we did. From the very first it is a record of agonies and aspirations,—hope and courage which nothing could overthrow, chained to every conceivable kind of suffering, of humiliation, of hope deferred. What poverty—and what pride;—what misery, and what constant nobility. . . . He always had, you know, the most uncompromising plainness of speech—and it is all there in his pages; everything set down so clearly that you live it yourself;—only no one could ever imagine any soul sent to earth could have thought and felt the things this boy of twenty-two and three did;—or that anything human could have kept such faith with himself, and lived internally so ideal—so absolutely removed and lofty a life as he did, under such circumstances. It is an infinite pity—a pity for the human race, that the books cannot be published as they stand. A great portion can, may and must be published eventually, for it is the history of an artist in a sense that no other book ever written has been, it seems to me. I begin to feel that perhaps this is why I am here and why I was given a gift of writing, that I may do this work for him. Perhaps the book can never be published in my lifetime—or that of some others. As he said in it,—with him Life and Love flow into one another. It would be impossible to write a Life of him and leave out the personal.

The absolute domination of his Art over him, the way in which it *was* him, is beyond belief. The pages actually glow with the fires he felt, and I think it would have killed me to read them, but for one thing. However and wherever I fell short, I believe I never failed him in one thing,—I never lost sight of the artist in him, nor counted anything before his art. He knew that my passion for it was almost as great as his, and I think this was the one comfort I was to him—I worshipped where he worshipped. He knew—he couldn't *not* know how absolute was my faith in his genius, and how everything else in life seemed a little thing to me beside keeping it alight and alive. And for this one reason I can bear to live—if I must. . . .

I have used the words "wonderful" and "marvellous" a great many times in these two pages,—but they are the only words which come to one's mind, in thinking of these journals. Everything in them *is* wonderful—as he was. He could write as well as he could paint and I have no doubt it is strictly true as he says in one place that he was "quite as much a musician as a painter." He speaks of composing music in parts, in his head, and being able to hear it orchestrally. It is not strange he did too truly hear it later on. Love and Art,—Art and Love,—were inextricably woven in him,—and Love to him meant what it means to only one soul in a million souls. He seems to have loved everything,—to have been full of tenderness to every living thing, almost *sufferingly* so.

He was the most gentle and exquisite of beings, with all his indomitable strength of will and power. I thought there was not a tragedy of his life I did not know, not a sorrow, but I feel now as if I had never known anything—when I read the long, long story of his patient, heroic struggle. It was the burden of debt—the never lifted poverty which killed him. If that one thing could have been lifted I believe he would be here now. And he had learned so absolutely to put all things under his feet. It constantly grieved me that he could not have—and would not buy—the things I knew he must crave;—that he had taught himself to do without nearly everything most artists have, (and in fact we both have,)—but when I read in these pages of the delight all beauty gave him, the poignant delight, I feel anew the cruelty which deprived him of even very small bits of beauty. Thank God—he did have Rome,—

Rome which was an incessant joy to him. And we had the voyages—which were perhaps his keenest pleasures of all. The sea and sky were free and he could enjoy them without thinking that it was somebody's rent diverted!—at least after the steamer passage had once been obtained. How I rejoice in everything I compelled him to do of that kind! He would have had *nothing* but for my insistance. And he died—looking forward to one more longed-for voyage. . . .

Faithfully,
G.E.C.S.[56]

NewYork—Thursday (the 23rd)
[May, 1912]

Dear Brother:

I am so glad you continue to enjoy the extracts and I purpose mailing more today. You say it will make a book which will interest many; before I have done with it—it will make a book which will *enthrall everybody*! It will be a wonderful book. It will embrace two continents and include many interesting people, and the material I have to draw upon is so rich. . . .[57]

. . . The thing which first fascinated and drew me irresistably to Walter was a kind of wonderful purity in his attitude toward life and love and every day facts, which he somehow transfigured into ideal things. It was purity like that of fire— vivid and beautiful, and I recognised then and reverenced ever after in him a quality which was all his own and which seemed only to grow brighter and brighter with the years of his life. Surely if anyone knows him,—I do; and I know that with him the ideal *was* the real, and that he did actually attain the things his early records show him striving so ardently for. His frankness was without limit; he was purely Pagan in a multitude of ways; and he was exquisite and lovely in the smallest details as in the largest facts and acts of his life. More and more I grow to have the feeling that he died partly because Life had no more to do for him. We do not see how he could have become more beautiful, more courageous, more selfless and serene than he was in the latter years. And we always had, and frequently put into words, our feeling that he was really living chiefly in some other world—some higher world than the rest of us, even while with us. . . .

We always send our love to you all.

Grace E.C.S.[58]

---

[56] GEC to EBK, April 2, 1912, pp. 1–4.

[57] Grace Channing planned to include discussion of Stetson's years in Italy, but, to the best of my knowledge, no diary material after 1888 is available.

[58] GEC to EBK, May 23, 1912, p. 70.

ENDURE

The Diaries of Charles Walter Stetson

. . . *time healed the wounds*

August 1883

WALTER STETSON WROTE the first diary entry on October 6, 1881, adding the following introduction several years later—August 1883. In it he briefly reviewed some of the reflections and events recorded in a previous diary, asserting hopefully that his earlier despondency, particularly the "ache and terror" accompanying the failure of his first love relationship, would be replaced now by greater happiness and self-respect. Stetson resolved to destroy his early diary, to forget his past, and to pursue instead the two great loves—Art and Charlotte Perkins—which seemed to promise greater "Truth."

The name of Stetson's first love was probably Anne Angell. Unfortunately, most sections of the diary which discuss this relationship have been removed or crossed out.

AUG. "83.

The 939 pp. of my Journal which I burnt were a painfully minute record of the morbid introspection of a strange boyhood and youth, when all the peculiar forces of nature, modified by environment, were working towards fruitfulness. It was a record not only of events—little at first, bitter as wormwood, and blinding as lightening afterwards,—but of all my ideas of the body, of the earth and men, of life, of death, of love, of art, of religion and of

God. There were strange dreams formulated into systems of religion, and accounts of astonishing symbolism and mystic rites performed alone—always alone. I could let no other into my heart and head, life. No one among my young friends could have sympathized, and my elders would have either laughed or gravely thought me mad. It is not at all strange that when one came, a stranger girl, banished from her companions by her father's business failure, from comfort to hardship of poverty that I pitied her. For months I kept aloof though she lived in the same house. But when Summer came with its outdoor pastimes we were brought together. I knew nothing of women save which I had read. I admired them, reverenced them, considered them something much nearer angels than ourselves. I believed them as a whole to be pure. She was soft, yielding, ease loving, lonesome. I conveyed my own heart—life to her by my astonishing property of idealization—a fault. She seemed after that in my eyes everything. She was downtrodden, sad, sick, oppressed by fate, *misunderstood*. The latter touched the tenderest chord. I became her knight. And never lady was served more faithfully. It seemed a *duty*, and as such I clung to it. She was perverse at times; was far from pretty; was ignorant; hated books and science and religion and art. Even at that time I was deeply in earnest about them all. But I felt what I thought to be love for her—and I was 16 years old—and set about to teach her what I knew. Wearing, horrid task! . . . [A] love of an idea I know now, for I loved the same thing after she was gone—but, *love* none the less, though not of her *as* her—the end of all was such heart ache and terror as makes me shudder even now. During that time sickness for myself, terrible sickness for mother with Death always near; the most bitter poverty, with moving from house to house on account of unpaid rent. And I was an artist, tainted, set upon by relations, with insinuations as to my honesty, and tales of my cruelty to my parents. The only comfort in all those black years was the knowledge that I was obeying the God in me, and was faithful to the light I had and to the love I felt, however mistaken it was. In 1877 I was almost crazed, if not quite. No, I must not think of it—. That love affair was settled strangely. I breathed for the first time in five years a *free* breath. Oh how I remember the first night after it! Such sweet sleep!

I'm sure I helped her. I taught her a deal: especially in the direction of physical culture. She loved me as well as she could with the mind she had. An animal love she gave fully, but there could be no happiness born of perfect union. I feel that I made the holiness of love dearer to her, and we did not dishonor it.

Then I was filled with doubts of everything—especially of woman, and hated heartily the shams of the world. Custom I warred with. I was morose, taciturn, but terribly in earnest. All my blessed dreams of golden living vanished completely, only remaining as a faint memory to mock the darkness. I was waging a war with that most dreadful enemy—self, hourly—myself, my desires. All I had cherished lay in ashes.

Time healed the wounds a little: young blood began to build anew. A deep hungering & thirsting for companionship came—for some one who could understand my speech and be glad of a brother like me. Also an aching for something pure to look upon and think of. Sidney brought this to me.* She [Charlotte] was innocent, beautiful, frank. I grasped at her with the instincts of a drowning heart, and—was saved for the time. I loved all that I saw pure in her. She was sweet air for my soul's breathing. She was cleanliness to long for. Yes, I loved her purity of innocence, or perhaps, ignorance of the world. I told her so, I'm sorry to say. It did not harm her— nor me. It was a sort of famished man's cry of thankfulness for bread. My faith in woman began to revive, and my belief in the good of the world. Oh I was brought exceeding low, almost to my heart's decay. But thanks be to God, I revived. This Journal commences just after that.

At last the grandest event of my life came—my Charlotte, holy wifely love! A woman gracious and grand in womanhood. Through her God gave me new power and cleansed all life for me. Beyond words is she. He knows: He will reward her. Would that I might.

I will leave my Journal just as it is without an attempt at relieving it of the passages which point at the weakness of hunger. Charlotte, if she ever reads it, may think me fickle, and weaker than I am. There is a weakness born of a certain kind of strength. I believe that weakness is mine.

My true love and what I am, God will reveal to her some day. And what I appear to be—I will remain, bearing the burden of it until the due time comes. She will not judge hastily: and He will judge correctly and with mercy.

There is peace. I have it now through truth and her.

———————

*Sidney Putnam, a Providence friend, introduced Walter Stetson and Charlotte Anna Perkins on January 12, 1882.

CHAPTER II

. . . *how blest in friends*

October 6 – December 29, 1881

IN FEBRUARY 1878, Walter Stetson, together with artists George Whitaker, Edward Bannister, and Frederick Batcheller, met in Bannister's studio for the purpose of organizing the Providence Art Club. They planned to bring together local artists, patrons, and collectors; to sponsor lectures; to facilitate exhibitions of their paintings; to provide mutual professional and personal support. Frequent meetings followed. They signed their charter for the Providence Art Club (PAC) in April 1880, and in May had their first exhibit in the Hoppin Homestead Building. As the youngest and least experienced of the early members, Stetson would pepper his diary with appreciative notes on club-based opportunities. He noted his talks with fellow artists—George Whitaker, Edward Leavitt, Sydney Burleigh; his contacts with patrons and collectors—Henry Field, Isaac Bates, William Weeden; and his own contributions to club-sponsored events. Despite occasional disclaimers, Stetson clearly was respected by his fellow artists. They included his work in their exhibits, elected him to the club's Executive Committee, and in November 1881 helped him to sponsor his one-man art show.

Meanwhile, however, Walter was only a marginally self-sufficient artist, yet responsible for providing both emotional and financial support for his aging parents. His mother, Rebecca Steere Stetson, suffered from repeated illnesses; and his father, Joshua Augusta Stetson, struggled with unpaid bills and accumulating debts.

In the fall of 1881 Walter once again began a diary—hundreds of narrow-lined, leather-bound, foolscap pages. In it he would explore his artistic commitments, his religious concerns, his needs in love and friendship.

OCTOBER, 6. 1881.

All day I have been very much discouraged. Since I wrote last our affairs have gone very disagreeably. During the summer I got so little money—I can't remember just how little—that I was not the slightest aid to father or mother. Dear man! he bore the strain with wonderful patience, and labored incessantly. True; I labored in my way very steadily, and to tiresome lengths: but his labor was far less pleasant in itself. . . .

Well, so it has gone on. My work has progressed steadily and my pictures for the Nov. Exhibition approach completion. Mr. Bannister* came up Sept. 18. and took tea—a meagre one—and looked at my pictures. I think that I surprised him with the amount of my Summer's work. Some of it he liked and some he did not, thinking it sentimental tho' pleasing in color. Whitaker calls nearly every Sunday on his way from church.† He has encouraged me a great deal. He gave me ten or 15 excellent mahogany panels, which, though small, I have turned to good use, painting some little figures on them with a clearness and force that I have never done before.‡ . . .

OCT. 13. 1881. THURSDAY.

. . . Monday evening was the 3d quarterly meeting of the Club. Though feeling unwell I went. Mr. Bates § came to me quietly and said: "I received a note from Mr. Weeden (WmB.); he wants us to call there this evening. Shall

---

* Afro-American artist Edward Mitchell Bannister (1828–1901), was a winner of a bronze medal at the Philadelphia Centennial of 1876, a founding member of the Providence Art Club, and a well-respected New England landscape artist. A number of his works were recently purchased by the National Museum of American Art, the Smithsonian.

† George William Whitaker (1840–1916), often referred to as "the dean of the Providence artist colony," was a founding member of the Providence Art Club, an early painting teacher at the Rhode Island School of Design, and one of Stetson's closest colleagues and confidants. They travelled together, painted and sketched together, and conferred on Art Club projects. See "The Dean of Providence Artists," *Providence Sunday Journal*, Jan. 10, 1915, Stetson Scrapbook.

‡ Grace Channing later wrote, "One of those little [mahogany] panels, I believe, is on my desk as I write—inscribed on the back—'To my friend, Miss Grace Channing, Nov. '84'—the very first gift he ever gave me, and this must have been on almost the first occasion of our meeting, when I went with Charlotte to see him and meet her fiancé. It is a marvellous scarlet Crusader, kneeling before a shrine,—the precursor of all the scarlet Seminarists of the future. I owe Whitaker a good deal.

"The colour of that little panel has been the admiration of painters for more than a quarter of a century—and the boy was only twenty-three when he did it. It is as beautiful as any colour can be." GEC to EBK, May 15, 1912, p. 43.

§ Isaac Comstock Bates of the Comstock Packing Firm was an early member of the Art Club Executive Committee, a generous art patron, and also a vital force in making the club a

we go or not?" I thought for a moment & decided in the affirmative, as I wanted to know more of Mr. Weeden. After getting Mr. Burleigh to attend to my secretaryship (I was Sec. pro-tem.) we started.* Mr. Weeden received us cordially and ushered us into his magnificent library. Every where were beautiful casts from the antique, good pictures, books, and photographs. Everything was elegant and showed the owner to be a student as well as a wealthy man. We chatted & looked at the works of Art until 10 o'clock. . . .

Mr. Weeden made me promise to call again. But he little expected I think that my next call would be on business. . . .

I have decided to overcome my excessive pride and sensitiveness. As a beginning, I am going to try to borrow $500—of Wm. B. Weeden—on a note!! I *must* have a *studio* downtown; I must have *models*. I shall never have them unless I have a sum of money at once. I wrote him a letter this afternoon asking for an interview. It is sent. There is no recalling it! and though I tremble I must now bear my part. My reason tells me that no harm can come of asking him—that is simply businesslike: that it is no more than right that I should have as fair a start as others, and nearly all I have read of have been helped in the beginning. But my sentiments of independence rebel terribly, and doubtless I shall make clumsy work of asking him. But it *shall* be done! unless something strange happens before I see him. I dare not hope that he will grant my request—I can offer no security, there's the rub.

I am sorry to find that I am growing desperate. My discipline thus far has not been of a kind to sweeten me. I try to be philosophic and trustful, and ever prayerful: but it is true that hunger and illness and continued ill fortune rob philosophy of its strength and make one doubt the benefit of prayer. Would to God my faith were stronger! If I could but live in my ideals all were well; but the real is pitiless.

I hope I shall have strength to push the matter with Mr. Weeden, and to be simply myself, covering no faults.

*　　*　　*

---

powerful influence in the community. From Stetson's point of view, Bates was a "dear, cheering good soul," a kind of "guardian," since he would eventually purchase over a hundred of Stetson's works (Diaries, Sept. 22, 1885).

　*Sydney Richmond Burleigh (1853–1929), another of Stetson's closest colleagues, was an active PAC member and the major designer of the Fleur de Lys building in Providence. In later years, Stetson would rank Burleigh as "one of the very best of water colorists of the country." CWS, "The Studio: Sydney Richmond Burleigh," unidentified clipping from the Providence press, ca. 1892, in Stetson Scrapbook.

Sunday evening I had [a] talk with Mr. Weeden about borrowing $500 — of him and opening a studio. I confess that during the day, and the days before, I was nervous in the extreme: but I knew that I must put the question fairly or be a coward. It was not that I feared what he might do or say, but I did have a foolish dread of his thinking less of me and misunderstanding me. I prayed all day for strength to bear whatever might come. I did not expect that Mr. Weeden would grant my request.

I reached 158 Waterman St. about 8 o'clock and was pleasantly received by him in his library. His family were at home & that embarrassed me a little. He divined it, arose & closed the immense doors. Then I began—how hesitatingly! It was told at length. He received my words very attentively and kindly, and after asking a few questions as to my life and Art he said that he wanted me to be sure that whichever way he decided I had his perfect sympathy. "It is not a matter of $500., but one of conscience with me," he said. "You know that true economy is true philanthropy: if it is a public want I should not hesitate to expend several times that sum, but if it is not it should not be spent." And to save me I could not make out how he was to ascertain if the public wanted me. He illustrated by examples that were familiar to me from my study of political economy, but truly I could not comprehend how the public could tell if it wanted a man's work until the work was done. However it was all very kindly put and *earnest*, and put the thing in a new, if obscure, light to me.

He said: "I am satisfied that you ought to go no further without instruction. It were well if you could study in Europe, but if that cannot be done there is the Boston Museum School." I showed him that it would cost as much to study there as in Europe. "Well, I'll look into it, and come up this week to look at your pictures." As I was going out he said: "It's a pity you could not have the proper instruction. Anyone can see that you have a true artistic spirit, a feeling for color, and a—I can think of no other word than 'go'." Then he continued: "With proper training and favorable circumstances there can be no doubt but that you would quickly reach a place where you should have no need of help from anyone: but whether you will ever go further without that instruction is in my mind doubtful." He bade me goodnight pleasantly, told me to come again and look over photographs with him—and I had gone with a fluttering heart.

He gave me a great deal to think of; and I am sure that the seed I sowed in his mind can bear no bad fruit: but that he will advance me the money is very doubtful as he will probably conclude that I am not "a public want." What *does* that mean? I am awaiting his visit with considerable anxiety: *but the thing is done*!

Yesterday afternoon, as it was so dark I could not paint, I called on Bannister. He was blue enough. He had not heard from certain parties upon whom he was somewhat dependent for his European trip, and things had gone awry considerably. I tried to cheer him up. He is my only confidant in Art matters & I am his—so I told him about my affair with Mr. Weeden.*
He prophesies great good to me from it, and extols Mr. Weeden's character in a way pleasant to hear. But he failed to understand the "public good" part. . . .

OCT. 21. 1881. FRIDAY.

Yesterday was eventful. . . . I had just finished my work for the day when Mr. Weeden called. . . .

Well, I showed Mr. Weeden my pictures and am glad to say that he was sensible & criticized them very impartially, pointing out what he thought defects with unflinching hand yet not quite leaving the good points unmentioned. Then he began the momentous subject. After some questions as to what I would rather do and some others indirect by which I think he managed to learn my idea of Art he said: "Well, I will do what you desired." I was much surprised & disappointed. I could not express my thanks, and he said it was not necessary. "It is only fair that you should have a start, Mr. Stetson, only fair," he said. I told him that I wished that he had more faith that I would accomplish something. "I have no doubt of it Mr. Stetson. I

---

* Following this diary entry, Grace Channing noted that there had always been something especially "beautiful" in Walter's friendship with Edward Bannister, "the elder painter of that tragic race," but that there had been a sad irony as well. For although her father (scientist and inventor William Henry Channing, son of the Unitarian minister William Ellery Channing) had known Bannister quite closely, Walter, for some reason, was never introduced. Grace wrote: "And here comes the thought which comes so often—Bannister was often in my home,—my father often in his studio. My father sought out and made a friend of every coloured man he could, in his profound sympathy for their wrongs and handicaps. Was it not strange—like a destiny—that with all that Walter and I never met! Bannister could so easily—(it would have been much more natural than *not*)—have brought him to our house. My father was always helping young artists—our house was full of them, as of young scientists; he would have been capable of sending Walter to Europe, of doing for him all the things I knew him to do for so many. He actually impoverished himself thus." GEC to EBK, May 15, 1912, p. 45.

will send you a check for $200. tomorrow and another for $200. the first of January." I asked him what interest he would charge me. With one of his fascinating smiles he said: "The interest won't trouble you—don't worry about it. If it's only paid in a reasonable time it will be allright." Further said I, will you tell me what is a reasonable time? With another smile he said, "When you can pay it as well as not." Then after some indifferent chatting he (with great politeness!) left. I could scarcely contain myself. . . .

MONDAY EVE. OCT. 31. 1881.

All the week past I have been getting things together preparatory to moving into my new studio, Room 4, 35 N. Main St. I found it a very weary-ing piece of business, running hither and thither so very much besides wor-rying about the things to be bought. And yet there was pleasure in it.

Withal I have not been well, and if the truth were known I am tonight as brokenhearted as any mortal that lives. Not but that—things have gone well enough as regards my furnishing & materials, but it makes me sad to think that it may make mother lonely to have me take all my things away from the house and to be away from it so much myself.* I can see that it already begins to affect her. I am homesick already. . . . Ham[ilton Mac-Dougall]† is so occupied with his music recitals that I see him little, and when I do I fail to get that sympathy from him I would like. Not, God knows, but what he is anxious for my welfare and would do almost anything to aid me, as I would for him, but his way of thinking daily diverges, I fear, more and more from mine. . . .

I am very lonely with no one who can understand me. Sometimes and often I feel that I must be very weak and sentimental to be so easily affected by everything. I know that it stands greatly in the way of my prosperity, but I cannot wish myself of harder heart. . . .

Tomorrow I move into my room.

The past week seemed more than long.

---

*Following this entry, Grace Channing commented, "That tenderness, which was suffer-ing, in him, informs every page of his journals, as it did every act of his life. Nobody realised how he loved his people, and what he suffered for and with them, and how the most joyous moments of his life were always and forever clouded and shadowed by his inability to make them too quite, perfectly happy." GEC to EBK, May 15, 1912, p. 47.

†Hamilton MacDougall, one of Stetson's closest friends, was an amateur musician from a well-to-do Providence family.

I have an overwhelming feeling of my bitterness and of the small value of what I have done. The more I read of great artists & poets the more perfectly I see that I am in complete sympathy with them: at the same time it depresses me when I think of how much is to be done & how little I have done. Think of it! Regnault was but four years my senior when he died. And what a record he left.* And there are others. Suppose that I should die to-morrow—my parents would be sorry, and Ham and one or two more perhaps. What else? *Absolutely* nothing! I have painted nothing, written nothing that deserves to live.

God almighty! Shall I?

I wish father & mother were happy! †

NOV. 15. (TUESDAY) 1881. 9:15 P.M.

. . . The pictures which I have in this exhibition (which opened tonight with a Reception) are my best.‡ They tell me that I have improved a great deal in the past year, and it is true. If nothing happens they can say the same a year from now. Models! Leisure! Money! I could not attend the Reception tonight as I had nothing suitable to wear. Those present would not enjoy themselves so well if reminded of my poverty by my old coat. . . .

I do not write a tenth of what I wish to say because my work makes so great a demand upon my time: and then my literary studies must not be

---

* Reference is to French painter Alexandre Georges Henri Regnault (1843–1871).

† After quoting this diary entry at length, Grace Channing wrote, "That early entry . . . seems to me to mark a distinct chapter in his life—the point of departure from which his fullest art-life may be said to have begun. And because it contains in brief the whole character of the man and the whole tale of his life,—all embodied in that moment of courageously securing what he felt to be a necessity for his work, and entering upon its attainment, not with the exultation natural to twenty-three years, but 'as nearly broken-hearted as any mortal that lives'—because of the loneliness he left behind him. That courage and that tenderness for others,—and that burden of debt—he was to carry with him through life and did carry to the very door of the Clinic—and past; yes, even to his last conscious hour and *past that too*, for even in his delirium and wandering agony he was full of sweetness and consideration for everybody, and to the last he spoke of his sisters and of his cares and anxieties about debts. The *habit* of the soul survived the conscious personality itself, and that characteristic never forsook him which led him to enter that studio 'broken-hearted' for the loneliness left behind him.

"Should we not rejoice greatly, my dear friend, that he did not *die* broken-hearted for the loneliness—he left behind him!" GEC to EBK, May 15, 1912, p. 48.

‡ Stetson's art exhibit, opening November 15, 1881, was one of a series of one-man shows sponsored by the Providence Art Club.

neglected. I should like to write my opinions about Art and other things that most interest me, but I find that it will be better to put my thoughts into some other place, leaving this as a register of feeling, and an epitome of the events.

I take more and more interest in my work and have a more exalted idea of the art-sentiment. I am feeling my way towards some subject that will absorb my whole soul: I feel it approaching. My color grows better daily, and I have a truer sense of form, and a more discriminating taste for action.

God is leading me. The spirit that pervades all is developing my soul. I have every reason to believe that in the end I shall be a master. . . .

I feel all the time as if [unrecognizable drawing] must be near. She may be in the city. I could not caress her now as I used, for though I worshipped her as a goddess, and such thought her, [she] showed me clearly that *for seven years* I *had worshipped* an idea which I deposited in her. No, no; she could not have been that sublime, holy, undying spiritual—venus which I thought. I will not—I cannot libel Love so. Had she been that being she were with me now. And yet she is not to be blamed: I owe her, God knows how much. O, may He reward her!*

NOV. 16. 1881. 11 P.M.

I have been at the Art Club rooms all the evening, and a delightful time it has been, for I met Mr. Weeden there and we had very interesting conversation about art and its kin. He seems to sympathize with my art-ideas closely, and I can but think that he is wonderfully versed in the subject for a man who is so eminent in business. . . . Mr. Weeden treated me far more as if he owed me something than as if I owed him. I like him wonderfully—not I fondly believe because he is kind to me but for something noble which I feel to be in the man himself. . . .

I have worked today only upon a 18 × 24″; a pleasure garden with quaint trees and shrubs, a fountain of marble, a marble bench upon which are two girls: by the fountain crouches fainting a beggar in brown. In the foreground recline two nude girls looking at the beggar. That is the senti-

---

* Stetson's first love was probably Anne Angell. He had been struggling to forget her, but thus far unsuccessfully. Several weeks earlier he wrote: "Last night I dreamed fearful things of [illegible]. I cannot forget her do what I may. I try not to let her slip into my thoughts, and succeed very well during the day; but in my dreams—" (Oct. 31, 1881).

ment, careless luxury and pitiless want. The color is going to be golden brown in quality with a cloud-flecked turquoise sky.*

My pictures are mysteries to many, if not most people. I think they take me for a "crank." The truth is the pictures by the other men here are so commonplace in subject or treatment that it makes mine very prominent by contrast. Then the power of my color attracts, and mystifies at the same time. My weak modelling (as a rule) and my lack of grace are quite apparent not only to all but to me. I cannot yet paint hands: *because I have no models.*

It does seem pitiable that in a city of this size models cannot be had. Good God, women for a few dollars will sell their embraces to the worst brutes, but to aid in the expression of beauty they can almost not be hired. However, I shall persevere until I find them. As a last resort I shall hire a harlot. And I will transform her into something only a little lower than the angels! ! ? . . .

NOV. 17. 1881. 10:40 P.M.

. . . I was at the Club this evening. I found Bannister there. He is enthusiastic about an Herodias that he is composing. He wants a model. . . . I will then ask . . . [Isa Read] if she will pose for him. Her husband will undoubtedly object. I know that jealous as I am if I had a wife who could aid an artist such as Bannister my consent would be glad and hearty. But the world only sees a lewd side to the occupation of a model. Unfortunately low women are about all that can be got for the nude. The more shame to women of "character" and eminent "respectability"!

Even men here seem to be very unwilling to pose for men: and yet they will lie the night through with bestial women!

Ah God! how the body thou didst create has been degraded! They blas-

---

* *Beggar in a Pleasure Garden*, one of Stetson's first successes, was accepted for the 1882 Boston Art Club Exhibit and reviewed in *The Boston Evening Journal*, Feb. 18, 1882, p. 4. He later quoted that review in his journal.

In his "Opera" Book Stetson wrote: The *Beggar in a Pleasure Garden* "as a piece of color has puzzled me more than almost anything I have ever attempted. The colors of my palette—which is an ample one—are really exhausted on it. I have not yet learned how to manage overly deep skies. To get the right value of sky puzzled me most. . . . I intend sending it to the Boston Art Club this week. I do not think it is my best work, but it is the only one for which I have a frame. They will say of it, that it is an imitation of the Renaissance painters—a weak one to be sure! But *I* know it is not." "Opera" Book, pp. 19–21.

pheme against thee who say that the human form is unclean and unfit for sight. . . .

NOV. 18. ''81 FRIDAY. 10:30 P.M.

Again I sit in bed: after finding that David in his Psalms prayed my prayer of weakness and crying unto God for help. He too was "shut up"—a prisoner, reaching for things that were beyond him ever. I think as I grow older I find more beauty in the grand poetry of the Bible; indeed, it were strange if I did not. One is glad to find anything that he can sympathize with, and if he is struggling with the opposing elements of nature, trying to overcome himself and all that can keep him from good and beautiful things, as I am, it is good to know that others have had similar longings and pantings, and that they have been comforted.

This morning I gave half an hour or so to calling on Bannister. . . . He . . . showed me his sketch for Herodias. She is sitting contemplating with the head of John, Baptist before her. The pose is excellent. It is profile. It suggested an entirely different composition to me. The dramatic moment when Herodias is whispering to Salome "Ask for the head of John the Baptist." The opportunity is tremendous but in the hands of so poor a painter as I it would meet with sad treatment I think: I shall attempt it however. It is so absolutely different in composition from Bannister's that he will not be tempted to say that he gave me the idea. We grew very enthusiastic over color & dramatic action. . . .

I learned to day for the first time that a good many people of good sense think that all I am for in Art & all I shall ever be able to do is "artistic gush." God alone knows what that means—I think: and God knows whether it be true or not. I hope that it is not. It seems strange that I should have cried unto him so earnestly for years to develope in me something grand and noble, something broad and sweet and tender in sentiment and yet paint only "gush." It is *not* true! I must have manliness enough to deny what I know to be false. I fail, yes often and often. But if I mistake not I shall not always fail. If I do paint a great picture it will be a very great one, I know, for it will combine with great power all of the poetic tenderness they please themselves with calling "gush."

There is no place where I am so "sentimental" and diffuse as in my Journal. The only person that seems to understand my Art ideas is Bannister: and I say more to him of my art feelings than to any other man. I am sure that he would be the last one to say that I "gush."

I am trying to make myself believe that I do not care what people say. I do not enough to make me be other than myself: but I cannot help its making me feel sad to know that it will take years to make myself understood in paint. Only a perfect technique will enable me to do that. And then perhaps not, for—people are so stupid. . . . [Here a diary section has been removed, probably because of references to sex.]

I must be dead to every human being—I must shut my eyes to palpitating flesh that prates of hot blood and good life—shut my eyes to all tales of other souls told by other eyes, that pant as I, and long as I, and are restricted by the same cursed thing that restrains me! And love—the instincts of sexuality are wrong they say. A *lie*! A lie, or else all nature lies.

I am shut up: my soul is caged. How long, Lord, how long! . . .

NOVEMBER 27. 1881. SUNDAY. 1:30 P.M.

Thanksgiving day passed quietly. I worked both forenoon and afternoon, sparing time however to dine from a delicious turkey sent me by some kind and thoughtful friend—who I cannot guess. . . .

Two of our painters have turned business men, and with flaming advertisements call attention to their wares. They are E. C. Leavitt, and A. J. Perry. Artists! they are not artists. Leavitt himself said to me, "After all, Mr. Stetson, say what we may, we are only dry goods merchants in another line." I could but reply: You may be Sir, but I am not.

Let them advertise; let them boast and lie. Art, daughter of God, lives on serene and unpolluted. They love but harlots: my mistress is the pure, passionate child of Love and Truth—ART, twin sister of—nay, Poetry's very self.

I will endure, and—*conquer*!

SUNDAY DEC. 4. 1881. 3:30 P.M.

. . . Saturday morning Mr. Bates called. I had just begun a landscape over a head that I started last month. He was admiring it when a knock sounded at my door. It was a note from Mr. Scott A. Smith,* saying that

---

*Scott A. Smith, Sidney Putnam's uncle, would later write of Stetson: He "alone has undertaken the revival of colorist art." He seeks "to express the totality of colors," to "teach you to see lines and depths and phases that before had seemed impossible." Scott A. Smith, "Mr.

he had written to his Philadelphia friends [Mr. and Mrs. George Cresson] about my pictures and that they wanted him to send on the *two* heads and also the *Monk with a Candle*.* He felt, he said, no doubt that they would take them. One of the heads was the one I had just painted out.† I told Bates and he said: "Never paint out anything: if you don't like it put it aside—somebody will. Then by [and] by you will have a lot on hand and can have a sale. I tell you, never paint out anything!" In one sense that is good advice, and would no doubt be pecuniarily more profitable: but I cannot bear to see a thing about that I know is poor: and really, because someone else may like it is no reason why I should keep it. They ought not to like bad things.

I have sold nothing since I have been in my studio: but I am not discouraged. Would that I could let father have money for family needs! But I think that will come.

[George] Whitaker wrote an article about the pictures at the Club, and paid me a tribute of which I am secretly proud. Coming from an artist it is all the better. It shows me what the most artistic people think of my work and of me. I know what the others think, so I may draw an average. It is not a flattering average God knows. I am absolutely sure that I am feeling my way towards some great thing. I know that many would laugh at such vague feelings, but take those from me and I have quite nothing to rest upon: I have neither fame, fortune, honor, and few real friends, and no lover. My beliefs, my hopes in God & Art are all I have. . . .‡

I have not seen Ham[ilton MacDougall] for a week.

Today I have made a sketch for a "Prodigal Son"—"And he arose." It is

---

Stetson's Paintings," Providence, Feb. 25, 1899, Stetson Scrapbook. Smith's comments, transcribed by David Goodale, were directed to the editor of the *Providence Sunday Journal* during one of Stetson's New York exhibitions.

*The *Monk with a Candle* was shown in the 1881 PAC Exhibit, and later purchased by George V. Cresson. The monk figure appears in many Stetson paintings. See particularly *A Pagan's Procession* (1892).

†Grace Channing noted that Walter "always" painted out his pictures—"for lack of canvas, and money to buy more. He *had* to paint pictures—if only on top of others. Alas!—he did this even in Rome. Katharine and I still mourn a superb great 'Aged Pan' on the shore of a lonely sea, with a great moon, and broken pan-pipes in his hand!" GEC to EBK, May 16, 1912, p. 59.

‡George Whitaker believed that Stetson was "perhaps the most gifted" of his Providence associates. He "had a thoughtful, poetic mind, an individuality all his own and a spirit that led him to please his own high taste rather than that of his less intellectual and intelligent public. He never painted down to gratify anybody's whim." "The Dean of Providence Artists," *Providence Sunday Journal*, Jan. 10, 1915; Stetson Scrapbook.

mostly landscape: the figure being comparatively small. But it is the *figure and* landscape which must express "And he arose." I think of painting it 4 × 6 ft. in size.*

SUNDAY, DEC. 11. 1881. 8 P.M.

. . . I have reached the point in Art of which my good friend Bannister told me—that of timidity. I hesitate before painting anything knowing that for the subjects I desire most to paint my skill is not sufficient, and even if it were that they would not be appreciatively received; and knowing also that if I paint things that the public demands my heart would not be in the work, so they would not be genuine expressions of my feelings and beliefs,— which all art should be, and all true art is. The buying public wishes for "still life" & prettiness of every description: It wishes something kittenish. It cares nothing for historical or religious painting; nothing for poetry and passion. I *cannot* make *pretty* pictures. I cannot remember that one of my works has ever been called that. Most people say that they cannot under- stand it: a few, (perhaps many) laugh at it, call it absurd and vow that I am ruined by being on the wrong track. A very few understand enough to see that I am aiming at something deep and true and pure. The appearance of extravagance is in part due to my lack of technical skill; but in great measure because they do not understand the idiom of my language.

I know these things so well that they depress me. It is truth what [E. C.] Leavitt says: "A man's work cannot be gotten out of a boy." I am truly a boy in art if a man in law and among my comrades. So not being able to paint prettily and not being able to express my true self I cannot make a living. It is some consolation to know that some of the greatest artists have been similarly situated, but it were the height of conceit for me to infer from that that I am one of the great. But I do feel that I can be as great as any of them: for the spirit which inspired them can inspire me. The great men have not been great in themselves. It has been through their love and their sim- plicity of faith. I have discovered the secret of the old masters. It is *God*. Men could love in those days without drawing scorn to themselves and without

---

*Charles Eldredge suggests that Stetson's "formula" for the *Prodigal Son*—"*And He Arose*" ("mostly landscape: the figure being comparatively small") was one he would frequently repeat in both religious and secular compositions. Charles Eldredge, *Charles Walter Stetson: Color and Fantasy* (Lawrence, Kan.: Spencer Museum of Art, 1982), p. 23.

being made to half believe that what they loved was bad. Now one can love nothing openly. Skepticism rules—*I* doubt even my love of the things I love most sincerely and passionately. . . .

I believe it a mistake to think that we can do what we will with our-selves. Souls have orbits like planets. We can go only in the paths planned at our birth: I do not *like* to believe that for I wish to be a very god and do what I will. I have grown old in the past year. Being deprived of all hope of true love and domestic happiness I am become still more intense (I can think of no better word). It may have been a good thing, but my heart sickens and faints. I need more than I can say love unlimited and wholly noble and sin-cere. I fear it will never, never be mine.*

I find myself renominated a member of the Art Club's Executive Com-mittee. As the number is very much smaller this year it is more of a compli-ment than it was last. I shall do my duty. My benefactor, Mr. Weeden, is nominated to be President. . . .

DEC. 22. 1881. 8 P.M.

Last week marked an epoch. Mr. Smith brought in his Philadelphian friends Mr. and Mrs. Geo.[rge] V. Cresson. Mr. Cresson came several times to see me and took to me wonderfully. To begin with he bought four pic-tures of me: "The Slave" \$75–;† "Monk with a Candle" \$25–; A female

---

*Grace Channing wrote, ". . . To nearly everyone *but myself* I think a great surprise in these Journals would be the strongly religious cast—Walter's terms of intimacy with the Deity! Not for nothing was he born of a long line of New England clergymen. In later life, he had cast aside the earlier form, but as a matter of reality, he was intensely religious *in his way*, and his devotion to the Bible was a family jest—which covered much more than a jest. Of course it ought to be easily gathered from his Art that this was so,—but his apparently contradictory skepticism misled most people, and his intense antipathy to 'paid religion.' I think he never changed in any essential that perfect reliance and trust, which *is* Religion, and which in these early years took the direct form of appeal to that which he later christened 'God, for short.'. . .

"The last months of his life he read almost nothing but the Bible, rejoicing in 'the cheek-teeth of a strong lion'—and the like,—but moved to so great emotion often that he laid it down. He was moved in the same way—and spirit—by the clouds and the sunsets and the moonrises,—and I am sure he had a perfect, unformulated faith, which did not even *ask* indi-vidual immortality, but which was an essential inheritance from the race of which he came." GEC to EBK, May 18, 1912, p. 65.

†The *Slave* was earlier called the *Servant of Royal Peacocks*, begun July 1881. *An Errand to the Sick*, begun in September 1881, was "a smiling monk carrying a bottle of wine in a green bag" (3½ × 5⅞ inches, mahogany panel). "Opera" Book, pp. 15, 28.

head . . . \$25–; and a tiny panel "An Errand to the Sick" \$15—total \$140–. But dearer even than that to me was the thought, the knowledge that he really understood my intentions and liked them, and had faith in me. Our talks were very pleasant to me. He told me that if I would come to Phil. he would see that it cost me nothing, that I might stay as long as I liked. It was not said in a cold way but urgently and sincerely. Mrs. Cresson is a lovely woman. Think of it! They want me to paint her. They have more faith in me than I have in myself. Paint her! But strange to say they do not care for absolute accuracy as regards form but as regards her sweet character. *That* I can do, I think. . . . One of the pleasantest parts of it is that they are willing to pay my prices without a murmur. Mr. Cresson even asked me if I was satisfied with my price and that he was willing to pay more. . . .

. . . I have started several new canvasses which promise much. Two in particular. *Out of Consecrated Ground* and the *First Kiss.** . . .

. . .

---

* *Out of Consecrated Ground*, later called *Burial of a Suicide*, was shown in the Fourth Annual Providence Exhibit, March 1883, and later purchased by Thomas B. Clarke. *The First Kiss*, later called *The First Caress*, was shown in the April 1882 Providence Exhibit.

CHAPTER III

. . . *a new heaven on earth*

January 1–February 6, 1882

THIS CHAPTER marks the beginning of the relationship between Charles Walter Stetson and Charlotte Anna Perkins. On first meeting, Walter was impressed. In his view, she was the ideal combination of "brilliance," "nobility," and sensuous beauty. His earlier love had been merely a projection, he decided; "I did not love *her*, but myself—that is, the thoughts, feelings, etc. which I projected from my own brain & soul upon her." But *this* love seemed "profound, enduring, [and] supreme."

From the very outset, Charlotte also was infatuated with the friendship. She was loving and enthusiastic, but also deeply ambivalent. "I *don't* combine, and I don't want to," she wrote him; the question is "whether I am most a woman or Charlotte A. Perkins."

For the most part Walter misunderstood the ambivalence she faced. And while for a time he kept a respectful distance from her struggle ("it is not for me to judge, for I should not judge with impartiality"). Clearly he assumed that she would eventually accept her woman's calling, and that in the meantime his more compelling struggle was to "tame" his passions and calm his mind.*

---

*The above quotations are from diary entries (including quotations from Charlotte Perkins' letters) of the following dates: Feb. 6, Feb. 1, Jan. 26, Feb. 6, 1882.

JANUARY 1. 1882. SUNDAY 10:30 P.M.

I begin a new year, and pray God that peace may rest on all the world. . . .

SUNDAY JAN. 8. 1882 8:30 P.M.

I am very tired but I wanted to make a note of last week's doings.

Mrs. Cresson came to sit twice, and I must confess that I never spent pleasanter hours in quiet talk than then. She is so soothing, and gives one such a perfect confidence in himself and in her that I really forgot all else. I am sure that she enjoyed the sittings also: and I think that she likes me very well. It is a great thing to be liked by such a woman. She has been ill for three days, so I have not had sittings from her. I cannot say how the portrait is coming out but I feel as if it will not be bad. I only fear that something will interrupt her sittings. . . .*

Mr. Weeden sent me a check for $200—the 3*d*. The evening of the 3*d* we had our annual meeting at the Art Club. I was elected a member of the executive committee another year. Mr. Weeden who was elected Pres. made an excellent speech. . . .

SATURDAY EVE. JAN. 14. 1882.

[For some weeks Stetson had been planning to give a lecture on etching at the Art Club. He was hoping to "illustrate" the etching process "by preparing a plate, biting it, and printing from it before the audience. It will be a

---

* Stetson's current diaries include a number of references to the growing friendship with Mrs. George V. Cresson. Unfortunately, as was all too common, Stetson did not refer to Mrs. Cresson by her first name. He had "grave doubts about the success" of her portrait, but found her a "very very lovely woman" (Jan. 14, 1882). Some days later he wrote, "We have become very much attached to each other even in this short while. One day in my studio after she had put on her dress, I playfully said: You look very matronly now. 'And, pray, why should I not? I am old enough to be your mother.' Don't you wish that you were? said I. 'Yes, heartily! May I adopt you?' Her face brightened wonderfully when I said: Yes, you may adopt me. Then we talked much. So since then she has been very motherly and takes a deep interest in me" (Jan. 26, 1882).

Stetson was of course aware of the potential value of the Cresson friendship; rumor had it that Mr. Cresson might send him to Europe. But he also felt a "horror . . . of fawning," he wrote, of purposefully acting "towards them so they might be drawn to help me in my studies. . . . I cannot do it. If they want to aid me I will accept aid, because I know it would give them pleasure. But the proposition must originate with them" (Jan. 26, 1882).

novel, and I think an interesting proceeding," he wrote (Dec. 22, 1881), but "I tremble, for it is somewhat of an undertaking" (Jan. 8, 1882).

As it turned out, it was a "very remarkable lecture," according to George Whitaker, and "was discussed days afterward by those who heard it" ("The Dean of Providence Artists," Providence *Sunday Journal*, Jan. 10, 1915. Stetson Scrapbook). Moreover, it was probably this lecture-demonstration which later secured Stetson the commission from Beriah Wall to make etched copies for a catalogue of his painting collection.]

My lecture came off Wednesday eve. and was a great success for me. I had an audience composed of the very best culture of the city, & have the satisfaction of knowing that I interested all and instructed some. Everything went to my desire. I find that I connected several to myself. After it Dorrance * took me to Young's where we had a delicious supper & a bottle of LaRose Claret at $2.50—at his expense.

The next day Mr. Putnam brought in Miss Perkins, of whom he has spoken often. She & I have taken to each other very well. She is an original: eccentric because unconventional, and well versed in almost everything, I guess! †

She invites me to take walks with her Sunday afternoons & many other things. She has a form like a young Greek & a face also resembling a cameo. She is an athlete—strong, vivacious, with plenty of bounding blood. She is an indefatigable worker—but I shall see some of her.

She has such a classic figure! She is moral, intellectual and beautiful!

She said frankly, "Mr. Stetson, I must know you better!" . . . I think that I shall like her much. . . .

26 JANUARY 1882 9:15 P.M.

I scarce know how to write all that I wish. I ought to have written daily, but the hours were full and the nights were weary, & my room so very cold that it was neglected. Let me see. . . .

---

* Courtland B. Dorrance was a PAC member and a confidant at times, but in Stetson's view was too "worldly" and "shallow" to merit much respect. Some time later Stetson did a portrait of Dorrance which he regarded as "a truly excellent likeness. Every touch on the head was painted from life, and it was an attempt to see how near I could come to a matter of fact production." "Opera" Book, p. 21.

† Grace Channing noted that this was the "beautiful first description" of Charlotte. Her letter continues: "That entry marked the closing of an entire period of [Walter's] life. Before the next was made he had entered 'a new heaven and earth.' He had been to see Charlotte; they had talked together as two such wonderful young people must and had covered in a week leagues of ground." GEC to EBK, May 23, 1912, pp. 77–78.

[After returning from an evening dinner with the Cressons] Miss Perkins met me at the door with a pen in her mouth and her hand thrust out to be grasped. Sidney tells me that she will not shake hands with him or any other young man that he knows of: I am glad, for she took mine warmly & in parting that evening let it linger.

"I have saved two cents," she said blithely, after she had assured me that she was glad of me. "I was just writing to you, but it is so much better to be able to talk to you!" (I had asked her to go with me to a concert at the Club last night.) She tossed the letter to me & I read it. She answered the question by saying "I will go; with pleasure"; and then she went on as according to the letter which I have put on file. Her conversation that afternoon was indescribable. I dare not try to give it verbatim, although some of her sentences burn in my heart. As Sidney Putnam says, 'I cannot forget what Miss Perkins says.' All is said so clearly, yet so picturesquely, and in a way that tells you that she has thought systematically and poetically, as well as practically. She said things which I am positive no other young woman ever said to a young man. She laid bare her heart to me as completely as words would allow, and ended by saying "There, I have been absolutely frank with you. You can now understand me. Am I worth knowing? You can be to me more than any one else. Will you? Will you accept what I can give you for your friendship and aid, etc." At some little remark that I made she covered her face and said: "It seems too good to be true!" And then in a deep raptuous way, "I like you—for what you *are*."

It seems that her life has been very sad and strangely like my own. She has suffered similar things; thought like things and conquered herself & grown in the same way.

She said [Stetson quotes the letter at length]:

I wish I could understand it: from the night of your lecture, when I first saw you, it seemed to me that I had always known you, and that you had only returned from a long journey. And then when I met you in your studio the feeling was confirmed, and I knew that from you, if from anyone, I must receive that of which my life has been barren. . . .

[The letter continues with Charlotte noting the fact that Walter reminds both her mother (Mary Perkins) and her aunt (Caroline Robbins) of a "young divinity student to whom mother was twice engaged, and he died when young. Do you suppose that I feel as if I had known you because you are like one whom mother had loved? *Did I inherit it?*"]

Time after time as we talked we were struck by the similarity of our lives. Would to God I could write what she said. It deserves right well to live, but to repeat it is to make it cold. I never had listened to anything so noble and good.

She is a poetess: a philosopher, and no mean one, and more of a mystic than she guesses. A warm, soft, sensuous nature held in check and overcome by a strong will, a sound intellect & a good moral nature.

Again I must say, O that I might worthily repeat what she said! Would—but the words will not come with proper fire & strength. But I must say that the words made a new heaven and earth for me. I came home & wrote her a letter Sunday evening and she replied with one which is as fervid as a lover's prayer, and as odd & unconventional as she is herself. I hold my breath when I think what has occurred this week. I cannot quite throw from me the feeling that it is a dream. To have a *perfect* friendship with a woman who unites the highest type of intellect with a perfect physical nature is simply over-powering. And yet I never felt such absolute repose and exaltation. I have worked better and thought better. And I know that she is happy. Witness her letter which I will copy so that it may not be lost. Should I not be happy causing such happiness? Would that the world might read that letter! It shows what a woman *may* be.

Last evening we went to the concert. It was bliss. To hear her words an unknowing mortal would think her passionately in love with me. I understand her and do not think it or believe it. I know that she does not wish such a catastrophe & suspects that it *may* happen—so is on her guard. It can be read betwixt the lines of her letter. I fear for myself. If I am much with her I shall love her grandly—not as I loved [name deleted]—not as I love [name deleted]—but supremely: for she combines the good of all women.*

I pray God that I may be to her all—yea, more than she has yet thought, dreamed or hoped for.

I cannot understand it: she seems my bosom friend from eternity. . . .

[The diary continues with a description of a visit by Mrs. Cresson. She had brought] a generous bunch of fragrant heliotrope & delicate maiden hair fern. Then she posed and talked—and she can talk beautifully. Her sittings have been my pleasantest hours for long—until Charlotte Perkins came—bright star!

They have been endeavoring to draw me to Philadelphia but I had made them no promises. . . .

She says that I must not consider that I am going visiting, but rather

---

*The first name was probably Anne Angell, the second Nellie Sanford.

that I am going to a sister's house where I may do my will. Where I may be in heart at home. Setting before me such pleasant things that I could but feel that it was my duty to give them pleasure: for strange as it seems to me, I do believe that it will give them pleasure.

We are to finish, then, the portrait there, I having agreed to go as soon as I can make my affairs in harmony. . . .

[Then she began discussing the possibility of spending the summer with them] ". . . whether at the Pier, Long Branch, the Adirondacks, or—"

"Europe," said I.

"Yes, in Europe. I was saying to Mr. Smith during breakfast that I could think of nothing better than going to Europe and taking you with me. Would you like to go?"

I repeated slowly her words, "would—I—like—to go!"

"O, I know you would: and you *must*! If I were a wealthy woman, in my own name—so that I could do as I pleased without asking anyone, you should go this week if you wished. Someday I *shall* have money of my own, and then—!" and her face lighted.

Mr. Cresson & Mr. Smith came soon after.

He did not like the portrait; but cleared me of feeling by saying that no man living could paint her; even a photograph didn't look like her. He is right. My portrait is not good although Mrs. Cresson thinks it is & asserts it strenuously. Mr. Smith also likes it and thinks I will succeed in getting something fine of it. I doubt it much but I shall try. I can work with my heart since Charlotte is mine to friend.

Here is her second letter to me. A letter that set all my soul afire & put life into every corpuscle of my blood. God bless her & make womankind her equal.

(I must say that I began my second letter to her with "Dear Miss Perkins" & then went on to defend my right to call her dear.) . . . [she wrote in return:]

"Dear Miss Perkins"

Is a paradox. If I am Miss Perkins the "dear" which goes with that is a mere formality. If I am—*dear*, then I am no longer Miss Perkins. Find me a name of your own.

Do you like having your letters answered inch by inch? . . .

I am going to be cruelly frank with you. If we are to come as near to each other as I hope we may, as I think we shall; there must be nothing between us.

Let me tell you then that I am not of the combining sort. I *don't* combine, and I don't want to.

My nature is the polliest of polygons, whose happiness it is true depends on the contact of its many faces, with congenial surfaces, but which keeps its own unchanging shape. (No, not unchanging, for every year new facets appear, and the whole grows larger.)

The rising happiness that I find in you is that you touch and cover many sides which had shrunk and shrivelled in comfortless neglect.

That we have suffered similar things is true: true that we love similar things—Ah! do we not!, but my goal (if you'll excuse a return to my small fable) is to make my music box the most perfect of instruments, and to help other people tune theirs.

My life is one of private aspiration and development, and of public service which only awaits to be asked.

There are now, (and I say it to you as freely as I own it to myself) [those] who look on me as "the shadow of a great rock in a weary land."

You, I greet as pouring unprayed-for happiness into a life that seemed wholly cold save for the warmth of gratitude and respect.

Having calmly accepted the fact that the happiness of most women was no happiness for me; having lost forever the one joy that made hardships trifles;* having bowed quietly to a fate that forbade the indulgence of each and every individual instinct; having settled my shoulders firmly to the yoke which grows harder to bear as the years pass; holding in control such of my wild horses as are already mastered, and taming new ones every day; plodding steadily on with no light save the self-made radiance of my future home—I turn a sudden corner, and find—! I cover my eyes as yet. Cover my eyes and plod on, but with a new light in the dreary landscape, a wild sweet music beating through the harsh noises around me, a glowing background for my thoughts to rest upon—when I dare to let them go.

No circumstance is changed, no plan disturbed, but as the difference between shadow and sunlight is the difference between my life two weeks ago and now.

No, I am *not* sorry that I am already very dear to you.

Do you see the towering selfhood that holds its own even in an hour like this? I am thinking of myself and of myself alone. Do you wonder that I boast of a force which is slowly but surely changing such a nature into quiet work for others?

With ears on the one side and pen & tongue on the other there wants only time for us to know each other. I hardly know which is more delightful, the ever new attractiveness of exploration and discovery or the rich peace between two souls when they have years of common experience behind them. We need not hasten, there is a world of happiness in both, and both are to be ours.

I half wish you were a woman. I have a haunting dread that in this joy there may lurk some danger. My life has been so filled with small denials that every little pleasure had its own uneasiness, and my heart stands still to think of the commensurate pain that would fall here if this went wrong.

---

*The reference here is to the "hardship" of losing her close friend Martha Luther. This woman-to-woman relationship was so warm and mutually affectionate that when Martha became engaged, Charlotte found it the "keenest, the hardest, the most lasting pain" she had ever known. CPG, *The Living of Charlotte Perkins Gilman: An Autobiography* (New York: Harper & Row, 1975), p. 80.

As you live, be honest with me! Let us count each step with sacred care, and taste the sweetness as we go; so that if we grow apart we can say as my lost friend and I do now, that the joy we have known has been thoroughly enjoyed, has ennobled us both, and has left no sting.

Happy as I am now; happy as you make me, it is the happiness of gratification only, a personal delight; and remember "those who have known the pleasure of avoiding pleasure, will never call the pleasure of pleasure, pleasure."

Until I am sure that this is good and right; sure that you paint better for it, and I work the harder; that the strength borne of new happiness is turned to noble ends, I will not *let* myself enjoy it.

Is it plain now?

The joy I have in you is the joy of *knowing you*; and you may have the same.

Furthermore, or rather *in that*, I will give and give and give you *of* myself, but never give myself to you or any man.

Truly I am in appearance a lady, in nature a woman, but first and always

Charlotte A. Perkins

There it is *verbatim*—as she wrote it. It seems to me that it is unique.

I am proud to feel that I am worthy of such a letter: for it must come from a noble soul, for, though it has the minor faults of a nature who is conscious of more than ordinary powers,—it requires a noble soul to write such. There are little asperities of feeling in it that time will remove. I understand them for they have been also in my life. The whole letter reads as if I wrote it some three years ago. I am proud of her.

Live, O Letter, and when I am dead may all maidens read thee and be as grand and earnest as is she from whose brains thou comest!

This entry is very long, but not a tenth is said.

JANUARY 29. 1882 SUNDAY, 10 P.M.

In the afternoon I was with Charlotte Perkins. She showed me a Gaelic love song, which is in the midwinter Scribner's and which I had admired before. Then she told me of her thoughts and desires. Later she took me into her study where there were many books and pictures. We stood near each other by the stove a few moments; both were thinking. At length she said: "There is one thing that I do not like." What is it? I asked. "I cannot quite formulate it yet: but I will before you go." Pretty soon she said: "Do you want to please me a little—" and she led the way into the parlor again— "want to give me a few sugar plums so to speak?" Certainly, said I. What do [you] wish? "Tell me why you admire me. I never was admired before and— *I like it*. I want to know just what you admire."

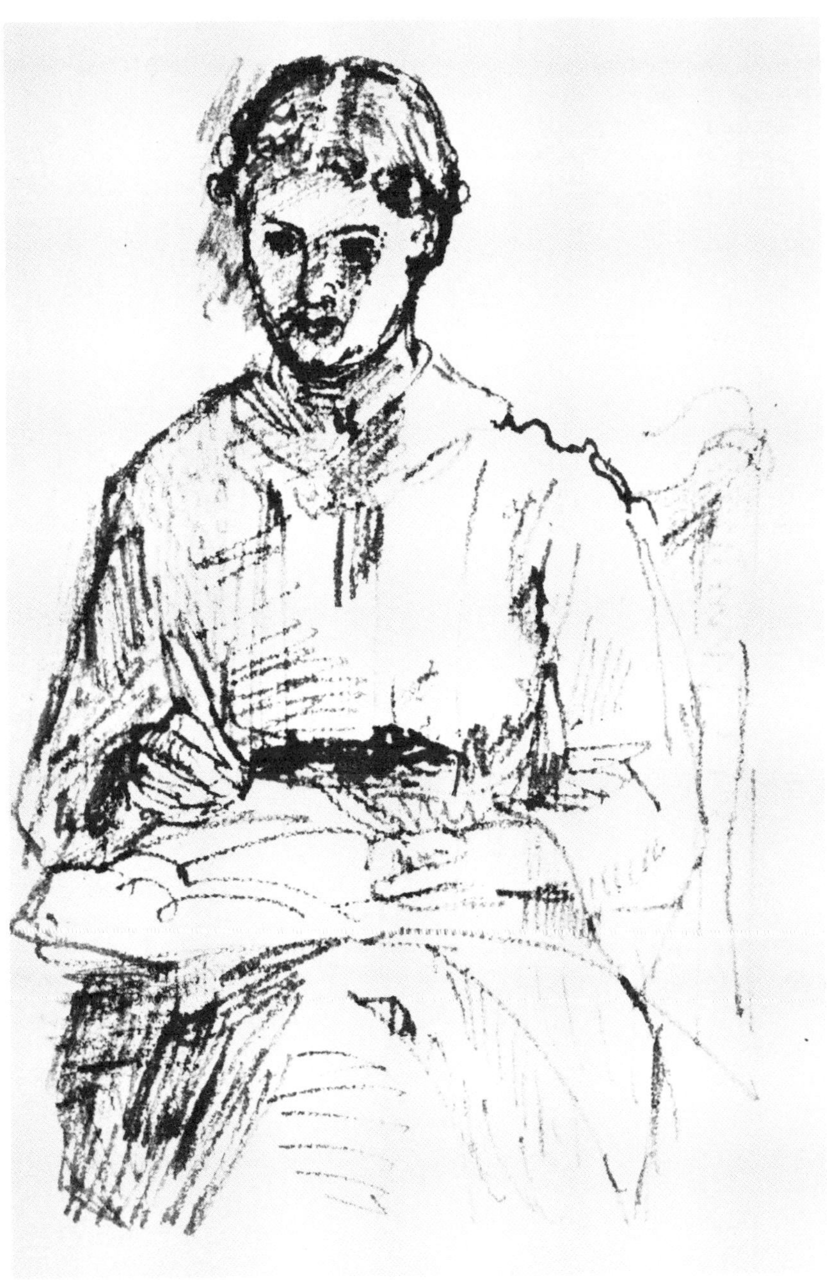

Charlotte Perkins (Stetson) Gilman. From Sketchbooks.

"Well," said I, "I admire you because you have a purpose; because you are perfectly honest in carrying out that purpose: because you dare to think for yourself—to *be* yourself."

"Good! I want more!"

"More? Of what kind?"

"I want now some artistic reasons."

"Do you want me to tell you what I admire that is physical?"

"Yes," she said.

So I made a soberly detailed account of her physical qualities that pleased me.

"I do heartily enjoy having you admire me!" She seemed peculiarly affected by it. At length after talking about a few other things I arose to go. After I put on my coat I saw that she had something to say to me, so I waited.

"The way you look at me sometimes troubles me," she said.

"How do I look at you?"

"As if you—might grow fond of me."

"Well, suppose that I should?"

"I can but fear that something will go wrong and mar our happiness. I *know* that I shall be very fond of you—very very fond of you: and I shall want a great deal of tenderness from you. I am afraid that it may result to both—in *love*: and that would be only pain. For—you and I are sensible people, let us talk plainly—for I cannot marry, although I am fitted to enjoy all that marriage can give to the utmost. Were I to marry, my thoughts, my acts, my whole life would be centered in husband and children. To do the work that I have planned I must be free. Nothing would give me more happiness of a certain kind than love—so—"

"Well," said I, "perhaps then it were well to part at once. I am fond of you already. But I can bear even more."

"Do you think so?"—and her voice was sad. "I am so fond of you now! I only mentioned this so that, knowing the danger we may be able to guard against it."

"But you cannot remove the danger; it will always exist, and it will be greater daily. If we are together as much, and are as near to each other & as tender as you and I wish to be, I am quite sure that I shall love you passionately—I *know* that I shall. But why need it disturb you? I will not let it pain *you*. *I* would rather bear the pain knowing that you were really fond of me than to be without you."

Dear woman! Dear woman! Her fondness and her previous plans had a severe struggle. [She said:] "Were I to part from you now I could easily over-come the pain though it would be great: but if we are together as I wish, you will so become a part of my life that the pain of separation would be fright-ful. But I need you—you can be so much to me. And if I could only feel that all would go well I could be glad and give you everything but my life."

"It is for you to decide," said I.

"If we should watch ourselves don't you think that we could keep from love? We could see that the next step would be too much—so we could separate?"

"Dear," said I, "by the time that we reached that last step we should have become so weak that the step would be taken before we knew it."

"You are right: If I were like other women I suppose I should have known that a friendship such as I had wished was not possible between a man and woman. And how I wish that it were! For I *am* fond of you now and cannot bear to think of parting from you. I know it sounds presumptu-ous for me to premise that you may be fond of me—yet truly I cannot see why you should not be when you admire me so much."

"But," said I, "are you sure that I shall not disappoint you, and that you can be as fond of me as you think that you shall?"

"Yes, perfectly sure!"

Ah God! how wonderful she seemed as she stood in that twilight look-ing into my eyes with her intellectual and passionate ones. The idea that she could love me I had not entertained, and now to have it from her own lips—! The slumbering love of her awoke. My fate was made known to me. The world and all vanished. I loved!

Said I: "Why do you not wish to be loved by me—to love me?"

"I think that you know nothing would give me more joy than to know that you love me. But—you know of my plans: you know of the work I have set about doing."

"How would my love hinder you? I can think of no good plans which true love ought to or would hinder."

"Oh, on the simplest of physiological grounds I know that a love begun should be consummated: and consummation would mean relinquishment of all my plans—and it would feed the side of my nature which I am holding in check. I am pretty evenly balanced, animal & spiritual. Were I to give up—I fear I should give all up and become of no more use than other women. If my life were made for happiness that would be well enough."

"Become like other women!" exclaimed I, "impossible! I cannot argue with you; I am glad you feel that you have a duty to perform. I will not seek to alter one of your plans: indeed, I will do all in my power to help you accomplish your work: but don't you see that if love comes we cannot prevent it?" (God thou knowest my heart!)

"Will you promise to tell me when you begin to love me *very* much—and—or—will you promise to *not* love me?"

She was so filled with the conflict that her usually clear, certain way of speaking was gone.

"No! I will *not* promise you! Because I cannot promise what I am sure I cannot perform. Listen: (I put out my hand) "The die is cast—from this moment you are changed: Put your hand in mine! *I Love You!*"

She put her hand in mine and held it close for many minutes, held it with a caressing pressure which filled my whole soul with peace and joy. . . . "If you do not see me again," said I, still holding her hand, "remember, I love you and can but love you always; for you satisfy every sense, and every intellectual desire. Do you not think that however good friendship is, that friendship & true love combined are a thousand times better? You have both; I give you both. Your life will be different from now, I am sure. You may not feel very differently now, but—remember this hour years hence!"

"I must not enjoy this though it thrills me. You know what my work is to be. Those who marry should coalesce—you would not want another man to hold my hand as you are holding it—nor should I. I should necessarily give myself—"

"You cannot give *yourself*: that part of you which is individual now would be individual then. Could I give up painting, think you, for any woman?"

"But it would not be necessary—a wife might help you!"

"*Might*, yes, but on the contrary not one woman in a thousand is fit to be the wife of an artist. Although I *hate* painting I could not give it up but with life."

When I said that I hated painting she drew back and exclaimed: "Hate painting!"

"Yes, but it is my only means of expression so is very necessary. I *must* express myself—so I paint. Now you, dear, have something which corresponds to painting: you cannot give it up for any man. It is not yourself, but your expression. Marriage need not rob you, would not rob you. But do we not talk of marriage prematurely?"

"Yes—and no: marriage would be the end; it is best to consider it at the beginning."

"Can you not see that you have already hastened my love by showing me that it is possible that I may be loved in return?" At length she said: "I will risk all." It seemed hard to her to let me go. She followed me to the door. A flood of moonlight and starlight came in at the opening; and how glorious her love-lighted face was in the moonlight! She went upon the porch with me, and though it was very cold leaned over the railing and looked at me, then said: "Have you held my hand enough—here, I want you to take it again," and she put it into mine.

As she did so my eye caught sight of a splendid planet in the southeast, and Keats' last sonnet flashed upon my mind. I asked her if she knew it. She did but could not remember it all, but said she would go in and read it. I repeated the first line so that she might be sure & read the right one:

"Bright star, would I were steadfast as thou art!"

This account of this evening is as tame as the newspaper account of a battle like Waterloo would be, or the tale of Paradise told by an idiot. I was a god—and she—ineffable!

Now I feel new energy in every atom of my being. She *does* love me. Even her friendship were better than the love of most women. She talked of marriage so nobly that to marry her, it seems to be now, would be to realize the ideal that has filled my life for years. She talked of children, the result of such union, so feelingly that it seems to be now that no other womb than hers could bear the child I have dreamed of and longed for.

It seems true besides that a chain of impulses since childhood has led us both to each other, and has given us lives which have fitted us for each other. She said something this evening which called forth from me:—I understand you perfectly: were you made a man you were not much different from Charles Stetson.

"I think you are right," said she.

And now I see the hard task which is before me: to love, and love passionately without allowing it to hinder her labor or my own: to desire her in every way, night and day, and know that I cannot have my desires gratified for very long if ever; to force myself to say less than my heart prompts, and to make tame my strong feelings.

Yet, with that mighty task before me, I never have known such rest, such positive calm, such inward peace as I do now. I have far more than ever to live for. I have far nobler deeds to do.

Art seems dearer since she loves it too, and understands what I am striving for. The external world, even at this drear season, seems fuller of heavenliness than past springs have seemed.

Yes, I do love her with a man's love. I am proud that my love is so wholly and grandly a woman.

I must be prepared for any fate. . . .*

.   .   .

FEB. 1., WEDNESDAY, 1882.

When I came downstairs this morning I found a twelve-page letter from Charlotte. *I am living in heaven.* I can imagine nothing nobler and more honest.

I copy it here verbatim because it shows her in a new condition, that of "the heart awakened."

Besides it shows my character as clearly as it does hers.

THE LETTER

Providence
January 29th 1882
[this date should be the
30th—C.W.S.]

Friend and Lover:

Whom, if I had given you the hand that lay so long in yours—that no man ever held before—I should now be addressing as my Lord and King—

I wish I could see you tonight. I want to talk; and was never more thankful for my utter freedom with the pen.

Let me say now that I think of it, that when I ask you especially on Sunday afternoons it is only that I am sure of seeing you alone then, and not at other times. But I shall be more than glad to see you as often as you care to come, running the chances of possible callers and certain family.

Please be *sure* that as far as my pleasure goes you cannot come nor write too often.

And now for my letter.

I've had twenty-four hours to cool off in and am more myself than I was yesterday! My Individual Self, the Soul that I hope you will meet when we are dead, is a thinking creature, and I hate to lose its cleareyed strength even for a moment.

She reigns tonight, strengthened by two victories this afternoon; the one over

---

*On January 29, 1882, Charlotte Perkins wrote in her own diary: "I have this day been asked the one great question in a woman's life and have refused." CAP, Diary, Jan. 29, 1882, Gilman Papers, AESL.

an illogical desire to go to your studio, (good reasons against it) and second over thoughts that *would* rest on you, while I was taking an hour of Egyptian History at the Ath[aeneum]. I could, this minute, give a clear essay on what I read in spite of the added difficulty of *reversing* as well as concentrating thoughts.

Then I walked home serenely in the cool moonlight, and feel that I have earned an hour or two for you.

And now I will tell you as clearly as I can first what I *feel*, and second what I think.

I feel surer than ever I was before that I am right in my ideas of the first question in every life; my highest use and happiness.

Gladder than ever of my perfect freedom, that bows to *nothing* but the Laws of God—and then *utterly*.

Prouder!—O prouder! than I ever dreamed of being, to think that my years of patient, unnoticed, solitary, misunderstood (and reviled as far as it was understood) ceaseless and undiscouraged work of self training and development have been so *grandly* crowned!

So grandly crowned!

I cannot find words (I *never* saw the time before when I had not words enough) to tell you the glory of it.

That the nature I have worked *so* hard to elevate and strengthen should at last be recognized and saluted—and by such a man as you!

I have no words.

Sure. Glad   &   Proud.

What more has life?

Can I complain *now* of the discord and restraint of *any* life?

Truly, my friend, you have given me enough already to fill my memory forever. And if you are as much like me as I find you so far, it will fill you with a slow, thrilling happiness to feel that you have poured such grandeur into the life of one you love.

Of one you—Love—

I pity those who do not feel as thoroughly as I do. In every uttermost filament of nerve—to the last drops of tingling blood—in soul and mind and body; truly I inhabit my house from starlit towers to deep foundation stone.

Now listen, you who are to me distinctly this: A window rather than a door—a high, broad window suddenly thrown wide in my dark life, through which I look and look, feasting starved eyes on every lovely dream I ever had; on every phase of dear loved sea, on every form of smiling meadow and high hills, cool woods where clear water sleeps under the trees, and hot bright sunlight beating down on every hand while the low chirp and hum of insects fills the nearness, and a distant cock-crow is the only sign of human life. You touch the springs of Memory and Imagination. You give me rich new happiness which bids fair to make up for the dear love which I have lost.

But mark me! If another could give me this (perish the thought!) I would take it as gladly. It is *through* the window that I look, it is the joy you give me that I prize, not you!

I am tenfold happier tonight than I was yesterday. And yet—and yet—I will tell you fairly that I thought no more than this of my lost love when I first knew her. No more? Not a hundredth part as much. She was merely a pleasant acquaintance for a year or so—then nearer and nearer, till—you know how near.

There is no reason in life why you, giving in your way perhaps more than she did in hers should not sooner or later be loved as well—perhaps better. I look tonight at what I yesterday called danger with different eyes.

If I am right—if I am what I think, and my life is what I think—then I do *not* fear any temptation, any bright alternatives of human love and joy. I have held fast my convictions under every adverse circumstance and I do *not* fear to try them in this new fire. And if they cannot stand—If I am wrong—why, it were better to find it out now than later.

It was cowardly in me to shrink so weakly from a trial which, unless I pass through, will haunt me all my life with a sense of possible loss and mistake.

Now, on the threshold of my so vaunted life, let me meet once for all the question which finds here its only answer—whether I am most a woman or Charlotte A. Perkins.

You, my friend, are nearer me already than any man I ever saw before. Come nearer still, try me for a year or so; you shall have the fairest and fullest of chances; and if I find my hopes and plans grow dim, new views of the relative value of things supervene, the polygon take another turn, as it has so often done before, and throw a new side uppermost—then on my honor as a Human Soul, I will tell you so.

Now I would fairly *vivisect* myself rather than deceive you—*as I look at this thing now*—*being what I am now*—what I would have with you is this.

For you to live your life at its grandest, and share with me what I can hold and you can give.

For me to live my life at its grandest; and give you the same.

For you to always find in me everything of tenderness and strength that a woman can give to a man.

For me to always find in you that which I *must* have from some quarter—Congeniality and Love. With this for an outline there is *no limit* to the glorious prospect.

And let if at any time we grew apart as souls do grow apart—too late, we could say goodbye with no harm done, and a world of joy to look back upon.

The idea is simply Paradise to me. Simply Paradise. And yet, my friend, if you, after giving this subject the earnest consideration which it deserves,—if you honestly think that to go on in the new country which *you* have entered, with the prospect which I believe to be true, and the chance which I admit to be possible & if you think that the possible loss would be more than the positive gain—if you see room for pain and wrong, and prefer to stop now before we both feel deeper—

Then come once more, and take my hand, and say

Goodbye.
Charlotte A. Perkins

There is the letter which I answered during the day. I painted better, thought better, felt better physically for it. I know that it is a noble work that she will do for my life. She loves me now, and will love me no less.

I should despise myself forever if I tempted her premeditatedly. It is glory & joy to me to know that I may aid her in carrying out the plans she has already made rather than to hinder them. Is not that true *love*. Truly, I would rather sacrifice my desires, though they worried me unto death, than to be willing to make her life less useful.

If she should grow to find that her love of me was stronger than her love of her plans, if she should find that she has mistaken her mission, I should be glad to meet her with all my desires & love, and she should aid me to conquer my foes.

God has been good to send this worthy companion and strong comforting woman after all my bitterness and the unrest of an untrusting and imperfect love.

I can only be worthy by conquering daily some fault; by living purely in true manliness; by making myself as far as possible her equal physically— *by living in God.*

FEB. 2. 1882—AT STUDIO

I have painted with some fervor today, although I have been haunted with the nightmare that has followed me so long; . . . that mother will have some kind of a cancer on her face or some otherwhere. . . .

It may be very foolish on my part. Every eruption or blotch or unevenness that I see on her face worries me anew. There is a kernel about as big as a diminutive pin head on her right cheek near the jawbone. Do what I will, vow to myself as I may to the contrary, my eyes go directly to that spot the moment I am near—at breakfast, at dinner, at supper—at all times. I sometimes fear too that I have something of the kind growing in my stomach. I pray God that it may be nonsense. That is the only disease that I truly dread. I do my best to overcome my fear. . . .*

It is a wonder to me how mother can remain at home so much. She rarely goes out. It seems strange to me that one can pass a whole life in that quiet way—I who long to see and do so much would chafe terribly. I wonder if women do accept their lot calmly and work on day after day, as mother does, doing the same things, seeing the same things, and I know not but thinking the same things from year's end to year's end.† It seems to me that it ought not to be so: that more change and gaiety ought to be infused into

---

*Grace Channing wrote, "I never knew he even had the fear;—but, in light of the event,—could it be possible the seeds of Death were at work *even so early*? He was never *well*,— or so rarely and for so brief intervals that it hardly counted." GEC to EBK, May 23, 1912, p. 80.

†Grace Channing added, "He had ceased to wonder; he had time to see the 'New Woman' developed, later on." GEC to EBK, May 23, 1912, p. 80.

our home life; but I confess that I do not know how to do it. More company would make more work for her. If one had money—. . . .

. . .

The storm was very heavy, for any latitude, but, although some of the drifts were over my head in height, and though the wind blew bitterly, I went to Charlotte—and was paid a thousand times over. For years I have not spent so holy an afternoon and so joyous an evening (for they insisted upon my supping with them). Charlotte revealed new sides to me; she showed just before and sometime after tea, a playfulness, a brilliancy tempered by thoughtfulness which were fascinating & exhilarating in the extreme. And I could see the symmetrical limbs move in enchanting rhythm—could see all the sensuous graces of her healthful body, and knew at the same time every one was held in perfect control by a strong and pure mind. And that added to the charm.

During the afternoon we discussed at length our relations to each other; defined clearly what we wanted of each other. She talked as freely of love, marriage, and the delights of both as if we were discussing the odor of violets or roses. It was such a conversation as I had dreamed of long but really never hoped to have. Every word she uttered, every look she looked, every frank touch of her hand, swept over my heart and stirred it as it was never stirred before—*never*! Not alone with amorous desire, but with the grand glory of meeting face to face a soul striving, longing, believing like mine; a soul full of noble energy and sublime sentiments.

She desires to educate herself in all things, developing every part of mind and body toward perfection—to live single so that domestic duties will not detain her—and to devote her whole life to doing good to all the world, serving whosoever asks or needs aid. She feels that her greatest usefulness and happiness lie in that thing, so does not feel that the loss of the enjoyments of a husband, home, and children would be a "renunciation." If she felt that, she says that she should suspect that her motives were not right, and that she was doing it for a very selfish reason.

I truly and unqualifiedly admire her for her resolve. Though I could love her in the extreme—and I can if I do not now—I love her too truly to attempt to injure her usefulness or her happiness. I confess that it seems sad that one who is so eminently fitted in every way to be a true, strong wife and mother should not give birth to a child—for such, I should judge would be better fitted to live than most children. But it may be that God needs her aid in the way she thinks; if so, it is well. It is not for me to judge, for I should not judge with impartiality. If my desire were attended, she should be my wife; but my will in this case is *her* good—*her* right. If she is wrong, she will be shown. My duty is to give her all the tenderness that I may; to aid her; to bear her confidence; to prove to her that, though a passionate lover, I can be a strong, earnest friend. . . .

FEB. 6. TWILIGHT

I have been examining myself to see how it was that I could think that I loved Miss —— [Angell?]. I believe truly that I did not love *her*, but myself—that is, the thoughts, feelings etc. which I projected from my own brain & soul upon her. And I think that that avowal "I love you" was only the cry of a starving man shouting for bread. It is a necessity for me to love *something*, even a worm or a flower. Miss —— [name deleted] was sweet, sentimental and gave a show of being profound. And she was pure—the *purity* of *ignorance*. A child's purity.

I am not apologizing for myself. I am not ashamed of what I did: I am not a "gay Lothario" or a "Don Juan." I am in earnest, and want to do pure & right things. . . .

And I have been searching myself through and through to see if I am not deceiving myself in regard to Charlotte.

Witness ye eternal spirits—God my Creator. I am *not* deceived. I love her with profound, enduring, supreme love. A love that swallows all other women—nay, a poor phrase: a love which covers all other women from my sight.

Charlotte, if you knew that so short a while ago I whispered those three words to —— [name deleted] would you despise me? God knows that you would not if you understood my heart. Ah, if you could but feel the weight, the glory, the strength of the love I bear to you, you would know that for the *first time* my whole being is awake. How can I make it evident to you? How? How?

It burns, burns—*burns*!

CHAPTER IV

. . . *it is hell to live thus*

February 8—March 21, 1882

BY FEBRUARY 1882, Stetson had tasted some of the success he was hoping for. He was beginning to sell some paintings, to receive an occasional positive review, and gradually to win Charlotte Perkins' love. "It is very much to have her look up to me as if I were superior: very much to know that . . . my love of her has conquered." But there were still some problems to contend with: how to earn money, to improve his drawing, to "check" his passions, to maintain his parents, to find and somehow pay for models. "All that keeps me in any degree calm is Art and Charlotte," Stetson wrote. "It is Hell to live thus." *

FEB. 8. 1882. 5 P.M. STUDIO.

I have been painting this afternoon—for two hours of it—from a naked youth of some 17 years. He has a passable form & a good ivory color. I *think* that my two hours' work is pretty good. He is coming again Saturday afternoon. He thinks that he knows of a maiden who will pose nude for me. I hope so. It is grand, I can assure anyone, this painting from life. The very symmetry and softness of flesh is an inspiration in itself. Ah, if I can but paint the nude as I can imagine it, my mission will be well fullfilled. And why may I not if I have models and time?†

---

*The above quotations are from diary entries of March 13 and Feb. 17, 1882.

† Stetson was at first optimistic about painting from this boy model, but later found him too "restless" and "uneasy" to be satisfactory. Diaries, Feb. 11, 1882; Feb. 18, 1882.

When I went from here last night I . . . found at home a letter from Charlotte which touched me strangely.

She commences it "Lover & Friend" instead of "friend & Lover" as in the previous one. She is humbled: she finds that love has broken her independent spirit in great measure. The first part of her letter is a comical account of her day's work. She wants me to call this evening—to see me again before I go to Philadelphia, which I had intended to do the tenth. Then she says among other things.

Do you know what would be *the* greatest temptation I could have? To give up my life with any show of honor. And I am just *21*.

I fear I am going to be cruelly, bitterly, utterly, disappointed in what I thought to find in you—with you. It is not your fault, dear, I would not have you a bit different; but the disappointment is in myself.

Then she continues by comparing herself to an aspiring young bird who felt the coming power to fly: he starts to cross a gulf.

Backward & forward looks equally far, and the chasm is bottomless. It must cross or return, and the new little wings ache already.

You bid fair to teach me the virtue I have most lacked, humility. I am in sackcloth and ashes just now. I feel what I have not felt for a long time—ashamed of myself.

I don't like it.

O why weren't you a girl!

Why weren't you a girl!

I want you *so much*, my friend, my fellow traveller, my compatriot soul! But when you come to me you are a man—and I? I am a woman. You have held my hand, and kissed it. Kissed it. My hand that I used to grieve over so deeply because it was so red, so coarse, so illshaped—I wouldn't change it now for the daintiest lily-fingers that ever wore gloves.

I shun your eyes—I shun your touch—because I want them. You are too much in my mind. You are beating hard at the door which I have bolted and barred, or rather which *I thought* secure because no one has ever tried it.

Cleopatra is waking and rising, stretching herself with a traitorous smile and a kindling gleam in the long black eyes. I thought to find rest & strength and comfort with you, & find myself face to face with the greatest conflict I ever saw yet. etc.

The whole letter shows that I have touched her heart and awakened her amorous desires. I am half sorry, and yet very glad.

I am going there tonight—what will happen?

While I can see that she has not been so calm & ready for work since she loves I am far more calm & can do better work. So could she if she would not struggle against it. . . .

FEB. 11. 1882. 5 P.M. SAT.

My call at Charlotte's last Wednesday evening was delightful, but not so wholly as it would have been had we been alone. She is absolutely unlike other women in her conduct. There are no hints, no equivocations & ambiguous sayings. She would not kiss even me now: and how much dearer her kisses will be for it, for I can but think that she will kiss me sometime. . . .

13TH FEB. 1882—MONDAY MORNING.

Yesterday afternoon I went to Charlotte's. Found her ready to take our Sunday walk, which has been long contemplated. It was *very* wet, & terra firma was not *firm* by any means, on account of mingled snow & mud; but I knew that I could go if she could. She went.

O, the delight, the unspeakable joy of being alone with her! There was freedom at last. . . .

We walked for two hours. Then I went home filled. . . .

I say I went home: it was to a strange task. I found that the time had come for me to tell her as fully as I could of my past life—of my love of [name deleted]. And I did so; unflinchingly; honestly. I am wholly my candid, frank self now. I have nothing to hide from her; because she can understand. . . .

In my letter, which she read yesterday, I incidentally mentioned that I could not "support" a wife. When she came to that she stopped—looked in my face with a blaze of light in her eyes and said: "You cannot believe that that would influence me at all; you certainly think better of me than that. *Never* mention that again—it must never be in our thoughts. If it were not for what you already know—my purpose—my mission—there would not be the slightest barrier between us. Remember it."

As we are going down Benevolent St., towards the sunset, she said in a low tone: "You have humbled me. You have taught me to pray."

"In what way?" said I.

[She said,] "Until a little while ago I never felt the need of prayer. I revolted from the idea of asking God for what I knew I could get myself, and what I was absolutely sure would be given me if I only lived as I ought. Even in those months when I grieved, for the first time, for my lost friend, I could not pray. I could not ask for strength to bear it, because I knew that I should bear it. So I have never prayed—except by striving. But—when you came—

what *did* you do! My heart was so full that it fairly burst from me and I found a prayer of thankfulness going to God: I found need of expressing my gratitude for what I had not asked for: I found the need of praying that I might be worthy of it all and appreciate it all. Yes, dear friend, you have made me humble, and taught me the blessedness of prayer."

I do wish that I could write as she talks: it is impossible.

There was a new peace stole in between us. The very heavens—the long salmon colored clouds in the west toward which we were going—the dull grey at the north and south, seemed bending to me, and whispering such comfort that I could have clasped them for very joy.

Ah, dear heart, you and I tread strange ways: there are hard roads, but—what inns we stop at! What singing of birds and bloom of flowers on either hand! What cloud-breaks and glimpses of heaven above! Better the foot sore way—better the burdened head and weary shoulders with such heart-joys and soul-peace.

Often when I look over my Journal it strikes me that the phrase "I pray" or "I have prayed" occurs very often. It would probably be misunderstood by most people who would interpret it as meaning that I prostrated myself in a gymnastic fashion and went through a certain formula: and that it arose from a desire on my part to cast off my burdens and have things done for me by a being called, for short, God.

It is certainly true that I feel the weakness of my soul as compared with the omnipotent. I have found that I have failed in many things: that I must bear many things. I have found that the failures were not because of a weak spirit but because I allowed my senses to be influenced by the material arguments of others. I too often for the sake of ease bowed to the dictates of custom: I found bitterness in it; found that it weakened my will and my intellect. But though convicted of my own weakness, I saw clearly that it was not an inherent weakness, but an acquired one; and that I could only restore the robust tone of my will by seeking to put it in harmony with the supreme will. That is the whole secret of my praying—a striving to rely wholly upon God, and upon myself because living in God—a striving to adapt myself to his laws—a longing to be more in Him, that is to approach more nearly to the divine perfections. It is a panting after my place in the universe—a panting desire to be instrumental with God.

I begin to feel that I am nearing my path.

My duty is to serve the ends of the universe. Not by being less an individual, but by being more of one. Not by being less self-reliant, but more self-reliant because feeling that self is right.

I want that distinctly understood by Charlotte and the world. It must bear fruit by *act*. . . .

WEDNESDAY MORNING FEB. 15. ''82

. . . The Executive Committee met last evening; after which Whitaker and I went to the concert of the Prov. Symphony Soc., upon some tickets given us by Mr. Bannister. How I enjoyed the music. The concluding number was the "War March" from Wagner's "Rienzi." Whether I was unusually sensitive at the time I can not say, but from the opening blast of trumpets to the end my blood fairly boiled and hair stood up. O how I want to hear Lohengrin—all the Nibelungen Trilogy. Perhaps it was more effective coming as it did after a soul-enchanting *Valse* by Strauss. What *is* there in the waltz movement that so excites all that is soft and sensuous? What a very wizard Strauss must be!

I would that I could hear music daily. I should paint better and think better. I am as much musician now as painter—though I can play on no instrument and sing with no excellence of voice. But I can *feel* and can tell what gives the effect, and can compose pieces of several parts in my head— that is I can originate & *hear* them. Would that I could write them! But alas! one can not do everything. If we could what gods were some of us!*

To work!

*   *   *

FEB. 17. 1882. AFTER WORK—NEAR TWILIGHT

. . . Yesterday I painted industriously & with some effect. Mr. Pearce [unidentified] brought me a notice of the Art Club exhibition—at Bos-

---

*It was characteristic of turn-of-the-century "Tonalist" or "Symbolist" painters to emphasize analogies to music, to talk about the "harmony" of color or the "rhythm" of artistic style. "The mysterious relation between 'sound music and color music' enthralled [Stetson]. Color and music both he defined as 'matters of vibration, controlled by a specially gifted soul,' and the colorist's palette was for him a 'stringed instrument,' the pigments thereon . . . notes of the natural scale upon which the artist played." [Grace Ellery Channing-Stetson], *Catalogue of the Memorial Exhibition of Works by the Late Charles Walter Stetson* (Washington, D.C.: Corcoran Gallery of Art, 1913), p. 14. At the time of his death, Stetson was working on one of his most ambitious projects, a large canvas entitled "Music."

ton—in which it said: "Mr. Stetson's *Beggar in a [Pleasure] Garden* is especially admired, both for its rich coloring and poetic composition." So I think that I have scored one. Mr. [John] Selinger says that it is very much liked, & that a gentleman was talking of buying it. I do expect pecuniary success from it.*

It certainly is pleasant to know that what I am striving for is in some measure recognized, but I feel quite sure that I could paint on and on for many years without recognition of any sort, were it not for the pecuniary inability to so do. . . .

This forenoon I devoted to making calls. Mr. Dorrance took me up to Walter Brown's studio. We have been trying to meet each other for some time. I was favorably impressed with him, although I cannot say that I think his work gives evidence of much truly poetic feeling. He seems to have joined the modern crusade against low toned pictures. His things are all light in key. Sunlight is an excellent thing but one tires of beating rays quite as quickly as of twilight gloom. Indeed to one who thinks much I must believe that the twilight gloom is most agreeable. Mayhap that he will dislike my work because it is so dim & "old master like."†

The worst thing that I can record is that my sexual desires are almost overpowering. Could I use a harlot? No—decidedly *no*! That is the pain: I am fastidious, moral, and tremendously desirous.

As yet my will conquers. But God! How my flesh is worn and how faint I am. Life at times seems scarce worth living because of it. And men—most men have surfeit.

I do not think it would be wrong to have a mistress if I can not marry: if I cannot marry the woman that I really love, it certainly would be an insult to make a woman believe that I loved her enough to marry her—to make

---

*Earlier Stetson had been pessimistic about the *Beggar in a Pleasure Garden*: "I suppose my pictures do not look very well beside the work of the Boston and N.Y. artists. And if they see any good in them probably, not knowing me, they think it copied." Diaries, Feb. 6, 1882. But as it turned out, its reception at the Boston exhibition was "decidedly a success in all ways." The *Beggar* later sold for $150 to a "first class buyer," thanks to the enthusiasm of Maud Howe Elliott, one of the first persons to recognize Stetson's "genius." GEC to EBK, May 23, 1912, p. 92.

†Walter Francis Brown (1853–1929), painter and PAC member, was illustrator of Mark Twain's *A Tramp Abroad*.

Some weeks later Stetson noted: "[Walter] Brown said that I ought to 'go to Europe' for he could see 'quick'n lightening that I had a thundering lot of stuff in me an' it oughter come out." Diaries, March 17, 1882.

her my wife. Whereas a simple mistress would be but a matter of convenience and of health. Those, the world considers, dangerous morals. I ask God to read my heart.

It is Hell to live thus.

[The following entry was added in the margin of the diary, Aug. 26, 1883: "Yes, they *are* dangerous morals, and even at the time of this entry I would not have *done* it. It was a mental affair. But now, my all is mine."]

All that keeps me in any degree calm is Art and Charlotte. Ah, if *she* might marry me! Then would be combined true love and passionate desire as they should be. But I must not hope that she ever will. I feel quite confident that I shall never marry anyone else. So it means—a mistress, I suppose. I shall certainly die if my desires are not gratified in some way.

It is strange that I can draw from the nude without a tremble or a desirous thought; it is a proof to my mind that I am not base in my desires, & that nudity has nothing to do with them.

No it is *not* baseness or its kin: it is simply a natural right to fulfill a fundamental law of our being.

I had a short letter from Charlotte yesterday afternoon. She liked my letter & my confidence, and says that she only wishes that I did not love her, for she could more easily have lived without my love than to live *against* it.

Charlotte—!

FEB. 18. 1882 — SATURDAY — 5 P.M.

This day begun well. How? I met Charlotte as I came to my studio— met her, saw her—ah, what a glorious woman, all light, all intensity, all beauty! What a goddess-like mien she had as she came toward me, the morning sun full on her unveiled face! And that smile and flash of eyes! I see them now. Was not that a glorious beginning. And tomorrow I call—on her. . . .

. . .

TUESDAY, 11 P.M. FEB. 21. 1882.

[The diary reports Stetson's first meeting with Charlotte's "greatly loved friend" Martha Luther and her fiance, Charles A. Lane. When Martha and Charles Lane arrived at Charlotte's home, Charlotte said,] . . . "This is Martha—the friend" then turning to the man, "This is the enemy, Mr.

Lane." The poor man was dumbfounded. But we made it all right. I liked Martha very much although I saw her but little. She took my hand in a way which said a great deal—and she looked into my eyes in a way that told me that she was a good soul.

I would not be surprised if Charlotte had told her of our relations. . . .

It rains & snows today—is horribly disagreeable: but I found beneath my door this morning a letter from Charles De Kay,* the poet; and it was very kind, very appreciative & frank. He has bought *The Brook* ($50−), and *The Flagroot Gatherer* ($35−) † & wants to keep the other two that I sent for a week. He sent a check for $85−.

I prize his letter very highly. It ends thus: "Congratulating you on your very evident talents & hoping that the public will not treat you with indifference, believe me yours very truly

C. De Kay."

He also says that he hopes I will try the Amer. Artists' exhibition this Spring: and that he has no objections to sending either of those which he has bought, provided his name does not appear in the Catalogue.

I had rather sell my two pictures to a man like Mr. De Kay for $85—than to sell $5000. by the advertising, boasting & bullying. . . . It is sweeter to know that I have been sought than the possession of $5000 could ever be. It is dearer to know that a poet sees in my work what I strive for than all the patronage of fruiterers & hucksters & the like could be.

I wish that De Kay could see more of my work. I think that he will.

---

* Some years later Stetson would describe art critic and patron Charles De Kay as "a poet, a collector of pictures, a true amateur, and a writer who sincerely tries to elevate the public taste and lead it to see beauty." CWS, "Criticism," A. E. Club Lectures, April 23, 1891, Club Papers, no. 143, p. 3, RIHS.

Writing for the *New York Times* in 1890, De Kay argued that "an individuality of the finest calibre was gradually asserting itself among American colorists," that Stetson was a "colorist bold beyond the ordinary." "Pictures such as he paints are the horror of all well-regulated academical artists and the good boys who find favor with the Parisian masters. Nor need it be said that Mr. Stetson would not be the better for more drill in drawing, more skill in imitating flesh and garments. But the question is whether he would be able to give us goose flesh with the dramatic quality of his color and compositions had he been forced through the molds that Paris has always kept ready for the destruction of originality since the beginning of the present century." Charles De Kay, "Three American Painters," *New York Times*, Dec. 12, 1890. See also [Charles De Kay], review of the Stetson exhibition, *New York Times*, Feb. 25, 1899, Stetson Scrapbook.

† Stetson called this *A Woman Digging Flagroot*: "Tone golden brown. Time twilight: woman . . . stooping to gather the flag. A knoll bordered with saplings & a blue & dull gold sky form the background." "Opera" Book, p. 19.

FEB. 24. 1882—FRIDAY: 2:30 P.M.

I have reached the point where I begin to count the days ere I shall see Charlotte. I have not heard from her this week, and the time seems long. . . .

The Boston Journal of Feb. 18*th* contained an excellent notice of my *Beggar in a Pleasure Garden* (which is, of course, at the Boston Art Club). I think I will copy it here as it is the first notice of the kind, the first unprejudiced notice, I have received.

It says:

Another unfamiliar name is that of Charles W. Stetson, whose "Beg. in Pleas. Gar.", No. 171, is a work which has strong characteristics. The tone of the picture is somewhat treacly, but the command of strong color in producing a rich and harmonious effect is quite unusual. There is an unreality about the work which suggests Albert P. Ryder, & undeniably has much of his charm; and the painting has an opulent glow about it which now recalls the method of Ziem's best work, and now has in it a faint reminder of Allston. Whoever this artist is, it is evident that with training and persistence to which is evidently an original habit of thought, he will yet do some remarkable work.*

What could I ask better than that?

Not a word is said of the faults. Ah, the faults—faults—*faults!* What if there are beauties and novelty,—what care I for all that save as a slight encouragement, when I know how much the work lacks? That bit of criticism is sweet to me, but it is the sweetness of a flower that vanishes in a day. I must struggle the harder and forget that my work has any good in it. . . .

27TH FEB. 1882—MONDAY MORN.

I am once more ready for work. The pictures about me disclose new beauties & new faults, although I saw them but a day ago. I have grown since Saturday night: for I saw Charlotte yesterday. And why grown because of her? She stimulates like sunlight, and wind—like wine, and the stimulation is permanent, and not at the risk of a following depression.

I feel perfectly at ease with her; perfectly at rest. . . . And she is at ease with me—I think. She has fully decided that her life must be a single one, and, as is well known to me, not for any low motive, not because she shrinks from the duties of wifehood & motherhood, but because she feels that her mission is still higher.

---

* Stetson was quoting directly from "The Art Club's Exhibition," *Boston Evening Journal*, Feb. 18, 1882, p. 4.

God knows that it is not for me to say that it is not. I know the force of conviction: I know what it means to feel that one has a calling that must be pursued at any cost. If she can help the universe more by being alone, that is as it should be. What if it robs me of light and supreme joy? I shall still have the knowledge of loving—loving in its very fullest sense—and if she is not my wife she will be loved nonetheless.

She was glad to see me yesterday afternoon. A soft glow of content and love shone from her. Her face was as mildly warm as the most sensuous mind could desire. The warm blood appeared beneath the skin; the supple neck bent & curved; the cream white throat swelled; the nostrils dilated, trembled, fluttered like the wings of a lighted butterfly. The eyes blazed when full of some noble emotion they met mine; then they softened into something more than tender and delicate before they turned away. We talked uninterruptedly all the afternoon, as only two beings who feel sure of each other can talk. It was an earnest [?] of some far distant paradise toward which we journey. . . .

I must not hope in the slightest that she will find my love & the thoughts of a life with me of more importance than what seems to be her mission. I must hope for nothing but strength to extract all my happiness from the thought of mutual regard and duty done.

Indeed it is somewhat like having a prison with a thick glass window looking out upon Eden. Behind, hell with nothing to separate me from it: before, heaven with a wall of glass—heaven offering all its sweets to this modern Tantalus story.

I do not quite know what to do this morning. I feel my lack of skill tremendously and the subjects that I have begun require just what I lack. Perhaps it were wise to wait until I *must* paint, skill or no skill.

I showed Charlotte Mr. De Kay's letter & also the article in the Boston *Journal*. She was far more pleased than I. Indeed what little pleasure they did evoke has entirely gone.

I and the insect on the Himalayas: miles & miles above, around stretch the giants. I am little, weak, and sensitive to the heats and chills. What can I do? Climb those miles to the clouds? . . .

FEB. 28. 1882. MORNING.

This is another atmospherically delightful day.

When I reached home last evening I found a little surprise in the form of a card, thus:

> *"Mrs. Rowland Hazard*
> *Miss Hazard*
>
> Tea Thursday March 2nd   5 to 8 o'clock"

Never having met the mother or daughter, I suppose that the invitation comes through or by (in some way) Charlotte.*

Now I must confess that such things are dreadful bores to me. I shall give up the ghost if this is only the beginning of many similar invitations. I want my time to myself. I cannot afford to waste it upon people whom I cannot benefit. At least I can't see how I can benefit them. Besides it is dreadfully awkward. I don't know what is expected of a fellow at an afternoon tea. Is it formal or informal? Must one wear a swallowtail to be au fait?

All together *I don't like it.*

There is another side of course. The Hazards are cultured, wealthy and in the right set for a poor artist to be with. Doubtless it will help me pecuniarily: and that is not to be despised when one has so much to spend for as I, and so meagre an income as I.

I must see Charlotte this evening & ascertain what I must do. I am a perfect child in such matters. To be sure I have always acquitted myself decently when with the "*fine folk.*"

THURSDAY, MARCH 2. 1882; MORNING.

Here I am, ready again to woo the witch of art. I slept quite well last night, although I was nervous enough when I went to bed.

I dreamt a strange dream. It was a clear starlight night with a suspicion of moonrise in the sky. I was walking by the open lots near Durfee's Mill when I heard a rattling sound like rifle shots fired in rapid succession. Out of the sky came a meteor—not a starwhite meteor but one black as coal. It came directly towards me. I jumped aside and it struck the earth, became dismembered, & bright as the sun was each part. And then each separate part became like a living thing chasing me as I ran. Every time I dodged it

---

*The Hazard family was very prominent in Providence in the 1880s. Rowland Hazard II was superintendent of the Peacedale Woolen Mills, scientist, man of letters, and philanthropist. On this occasion Stetson did not accept the Hazard invitation, but later attended their social functions, and even said that he admired them. He found Mrs. Hazard (whose portrait he painted) "full of refinement, kindliness, and all the loveable qualities"; Caroline Hazard (later President of Wellesley) was "refined, kind, sweet-voiced, [and] dignified." Occasionally, however, Stetson was deeply antagonized by the Hazards' "high and mighty" manner. See Diaries, Oct. 18, Dec. 1, 1882; Nov. 22, 1886.

struck the earth, and with every such contact it multiplied. Not once was I hit until after many dodgings. I was tired out & fell: then the strange substance with a thousand explosions turned to a fine granulated matter & covered me. O, how each morsel stung me to the very bone with its fire! I awoke—as I ought to have done before.

What interpretation would the dream readers put upon that. It is a little like the dream recorded of Nimrod. Only the stars of heaven fell upon him & then a strange Being stood before him—with claws.

I went to see Charlotte as I purposed. She was not home when I arrived so I had a pleasant talk with her mother. I like her mother very, very much; she seems very tender and spiritual minded.*

By & by Charlotte came. . . .

[Walter continued to worry about the Hazards' invitation to tea, and Charlotte tried to reassure him. The best solution is to "go as simply as possible," she told him.] "They know that I am poor and that I am Charlotte Perkins. I think you had better go, as they want to know you, and it is the most informal of formal occasions. I shall be at work all day—out all the afternoon, and shall positively wear the dress I have on."

"The Hazards have done a great deal for me."

Then she smiled & enumerated the things they had done, and I confess they were many. Women less sincere than Charlotte would have been ashamed to own some of the things they have done for her. . . .

AFTERNOON   . . . Charlotte was showing me something and while doing so my hand touched hers, and I held it. After a little she drew it slowly away, and blushed. It was a blush of pleasure. Then she said hesitatingly—. . . which was a great contrast to her usual positive way of speaking—"I have been wondering if it is quite right for me to let you hold my hand as long as—as long as—I am not going to give you my whole self." Then she told about how delightful my touch is to her; of how much she wanted it. I could not clearly see what she was trying to express; indeed I have my doubts that she did. I think however that she feels herself growing weaker and more needy of the expression of love. . . .

[She said,] "O, it is so hard to keep from giving way to my feelings!— such a conflict: and I am growing weaker!"

[Stetson replied,] "My heart, Charlotte, says to you, give way! My mind says, if you have your conviction still of what is right for you cling to

---

*In an earlier entry he had written: "Mrs. Perkins told me of her past life. And what a romantic one! Perhaps I shall utilize it in some novel sometime." Diaries, Feb. 27, 1882.

your conviction at any cost. I think that you could do better work, more acceptable work if you would allow your physical desires, yes, your mental desires to be gratified. They would then be at rest and your mind would have freedom for work. . . ."

"I know it! I know well that I must have love from *some* source sometime: and if it were not that I fear that I should want my old freedom back again as soon as the first blush of happiness was gone, I would relinquish at once. I fear that my individuality would be too strong &—and—and—. . . . Do you think I can do it?!"

"Do what—resist?" I asked.

"Yes," said she.

"I think you can," said I: "and if it is right I hope you will."

Then she rose. . . .

Time will certainly prove my love to her: and today for the first time— I dare *hope*!

I think it is clearing up. Tomorrow I expect to go to Boston.

P.S. Some of my entries read like the sentences in a primer!

FRIDAY, MARCH, 3; 1882. 8 A.M.

. . . Last evening at half past eight I went to Charlotte's. . . .

Charlotte had been thinking a great deal about our love for each other & was glad of an opportunity to talk of it. She said that she had come to some conclusions. I dare not attempt to repeat the words which she said but they were to the effect that she was still more confident of the genuineness of her mission. That, although she loved me with all her heart, yet she must not give me her body. That we were in most things *one*: that I filled a place which has been cruelly empty. But that she could not marry me, or even grant me the caresses of a lover—the major caresses.

That she was satisfied with me; that I was the first man whom she had ever felt to be her equal, and that she felt me to be her superior. She could look up to me etc.

I must be stupid this morning for I cannot remember with distinctness all that she said. I know however that it meant that she had found that she really loved me and that she was ready to give her highest self: all that she now could give. That she felt a great inward happiness in my love.

I was very, *very* deeply touched and knew that she meant every word uttered, and they were noble words. . . .

Charlotte seems to desire to impress me with the fact that she is making an enormous sacrifice (as perhaps she is) and that she is as much as any woman pleased by the pleasures of her senses and of sex. She is without a shadow of doubt quite honest. . . .

Such love is absolutely noble, and how rare! *Her* love I mean.

I wish that the rest might be added so that the unity might not be marred, and yet I have all that is best of her to commune with, love, care for. The things of her which I should most love she gives me: the lasting attributes, the eternal.

No life, however hard, could be too long to live with her.

Better a wasting body—better an uneasy desire unsatisfied, with such love—O God how infinitely better! than all else beside.

Charlotte, loving me so you will find your way of life harder even than you think to bear—you will have almost irresistible impulses to give me your body as well. But I must help you to bear it: for if I should do what I could do you would fail. God keep me from that. . . .

· · ·

WEDNESDAY, MARCH 8TH 1882 AFTERNOON.

. . . I have read some of Dante Rossetti's sonnets. There is a wonderfully sustained fervor and solemn loving in them. It is not the expression of a hysterical youth but the expression of ripe manhood which feels sublime love in its soul. How like tinkling brass my own weak sonnets sound beside them. And yet I knew that my meaning is just as pure & high as his. He has the full measure of the singer's gift and I have only a little. But we work I think in the same spirit and for the same end—the glorification of Love, of woman & of God: of all that pertains thereto.*

Charlotte has been in my mind all day: not to the exclusion of my duties but as a helping spirit—a lamp to guide my effort; a strong wine to vivify my half fainting spirit.

Yesterday's mail brought me a very good & sympathetic letter from Mrs. Cresson. It seems odd to read at the heading "My Dear Boy."

I know that she thinks a great deal of me. And I am glad. She surmises that I am loving Charlotte, and she says that she is half sorry, for she thinks her not suited to me, being too near like me. . . .

---

*Grace Channing added: "To *me* it [is] a deeply interesting entry as the first touch of Rossetti in his life; he loved his poetry always; in London we came to know his pictures; and in Rome the present generation of Rossettis were to become our dear friends. It was Olive Rossetti Agresti who looked last upon his face with us; she alone went with us and stood beside us when the doors of the furnace closed about him." GEC to EBK, May 23, 1912, p. 89.

MARCH 10. 1882. EVENING. 5:30 P.M

. . . I saw her Wednesday night. . . .

. . . She told me that she loved me so earnestly that I could not doubt it in the least. I read to her some of Rossetti's sonnets which seemed to be utterances of my own soul. They affected her deeply. Then she put her hand in mine & looked with a pity that smote me sorely: tears came to her eyes: to *her* eyes—eyes which shed tears at no self denial, no privation & pain.

I am so jaded with my work tonight that I shall not be able to write clearly. I will only say that I can see that I give her all she has ever dreamt of love & its fellows, that I give her complete happiness. . . .

I have been painting from Mrs. Nye* again this afternoon (and it is becoming a bore: I do not enjoy it a bit) & also during the day upon what I intend calling *The Honey moon* (6 × 11″). A golden glow with spring trees & a man & woman nude clasped in each other's arms beneath them. It seems to me to convey the sweetness, purity, solitariness & holiness of love. I like it best of anything I have now. I shall try to exhibit it in our coming exhibition. It may not be accepted on account of the two (too) nude figures. But I think that it will be liked. It *ought* to be, and that is what I can rarely say of my own work.†

MARCH 11TH 1882. 11:30 A.M. (SAT.)

When I reached home last night I found a delightful letter from *my* Charlotte. She wrote it at 9:50 the night before—so two letters that day, one at sunrise, the other at bed time.

I cannot find words to make apparent the feeling that she gives me. It comes very near the ideal I have always had of love—feeling. She has given herself up now to love, and finds pure rapture in it. It is her first love of the kind. She finds hot tears coming even at the thought of losing me, she says. She finds that the knowledge that I love her brings body-rest & soul-peace. . . .

What harder work I have to do! Success means mightier struggle. Bannister says that few men who have painted as little while as I get as good prices for their pictures. I think it is true. I do not feel that I get too much

____

*Mrs. Nye was a model for Stetson and a number of his colleagues.

†Very likely this is *Saturnian Honeymoon* (6 × 11 inches, cherry panel): "Male & female nude figures by a river bank at twilight, embraced. Crescent moon above. Tone golden brown. . . . Sold to the George V. Cressons, May 22, 1882." "Opera" Book, p. 25.

for them. I sell very few & if I got but 5 or 10 dollars each for them I should almost starve. I think that at some time—perhaps a date far distant—my pictures will bring somewhat large prices. But it is a mere feeling, as vague as many are that I have. . . .

13TH MARCH, ''82, 5:30 P.M.

. . . I am discovering gradually many of the kind offices she has performed among the sick & poor: I am discovering new beauties in her character & new qualities of goodness. My heart fills unutterably full when I realize that I can walk hand in hand with her, sympathizing, loving, believing. It is very much to have her look up to me as if I were superior: very much to know that she confides in me; that she feels humble towards me— that she *loves* me! That my love of her has conquered. O, Charlotte, Charlotte, you say that you are very "happy." What have I done to you or for you? . . .

MARCH 16. 1882. THURSDAY 10 A.M.

I thought I would write a few words before commencing work, as it may make me calmer. I do not feel much peace this morning—I mean *quiet*; my soul is not very vexed. It is more the mind & body.

I am feeling somewhat of my fear as regards mother's face. And she is not well. I may be in one of my morbid fits (and I pray that it may be so) but that tiny kernel looks this morning like a huge volcano to me. I am surrounded by talk of disease and decay. It eats into my mind & fills me with vague irritation. I feel satisfied that I do not fear the act of dying. I feel satisfied that if I should die today I should not lose my love.

Sometimes—& not infrequently—I feel as if I were one of those whose life is simply promise: one of those who die before the fulfillment. Such as Keats—such as Monticelli, such as Regnault & Géricault, without, perhaps, much of their talent and genius. This morning such feelings taunt me with what I have done. Ah, how little it is! What I have not done. How great!!

I know that all of this is useless. I must live until my organs fail. I shall live no longer than that; I must bear pain of body & that far more excruciating pain of watching the suffering of others, of those I do not & do love. The temper of my soul will be tried. I fear that it is all too soft for buffeting. . . .

.   .   .

MARCH 20. 1882 MONDAY

Yesterday I went to Charlotte's. Mrs. Perkins met me at the door & said: "Have you strong nerves?" I realized that I turned pale; but I said, "yes; what has happened?" "Charlotte, poor girl, has met with an accident." "At the Gymnasium?" I asked. "Yes; but not while exercising." "Is it serious?" said I trembling inwardly. "Somewhat so." "I think you had better let me see her," said I. "O, yes; certainly. I thought that I would prepare you."

Then I went in & found Charlotte lying on the lounge in the sitting room, looking little like an invalid, but more womanly than ever. I took her hand in both mine & said nothing for a little while.*

Then she told me how it was done but not where. I suspect that it was about the pubis. She thought she would set the clock at the Gymnasium, so she mounted a chair & was about to put her foot upon the top of the up-right piano when the chair went from under her & she fell upon its sharp edged back. The loss of blood was considerable; but after telling Dr. Brooks [Providence physician] about it, he said that with her absolute health . . . she would find but little difficulty. She was quite comfortable yesterday.

So I sat by her all the afternoon, excepting the half hour in which I did an errand for her mother, holding her hand, stroking her head & caressing her as I must. She enjoyed it I know & I am sure it made her tenderer towards me. I laid my head upon her breast & she did not wish it removed. I put my arms about her, & she found it good. It was very hard to keep my lips from hers, but I did it, because I knew that she wanted to keep them until she could give her entire self. . . .

It is a hard fight she is fighting. It will be hard for her to give up to me & it will be almost as hard to keep from it. . . .

TUESDAY, MARCH 21ST 1882

. . . Charlotte has acquired new tenderness since her accident. She talked to me tenderly, lovingly; and said that she wished she more fully repaid my love of her: wished that she was more of a woman; wished that she

---

*Charlotte wrote her friend Charlotte Hedge on the occasion of this "accident": "I, the strong and impregnable; I, the budding athlete and Chief Performer at the Providence Ladies Sanitary Gymnasium; I, the surefooted and steady eyed, ignominiously tumbled over a chair, and so injured myself that I was laid up for four days. . . . I have been blessed with more callers than I have had time for in all winter, and with bananas, *strawberries*, oranges, candy ice, and flowers in abundance. Should like to do it again sometime." CAP to Charlotte Hedge, March 26, 1882, AESL.

could make me understand how great she felt my love to be and what an honor to her, etc. Then, notwithstanding her lameness she arose & followed me to the door. There was a piteous look in her face (Ah! how different from the triumphant conqueror's look of sometime ago!) which thrilled me. Then she put out her hand & laid it in mine; then drew it to her breast—and I lifted it to my lips, & looked into her pure eyes meanwhile; then—Ah God!—then—she put her arm around my neck & laid her cheek against mine, & I kissed it. O, what an embrace was that! Our first embrace. The first time my lips have touched her face. March 21st.

I withdrew myself with a fuller heart than she could know but calm outwardly & said; Become well soon dearest, Good night, left her standing with an indescribable humility in her face and a surpassing sweetness.

But there was not an atom of joy in my heart. Her act, her soft skin & the purity of her nature exalted & thrilled me: but joy was not there: for I could but feel that it was only preparing a bitterer day for me. And why? I know not. I know that she loves me; but I am sure that we shall both suffer more than we have yet.

I shall meet it & face it & if I fall my face shall be towards the foe. . . .

CHAPTER V

. . . *of tender love and selfish struggle*

March 22–August 12, 1882

IN THIS SECTION, Walter seems particularly intense, particularly
exalted in his passions, particularly exacting in his standards for himself and
friends. In part it was because of constantly recurring illness, but clearly it
also was because of Charlotte. For while he occasionally was able to focus on
some outside interests—preparing for an Art Exhibit, visiting the Cressons
in Philadelphia, taking a sketching trip to Nova Scotia—for the most part
love-based struggles occupied his mind. Self-righteously, he copied Charlotte's lengthy letters, explained his own perspectives, and provided in the
process a novel-like record of roller-coaster struggles in love. "O I hope that
the world may know of those letters some day," he wrote.*

WEDNESDAY, MARCH 22. 1882. 1:15 P.M.

[The evening before, Walter and Charlotte had exchanged letters and
read them together.] . . . Hers was long—12 pages—11 pages rather, and was
a curious, passionate mixture of love, yielding and rebellious, of tender love
and selfish struggle. She calls me in it a profusion of endearing names—beginning with "Good morning, Sweetheart" and ending with "my love." Yes,
she has called me everything but husband.

---

*The above quotation is from the diary entry of April 8, 1882.

Ah, but after all that sweetness she said she was preparing to give me up. I will quote from the letter as I have it in my pocket.

8 A. M.

Good morning, Sweetheart!

It is cold & bleak enough outside, but my life is full of sunshine, & I want to send you a little if possible. I am up betimes, as you see, and have just breakfasted luxuriously on big crimson bananas, like a lively young Sybarite as I am.

Now I want to know, dearest of brothers & lovers and friends, if you have a "real living sense" of my state of mind?

Only two months, and I am getting to love you as well as I foresaw that I should in our first talk.

But O my dear! my dear! the more I love you, and the more I grow accustomed to the heaven of your love, the less I wish for anything further. My life remains all that I have dreamed it, only in sunshine instead of shade, but you—.

O why wasn't I made like other women, that I might come to you like Lady Geraldine, only wishing myself the worthier to reward your pain and patience as it deserves!

Please forgive me if I hurt you, dear—I know I shall both now & always. That is the sad truth underlying the little porcupine ballad,—the more I wish to please—the more I love a person—the more I *hurt* them without ever knowing it.

Dearest (you are the dearest even now I think, & grow dearer every day) I cannot, I fear never can, give you enough to make up for the love which almost appalls me, as I begin to see its whole grandeur. Not the whole yet, I *cannot.* . . .

I should be ashamed, dear, if it were not that simple truth can know no shame. See then. Firstly. I love you better than anyone else. You have first place in my heart, first place in my confidence, first place in my life, as far as I can see. To you I turn in pleasure and pain, helper & comforter, friend & lover: with you at hand I ask for nothing else. And what do I give?

Well, you know how I loved my friend. For you the same—only more.

It was enough, between us girls, to almost tip the scales against her lover. And between *us*! through years & years—Ah! I was wrong to underrate myself—I *can* love, and I love you!

You have the advantage now, but give me a few years grace, & it shall go hard if I do not love you as well (though differently) as you love me. I cannot help it, dear— I cannot, *cannot, cannot* be any different!

It is not that you are not the one—'be that should come'; if ever any two people fitted each other we do. But I am sure with a certainty that grows with my love, that my life is not for any *one*, or any *few*; but for as many as I can reach; for action & responsibility, for the outside of the ring in running. It is as natural to me as air to birds & water to fishes—to carry the bundles, & hold the umbrella—to care for myself and others. There is a sense of dislocation & incongruity in *my* being done *for*—you can't see it of course, for you see the soft & feminine side, what there is of it.

Would it not have been better, dear, if you had "come once more, and no more" & said goodbye while yet there was time?

Could you do it now?

It is a cold, white, sickening pain to *think* of it, but if you cannot be satisfied with what I can give you, do not for God's sake waste a great life without return. Rouse yourself before it is too late, and leave me.

I can live, sweet. Your love & the splendors thereof are *added to* my life, & I hardly dare believe—I have not dared believe that it was mine forever.

Don't misunderstand me now of all times—what can I say to make myself plain!

You *must* believe that I love you, if you feel still as I do now, the touch of cheek to cheek & hand to hand—your kiss is warm on my neck, love—your eyes are ever with me. But much as I love you I love <u>WORK</u> better, & I cannot make the two compatible.

Now I am afraid you will misunderstand this, & think that my love is like yours. It isn't, dear, it isn't. Sitting by my side, holding my hand, alone with our common thoughts & fancies you were not contented—*I was*.

To have you as you are—with love & trust, with mutual confidence & respect—with all the thousand ties of kindred heart & brain—dearest, you would give all else to hold me in your arms & whisper "wife"! While I am more than contented with the honor of being your *friend*. "The *pity* of it." I feel as if my life were shadowed by a curse, that I must needs bring pain where most I love. The thought haunted my girlhood, was forgotten in a two years' happy love (Martha's) & now returns with a dreary reiterance that sounds like fate.

It is no use, dear, no use. I am meant to be useful & strong, to help many and do my share in the world's work, but not to be loved.

And I almost dared to dream that I *was* what for your sake I wish I were.

Where now is the sunshine with which I began this letter?

It was the happy consciousness of your love, dear; and now I am making up my mind to go without it.

I am sorry. *So* sorry!

"And still she sobbed,—
'not for the pain at all,' she
said, 'but for the Love, the
poor good love you gave me.'"

Goodbye, my love.

Charlotte A. Perkins

I have copied the chief part of her letter. I read it twice while she sat reading mine. Now & then I would look at her & I could see tears in her eyes, & I remember that her bosom heaved sobbingly.

The latter part of her letter seemed to freeze me—and stab me—&

wither all my hope. O, the pity! A woman so grand so lovable, so truly noble & gentle to not be able to love as she would. I really think that she loves me better than she knows herself. But I concluded in my own mind that it were well to leave her. If she was settled to her choice, it was enough. My throat was dry & swollen. . . .

. . . I left her, God knows how.

I went to the Club: but could not sit still. I reread her letter. Something told me to go to her—that she needed me: that she was suffering—that I ought to ascertain precisely what she wished me to do. So getting excused from the committee I took a car to her house. . . .

I told her that she mistook me when I said that I was not content that afternoon. I was content with what I had, but not with my life as a whole. I told her that she had given me enough already to last me very long: that she could not be expected to give what she had not; that if she gave all that she could it was sufficient. "Of such as I have give I unto thee etc." That it seemed to me a poor love which was only of what it received. That I should love her if she gave me nothing in return.

"I cannot understand it—I was not made to be loved—it is not for me. Are you *sure* that it is *me* that you love?" said she.

I am as sure as I can be, I told her. That it might be that I loved a certain idea which I projected on her I could not say with positiveness, but I thought not: that I was as sure that I loved *her*, as of anything.

Her love of me conquered her!

"O, I do want you!" she exclaimed and she put her hands in mine.

She said that she had lived a year in the last hour. Lived it? said I, yes, but you have not done a year's '*work*'! She looked into my eyes with a deep intelligence.

Then we settled that she should give me all that she could; and she averred that she *loved* me.

The truth is she has so high an idea of what is due to a lover that she feels herself insignificant. I am more than satisfied with the love of so pure & high a soul. . . .

. . . My true love *shall* conquer, if God prevents not.

MARCH 25. 1882. 2 P.M.

This is my 24th Birthday.

Last evening I found when I reached home one of Charlotte's letters. I think it almost the most delightful that she has yet written to me. . . .

APRIL IST 1882 9:30 A.M.

It seems a long time since last Saturday, because I have been ill during it—and also, I suppose, because I have received many letters from my Love.

I say I have been sick. O yes, with what looks like an incipient consumption of the lungs, but what in God's name I hope to be but an influenza. . . .

[Charlotte came by his home to bring kisses as a surprise "remembrance" for his birthday.] "You shall have twenty-four!" said she. Then she kissed me again passionately.

Said I after a little, Save some, Darling, for a future time.

"Ah," said she "they are inexhaustible." The afternoon was simply a foretaste of Paradise—O, yes, paradise itself. She came time & again & knelt at my feet, & embraced me, as only an intellectual woman who loves can embrace. . . .

SATURDAY, 4 P.M. APRIL 8TH 1882.

How good it seems to be able to enjoy the tender spring air after my short but severe illness. . . .

Dr. [Edward] Allen has been very kind to me.* I think I have won his friendship completely. And mother & father were never tenderer & more solicitous. I think at one time in my illness it seemed to them all that they were about to lose this "young man of remarkable promise as a colorist": and they all began to feel that they should indeed *lose* some thing if it were so to be.

It was a great thing for Charlotte. She for the first time fully realized what I have become to her. And when she saw the possibility—of losing me her heart for a moment sank in a way that was new to her—as her letters show—and with a passionate pain, as her letters show. . . .

I am glad that I was ill. I have learned many things by it & it has strengthened me wonderfully in all my better qualities. . . .

. . . And how broad the future looks! How full of great & good deeds & tender thoughts & noble thoughts and of friendly & sexual joy with her.

I have managed to get four pictures ready for our exhibition of this month. *The First Caress, A Saturnian Honeymoon, Sacrifice,* & *Portrait of Dorrance.* . . .

---

*Edward S. Allen was a medical doctor, an art patron, and a long-term friend of Stetson's.

WEDNESDAY, AP. 12, 1882. 3:30 P.M.

I have been so busy helping arrange the coming Exhibition at the Club that I have not had time for any other work. Two evenings I have not been home before twelve o'clock. Most of the work is done now, however; and we have the best exhibition of contemporary American art that has ever been held in the city, I think. . . .

My three pictures reproach me somewhat—indeed very much, when I compare them with Wm. Sartain's "Revery," and A[lexander] H. Wyant's "Evening,"* and some others. I am not so blind that I cannot see that my work has a certain kind of merit that nothing else here has, but taken as a whole I think it falls far short of the standard set by this exhibition. I was a little depressed by it the first day: gradually the depression has worn away until now I think that the better work encourages me to new effort. . . .

[A large section of the diary has been torn or cut out here.] Great God, love the holy sanctifies all for us. Blind men only see the sensual while such as I, feeling love's truth and essential goodness, see through the sensual to that soul-delight of spiritual love. It seems to me that there exists for me no material thing, and that love as expressed in the body is but the joy of two souls uniting in creation. And it is a god-like joy.

Charlotte is growing more and more to understand or feel the full benefit of love, as she told me in a letter which I read Monday afternoon. I think that ere long, with her strong nature love will occupy in her life as much space as it does in mine: and in me love and life lose themselves in each other. . . . [Again, sections of the diary, apparently pertaining to his first love relationship, have been removed.]

Charlotte said the other day to her mother & Mrs. Robbins: "This is the only man whom I have met who has not been afraid of me. He does not frighten worth anything."

Charlotte, after she has been talking, say about philology, the germ theory, Egyptian history, has a way of talking as childishly (not weakly) as can be imagined, in a charmingly playful way. It is a startling contrast. And contrasts seem to rule in her nature. She is independent, but she likes to nestle by my side and depend on me. She is at the head of the Gymnasium, yet she can be as soft & gentle as a weakly woman. . . .

----

*Landscape painter William Sartain (1843–1924) was a founder of the Society of American Artists, President of the New York Art Club, and later a teacher at the Art Students' League in New York. Alexander Wyant (1836–1892), landscape artist, has well-known works in the Metropolitan Museum of New York, the Corcoran Art Gallery, and the National Gallery in Washington, D.C.

FRIDAY, AP. 14. ''82 3:50 P.M.

Charlotte has just been here. She called to ask me to come to her house this evening, as Mrs. Robbins* & her mother were going to be out, and we could have a longed-for private tête-à-tête. . . .

Charlotte has awakened me a little & the prospect of a long evening with her is charming. The gods keep other callers away! We never yet have had an evening wholly to ourselves.

This morning I corrected the last proof sheets of the catalogue and painted a very little. This afternoon I have painted some but not in a vigorous or satisfactory manner. . . .

APRIL 19. 1882. 3 P.M.

Owing to the Art Club Reception and a hundred little things I have not been able to write.

Last Saturday was one of the saddest strangest & most horrible days that I can tell of. During the early part of the day Miss Anne A[ngell?] called. . . . [Although most diary entries discussing Miss Angell(?) have been removed, there are enough remaining to indicate that she still called on him occasionally, attempted to reactivate the friendship, and even urged him to marry her. On May 9, 1882, Stetson wrote: "Miss (name deleted) was here when I arrived this morning. She will soon have another of her insane fits I know—God pity her! She wanted me to kiss her goodbye but I could not because of the environing spirit of my love. I told her why I could not. But she said I was a Roman priest—and she came and kissed my cheek—'in reverence' said she."]

APRIL 22 (SATURDAY) 1882. 2:30 P.M.

. . . I feel very strangely. Life looks more serious than ever. A thousand ideals that I have had are low in the dust. Morality seems almost without foundation (although I could not be immoral with out disgust). I doubt some of the very best things of life, Charlotte remains like a fair star shining in all my darkness.

I hope to be with her tomorrow. Charlotte! Charlotte! Stretch out the hand of your pure womanhood and lift me from my dark place!

In regard to Art I feel despondent. And my money is almost gone. Charlotte!!

---

*Caroline Robbins was Charlotte Perkins' aunt, Mary Perkins' half sister.

MONDAY AP. 24. 1882 9 A.M.

I was with Charlotte yesterday. . . .

. . . [H]er mother, good woman that she is, is very conventional, and she tells Charlotte that unless she means to marry me she has no right to show me any more attention than she does other young men who call. And that she must not see me alone & a hundred other trivial things. Charlotte at first tried to reason with her, but found it to be no use. Charlotte asked her if she could conceive of no middle ground between an accepted lover & a friend merely. Her mother said, yes, she could, but it should not be done in her house. Now Mrs. Perkins is a gentle woman & means well, but she does make a perfect hell for Charlotte simply because she does not understand her, and does not sympathize with her ideas as far as she does understand them.

I know that Charlotte tries to bear it all pleasantly & patiently but her impatience will come out at times. Charlotte is not happy in her way of addressing her mother, because the mutual differences of two strong individuals have been fostered religiously. Poor girl! Strong though she is I pity her.

Now Mrs. Perkins & Mrs. Robbins like me very well. I know it. But as for going there in an unwelcome manner I will not. I shall not practice hypocrisy. Unless it can be seen by them that Charlotte loves me & I love her, I shall not go there except to call for Charlotte to go to walk or the like.

And I wrote a letter to Charlotte last night and said things to that effect. I *will* not act such a lie. I should lose my self respect & my freedom & I do not want that effect.

I also told Charlotte that I should, if I were situated as she, have it distinctly understood that I loved Chas. W. Stetson better than I loved any man: and that he knew my feelings & thoughts regarding matrimony, & that I should not marry him unless I could fully believe it to be compatible with my life work & character. And that we were to see & have as much of each other as possible under such limitations. . . .

IST, MAY ''82 9 A.M. MONDAY

Yesterday I was again with Charlotte. We walked to Hunt's Mills & back. I really think that we were in heaven. I have never known a tenderer day or a holier one. There was neither fear nor unrest. The sky was full of a soft warmth, and our hearts must have felt its influence.

A thousand beauties appealed to us both from among the opening buds & the flowers, the tender rushes pushing themselves from the swamps:

the glorious trembling of the amber water with its resinous but clear shadows, over the dam & the big rocks at the mills. But I have not [time] to write much. I can do no better than say that it was wholly without a jarring word; wholly without even the faintest intimation of wrong or distrust. Our souls I am sure were interfluent.

We talked of nature, of pictures, of ancient literature, of Love. And she talked ah, how tenderly & purely! of the goodness of bearing to me children; of training them: and also of a home that we might have. And she said: "You would not mind if I supported myself?" An interrogatory semi-assertion hard to describe without the sound. It took me some minutes to answer. And the answer was that I should rather support her; besides if she bore to me, she would have little time to earn for herself: except by writing, perhaps; in which case I should not object. Then she smiled.

I think that the idea of being my wife & the mother of my children is taking deep hold upon her. I *know* that it is. . . .

I can well believe that Swedenborg lived in Heaven. How can I doubt, since I have been there—and walked with my body over six or seven miles of varied landscape?

Now, with a prayer, to work.

THURSDAY, MAY 4. 1882. 4:30 P.M.

. . . Charlotte is loving me more than she is aware herself. Her ideas of life are certainly changing & changing rapidly in my favor. It is true that I have directly done little or said little in the way of attempt to change her. It is rather the mere fact that I love her & the softening influence of the varied manifestations of that love which are doing the work. . . .

She talks of my children & her children: a talk alas! which is dangerous to her if she really does not expect to marry me. And she is cultivating herself in body & mind so as to be worthy to bear such children & to train them when born. Such cultivation will indeed be excellent if she has no need of it for the particular purpose.

And I too am trying to live 'worthily & nobly.' It grows heavenly sweet to think of!

Why should I hide from myself the truth that I am making her life still more serious & beautiful than it ever has been? I know that my influence over her has been the best: I know that she has grown less anxious to say bright things & things degrading though witty of high & holy things: not that I think she has ever had low ideals (I *know* that she has not), but she has had a delight that belongs to clear heads in picking flaws in doctrines & theories & taking the step from sublime things to the ridiculous. She will overcome that as I have. The temptation in me to say sharp things about sublime subjects is immense. I have been able in good measure of late years to overcome it.

(Her fun is of a hearty kind & I appreciate it.)

Well, we have done each other good. She glorifies my life & gives me what I have always needed. A love which is whole & which I could trust to any length. . . .

SATURDAY, 4 P.M. MAY 6. 1882

It seems to me that I have done very little manual work this past week. My 30 × 40—Autumnal Sacrifice is growing & will eclipse almost all my other work as to color & dignity of composition.* Whitaker was in this afternoon & said apropos of it, that he could not but feel that sometime my work would be appreciated. I do really think that there is far more in my work than the people as a whole see. But such things cannot be hid forever, and if there is that which is good in my work someone sometime will find it. I can but wish that it would be better liked now so that it would sell for one reason: tonight I am out of money, & father has promised to pay the rent which was due last Monday. It will not be paid—and so a howl from the landlord. If I could see Dorrance I would try to borrow ten dollars of him.

Thursday evening my Love & I called on her dear friend Martha Luther.

I met her at the Atheneum at seven o'clock then we took a long walk until eight. . . . Daily she grows more & more of the feeling that she must marry me & bear to me children & how nobly she talked of it!

She wanted to know if I thought that we could arrange it so that that thing might be done & yet neither of us be bound to subjection in any way—that is, so that we should be free to carry on our life work individually & etc. . . .

Our call at Martha's was delightful. Martha knows how Charlotte & I love each other, and as Mrs. Luther was out Charlotte had an opportunity

---

*Although *Autumnal Sacrifice* was shown in the 1882 PAC exhibit, and then sent to the Academy Exhibition in Philadelphia, Stetson did not always like it: it "somehow looks rather mahogany color and otherwise mean. Can it be that I have mistaken it for a good piece of color?" Diaries, May 13, 1882.

for showing in her frank way that she did love me. She sat by my side and held my hand, & while Martha played a beautifully tender revery on the piano she lay her head on my shoulder & seemed perfectly happy. There was an indescribable heavenliness about that understanding of three persons—however incomplete it may have been. . . .

. . .

TUESDAY; 11:15 A.M. MAY 9TH 1882.

. . . The morning's post brought me an unexpected letter from My Love. It is a letter to pray over, to take oath upon, if such were needed. And as it marks a new day in her life I shall quote it here verbatim. I like to make doubly sure the preservation of such words of hers. . . .

THE LETTER.

5.5 A.M.   May 8th 1882

Sunrise greetings, my Lord & King!
I am yours with none to sever.
I wear your kiss in place of ring
And am yours forever and ever! . . .

I have no time to stop for words, dear, so rhyming must stop, but the thoughts go on in endless music of whispering pine trees and soft winds. Under God's blue sky and on the breast of our Mother was fitting time & place for me to receive my first Kiss—that Kiss which seals me yours.

First for God and the world and then for you, and serving God and the world through you the most—I fancy. Ah! have I not prayed!

Bowing low before the grandeur and the glory of it, and praying only to be more worthy.

And so help me Heaven! If I am not as worthy as a life's concentrated effort can make a human soul, then may I lose it!

When the time comes for you to take me to your arms, I shall be five or six years more deserving than I am now, and I will grow to you, dear love, through all the ages.

O my grand lover! My heart's King! Truly I was ready to have you turn my face to yours with gentle force; ready to give my heart to you when our lips met. How in the name of all that is holy *can* men and women trifle with kisses as they do! I think it must be a long step towards sensual excess; for after using such sacrament as has filled our soul with glory ineffable for *pleasure*, it would not take much more debasement before sacrificing God's highest and holiest ordinance for the same end.

And I have found a man even higher-souled than I!

My Friend, My Lover, My Husband that is to be—aye, and is now in God's sight and mine—let us thank him continually; consecrating our united lives to the service of humanity, as some proof of our recognition of the glory that has befallen us. And thank him even as I do for every hard-won battle and slow-climbed hill which has placed us where we now stand, in some poor sense deserving.

I wish, O how I wish that I had done better; but I know that in many things I have done well, and that alone makes the crown bearable. I am one who ne'er prayed "God be merciful," but now pray "God be thanked."

Goodbye for today, and perhaps for the week. Ah love! I am with you always though you get no letters; and now more than ever we must both *work*.

For what, dear, and for whom? Hush, love! For a home that shall be heaven, & for that little girl with eyes like mine!

Goodbye: and I love you more in stopping than in writing, because it is right. In love and truth, your own Charlotte A. Perkins.

P.S. Need I tell you that I dreamed of you and woke in your arms? Woke in the cool gray dawn after about 5½ hours of sleep as fresh and tireless as a waterfall (!) and lay there just five minutes, in thoughts too glorious and fair to formulate. Then up & to work with a new vigor, for I have a new interest in life now.

I wrote till ten last night, too.

Goodbye.

Yours ever
Char. A. Perkins.

Is not that letter, O my heart, more precious than gold or rubies? . . .

Just then a vision of her as she ran fleet as Atalanta down that woodland path, full of rich health and joyous spirit came strongly to me. And of how she waited at the end and came to my arms radiant with pure spirit and healthy blood. And then again a vision of how we ran side by side along that dusty road something like an eighth of a mile I bearing a bunch of anemones gathered by that woodland pool, and she covered with the late sunlight. O the true joy of it!

I am a true Greek in my likings, and she is even as I am.

That jointure of great soul and strong supple body, in both of which I can participate, is a very Godsend to me. . . .

SATURDAY, MAY 13. 1882. 10:30 A.M.

. . . I have received three letters from my Love, each of them very excellent . . . with the exception of one paragraph in which she referred to my health in a way quite unbearable. . . .

She has a very amusing although almost sublime conceit of her physical strength. Dear Love! I hope it will continue as it is—sound and vital. And the way in which she sets herself up as a pattern of industry and adherence to duty is also just a little amusing. It is only the pride of a young life which

is beginning to feel its strength. A few falls—a few mistakes will make her to
see I think that there are ways equal to hers. (Though she to me is un-
equalled among women.) They are good traits, God knows, only they "stick
out" to a fault! The tree will blossom. Has it not begun? Four months ago
she knew very well that her ideas of her life were fixed—although she granted
that something *might* change them. And now they are changed in all the
important particulars. She was to remain unmarried because she believed
that marriage was for having children & caring for them & the husband:
and she had a conviction that her work in life was even higher than that. . . .
After some one hundred and twenty days of being loved the green is turned
red—now she feels that she *must* have children & that she fancies her best
work will be done through me.

Now that change does not show a weakness but a strength. She thought
herself less a woman than other women when the truth was she was more a
woman than they. I saw—she could not.

She had sat in her house or gone into her own mind to see life & to find
out how she could do the most good. And she firmly believes to this day
that it was her *head* that told her that she must love me. A pretty delusion:
Ah! did I not see the heart awaken & given new reasons to the dear head?
Yes, the heart—the pure spirit of her has conquered: She is mine. She even
said, . . . "that sweet sense of being owned by somebody" as she worded it.
Only a short while ago she could not entertain that idea because it made her
less independent.

No doubt there are a few seasons of struggling in store for her, but so
long as she feels my love her heart will conquer.

And that proves her to be a woman & causes all her other qualities to
add to her nature; while if she was not a woman & had all the parts of
a woman's body quite perfect, and had a simply cold intellect she were a
monster.

O woman of all women! Bride elect! . . .

Father has repromised the landlord to pay him the rent tonight. He has
no money and I have no money. A person promised to pay him today: I pray
that he may. Our financial affairs are darkening again quite rapidly. . . .

I have 30 or 40 pictures in my studio. How to get rid of them I know
not. . . .

I am wondering if my life is to be a counterpart or likeness of my father's. A man of eminently good parts who accomplished nothing great because of his ideality and fear of hurting someone? God No!! If I grew mad-

dened Hell shall revisit earth once more—I shall grow mad if my end is not accomplished. . . .

20TH MAY, 1882. 10:15 A.M.

. . . A letter [from Charlotte] which came yesterday—partly written day before & partly yesterday morning had a somewhat new tone to it. It seemed to me a little *sad*, with the sadness of one who has dreamed of being great & famous & world-beloved and who finds that the Right after all appears to be that she must be "one of many and not one alone." That is just Charlotte's case. Her dreams were very good but very brilliant and almost impracticable: she as I have so often written thrust love aside as unnecessary and determined to be alone & win fame by I know not what sort of good deeds.

Then I came—: and she found that she was ignoring quite as high a law in keeping herself from love & marriage & longed-for children, and it brought her to her knees before God. As I told her it would, a new view of life came and love was added changing all else only to better it. And with her characteristic honesty she openly tells whoever asks, that it *is* true. . . .

. . . She says that no one says a word against *me*, but they like to "poke fun at her" because she has changed her mind so suddenly after telling all who cared to hear that she was to remain a maid and live for many instead of for few.

The very openness with which she avows her change because she thinks it *right* proves her of noble mind and sound heart. Then in this sad (?) little letter she says, after telling how honestly she had expected to be known to the world she asked: "And can you, my love, fill in my life the large place I had hoped the world would fill? Yes, my dear, you can and will; furthermore I shall hold you so near to me that by the invariable laws of perspective you will be larger than all the world beside." That is the substance of it—but not *quite* the words. Then she is trying to cultivate self forgetfulness. It is one of her peculiarities that as soon as she is well aware of a fault she immediately sets about curing herself. And she always succeeds.

The strangest part of her letter as compared with some of the first that she wrote me is its lack of self. Or to make it clearer, its lack of assertion or suggestion that she is superior to most women and men. It is true that in mentality she is far superior to the average man or woman—that is what she really *meant* but it *seemed* as if she thought herself superior to all. She rather looked down on men until she met me, and I know why. My "quiet nobility" brought her to her knees before God, she says. Yes, my *quiet* nobility. She had been used to boasting and noise from men who had not learned that they were but a part of a tremendous whole. My "quiet nobility"! I liked to read that immensely. . . .

. . . [Her letter] closes with

"Yours when I am good enough." O, how that spirit is broken. The false pride is melting before love rapidly. And love building upon such strong rich foundation will rear a superstructure of surpassing splendor and beauty!

If our love letters could be printed verbatim, and side by side, there would be a novel of great truth and philosophical worth. It would give the exact relation of the whole minded of both sexes. I would not be at all surprised to know that Malloch's philosophical novels were actual experiences of someone—either himself or another. . . .

29TH MAY. 1882. 11:10 A.M. MONDAY.

Again with Charlotte yesterday—and a shadow was upon us. How to tell of it I know not.

I was at her house by 3:15 P. M. She met me at the door—looking a trifle sad, but her greeting was as warm and tender as ever. She said that we were to stay at home, instead of taking our customary walk—for hygienic reasons, doubtless.

I, barometrical creature that I am, saw or rather felt that her mental state was scarcely enviable. And at length she tried to throw it off by getting the letters which she wrote to Miss Luther last Summer. Bright letters they are. She read several—until she came to one passage which she did not read any of only—"This delightful sense of freedom." She stopped, folded her hands, and looked as if confused mentally.* Then she went on to say that for the past two days she had been very unhappy. She could *not* become used to the sense of being "appropriated." All her old hopes, longings etc., had

---

*There were striking differences between Charlotte's letters to Stetson and those she wrote to Martha Luther the summer before (1881). Clearly she had been ambitious and self-respecting when she was writing Martha, whereas recently with Walter she felt "weakly" and ashamed. The process of reviewing those old letters, and in Walter's presence, must have dramatized the contrast between the "delightful sense of freedom" she had known with Martha, and the "feminine" approach to Walter as her "Lord and King." No wonder she suffered "acutely" and felt "mentally confused." She was trying to resist pressures to twist ambition to acceptable wifely norms. For discussion of the letters to Martha, see Mary A. Hill, *Charlotte Perkins Gilman: The Making of a Radical Feminist, 1860–1896* (Philadelphia: Temple University Press, 1980), Chap. IV.

arisen and rebelled against my love. . . . She loved me deeply—it was grow-ing steadily, rapidly, surely, but she could not yet feel willing to give up all her past for the "glory" of being my wife. . . . She asked all sorts of ques-tions regarding my love of her & what I expected of her, and the old matter of her work etc. was rehearsed in detail. She wanted reasons and I could give few. Then she wanted to know what I should do if she were dead, etc., etc.: she was certainly at her very worst, and no doubt in my mind that a good deal of her trouble came from her physical state, for I remember at her last there was something a little like it. . . .

She has changed her language regarding the whole thing (honestly too) a dozen times. She has lots of fights in store and will suffer a deal. That suf-fering will teach her that the best of all that she can do is to love purely, devotedly and bear children to be trained to something noble. That may be a premature saying, but I think not. . . .

I wrote her a letter last night in which I stated as clearly as I could under the circumstances what I should want her to be as my wife. It made me intensely unhappy, for I took it at the time as a sign that again fate placed the happy cup at my lips and snatched it away at the first sip—that I was to have a new burden to bear and that God tortured rather than pitied.

Those feelings made my letter rather too passionate perhaps.

This morning I feel calmer about it, and think that even now her love is stronger than her fears. And as for mine it is immeasurable.

In a few months she will have grown more used to the new life and what now looks like a chain to bind will be but a chain of gold ornaments.

Whatever comes she is a gloriously honest woman—and my Love.

TUESDAY, MAY 30. ''82. 2 P.M.

The streets are full of people going to & fro aimlessly. It is the day when dead soldiers' graves are strewn with flowers. I have had no part in the cere-mony. I have been alone strewing the graves of my own dead hopes; I seem a thing apart from all the world's ways and yet I know that I am not but that I am just as dependent as most upon what the world does. I am glad that I have this quiet room to come to—with horse-chestnut trees reflecting green lights on its wall, with birds singing beneath its windows, and with the sounds of a distant hymn from a house in the rear floating through the casement. I am glad of its dark maroon walls, of its filmy curtain and my poor pictures round about. For here I can uninterrupted commune with God and seek out those threads' ends which seem woefully tangled. . . .

I rather hoped to find a letter from Charlotte, but was disappointed in that—so I wrote one to her. Then I read "Two Gentlemen of Verona" until 9:45; and so to bed, full in the heart of prayers that God would make her love me unintermittently.

This morning two letters from Charlotte. . . .

. . . Dear One, she feels that something is wrong with her. . . . [H]er old thoughts break out again and again, but I can but think that they will come to the surface less and less frequently and at last die. . . . Heretofore I have not tried to influence her save by my quietude: it is time now to do those fair things which shall keep the love of me uppermost in her mind. She prays that her love may grow—a great help that. If she perseveres in her prayer she will find herself loving me very devotedly, for there is something in the fixedness of mind which prayer gives which produces marvellous effects.

Evidently when that letter was written she felt very tenderly towards me even if a flaming love did not fill her, & by night it had grown. . . .

MAY 31. 1882, 10:15 A.M.

My writing was interrupted by a call from that poor unfortunate bore, Miss A., and soon after by Mr. Hazeltine.* [Charlotte also called, but "she would not come, Miss A. being here."]

. . . Miss A. . . . certainly talks well: but though water is excellent to drink one does not care to be drowned in it. . . .

JUNE 1ST 1882. 11:50 A.M.

A letter which I received from Mrs. Cresson yesterday decides for me that I shall go to Philadelphia Tuesday night—the 6th. I cannot even guess how long I shall stay but probably two weeks will be the limit. I think that I shall leave my studio key with Charlotte, so that she may come here if she chooses to think or work or do neither. And then too I shall feel better to

---

*Years later, Stetson wrote to a mutual friend about his memories of artist Charles Hazeltine: "He came to my studio in Providence when he first ran away from New Bedford,— I think that was just 20 years ago. From that time until I left for California I knew him intimately—perhaps as much as anyone, and had the pleasure of tiding him over a few pretty hard places. He lived on five cents a day at one time: then suddenly one day . . . he came and nearly paralyzed me by buying one of my pictures! Nobody can guess my sensations. I had only a week before, I think, loaned him $2. to keep him alive. We both drank port wine . . . and felicitated ourselves upon his success. I think nothing ever did me more good than to see him with money to spend—for *my* work!!" CWS to William Macbeth, Dec. 19, 1898, William Macbeth Papers, Archives of American Art, Smithsonian Institution.

leave it with her, because it will be safe & save trouble if I should be accidentally destroyed on my journey.

And I think she will feel pleased at it—I should were I in her place.

As my Journal is here she can read that if she chooses and know for sure the most hidden parts of my life. Why should she not know them? If after reading them she thinks me weak, fickle, unworthy of her virginity, why, 'twere better found out now than when too late. . . .

.   .   .

MONDAY, JUNE 5, 1882 10:30 A.M.

This is the last entry I shall make until I return from Philadelphia. . . . Yesterday I was with her from 3:15 to 10 P. M. And it was one uninterrupted session of pure joy. . . .

She read to me. Once she stopped and looked up—leaned toward me and said: ". . . Does it seem, my darling, as if we could ever be worthy of so much! I have been too self-confident—and—that which was highest and best in me I was trying to crush out: you rescued me—and *now!*"

Those tenderer things, were they expressible, I would not write. No being under God has any right in our holy of holies. And such might get in, for sometime, if I do not destroy all before I die, someone will see my words. No matter how literally honest my record is I cannot be so exceedingly minute as to be to my love sacrilegious. She, God, and I above—we know the height, depth, breadth of the peace, joy, holiness of the innermost of our Love. And we alone shall ever know it. . . .

JULY 1. 1882, SAT.

Home from Philadelphia [where he had been staying with the Cressons], and have been since last Sunday morning. . . .

Mrs. Cresson became very dear to me and I to her. Our communion and intercourse were inexpressible. O such delight as I took, such luxurious leisures with her & with nature and with Art. I knew that they were comfortable at home—I was comfortable there and the result was that I was able to just give up all and be open to the dear influences about me.

I was cared for as if I had been a young prince instead of poor me. Every thing was given to me, every thing done for me. It did not cost me a cent while I was away & Mrs. Cresson bought for me at least a hundred dollars worth of presents. Love reigned. My dear Love sent me some good letters and some disagreeable ones but they did not discourage me as they might have done. . . .

Since I came back she has grown tenderer & more wholly ready to give up herself. She missed me while I was away & it made her unhappy. Our interviews have been very good. We do not caress now—a plan that she inaugurated at her father's suggestion—so our communions are rather peculiar. I think that she will not keep it up long, but she will be the first to relinquish the idea. She will be dammed up so long that when she does give up she will be simply deliciously loving—so perhaps it is well. She loves me better & better.

I have had two excellent letters from Mrs. Cresson. She confides so in me that I gain strength & it is good to have a true friend to whom one can pour out one's heart. . . .

[Another break in the diary occurs for several weeks, while Walter was vacationing in Cape Breton with his friend George Whitaker.]

AUGUST 2. 1882

It seems strange to write again in this book. Of course I am back from Cape Breton and am fully of the glory I saw there! I never had so simply an enjoyable time before . . . 3 weeks of it, that seemed 3 years, so full of sights and incidents they were—!

I grew well—I was absolutely well without a morbid thought, full of bounding spirits. It is a place of light in my usually tainted record.*

I made many pencil sketches which I am now interpreting into color, for Geo. & I hope to have an exhibition together this Fall.†

I got no letters from Charlotte while away because she did not know where to direct them. . . . She spent the same 3 weeks at Ogunquit, Me. and much to her betterment I think, for she came back with fresh vitality and desire to work and a brown complexion which would do credit to Castile.

---

*Grace Channing wrote: "Alas—so much for getting away from home, for having a little peace of mind,—a small 'vacation' from the life-long strains! Exactly the effect every one of our voyages had. He *could* have been well—with half a chance but that half-chance he never had." Grace Channing also noted that Stetson described this Cape Breton trip "in a narrative apart, written in fine pencil. I shall by and by copy it all out, and it can then be inserted in its proper place. It was the first important outing of his whole life and remained an unimpaired memory ever after,—and it had an immense effect upon him." GEC to EBK, May 23, 1912, p. 99. The Cape Breton journals are probably among the Stetson papers still in the possession of Dorothy and Walter Chamberlin. I have heard tape-recorded transcriptions of them, but have been unable to locate the originals.

†For the next several years, Stetson worked extensively from sketches he made in Nova Scotia. *Blomidon from Near the Shad Fishery, Grande Pre*; *Sketch at Baddeck, Cape Breton*; *Fog Coming at Sunset, Baddeck, Cape Breton*—these are only some of the works inspired, as he put it, by the "idyllic peace and wonderful beauty" of the Maritime countryside (Oct. 24, 1882). "If

She wrote me letters all the time and I found them when I returned and I wrote to her and her mother forwarded them to her.

Since I returned I have been with her twice and found her quite herself with a softened way, I feel, and a better hope of being my wife. She still puts into practice that advice of her father, not to caress more than she does before her mother—and it suits me well enough. . . .

But there is no peace with her. Her ideas about love, and about the meaning of the word "your," and the burning desire to go into the world to assist people keep her from being as comforting as she might be. There is an uncertainty about what she will be in the next half hour which is not all pleasant. But I am sure she loves me, and quite as sure that she will change her mind about many things which now make her company not everything to be desired. Meanwhile I love her ardently, and try to crush down the feeling that maybe after all my ardor will be wasted, and that she will decide that she can "work" just as well alone.

She is very hard to understand because she constantly contradicts herself and mostly because she does not understand herself. . . .

I became some what discouraged when I began sketching at Grand Pre.* I did it in water color and I could not get what I saw in nature. After a

---

European scenery is better than this I should die of a rupture of the heart." Unidentified clipping in the *Evening Star*, Feb. 8, 1913, Stetson Scrapbook.

Although Stetson had reservations about his Nova Scotia sketches, his travelling companion George Whitaker was impressed with Stetson's "quick . . . observation of things, especially fugitive effects like cloud shadows falling upon the landscape. . . . He could give a transcript of them to a nicety." The dikes along the Bay of Fundy, the mossy gabled barns, the tall poplars "like gaunt sentinels over the plains and hillsides," the rustic bridges—"all these were idealized by his facile brush." Citations from [George W. Whitaker and Sydney R. Burleigh], "An Appreciation of the Late Charles Walter Stetson," *Providence Sunday Journal*, July 23, 1911, p. 10; George Whitaker, "Charles Walter Stetson, Artist," Providence A. E. Club Lectures, Nov. 21, 1895, Club Papers no. 263, RIHS.

According to Charles Eldredge, the Canadian visit marked a turning point for Stetson. His Nova Scotia watercolors showed a "marked loosening of style" from his earlier landscapes, Eldredge wrote; "the translucent watercolor washes permit a new luminosity unlike the more heavily worked oils of the late 1870s. The emerald greens and heavy blue washes are clumped in color masses which provide a clue to Stetson's abilities with intense hues, which were to become more prominent in later years." Eldredge, *Charles Walter Stetson*, pp. 26–27.

* Stetson tried to rework this Grand Pre scene in a number of paintings. Some weeks later he wrote: "I have started a 12 × 14 canvas of Blomidon seen from a hill at Grand Pre. Shall try to get the golden atmospheric effect under which I saw [it] at the particular time of sketching. I believe I have 14 oil pictures from my sketches underway: and perhaps a dozen watercolors." Diaries, Aug. 23, 1882. *Blomidon from Near the Shad Fishery, Grand Pre* was shown at the 1884 PAC Exhibit, and is now owned by the Aaron Gallery, Providence, Rhode Island.

while I found by remembering sketches of great artists that I had seen that none of them got much in their sketches; so I came to the wise conclusion of getting only the skeleton etc. & putting in what I felt when I got home.

And I have had all my upper teeth out! And must eat liquids for something like ten weeks. And I am hoping to be a bridegroom to Charlotte! To be sure she has defects, but that does not make me wish myself imperfect. I can excuse a fault in her much more easily than I can in myself. . . .

AUG. 8TH 1882. TUESDAY. 6 P.M.

My day's work over. Mother ill, just as she was getting ready to go out of town. Hot as the tropics, though I ought to be thankful for a cooling breeze that steals through my room. Have been working hard all day: part of the time on *Blomidon seen across the great meadow at Grand Pre*; partly upon *The Stone Picker*, and a little on some willows sketched at Annapolis, N.S. . . .

. . . Mr. Waterman called as I had requested & we had a talk about the commercial side of art.* He seemed to think it would be a good idea to have a sale of all the pictures I have on hand as well as those of Cape Breton & N.S. which I hope to have. Said he would do all he could for me. . . . Mr. Purinton called to tell me more about the girl [who is to pose for me]. Seems she is sensuous, blonde; about 18. Has led a rather fast life but is nevertheless modest in a way, quiet, yet active. He thinks she can be hired cheap. Will bring her up Thursday. Then we talked about art of all kinds. Strange how people like to talk with me upon art philosophy. *I like it*—like to have them feel that I have thought enough about it to want to know what I think.

. . . I have reached the point where I believe that I must assert myself a little more—where I believe that it will be right for me to so do. Heretofore I have not asserted myself at all except where some moral ground was being entered upon. I am nearing 25—and it seems to me that I am justified in saying things a little more positively than I could as a youth of eighteen. *I must win* not for myself, but for Father, Mother, & Charlotte. . . .

THURSDAY, AUG. 10. 1882

With Charlotte last evening. Went from here home about 4:30 after a very full day's work. Notwithstanding I left an hour and a half earlier than

---

* Marcus Waterman, Providence artist and early PAC member.

usual—went because I was tired for one thing and so that I could take a bath for another: for it seems fit that, no matter whether one is clean or unclean, that he should bathe before coming to his beloved. May be a whim of mine, but it's in the blood I fear. Well, supped: took car and started at 6:30—arrived at 7. . . .

. . . How beautiful she looked! Wore an ecru dress with a bit of red about it somewhere, and some dull white low around the neck. A coral necklace which was precisely the right tint of red to intensify the flesh tints; a neat little straw bonnet. She was glad that I came—showed it in every look. . . . And she talked a deal about what we would do when we were married: and she said—"*Wouldn't* it be fun to go to a minister quietly—let no one know of it—be married according to the law and then live as if we were defying the law: that is live together as if we had no certificate. What fun to listen to the cries of friends—the warnings—the condolings etc. & then when things were at the climax quietly open the certificate and say: Why all this fuss? Is not *that* right!" And she laughed in an intensively satisfied way, then looked up after my high approval, and said, "I suppose that's a queer proposal for a young woman to make to her intended bridegroom." Although it was unusual I could sympathize with the feeling that prompted it very fully and should enjoy the overthrow of our fault-finding friends thoroughly. . . .

Mr. [Frank] Purinton* sent me a letter Tuesday saying that he had come across a girl who would pose for me if I wanted her. It was a kind but queer letter. After the business part of it he went on to warn me against the seductions of the flesh and to use her for a model and nothing else, and a whole lot more such as my grandmother, if she knew nothing about the drudgery of art, might have proposed. I thought first he was joking but upon second reading I concluded it to be earnest. So I wrote him a note in way of thanks and resentment of the implicitly imputed charge of wanting a woman to use for sexual excitement. Poor fellow! he meant well. . . . Well, I read the letter to Charlotte last evening, and she laughed in a delightful way about it. Not one woman in a thousand is so fitted—nay in ten thousand women, could not be found one so fitted to wed an artist as she. To think that she is willing, glad that I can get nude models! Indeed she would be joyous at getting them herself for me—or in being one to me herself.

Where is another woman like that? I know of none. Whether she is without the sentiment of jealousy (which I doubt) or whether she reasons about it to that end (which I think) I cannot say. Either way it is a rare and

---

* Frank M. Purinton, local painter and friend.

adorable quality. I think it is rather because she feels the art impulse so strongly in herself that she can understand it in me. She has much talent for drawing. She made some sketches at Ogunquit this Summer which evince that she has a rare gift at sketching. That which most people, even some professional artists, have not. When she paints flowers she marvellously delineates the most subtle convolutions of petals and the torsion of tendrils: and she well sees their natural colors. How she would be at invention and composition I cannot say, but knowing of her imagination some what, & her inclination to dream dreams, I think I may say that she would succeed. I can think of no happier combination in man & wife than that each should have the same pursuit and follow it conjointly. It would be a constant bond. Then how both of us love literature! What a treasure therein! . . .

SATURDAY, 5:30 P.M. AUG. 12. 1882

. . . Mr. Bates came in this morning and saw a few of my pictures: one looking over the Grand Meadow at Grand Pre towards the Gaspereaux river pleased him much and he said he felt as if he wanted to buy it: would be in again & decide.*

Begun the day with a good short letter from Charlotte. Yes, a good letter in which kind love shone sweetly. She goes to some secluded place at Martha's Vine-yard on Monday, from which place she can write no letters as it is some six miles from the P.O. She will be gone two weeks. . . .

. . . This I recognize in my work—a more just appreciation of the relative planes of my pictures: I can get them more readily, doing at a stroke what a year ago it would have taken half an hour to do. My outdoor looking & working this Summer has helped much in that way. The colors of nature rest the eye, and one must observe the relative values or nothing. . . .

. . . Fall comes apace, and I must forget the heavy demands of clothing and fuel in hoping that it will bring purchasers for my pictures. I wish I might sell nothing until I could paint better—but hunger urges and the coming cold & nakedness make me almost shameless about selling them. I would sell them all for ten thousand dollars apiece if I could get it—so shameless have I grown. For I want Charlotte to wife, and Mother & Father & all to have some latter comfort. . . .

---

* Some weeks later Stetson wrote: Mr. Isaac C. Bates "bought the Grand Pre canvas for $10—after ridiculously offering me $5—for it. I will have my revenge some day but I suppose it was kind in him to even offer me that. At any rate it was worth a dozen pictures to see father's brightening face when I gave him that money towards the rent." Diaries, Aug. 22, 1882.

CHAPTER VI

. . . something mighty stirring

August 14 – October 9, 1882

As Stetson faced his troubles with "Art and Charlotte,"
he turned to outside sources for support—to music; to literature and poetry; to biography and history; to artists and writers he could emulate. His
current reading (about Dante Gabriel Rossetti, for instance) fed his hope
that "stirring within" would "find utterance" someday. Thus far Stetson's
most effective work was of Nova Scotia landscapes; but his more important
aspiration was to capture the "mysterious attractiveness" of womanhood.

Meanwhile, however, Walter had to struggle with Charlotte's unpredictable behavior, and with his own "ravishing thoughts" and romantic aspirations as well. As he put it to Sidney Putnam, love is almost always "humiliating": "every weakness & fault of a man stands forth before him when he
realizes that a woman loves him & that he has nothing but his character &
the deeds thereof to give her!"

In some respects, Charlotte tried to bolster Walter's faltering ego—and
in appropriate womanly ways: by sending him effusive letters, by improving
her manners, curbing her wit, and temporarily comforming. "It is wonderful," he wrote, how love had "brought that strong woman so that she is as
dough to the kneader or clay to the potter, to be fashioned as her love wills."
Still, there were some forceful undercurrents that Walter couldn't manage,
for in fact, being Lord and Master left him feeling insecure.*

————

*The above quotations are from diary entries of the following dates: Aug. 17, Aug. 23,
Aug. 21, Oct. 9, 1882.

MONDAY AUG. 14, 1882

Am just down to my work, and while awaiting the calming of my blood (I walked fast) and the going of the sun from in front of my easel, I will just jot down yesterday's doings. Somehow it was not an irksome a Sunday as usual. I have not solved the problem, why Sunday is more irksome than other days: I see no reason for it. Took bath in the morning, of course; then read some in Shelley and studied Pure Logic a bit: but somehow I couldn't fix my mind on it, [then] went to Shakespeare, the never-failing, and read a few sonnets & snatches of *Pericles*. It seemed to do me some good: felt brighter after it. . . . Then began a letter to Dorrance when I was interrupted by the bell announcing the coming of a divine named Burroughs who was to share our board with us for that afternoon. Father preached for him at the Bethel, and he preached for father somewhere. He was an acid gentleman with a strangely alkaline reaction in the countenance. Certes some chemical change was going on there or there would never have been wrinkles like a power explosion around the mouth or such siding & undulating strata, on the forehead; sort of a mean face, it was, and I could do no less than compare it with my father's gentle, intelligent, and *taught* face. Why! to look from him to father at the table was like looking from a treacherous morass to a clear mountain height lit by the setting sun. Father stood up clear, rugged with past & present conflict, but with nothing to conceal and already feeling the sinking beams of Day. The other hung his head over his plate, looked sidewise at one, and had the sun at his back. Thank God for a father who had the blood of honest, pure minded generations in him: for one who is more moral than witty, more intelligent than smart! Ah! I see him more clearly now than I used. What scars I have had make me understand him better. He is a man who if he had been surrounded by the right influences, had a more demonstrative wife would have been a light in the world. I know that. I am not deceived: it is *not* because he is my father that I think thus (I didn't used to think so) but because he is a man trodden down by what he *could* not throw off: his feeling of duty to his children silenced all that he wanted for himself, and he has toiled patiently that we might be somewhat more than he. If we are as much as he, God be thanked!

Well, dinner passed as such affairs do usually. Father is always merry, despite his care when company is served. But, strange, Mr. Burroughs, unlike most ministers, seemed to have no feeling of humor. So father settled at last into Church statistics.

Heaven keep me from many graces as long as that Mr. B[urroughs] "of-

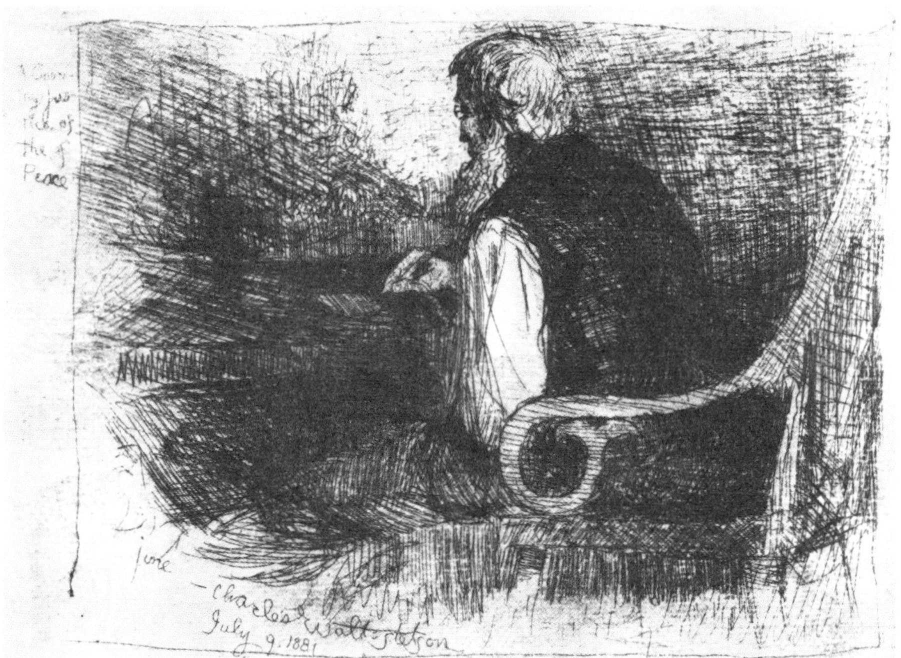

A Country [?] *Justice of the Peace.* Courtesy of Mary Armfield Hill.

fered"! Excellent for a boarding house, because, no matter how poor the food, the boarders would eat it gladly by the so acquired appetite of waiting.

What a foolish custom that is! Did very well for Kings & their ilk, but for a laboring man who is surely entitled to the food he earns by hard work, to thank God for the food he has gotten for himself is to my mind absurd! . . .

[Here part of the diary has been removed. A later entry describes a discussion about Charlotte's family's disapproval.] She told me about what they said at home, among other things they said that they didn't believe that she loved me or I her. What can they think we say so for and act so for! I exclaimed. "I cannot tell," said she, "but they hint that they think we do it for the animal excitement of it." O'o! said I. She smiled significantly—that is as much as to say—how little they know our hearts. Then she said that they made fun of her for wanting to wait six years. And she said "Now mother if he waits six years for me you'll forgive him, won't you?" "Yes, I will," said her mother, "for if he is foolish enough to wait that long he certainly loves you & deserves you."

Her mother is very much opposed to me now—as long as I was a friend she liked me much—and she bases her opposition on the ground that I was not a gentleman & acted dishonorably because I did not go to her and ask her permission to *love* Charlotte: As if it were possible! If she knew how our love grew and came to me like fire she would see the impossibility of it but she will listen to no explanation. I offered one & she would not listen—said it was too late to make friends with her then. She treats me courteously, but I know that she makes it very unpleasant for Charlotte. I have good reasons for thinking that if I were not an artist & had a fat bank account that I would be far more in the past tense. . . .

Why, I've *won*! Won as certainly as I live! No woman, strong minded, strong bodied, pure souled as I know her to be would dare, wish to do, the heavenly things she does—all pure, but ardent, hearty. She is won—she has surrendered almost all. The day comes—so be it God takes her not from earth—when she shall lie in these arms in supreme surrender. Do I dream— do I fabricate such certainties from the strength of my desires? Can it be that that so wondrous body shall be offered as the supreme expression of that so great soul to *me*? To *me*! Ah, that I may grow into some more near semblance of worthiness! . . .

One thing she said Sunday night during our walk struck me as an excellent symptom in my favor. Suddenly she said: "Have you ever been ashamed of me, dear?" So seriously that it must have meant a great deal—of how she wanted to be perfect that I might see her so.

I assured her I never had been ashamed of her, and I should be never so long as she did what she really believed to be right.

There it is: right in the midst of my most ravishing thoughts of her comes that other thought: Thou canst not take her to wife until thou are assured of money enough to support & educate your children! I could marry her tomorrow were it not for the children: she said so. But I feel sure that she would not marry me and go without them—and *I know* that I would rather bear the pain of vain desire than do it. I *want* the children— and *I will have them*. I do not say that I would not marry her that I might be ever with her & for the bodily delight: I think it would be a right thing to do—she would then be simply—my mistress. Not an ugly word when so much love is hid in it as in this case there would be. But to have it a settled thing that no children were to come—neither of us would do it. *Could* we? I think not. . . .

1882. 17TH AUG. THURSDAY.

. . . Spent last evening in looking over my poems: What weak things they are—and how little like the strong thoughts that prompted them! People who do not like my pictures would think my poems even far worse— they have not even the merit of rich color. If people could have understood me during my early youth and educated me for Poet & Painter how different would all be. I think surely that our "system" of school teaching causes many who might rise above it to stay at mediocrity. Wait! If I have children!! A man must be a sublime genius in poetry or he cannot do much nowadays. Can't I conceive of as grand things as Herrick (sweet things in this case) or Milton? Can't I run into the very ends of an ideal existence as did Shelley? Why can't I express myself? Because I was taught at school a lot of stuff that hangs about me—half taught, half learned, and it makes me afraid to speak all the words that come. Maybe I shall outgrow it. I hope so: for I know that I have very many poetical thoughts & emotions. . . .

SATURDAY AUG. 19. 1882

[Stetson has just finished reading an article by Edmund Gosse in the September *Century Magazine*.] . . . It seems very good to have Mr. Gosse confirm all my feelings regarding Rossetti. I *knew* the moment I first read his poems that we could clasp hands & be friends, for, though it might seem vain if any saw this, I know that I have very much that he had. I lack most his circumstances & a certain what looks like ease of diction. But I know that I have his religious fervor, his mysticism, his imagination: and then his color must have been somewhat like mine. I almost feel—though I am very de-spondent about it often—that I shall some day write good poems. Not so sweetly, beautifully, tenderly done as his perhaps, but done in my way and in an equally reverent spirit. . . .

Just as I was finishing reading about him I heard female voices in the corridor & someone say—"room 4." My screen was across the door & I arose saw two young ladies clad bravely in pink lawn. I surmised at once that one of them might be the model *in prospectus*, so I went to the door & she thrust out the card I had given to Mr. Purinton. They came in. I think I must have acted bashful. It was rather hard to begin: but it was far from shame that made it: it was a long descent to make suddenly, from Rossetti's heights to these damsels of the demi-monde. But they were not ill looking only wearing that stamp which any trained Eye may read. But I said to her of the card: I suppose you know what I wanted of you? "Well yes, a little."

Well, said I, I want you to undress for me so that I may draw from you. "When do you want me?" said she. First I shall want you to come and undress for me so that I may see if you have such a form as I want. "When shall I come?" When can you come? "Tomorrow?" Sunday? "No, Monday." All right, said I. "I'll come Monday afternoon at 3 o'clock," said she. Now whether she will who can say? I think Mr. Purinton showed poor taste in choosing her, judging from what can be seen through pink lawn & hoops.

Yesterday afternoon in the midst of my painting, [Sidney] Putnam walked in. Had not seen him for long. Is looking first rate. Got letters to go to N.Y. to teach school. . . . We stayed talking until 6:30. Just before we went he said he had a long story to tell me. Wanted to know if he couldn't bring down some supper for both of us today so that he could tell it, as he is going to leave the city so soon. Of course he could so I am expected to meet him at 5 o'clock. Hope he'll bring a lot to eat for I'm hungry having been presented with a good appetite by this beautiful cool Sept. like day and having not had a very large allowance of food at home owing to father's & my ill fortune.

I can't guess what Putnam wants to tell, but I'll wager it's something to do with a woman.

Where's the money for the model to come from? I must go for Mr. Bates to see if he won't buy a picture. Don't like to do it but I can't afford to let the opportunity to draw from the nude slip through my fingers so. . . .

MONDAY, 11:30 A.M. AUG. 21. ''82.

. . . Yesterday as agreed I met [Sidney] Putnam here at 5:30. He seemed somewhat agitated & I knew at once that he had eine Liebe-geschichte to tell me. Such was the case. After drinking some ginger ale & eating an apple he told me that I must stretch out on the lounge so as to be comfortable for it was a long story. It *was* a long story—2 hours and a half at least: told with a fluency and pathos rare enough. And it was a wonderfully beautiful story— idyllic, tender, of the birth & growth of his first true manly love for a wonderfully pure, patient, wholly lovable woman. He was deeply affected. There is no doubt in my mind that at last he knows the meaning of love in its best form. Ah, how good it is to feel that some respect me enough to come to me with their hearts' burdens, and believe enough in me to expect me to aid them by advice or sympathy. Such things tell me more what I am than anything that happens. When men like Mr. Cresson, Dr. Allen, Putnam, & the like come to me, young man as I am, and tell what I have reason to know they tell to no other it *is* something to be proud of. . . .

Putnam at last feels that great passion at once man-making and humiliating. How clear the every weakness & fault of a man stands forth before him when he realizes that a woman loves him & that he has nothing but his character & the deeds thereof to give her! It *is* humiliating, and as my love of Charlotte did for her, as my love of her did for me, as the love of *all* men who are in some sort true to themselves & God brought each to his knees in prayer so has it brought Putnam. How weak he seems to himself—how noble & strong to the woman that loves him. His true character is now defined and I like him better than ever.

I think I helped him some. Who appreciates strong love enough! I fear I do not—even I who find it the innermost of life. . . .

[Subsequent diary entries also refer to Sidney Putnam, this man of "strange nature," as Stetson viewed him, "full of yearnings and discontent with self. In the afternoon Putnam called & read me several letters that his lady wrote him. She rebels against his love and the poor fellow is nigh distraught. It is bitter I know but it will make him more of a man. I wrote him a letter last night" (Sept. 2, 1882). Through the next several weeks, Stetson tried in his own way to offer Putnam his support and sympathy: "[I] read to him some of my verses. I think he really liked some of them—at any rate he was pleased to copy three or four. I also read him Ham[ilton MacDougall]'s 'review' of 'death' etc." But given Stetson's feelings about the "bitterness of love without marriage" he realized, "[I] must have been some poor comfort to him" (Dec. 22, Sept. 2, Aug. 30, 1882).

For a time, Stetson argued that such "passionate pains" had some value; at least they were "man-making." But as Putnam's depression intensified, Stetson worried: "Poor fellow! Life looks very dark to him. I never had seen him quite so melancholy. I think he has some reason. Love pains him, inasmuch as he is engaged, feels himself unworthy, and sees no way of making himself worthy. (Do I not know? Ah, God!) Since his return his mother has shown anger at his daring to engage himself. She tells him that soon she will be unable to support herself, and that the burden will fall on him. With his meagre salary, with little hopes of having a more adequate one soon, it seems almost wild to think of marrying. And yet—is it not less bad than my case?—and yet—and yet, no, for my Love is a strong woman and likes that sort of thing. His is not robust and could scarcely bear it, I judge. Then his health is very precarious, he says. Poor fellow! It does look dark for him;

more so that he has not that vital energetic stamina that belongs to those who successfully battle" (Dec. 28, 1882).]

AUG 22. ''82 TUES. A.M.

Well the model came—and alone. Walked in modestly enough & sat down. I also sat down and said: "Are you ready to undress for me?" "Yes." Therewith she proceeded to disrobe, if such may be said of denuding herself of stockings, shoes, chemise, skirt & corsets. There she stood on that wild cat skin. All I can say is that I am at last fortunate. Her form is very very beautiful: symmetrical, delicate: graceful, lithe. Not one woman in a thousand I am sure can equal her. She assumed all sorts of poses at my suggestion and in not one of them was she anything but beautiful. Her color is a delicate pinkish ivory—not so rich as one could wish but just right for her silvery-gold blonde hair & pale eyes. Her face is not so good as her form, although I can use it by making those concealed alterations which every artist of feeling always wants to make.

Then as to terms. She did not know. I told her I should want her for two hours at least each time. Would $1— be enough for a sitting. It would. That's as cheap as a man could wish I'm sure. I think also she can be depended upon.

Though a harlot, and professionally so as she told me, she bears no evidence of it save around the eyes & lips. The nipples are fuller than they otherwise would be—but she is young, 18 or so, and her breasts are that beautiful erect kind—not flabby as in most women. She is a treasure to me that is true and if I can but get the money to pay her I shall use her often. Better than all that (in one way) is her quiet unassuming demeanor. No matter whether it is feigned or not it answers the purpose of genuine modesty. . . .

The evening I spent at home, and in writing a sonnet on the picture of a nude dancer resting. I *cannot help* writing. I do try not to do it—but before I know it I am at it. It does seem that what I do in that way ought to be better than it is. Ah, if I had but had proper study in my youth! I am doing all I can to make up for it now. . . .

WEDNESDAY, AUG 23. 1882 P.M.

. . . I feel something mighty stirring within me. I think it will find utterance. Daily I see that my honest opinions are having influence. I find that without any premeditation I have already influenced several of the older artists & I know that my enthusiasm is kindling something in my circle of acquaintance. Oh, if I may persevere and keep my heart ever on my goal, let men say what they will and society hate me as it will. . . .

Wish Charlotte were home. It seems very long since I kissed her. What a wonderful love she is; and how is it that she has come into my life so powerfully. No man in these days could deny that there is a sharp pain in love; but Oh! how grand it is & how much better than all other pleasure. . . .

FRIDAY, 25TH AUG. 1882 9:10 A.M.

[In the afternoon, Hamilton MacDougall called and talked with Stetson about some books and articles he had been reading; also, MacDougall mentioned that one of Stetson's poems—"The Hunting Song"—had been put to music and was going to be sung by the choir at the local Baptist Church.]

. . . After that and an unusual amount of fun on my side—I was *so* glad he called for I am growing morbid for lack of cheerful society. . . . I walked home with him. It was a lovely moonlight. We talked of Art, of women, of the Summer travel, & had a short discussion of the wearing of thin apparel by women, low necked dresses & the like. Ham said he was sure that it did him harm while at Saratoga to see so many women in low necked dresses— still it might be his fault. He was all mixed up on such subjects. He was sure that he could not control himself enough to draw from the nude. Then I proceeded to tell him that after he had seen the utter most of woman's body—(*utter* most is not just the word) after he had become perfectly familiar with all her parts & their ways that there was still a veil beyond—she was still just as much a mystery and sweet delight as ever: that it was not because her parts were different from man that made her so mysteriously attractive but because her nature was different—because she was a *woman*.*. . .

----

*Grace Channing wrote, "This I think eminently characteristic and beautiful. . . . This impersonality of the artist went so far that Charlotte, years after, gave it to me as her excuse for not liking to sit for her portrait to him, when I thought it her duty to do so. She said she hated to have him paint from her, for the moment he began 'he looked at her as a stranger; something coldly impersonal came into his gaze.' I have never forgotten it—and often quoted it to him— and I know exactly what she meant. He did seem to go off into remote and superior spaces and gaze at you from them without any of the usual silent language of the eye, and with an awful *concentrated* vision. The only difference being—that *I* loved exactly that: it made one for the time a part of his creation." GEC to EBK, May 23, 1912, p. 109.

Ham was pleased to laugh at some of my jokes of which I was unusually happy. It was very flattering because he rarely perceives them: either because they are too subtle or else because only my own mind considers them humorous or witty! It is very chilling(!)

Now for work.

*   *   *

30TH AUG. WED. A.M. "82

. . . At 6 o'c. I went home; supped; went to Charlotte's. . . . [She] met me with strong open arms. How rapturously she kissed me again and again as if she could not be satisfied. . . .

. . . I sat holding her hand and stroking the dark brown arms from which the skin was beginning to come off. Said I, I like your arms to be brown. "I'm glad," said she, "I was afraid you wouldn't and I felt half ashamed of myself—as if I were taking liberties with someone's else property." It was a startling statement for her to make seriously—and it was so made. I assured her precipitably that *I* had no property save her love.

But she talked & talked, and I sat and stared inanely either into space or at her. O what a stupid love she must think me! I can't talk with her now. My feelings, thoughts, will not become formulated! She wants things expressed—even the subtle sentiments—with logical precision and that I can't do. If they are not so expressed away she goes at them with microscope and scalpel and I become a good specimen of the illogical young man for her cabinet. And then her mother is always 'round—and she almost hates me now—and I *can't* talk for her to hear. What a way for lovers to learn of each other's hearts! Well, I felt heartily disgruntled with myself: there were burning thoughts filling me, but to put them into words was quite impossible: they floated before my mind's eye in beautiful symbols, but I could not, were I to have died for not doing it, have translated them into any English she would understand. It's a bad case. I don't know what to do about it; for she needs someone to convene with her about all sorts of things. I told her— she said half in fun, but it was serious in intent, that soon a certain gentleman would return to the city who liked to talk as well as she, and who could appreciate pure nonsense (of which she accuses me in default) and she was going to see a good deal of him. I should be jealous should I *not*? I said, well, what then? I am naturally jealous but I have some reason as well, and I think whatever jealousy I might feel you would know nothing of, and it would be sorrow, rather than anything worse because I was not able to supply all your needs. And I told her that I wanted her to associate with young men who could be of any service to her in her development. Soon after I left. It was with a glad sense of her love but with a sad feeling that after all I was perhaps robbing her of more than I gave. There can be no doubt that she is going to be either a very marked woman for good things or a great pedant. I can't say quite which yet: my love of her makes me think the former. Well, feeling this disagreeable I went home afoot and pondered upon what I must do—or rather *ought* to do. I knew that she could not understand my manner, why I said so little, or why I made my clear thoughts muddy in the saying. And by the time I was in bed I decided to write to her with utmost barefaced frankness, tell her what there was about her, her mother, and my life else that forbade the utterance of my all.

The next morning I did so. It took me all the forenoon. If any letter was ever plain that was. I knew she could not misunderstand a word of it.

Tuesday morning I received a response. She said she felt as if a great wind had swept a cloud from between us. That so long as she knew that I could talk she did [not] mind if she did not hear. So long as she knew that I loved her she did not care for the thousand tender things I might say. . . .

It was a good letter. If I am not mistaking she now loves me with a love that can overlook a few lacks for what I can give her. But that makes me feel nonetheless the loss she must suffer. I told her in that letter that I wanted her to associate with young men who can converse as I cannot, so that she may have exercise of her thoughts and wit. And that if I was jealous—that was my fault: and if she learned to love any of them better than me, why, if I am not full man enough to hold her by my manhood I want her to go: and if she is not nobly enough a woman to be true to her womanhood most certainly I should insist on her going—I think there was no mistaking what I said. . . .

31ST AUG. 1882. THURSDAY 8:40 A.M.

My studio looks brighter this morning, but only because I was with Charlotte to my good last evening.

It came about in this way: I painted all the afternoon . . . then as it grew later I sat looking out at my window, and had the delectable vision of a woman in the rear go through a, I hope not unusual, toilet. From taking a nude bath to putting on her corsets. Now heaven knows I'm not a "peeper," but when one sits at his own window and when a woman has not discretion enough even to pull down a shade when she takes her bath I have not moral courage enough to go away from the window: for certainly if she was very chary of her charms—which are undeniable—she would close either her blinds or have a shade down: and I am not, as is well known, averse to the nude in nature as well as Art. So I saw her; & her limbs and the rest were beautiful beyond question. And it didn't hurt me, rather did me good by calling to mind from my brooding thoughts of the inexpressiveness of my handicraft and my inefficiency therein. But the moment I did take my eyes from her they all came back with a tidal force. I saw that though I had worked faithfully it had resulted in expressing not an iota of my thought Then, thank heaven! Charlotte intervened. Her dear spirit seemed to come very near and I felt almost cowardly. I resolved to go to see her that evening, even if it were only to the door, and long enough for a kiss.

Immediately after supper I started, it was 7:30. Walked all the way because I didn't have money for horse cars. As I went up Waterman St. by the colleges the moon rose. O the bewitchment of it! Always new tho' seen a hundred hundred times. What mystic shadows under the great elms, and how weirdly the not yet extinguished gas lamps lit the under side of the leaves and mingled with the other! Some slim twigs run straight up and across the moon. It was a haunting poem, & followed me all the evening. Charlotte opened the door and with glad looks said "Oh! I'm so glad to see you! I was just wishing you were here and thinking about you never so hard." And she drew me in but did not kiss me. Into her study and made room for me in a chair filled with manuscripts. I never had seen her quite so evidently glad. It shone even in her fingertips, and her eyes—"Stars, stars, and all eyes else dull coals!"

Then she came and kissed me: How do women who have had no lovers learn to kiss with that delicious, trustful, senso-supersensuous pressure and melting tenderness? She has learned it in a short time. Is it not the truthful expression of the yearning love within? My sensitive lips can tell the tenor of a kiss most positively, and all along hers have revealed more of her real heart to me than all her logical (?) expressions of her feeling.

Oh, but she was glad! And being glad perforce I must be glad also, and that melancholy which I had expected to give in lone thoughts to the night vanished apace. Joy came, *words* came—not very plentifully but more abundantly than usual. I talked more with her mother than usual. Charlotte was just running over with love. So full that she could not contain herself, as her ever coming arms and looks testified. And such tones, such kisses! I, even I, ask for nothing better. Well, I carried her [William] Morris's "Hopes & Fears for Art" to read. . . .

That letter I wrote must have been an inspiration. It has brought us nearer together than anything else has ever done. Especially the part telling exactly of my financial hindrances etc.

It was the best evening I have spent with her for very long. I went home with the world changed. There was new meaning in the tree forms and cloudlets, in the deep shadows and glimmers on the college campus. And the city with its silent spires & domes and strong lights lay off and under me like some peaceful hamlet of which I was but a guest soon to leave for shores more blest.

All the way home it followed me: and is with me now.

The letter came this morning. *I like it*. I will copy it, it is so characteristic of her more loving moods.

Sweetheart—Darling! . . .

My dear boy! My heart is very warm to you this week. To find you so entangled in a world of little troubles very like my own makes me feel as if we were indeed united. (Strange word for her!) I don't wonder a bit at your being sad and preoccupied: and it shall be my part to make you as happy as I can irrespective of your precise expression. I think one reason I noticed it, is because I naturally want to feel that I *do* make you happy: and to have you sit with my hand in yours and look as if this world was a dismal delusion isn't exhilarating. Let me recommend that you mildly ignore these present difficulties, and fix your eyes on a pleasant picture of ten years hence: by which time you will have gotten well used to my eccentricities and me; and be surrounded by divers little folks imaginative and logical as it happens.

Just think of all the years you've got to live and all we shall be to each other; and this little period won't seem so dark.

I thank you very much for that letter of yours. Someway I feel as if I could touch you now; and we had something in common besides love. . . .

Ah-h! This winter just blazes before me, so *much* to do, and such effervescense of power to do it. . . .

2D SEPT. 1882. SATURDAY.

Am down early. Yesterday at ten o'clock Charlotte came to give me the first sitting for her portrait: with her Miss Luther—Charlotte's "dear little duenna." The moment I saw them I was happy. Here on my own ground, surrounded by the familiar tools I could be just myself. And Charlotte was so softened, so unlike what she was when she first came to my studio that it seemed as if indeed we two had by some divine thing been united. It was a beautiful sight, these two women each intellectual, each tender, yet wholly unlike in many things. Ah, the man that can often have such visitants and companions must grow apace in good things.

After some banter, and much posing I fell to work on Charlotte, in a pose that I think will enable me to show the thoughtful side of her nature, and as it was yesterday with a deep half revealed loving tenderness.

O what looks she gave me while I worked, speaking volumes of the love she bears me, of the hopes she has, of all fears vanished. And how she talked in that undercurrent tone of hers to Miss Martha about *our* lives, about what *we* had before us. It was very apropos as Miss Martha is preparing for a marriage in Oct. She said it all in a way which showed how decided she was that it all would be.

Then during the little recesses I gave her she came, leaned over the back of my chair and drew my head back upon her firm bosom and kissed me: not in an objectionably open way, but even as a wedded wife might. Charlotte is so frank before Miss Martha that one feels her real purity very strongly. And Miss Martha is so kind and thoughtful that one never feels that she is present in an intrusive way, but rather as a sweetening spirit. I cannot remember when I have passed a more congenial forenoon;—my love and work side by side and intertwined. O what a help her constant presence would be! . . .

4TH SEPT. 1882. 5:45 P.M.
. . . Saw Whitaker this morning. He saw Bates yesterday and asked him what he thought would be a wise thing for us to do in the matter of our Exhibition. Bates thought that it would be best to exhibit & sell our things at Doll & Richards in Boston; and gave good reasons for it. He said that he would give us a letter of introduction to them and they might send a man down & look at our work. . . .

FRIDAY, SEPT. 8TH 1882
Last Tuesday morning & yesterday morning I had a sitting from my Love. . . . How that picture of her sitting on my rug on the floor with her hands clasped around her knees lives with me: meanwhile she talked so confidently of the future! She wants to have me buy that peninsula at Malagawatch [Nova Scotia] and put up even a log house upon it; we can originate & have a village carpenter make all our furniture. And we should have to buy would be bedding. And then into such a place, a true creation of our own, take our work—writing & painting & live simply; rear our little brood, and after we had earned enough to warrant it return to some place nearer city life and buy a place. "And so keep our expenses *under* us instead of over, as most people do." "And how happy we could be so living *natural*

lives!" I asked her if she thought she could be happy & live with only me as companion and so far away from the excitement of city life. She simply *looked* at me—but how eloquent of love and surety was that look! I felt as if I must clasp her wildly in my arms and tell her how proud of her I am. . . .

I do not advance with the portrait as I ought: her face is very difficult to paint. May be it being hers I want to say it so well that at the thought of saying it at all I stammer. . . .

*   *   *

12TH SEPT. TUESDAY MORN. ''82.

It rains, but not as it did yesterday in dark sheets obscuring my light so that it was almost impossible to work. In the morning I worked some on my Love's portrait and also glazed on Baddeck & the Caribou Cove woman.* Geo. [Whitaker] came over about noon, and just as I received a letter from Doll & Richards which to be sure concerned him as much as it did me. They will send someone down next week to look at our pictures. Geo. still is very sanguine of the result but as for me I am still pessimistic.

Sunday evening with my love. . . . She had composed a poem on receipt of my last letter which she read me. It is virtually a prayer. . . .

Then she read me the first part of a partnership novel that she and the Channing girls [Grace and her sister Mary] are writing.† I can see that she is going to make it rather autobiographical. It already shows a good observation of character, an easy style—tho' not quite concise enough to suit me—and a reserve of dramatic force which will show itself someday—perhaps later in this same novel. I am glad she is getting her hand in: and I think I may expect from her some high good writing one of these days. She has not had experience enough yet with different sorts of people to give it the highest force but I think she is doing well. (Not said in a patronizing way, nor because she is Mine.) . . .

15TH SEPT. FRIDAY. 3 P.M.

This morning had another sitting from Charlotte. What a dear girl she is! Her love is so good & strong now: there seems to be no alloy in it—it wells up warm, and she allows it to gush forth richly.

---

* Quite a number of Stetson's Nova Scotia paintings cannot be identified.

† Grace Channing and Charlotte wrote a number of novels and plays together. Two unpublished ones—"The Test Case" and "A Pretty Idiot" (1890)—are in the Gilman manuscript collection, AESL.

Speaking of wells. There was a Mr. Wells who called on her some last Spring whom she liked much, and solely I think because of his "nonsense"—that in which she thought me lacking. Of course she was separated from him by vacation, but since his return he has called. Wed. evening as we were going to visit Miss Gladding* Charlotte said: "Mr. Wells called the other night and—I didn't like him so well as I did." Why not? said I. "That which used to amuse me and make me laugh seemed shallow—it was not enough—I wanted something better. And I am glad because it shows me that I *have* grown ever so much nearer to you." If Mr. Wells only has his fun to recommend him I am sorry for him then. . . .

. . .Miss G[ladding] I found to be a very lovely woman, dreadfully lame. She is so well bred that she doesn't seem to realize it, and you scarcely think about it. Just the woman to make good Charlotte's lack of those little, conflicting manners; I am glad to have her with her.

Miss G. played for us—at my request (which she felt glad of) Chopin, Etude & Nocturnes and two of Mendelssohn's "Lieder ohne Wörter." It did seem to please her mightily, that Chopin was one of my favorites.

While she played those sweet things Charlotte leaned herself into my arms and lay there like a child. Miss Gladding seems to have virtually adopted Charlotte, and so it was not making herself "too much at home." . . .

SATURDAY, P.M. 5:30. SEPT. 16. 1882.

End of the week—and I am very tired of all but Charlotte and art in esse. I have been thinking over what I have done—been looking it over: it is not of account. Had another sitting from Charlotte this morning: while I improved one part of the face I injured another so I can scarce see any progress.

The faults of my other work glare at me, but I do not know how to better it. . . .

Last evening I wrote her a letter which I fear was wildly passionate and much like the cry of a hungry man. But when she read it this morning she put it to her lips. I think she understands.

It seems almost hopeless: so much money will be required ere we can marry. Father & mother to look out for, Charlotte and possible, yea, probable little ones, rent of studio, and care of myself. And I am simply sick for

---

*Charlotte Gilman later described Augusta Gladding as "one of the older friends in whom I delighted, . . . a white-haired sweet-faced lady with mysterious iron legs!" CPG, unpublished autobiography, AESL.

lack of "conjugal rites" and Charlotte's companionship. There can be no doubt of it: desire of her rages within, although without is calmness, and I have self control. I wish I might understand why I am debarred from it: I wish I could know what part in God's economy is played by separated lovers who do love truly and would gladly live pure lives & rear good children.

This morning Charlotte unbound her hair and let it fall over her shoulders. How it fell away in rich dark waves and framed her rich complexion and intensified the soft ivory of her neck! I have never seen her so beautiful. . . .

[Four pages have been removed. The diary resumes with a discussion of the Cressons' offering him encouragement and support.] . . . They want me to send two 30 × 40's, the *May Measures* & *Sacrifice in the Afterglow*.

. . . They want to buy the Cape Breton Girl & the Twilight—or rather Sunset in Fog at Baddeck * if I do not sell them in Boston. I promised them to go to Phil. by the 20th of October.

How much good they do me! It is almost my only hold—to feel that someone has such faith in me. Charlotte's mother "rails" at me—they encourage me in that way: what extremes. Charlotte herself does not quite understand my art. She has not had *wide* enough culture yet. . . . If I had money enough I think I could ask her to marry me next month & she would do it. It seems mean to have money such a power in the fate of lovers. . . . I cannot now see much hope. If I earn more—my debts must be paid. I owe say $800. now: and if I earn yet more father & mother must be taken care of. . . .

I feel as if I had committed a crime when I think of trafficking in Art.

---

* *Fog Coming at Sunset, Baddeck, Cape Breton* (16 × 30 inches; see reproduction in this volume), was first exhibited and listed in Boston; New England Manufacturers and Mechanics Institute, *Exposition of American Painting* (Boston: The Institute, 1883); then again (this time as *Fog Gathering about Red Head at Twilight: Baddeck, C.B.*) at the 1884 PAC Annual Exhibit; and a third time (as *Fog Gathering at Twilight; Baddeck, Cape Breton*) in the *Stetson Exhibition and Sale* (Providence, R.I.: n. pub., 1888). It was first purchased by Mr. and Mrs. George V. Cresson, and is currently owned by Mr. and Mrs. Joseph K. Ott.

Art critic Charles Eldredge suggests that the painting shows the importance of Stetson's Nova Scotia travels, his growing interest in color and light, his evolving "Turneresque" techniques: "The sun's glow, filtered through fog and mist, intensely illuminates the scene, providing a golden tonality overall; the backlighting, casting dark shadows toward the foreground, is vaguely reminiscent as well of Washington Allston's coastal views, of which Stetson was an admirer. The Baddeck motif is similar to those painted by [George] Whitaker," Eldredge continues, "but the Stetson work has a greater luminosity and a looser sketchier quality." Charles Eldredge, *Charles Walter Stetson: Color and Fantasy* (Lawrence, Kan.: Spencer Museum of Art, 1982), p. 27.

Selling my works! Ah, why *can* I not *give* them—they are for all. The idea of making a *business* of thinking and feeling is simply shudderful to me.

I am in no mood for painting today.

The article in Harper's Mo. for Oct. on Rossetti pleases me much.* I love that man. His love, his hope, his despair are so much like mine that I long to call him brother. And yet—what hope have I for such genius?

25TH SEPT—MONDAY—1882 A.M.

. . . Last Wednesday or Thursday Mr. Hatfield of the firm of Doll & Richards came to see Geo[rge Whitaker] & me. Geo. came over here with him. I have not met a man for long who so formally impressed me. He is tall, well formed and to my thought handsome. He has an air of good breeding, which gives him a charming simplicity of manners: his voice is that of culture, and has a gently authoritative tone very pleasant to hear.

I showed him all my C.B. & N.S. [Cape Breton and Nova Scotia] sketches. He *said* very little, but I was watching his face and could see what he liked and disliked most. Once in a while he would make some comments very much to the point. After I had shown him all of them, as he had said so little, I told him that I wanted him to be perfectly frank with me for he would not hurt my feelings no matter how adverse his criticisms were. He thanked me and said that that would put him at his ease, and that he wanted to speak frankly because it was his way and he thought it best. Then he kindly told us that he thought it would not pay for us to have an exhibition of our work because it was not what the public wanted: and he knew that it would be discouraging to have all our things framed with the hope of selling and at the end, having sold but little, be confronted with a bill of expenses. He said that be as charitable as we might we could but feel that in some way the dealer might have done better. He also said that we must not think that he did not like our work as a whole, for he did, and that it was not because the things were *poor* but because they were "too good." Which he explained by saying that they depended wholly, or nearly so, upon their artistic *qualities* for their interest, and people demanded incident or anecdote, and such were the things that sold best and paid in a pecuniary way. So he showed me that my things had nothing to recommend them to the public as a whole.

---

*Mary Robinson, "Dante Gabriel Rossetti," *Harper's New Monthly* 65, no. 389 (Oct. 1882), pp. 691–701.

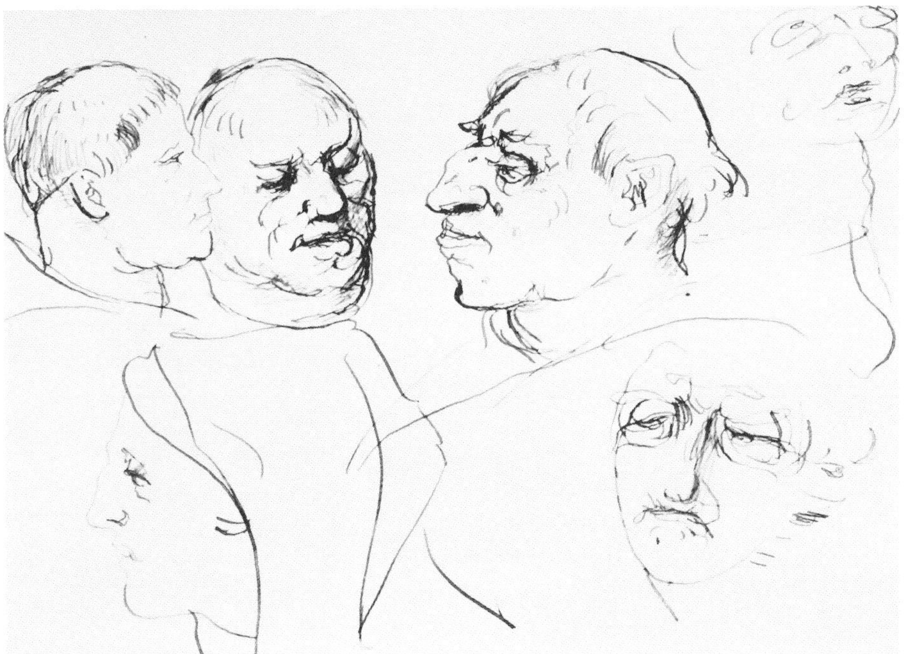

Drawing of unidentified faces. From Sketchbooks.

He showed that it would be different if we had a little clique of a few influential patrons in Boston, for they were all like sheep, went as certain men went.

Then he wanted me to show him all the canvases I had: which I did. The dancing girls [*May Dance*] which I was going to send to Phila. he liked very much and asked me to send it to him as soon as it was completed as he thought it would make quite a stir in Boston, and that he could sell it. He also grew enthusiastic over my *Mystic Rite* and called it "superb" in tone & color; but said he scarcely thought he could sell such a picture, it was so different from the art in fashion. And the *Fading Light* of last year, he would also like to have in Boston.* And he selected five water colors to take with him.

---

* *Dancing Girls*, later called *May Dance* (30 × 40 inches; see reproduction in this volume), was originally purchased by George Tewksbury of Topeka, Kansas, and now belongs to Dr. and Mrs. Rodney E. Sanneman, Burbank, California. Stetson wrote of *May Dance*: "two whirling in a dance & one standing by piping. All in a vaporous manner. Rather grayer than I usually paint." "It is generally liked by those who call on me." "Opera" Book, pp. 29–31.

Geo.[Whitaker] took us to the Hotel Dorrance to dinner & I left them after it. Mr. Hatfield told Geo. more about my work than he did me, & Geo. good naturedly repeated some of it. He told him that my color was very exceptional indeed; with his wide experience he did not know of another man who painted as I do. My individuality was very decided. Also he said I would make a great success & a decorator in the Tiffany-Latage way, but he didn't want me to be encouraged to do so, as he should feel sorry to have me give up picture painting.

It was a red letter day for me, as it is the first time I have been recognized in that way. No one who *knew* has said such things about my work, and no one has seen what I wanted seen in it. I must confess that I am not elated over it. It only shows me that my purpose to paint what I believed to be good has been in great measure kept to. And it is encouraging to have some one recognize what I am *trying* to do. And also it shows that I have made some advance or such dealers would not take my work.

No one need tell me how poor it is: I never felt it more strongly than since I began to paint my Love. I went home Saturday night feeling deeply my weakness & these sonnets came.

These many days I've tried to fix the face
   Of her I love on canvas, that it might
   Remain to tell of her and glad the sight
Of those to come with intellectual grace.
Most patiently did she sit, and I did trace
   And study the marvellous eye that's dark & bright,
   The curve from the wide clear brow's fair height
Along the cheek to the eloquent lips' red place;
   And then adown the delicate smooth chin
To the supple throat, until it was so lost
   In the hid and heaving breasts' cream white high mounds.

Stetson wrote of *Mystic Rite* (30 × 40 inches): "The values are rather subtle but I think for the sentiment intended correct, or nearly so. . . . Consider it one of my best studies of quiet rich color." "Opera" Book, p. 27. The painting was exhibited at the Pennsylvania Academy of Fine Arts in October 1882.

Stetson wrote of *Fading Light* (landscape, 30 × 40 inches): "This is my best and most important picture (if anything of mine is important) thus far. . . . It was begun many months ago. Indeed, for at least two years the subject has been brooding over my mind. I had done all that I can with what knowledge I possess—but the possibilities of the subject are only hinted at." "Opera" Book, p. 28.

But Oh! today 'tis not more like to her within
My soul, nor like to what her soul surrounds,
Than 'twas when first my brush the canvas crossed.

II

O what in me the fault, or what the sin,
That dulls my sight or warps her image fair
Until my hand may not her loveliness declare—
For which I've prayed e'er since I did begin?
Ah, Lord, and hath it always suchwise been,
That ne'er within my heart I yet did bear
An image true of all her shape so rare,
Tho' sure I know her spirit dwells therein?
What then the hope for eminence in Art
When what I love e'en as my very soul
Is not seen clear, is scarcely understood?
And while I cannot fix the smallest part
Of her great loveliness what can console,
And what of all my life and Art is good?

Sunday I did little but read. . . . After supper [I] . . . started for Charlotte's. I can't say that I felt remarkably well. She met me at the door radiant. . . . We sat in her writing-room and as the hostile relatives were in the adjoining apartment we wrote our inner thoughts, our love expressions on a pad, as we did the week before. There were some beautiful tender & high things written so. We grew closer together thereby.

She gave me a letter she had written Saturday evening in which she thanked me for [pointing out] certain things I had thought not beautiful in her talk—and she said that it showed her that I was indeed "for her." . . . Our evening was quite broken [by callers] but Charlotte seeing that it was all to be wasted in mere commonplaces drew me to her room and we finished our evening there in quiet communion that scarce needed speech. Her parting with me was so delicately passionate that I could almost wish for a life of partings.

THURSDAY 11:45 A.M. SEPT. 28. 1882

Yesterday afternoon Charlotte came to sit again: of course Martha was with us: Charlotte was more quiet than usual, but *I* talked more, and once when I stopped she said "Don't stop; I like to have you talk." And she said also that I was unusually pleasant—and that she liked to have me so. Well, I painted & painted but I *could not* get it to come right. At last in sheer desperation and despite brushes I went at the cheek with my palette knife and in ten minutes I had it more like her than it has yet been. But still—how far away from her loveliness.

During the sitting she tried to get me to promise to go that evening with her to see the Misses Channings, but I didn't want to.*

[Several pages of the diary have been torn away here. A long discussion follows about the wisdom of postponing their marriage. Walter was impatient, and Charlotte felt herself "easily satisfied" with the current situation. He quotes her letter:] . . . only 2 years! It doesn't seem long to me, time *flies* so, and it makes the time like one long-drawn pleasure to look ahead. I'm an easily satisfied sort o'body I guess. . . .

Monday at 2:15 [Charlotte] & Martha came to the studio for the last sitting before [Martha's] marriage. Charlotte is very philosophic and sees much to amuse her in the way they treat her at home. As Martha knows all about it, and indeed has been treated in like manner by Mrs. Perkins herself she could understand. Miss Martha though a sweet little body has much energy and what is colloquially known as *spunk* and she took up a bold lance against Mrs. Perkins. And told Charlotte a great many plain truths about dealing with her mother. It is astonishing how patient Charlotte is and yet has so aggressive a character. I'm afraid I shall be obliged to make some blue fire for Mrs. P[erkins] if she does not cease talking as she does and telling untruths about my engagement to [name deleted]. . . .

Am wearing my false teeth today for the first time. Bah!

SATURDAY, 7TH OCT. 1882. LATE P.M.

. . . There can be no other woman who is at once so childlike and so wise. There is no sentiment of love that [Charlotte] hides from me, from the passion of love and mutual sleep, to the grand heights of intellectual communion. She wants to live with me, said several times, simply, that she wished we were going to *our* home and that I might stay with her all the night; that she was growing lonesome without me. And told of how happy she felt sure she could make me, and of what a great longing she had to supply all my wants—indeed to have her own supplied.

______

*"The Misses Channing [Grace and Mary] wanted to see Charlotte's fiance!" GEC to EBK, May 23, 1912, p. 115.

Then we talked about her mother and she told me what I had noticed—that she had little fits of a sort of insanity—owing doubtless to her former family trouble. So I must make many perfect allowances for her treatment of me. Charlotte had never breathed a thought of it to anyone before. It is not a bad case yet, but I should not be surprised if she grew worse. She needs a husband; I think that is the main cause of her disorder. . . .

9TH OCT. 1882—MONDAY 2:30 P.M.

Yesterday . . . at home after a brief call on Caroline; and in the evening as usual went to Charlotte. . . .

O how marvellous it is to see her wholly melted in supreme surrender to Love's power! Not mine the victory but Love's who worketh in me: it was not the influence of this meagre body or unsettled mind that brought that strong woman so that she is as dough to the kneader or clay to the potter, to be fashioned as her lover wills. Thank God that I will that she should be fashioned into the utmost of noble womanhood, and with the tenderness that passeth all understanding. . . . [Here, 8 lines of the diary have been deleted.]

This morning a letter from Doll & Richards stating that they had received the "*Fading Light*" and "*A May Dance.*" They want me to give them some idea of a price for them to work from. It was a courteous little letter. . . .

. . . *spirits plot and counterplot*

October 11, 1882 – January 19, 1883

BY OCTOBER 1882, Mary Perkins had decided that she approved of Walter, and that he and Charlotte should marry quickly before "passion" overwhelmed. Mrs. Cresson, on the other hand, wealthy friend and patron, favored travel to Europe instead. Charlotte was a hindrance, Mrs. Cresson argued, "unless [she] could *give herself* up—become as nothing for [his] sake, it would be an ill thing." Apparently this was the first time that Walter thought of Charlotte as a burden; and it was the first time also that he saw a conflict in his goals. He wanted desperately "to go to Europe, to get out of home ruts, to study." Yet clearly he wanted marriage as well. "The whole world grows dizzy and it all seems so mean," he wrote. "Why *was* I born an artist and a lover too!!"

Meanwhile, Charlotte continued with her own vacillations. On the one hand she "feared that [he] would not satisfy her. She even said so." And on the other, she responded with a "child's faith" in her "King": "I could scarcely have foreseen so complete a subjugation of self, or abnegation rather." "She wants to be treated more as a child now than as a woman." *

---

*The above quotations are from diary entries of the following dates: Nov. 25, Dec. 4, Dec. 21, 1882; Jan. 19, 1883.

11 OCT. WEDNESDAY 2:30 P.M.

Such wonderful letters as I am having at this period from Charlotte: letters full of trust in me, permeated by love's hungering passion, frank as a child's, strong as a woman's. One yesterday, one today. . . .

16TH OCTOBER, 1882 MONDAY.

[Walter had written to his former lover asking her to return his letters and class ring.] . . . I sent a letter to——[name deleted] and in a few days my letters from the first came—. . . It burned my heart: for it must seem to her that I am untrue to that good love I gave her—and what would she feel if she knew that I had found a woman who *is* what I thought her to be— who is sunlight to starlight? Oh! ——[name deleted] was a good girl, tender, loving, but what unhappiness would have been mine & hers to live with her always. She *could* not understand me in my best self. . . .

She loves me yet, and I love her but not as I thought. Clearly I see that; and the pain of knowing how my self deception and too ready faith to believe the utmost good has wrought this thing making life darker for her and me is Hell.

I must ask Charlotte what to do. I must answer the letter, but how to do it without paining her I know not. If I tell her of my vast love of another it will be horrible at this time. God help us both.

Charlotte I *do* love above all the earth.

OCT. 18TH 1882. WED. MORNING.

Monday evening I met Charlotte at the Public Library, as agreed and she went home with me to supper. There was something beautiful in walking home with her. I think that father & mother were glad to have her. Mother to be sure is somewhat cynical but she says nothing against our evident love of each other. Charlotte gave me a dear letter at the library in which she told of her mind at present: and of how Sunday night she awoke and could really not tell whether she were herself or me. . . .

[On Tuesday Walter found Mary Perkins, Charlotte's mother, waiting for him at his studio.] . . . I *felt* at once that she had come to confess and find pardon: but I was not quite prepared for what did follow. Saying she had come to have a talk with me she came in & sat on the edge of my lounge.

I took off my things slowly, seated myself before her & told her that I was ready. It is useless for me to remember all she said for it was not all clear and was full of long digressions about things which only remotely bore upon the subject.

I listened with utmost patience. The substance was this: She had come to tell me that she had given up all resistance and from trying to hinder was now willing to help me or us. She had never resisted *me* but that in me which she had mistaken. She saw that she had placed me where all that I did was dishonorable whereas she now said that I had been honorable. And it was all because she deemed what we were doing "disorderly." Love she thought supreme and holy as long as its ways were regulated by order but Love disorderly she would fight as if it were the devil. She thought our love was Lust (!!) but she had learned to see that it was Love and remembering love she could no longer resist. She had watched Charlotte, and had found that she loved me wholly, and, she said, "for her to love is not a little thing: when she does love it is with her whole being. You have that love." It was all mixed up with analogies drawn from her own life and the Scriptures. She revealed secrets regarding her husband which were she healthy in mind she never would have revealed. She told all about Charlotte's life—things that Charlotte had told me—only from another standpoint. She told how she had guarded her and loved her ever, and how at last Charlotte had turned from her, ignored her—thus she had lost all faith in her. Her care over her was ended. She had given her to the Lord. Well, said I, if you still have faith in the Lord surely you must feel that he will care for Charlotte. It came just right: and she acknowledged that even her faith in God was not perfect. Well, it was a painful thing to me for I could say nothing in my own defense. . . .

But it all resolved itself with the climax. Charlotte was passionately loving: her whole sexual nature was aflame. I too was passionate. There was danger to us of the worst sort, wrecking to moral & physical well being. If we were together we would be constantly tempted to sexual intercourse (which certainly is true) and she felt sure we should yield and thus do some "disorderly" thing. Thereupon ensued a digression about the relation of civil to divine law. As she had given her to the care of the Lord she felt sure that I had a mission, that all this was providential and that in me was to be made manifest the care of the Lord. It was my mission to guard [Charlotte], to humble her pride and to save her from the damnation of disorderly sexual life. Therefore what better could be done than *to marry at once*. She could see no reason why we should not. We could each go on with our work just as now, or better; temptation would be no more; two hearts would be saved: she had rooms at the house, why could we not take them and live there. Charlotte was in frightful danger she said—being so passionate & so loving, yet having a sublime idea of the holiness of the relation of lovers. Why should we not marry?

I thanked her for her renewed confidence in me, and told her that . . . poverty was alone in the way: were it not I would gladly marry at once.

(O woman how consistent art thou!)

Thereupon she "went for" me with:—"You are too proud—you place money ahead of Love which is first, and being first is to be obeyed above all things and when obeyed God who is its author will proper the lovers." "Poverty is no obstacle in this case: Charlotte's besetting sin is love of money (?) and this will cure her. I am astonished that you say this—you who have so much of love and reverence in your nature." I tried to convince her that she was mistaken: that I would to God it were just as she saw: I did believe Love to be first of all; yet what were gained to marry and for lack of money find anxiety and unhappiness, for one in such case would doubtless be unhappy, & if one then both. And whether it was justifiable for me to assume new obligations until the old were paid I knew not.

I asked her if she was sure that there was as much danger to Charlotte as she thought. She still thought so. (I think she exaggerates a deal unconsciously. She broods over things until they assume gigantic dimensions.) She talked & talked until Charlotte & Miss [Augusta] Gladding came. Charlotte was greatly surprised, and somehow it was awkward all 'round.

During a moment when Miss Gladding and Mrs. Perkins were talking Charlotte . . . in facial pantomime . . . expressed curiosity to know what her mother's visit meant.

Mrs. Perkins stayed until after they had gone & went at matters again. Heaven only knows how long she would have stayed if Rev. Thos. Slicer D.D.* & Sydney Burleigh had not come in. She glided away. Her visit set me into a vast uneasiness. I firmly believe that her troubles and may be some bodily disease have injured the health of her brain. Her talk lacked perfect coherence and was rather hysterical. She meant every word she said—that I doubt not. I am thankful indeed that I can cease to feel that I am an intruder when I go there. But I fear that her assistance will be as troublesome and embarassing as her resistance. I must be firm. I want to do right & injure

---

*Thomas Slicer, a local minister, supervised Charlotte in teaching Bible classes in a program sponsored by a local chapter of the Union for Christian Work.

none. True it is that I love her as my very life: but father & mother are not to be forgotten: my debts must be paid.

But if there *is* danger to her health either of one part or another, all must be hazarded & she must come to my arms. Our dreams of our early married life will be all destroyed—our delightful plans done away—and the hardest of realities take the place. It means browsweat and soul-ache, pain and anxiety for both—but verily what is all to Love?

I wrote her a 21 page letter last night in which I told her all.

Stetson, even you have strange experiences!

19TH OCT. 1882. AFTERNOON.

Rains again: hard weather for us with our exhibition on our hands. When I got home last night I found a delightful letter from Charlotte. Her mother had a talk with her after they were home, in which she told her things much as she did me. Charlotte said that if her mother had always treated her with the same loving consideration she never could have been so cold towards her: but she fears that this mood of her mother will be of short duration. Charlotte cannot tolerate the idea of going to board with her mother—rather, she says, hire two rooms "down on the hill" and cook with an oil stove than to have our early married life open to ceaseless criticism. Besides she does not like taking me to *her* house—much better for me to take her to mine—but best of all to have a home of our own. She wants to be married soon—that she does not deny. . . .

23D OCT. 1882—MON. MORNING

I did but little yesterday until evening when I went to Charlotte's. She was mightily glad to see me and said that she found it hard waiting for me—a new development, I fancy. Her mother greeted me with genuine pleasantness and really seemed glad to see me. Charlotte then showed me some sketches of flowers she had been making—different from her water colors, being broad and simple, as masses of light against dark. She has lots of talent, dear girl, and please God, it shall be brought out when she can share her studio with me. If I cannot paint well myself I know that I have the power of making others do their best.

Then we sat down by the table. . . . [Her mother and her Aunt Caroline Robbins were present.] There was considerable talk about our marriage, mostly done by them. It did nothing but show me that they were really interested in it and goodnaturedly disposed towards it. For a wonder I said *very* little about it. How could I talk, so to speak, of the sacred Phallus and Golden Eggs so publicly. That was for her & I only. [The rest of the page has been blotted out.] What a marvellous work my Lord Love has worked in her, my Queen! What was harsh has become tender as spring flowers, and what was rough like thistle down. Her very body seemed to emanate light last evening, and verily an aureole surrounded us—hallowing bodily passion for the sake of prayerful spirit and true love. . . .

My two pictures were accepted by the Penna. Academy of Fine Arts, I suppose, as they sent me an exhibitor's ticket. Verily that is an advance. Now I hope they have hung them well: at any rate people will *see* them as they are powerful in color and different from any man's work there—without doubt.

Our exhibition at Waterman's has been very well attended—very well indeed, and our reputations have been raised a deal thereby (tho' that's of little account as regards the right spirit of Art) but nothing has been sold. It will be a hard case for me if nothing does sell. I have a large bill for frames, advertising and catalogues. . . . [Walter figured that the pictures he had at the various exhibits should sell for roughly $1950.] It does seem to me that out of that amount of work I ought to get enough to pay my debts and expenses. Somebody sometime will get something for them—so I suppose it's just as well: but how much I would like to have mother & father and my Love be benefitted by it while I live so that I may see the good it does. Shall I not see it if I die? Verily it seems to me that I *must*: I *love* them so.

(O how tenderly and fondly she came to me last night and whispered "My husband!") *She* is very happy: Thank God.

24TH (TUESDAY) OCT. 1882

It rains and is gloomy again today, but the sureness of Charlotte's love warms my whole soul. I am thinking of how earnestly she awaits sweet May for our marriage, and how glad she seems to think of going to Grand Pre to spend the first few months of our new life. Remembering the idyllic peace and wonderful beauty of Grand Pre it occurred to me that it would be just the place for the early growth of conjugal love—far from tumult, far from traffic, in beautiful light, sweet flowers and pastoral gentleness—should not we be more wholly each for each, and should not, if it so came, the child conceived amid such things be an incarnate poem? So it was settled that we were to marry, say in May, and go to Grand Pre and live until say the 1st of November—working, dreaming, loving. Ah, were not that an Elysium! . . .

24TH OF NOV. 1882 FRIDAY 11:30 A.M.

[Stetson has just returned from a four-week trip to Philadelphia, where he painted, went to museums, plays, and symphonies; and also enjoyed his growing friendship with the Cressons.] . . . They learned to love me better; they showered good things upon me, made me feel as if I were indeed "a son and heir." They enjoyed my visit as much as I did I am sure. And Oh! such things as Mrs. Cresson did for me, showed me, helped me too.

And they were satisfied (they said) with the portrait. . . .

25TH NOV. (SAT.) 1882 MORNING.

. . . My Philadelphia visit seems to me now as if I must have been wafted in sleep to some enchanted isle, the unpleasant things of which were only little dreams that fled. And best of all there were my letters from Charlotte. They were perfect; full of rapt love, and passionate longing & wide hope. She wrote to me every day, with perhaps two exceptions. There was much talk in them about our marriage in the spring—plans for home-furnishing and the like—talks about ways and means. Her love has grown until it is marvellously strong. . . .

Well, I soon found out what I had suspected, that Mrs. C[resson] was sorry that I am going to marry Charlotte so soon—no, not marry *Charlotte*, but marry at all: at the same time, as we love each other so—Charlotte & I—she says it is the only right thing to do. (Ah, dear Charlotte, she begins to feel in large measure the lack of ultimate expression: how *can* I help her?)

Of course it pained me to know that one whom I love as well as I do Mrs. C[resson] should object to anything so glorious and needful. And it almost maddened me to feel that it was only from a worldly point of view— only because it would hinder my advance towards "fame" and my studies. The idea that "practical things" must be considered when great love called so loudly made me indeed faint. And I told her that if my whole art life were ruined by my marriage it must be because my art life was not for me; for it could not be that *love* and *right doing* could slay any really good thing. . . .

She [Mrs. Cresson] wrote me a long letter Sunday telling me just what she felt about it. And it was that unless Charlotte could *give herself up*— become as nothing for my sake, it would be an ill thing: if she could all would be well she thought. She spoke very sensibly & feelingly. I read the letter to Charlotte.

Charlotte was overcome for a while. It had not occurred to her before that she could possibly be a burden and hindrance to me. I am glad I read the letter. It set her to thinking in a new direction and the good effects are apparent already.

In the "Boston Advertiser" of the 18th was an article on the Philadelphia Exhibition: and the critic gave my picture about a third of a column. That is, he began with mine for a text and preached a sermon to a lot of people in N. Y. & other places because he said my "Mystic Rite" represented a class of pictures that was increasing—those in which the purely sensuous element of color was the thing aimed at to the total neglect of beauty and the intellectual quality of drawing. There was a deal of truth in what he said surely. It is more than true that I cannot draw—but the picture mentioned would have been spoiled if it had been drawn hardly or even firmly. But the truth of his statement is apparent. But how am I to get out of the mire? They tell me I'm in up to my neck and stand on the shore and cry unto me to get out. No rope is thrown—or else it is one of sand.

Learn to draw I must, or I might as well be painting geometrical designs on walls for decoration. How to buckle down to the drudgery as long as I have my living to get I don't see: and no one who is questioned can tell me. They all say; get the money & go abroad, and do nothing but draw for a year or so. Who tells me how to get the money? I believe there is more intellect in color than the critic does, but I nonetheless believe in absolutely accurate drawing. It will be hard for me to learn because I am predisposed to the other extreme; but I feel certain that I *can* learn. . . .

2 P.M.   Well, I sent the "Advertiser" to Charlotte, & a letter; and in it frankly told her that I feared a time was coming in which I should stand divided between the call of Art and my Love of her. Told her how necessary it seemed to me to go to Europe, to get out of home ruts to study and how I did not see that it could be done for long if I married her. I told her that I thought my love of her would win—that I knew I would stay here and plod on rather than leave her and go away: and I told her what Leavitt had said regarding my going abroad that very morning[:] . . . "I tell you what *would* please me; that is to see you supplement your very evident power of coloring with knowledge of drawing. Why sir! two years off one damnation grind in one of those French A[cademies] would put you head and shoulders over all of 'em." . . .

[The comment of Leavitt and of] the "Advertiser" man upset me entirely. Confidence in myself had all gone. I couldn't have told whether a nose should be ⅓ of the face or not: and in that mood I wrote [Charlotte] a letter.

This is an extract from a reply that I received this morning:

You shall go. And I will go with you! My first thought was, you shall go and I will wait for you. But I fear the separation, longing, worry and letter writing would hinder you sadly. But with me at your side, me to go with you to the atelier, or await you in our humble lodgings if I could not go out (I'm considering the "consequences" as well you see.) I think you would do well.

Let's go, my love. As to money, if you can get enough for yourself I've no fear but that I can do the same. At worst I can surely raise 2000 by mortgage on the Hartford estate; and if I can't invest what little I possess in my husband's genius I'm not worth his least esteem, to say nothing of the great great love with which he honors me.

Let's go, my love! We'll be married as we intended and take ship for France straitway. You've no idea what a great wave of hope and strength and courage I get from your letter. I haven't felt so strong and awake for months.

The idea of your suffering or losing anything on my account maddens me.

Shall *I* be a hindrance in your path to greatness and success? Never, my dear. I'm going to *help* you to live, & I *will*: Beside all of which laudable sentiment I am animated by a lively desire for just such training myself. . . .

. . . There is something very beautiful in the thought of us two pursuing our studies together in Europe.

That we're indeed to be *alone*! I fear for her the hardships that would inevitably come. I know she is strong to bear them. But I have noticed that a great deal of her strength is fictitious. I mean that after she finds me able to bear she will give way that I may comfort her. It is for me to be doubly strong because of her strength. There is no use in my fretting myself about what to do if I get there, for I don't know what is there for *me*.

· · ·

DEC. 1 1882. NEARLY DARK

[The diary continues with a description of a Thanksgiving weekend trip to Boston. They went to the art museums ("Charlotte made very apt and charming criticism"), visited friends (particularly Martha Luther Lane), and walked a great deal: "Charlotte for a rare wonder was tired. That ought to be written in rubric." Charlotte stayed an extra day in Boston with her uncle Edward Everett Hale and his family, so Walter returned to Providence alone.*]

---

* Edward Everett Hale and his wife, Emily Baldwin Perkins Hale (the sister of Frederick Perkins, Charlotte's father), frequently invited Charlotte to visit them in Boston. But after enjoying the lively atmosphere of their large, energetic family, Charlotte felt less tolerant of Wal-

. . . I found at home yesterday morning a letter from Mr. Hatfield of Doll & Richards in reply to my inquiry as to the best way of disposing of the pictures I have on hand. It was most kind. He said that I could count on him to do everything in his power to help me: And one could always *sell* by putting things into the auction room, but the results were rarely satisfactory. He thinks knowing my wishes that he can dispose of some of my things during the season. Already he had sold two water colors for $40—, for which he had asked $50—. Then he said I might have a sale in the Spring, preparing for it during the Winter. It was a very interested & manly letter. I like him much and I congratulate myself upon having him to friend.

That and the letter from Charles De Kay saying that he should not send back the two canvases . . . encourage me a good deal. It is pleasant to know that after so long a time he still likes the two he bought enough to want to buy two more. . . .

*   *   *

4TH DEC. MONDAY; NEARLY DARK

Last evening with Charlotte after a dull day at home. It was very biting cold when I went over and worse when I came back. I cannot say that we spent the evening pleasantly. There was too deep a meaning, too terrible a meaning in it for pleasure. I found almost as soon as I went there that she was not in harmony with me. And I guessed the cause—her late visit to the Hales'. It is a sad peculiarity of hers that she is so easily influenced by the people she is with. They were all healthful jollity, and a certain animal enjoyment: now while she declares, and honestly, I doubt not, that there was not a moment of the day in which she had not rather be away from there than with them, yet the cheer and gaiety wrought their work in her. She came back, found instead of the tall muscular Hale fellows poor slight me (and who *could* blame her?) found that I did not supply her wants on that score and—feared that I would not satisfy her. She even said so. O how my dear Love wrestled with herself. She doubted & doubted and still loved me, but

---

ter's somber moods. After one Hale visit (at age 19) Charlotte wrote, "I was never so courted and entertained and amused and done for in all my little life. It seems as if the memory of today would last me in solid comfort through all of the ills that flesh is heir to. . . . Why to think of its being *Me!*" Or, as she put it in a letter to her younger cousin Houghton Gilman: "What joys were mine! I went sleighing, went to the theater, I went to parties, and I received calls. Bye and Bye, when you 'are old and hideous, and the hairs of your beard are mostly grey,' as the poet says, you will understand the joys of such an existence." Mary A. Hill, *Charlotte Perkins Gilman: The Making of a Radical Feminist, 1860–1896* (Philadelphia: Temple University Press, 1980), p. 58.

the doubts hid her heart away and an atmosphere surrounded her which I could not penetrate. To be sure she kissed me, but the passion was gone: they were grief-stricken kisses.

My heart sunk away, clutched itself, and tried to be strong. That is why it was so much colder when I went home, I think.

She was in a terrible state & did I not know her to be well I should think it some physical disturbance: indeed, I am not sure now that it is not.

She asked me all sorts of questions as to what I should do after we were married under various circumstances: VIZ.—If I should be unable to get money & she was sick, and perhaps the children also—how would I act? Would I be cheerful or unhappy? And many others that were equally useless.

I tried to treat her patiently and tenderly, and can not feel that I allowed myself to wound her in any way. She asked me to be patient, to love her, to pray for her. Ah my God all of these will I do tho' my heart aches to think of what may be. It is true, she may with equal facility turn & love me even more than ever. It is dark living so. It is enough to feel so hellishly uncertain about the future, and so dark because of insufficient skill, without having the added despair of doubting my Love's love.

But I will bear it. *I love her* that is *sure*.

This morning a long letter from Grandma Cresson. She misses me—wants me with her. She will try her hardest to influence Mr. Cresson in my favor. He at one time thinks it the best thing for me to marry; says that Charlotte has the most "grit" of the two—that it will be the making of me: and yet does not feel willing, or able, to advance me more money wherewith to consummate things. Grandma herself thinks it unwise for us to go to Europe together and draws a pitiful picture of possible children suffering in this "stern world," and my father & mother also. And she thinks it wiser for me to go abroad alone for a year and Charlotte stay here and wait for me.

The romance of it she thinks perfect and she feels that if she were rich she would send us, let us be happy and help us out of any snarl. She says she knows I will not like the advice.

Oh Grandma! How *could* I leave my Love?

I do not know what to do. The whole world grows dizzy and it all seems so mean—it is all made a matter of convenience. Why *was* I born an artist and a lover too!!*

---

*Grace Channing wrote, "I could have answered *that* for him; Because never since the world was made was his kind of an artist born anything else." GEC to EBK, May 23, 1912, p. 122.

All I can do is to try to trust God. I cannot pray believing that my prayer will be granted. It is as God wills: and he will do his will, prayer or not. I am growing to say "Kismet."

But perforce the cry comes: God help us! Oh be merciful! Keep her even as I would keep her and let her be my very loyal & everloving wife! And let me be able to satisfy every part of her. O let me be worthy! Do not, O do not, make all my, all *our* efforts towards pure living and noble character vain! Where fore dost thou vex us? . . .

5TH OF DECEMBER. 2:30 P.M.

The morning was spent in cast-drawing and in writing a little on a ballad. Last night I was very sad because of the uncertainty of her love of me. I could see as many reasons for her not loving me as I could for her doing so. It worried me strangely, and effectively. I have not half the physical energy that I had a week ago. It may be in me but it is grief stricken and hidden to lament its seeming uselessness. I slept ill and awoke tired this morning. I wrote a 16 page letter to Grandma Cresson and a short note to Charlotte simply telling her that if I could not make her happy, if I could not approximately satisfy her I would leave her forever. I wanted her to be happy even if I were not. I had thought that I would not write to her, but my poor heart yearned so for her, to comfort her and to be cared by her that I *could* not refrain.

This morning I had a dizzy turn. Simply, I am tired of thinking about my present and future. It is tangled in the extreme. There must be an end somewhere.

6TH DECEMBER 1882—MORNING

I did not rest last night. I tried to be philosophic. . . . But reasons to a yearning heart are like stones to the hungry. And what could that life be whose very root was cut—what could life be where all faith in love was injured as mine would be. I can see physical reasons why her love should stop—aberrations of the brain caused by bodily disturbances: but I can see no reason why if she is as well as she appears, love could stop. *My* love knows no ceasing day in and day out: but then, may be *that* is disease and the healthy way would be to stop at intervals. And also I can see why it should stop if it is simply a physical love: I don't think—can't think it is that.

No, surely, it must be that I have not yet been proved to be indispensable to her best living. And perhaps I am not. . . .

And during the evening I read Othello. I never understood it so well before. Why, I could *feel* it all from beginning to end. Not that I was *jealous*: no, but I could realize how upon circumstantial evidence a lover, a husband might accuse his innocent Love of the most horrid crimes. It was a salutary thing for me to read: for, shame though it be to me to think it, it has occurred to me that she *might* be playing with me. God pity her if she is, it would be the sorriest game she ever attempted.

Well, as I had some toilet operations to perform this morning I did not leave home until after the postman had brought me a letter from her. It is a sad record of her feelings written with a terrible calmness and candor. She says that I am strong and noble, also hasty and passionate. (The reason I am hasty is that I have so little faith in anything pleasant coming to me that I want to hurry to the worst to have it over rather than a long-drawn-out misery.)

She asks me not to leave her because she is again possessed by the evil spirit which baffled me so often in the beginning. And she says that somehow she has escaped me just now—:

I do not *feel* you—the strong chains of love which bound me closer and closer to your side have relaxed; and if it were not for memory I should feel a blank amazement at my situation. But memory serves me well: I remember the heaven of high purpose, daily progress and ever present love to which you have led me, and know that it was good and right.

What ails me now I cannot say: I have lost my love as one loses a quotation familiar as the Lord's Prayer—*knowing* it to be there, but unable to find it.

If you find it hard to bear, hard to "love me, wait for me, pray for me," just look over a few of my letters to you, away; and remember how you yourself said—"I had never seen any one so happy etc."

I am too apathetic and senseless just now even to be sorry for this state of mine, even to pity you for what you must have been through before writing this letter to me. But this I know, that it would be wrong to take any great step just now, for I am not my true self. If I have any?

It may be too that this unreliable vacillating nature of mine would bring you more misery than joy; and to load your life with the burden of my caprices be a sin. . . .

O my dear Love! I *will* wait—wait to I know not what end. It is just as likely to be to giving you up as to finding happiness with you. And meanwhile I feel as if a jury had gone out to find my sentence—death or life. And which—which? Death or Life? Loneliness or fruitful companionship?

Yes, I will wait. Verily I were more of a coward than I am if in the face of a possible uneasiness and danger I should flee. Who dares the shark gets the pearl. Who dares the fire damp gets the ore; who goes over the sea in ships smells the Arabian sweets; who dares the cross is lifted up though he bleed. And more than all, who loves and suffers—Who loves because he loves, glorifies love; and, Love, thou art to be glorified above all the world.

8TH OF DECEMBER, 1882. NOON.

Yesterday was a dreary day, but I worked upon a moonlight water color. I am working now towards a probable sale in March at Doll & Richards in Boston. They will want 125 [water colors]. I don't like to *manufacture* but I shall have to do almost that. If it will only end in giving me money enough to pay my debts & take my love to bed it were indeed great. I will try & work, and pray. . . .

My Love haunts me everywhere and all times. I would that I knew just what her fault is and just how to remedy it.

I incline to think it is half imaginary. If she were any other woman I'm afraid I should think it were a ruse to bind me more closely to her and to hasten our marriage. . . .

12TH DEC. TUESDAY, 1882

. . . I have not yet written about Sunday. There is a deal that might be said: but I must sum it up by saying that Charlotte was dazzlingly beautiful: her face shone with purity and truth. She welcomed me in her peculiar manner, chided me sweetly for coming so late, . . . showed me some newly painted cards & read me her short paper upon the Jews in Egypt which she read at the Slicers' Bible Class Thurs. eve. . . . After that reading . . . she asked me to read her my letter, which I did.

I clearly saw that the letter was a mistake: that I had hinted at things which were wholly unworthy of me. I felt very shamefaced. Then after I had read it she rose, with a heavenly look, came to my side, kneeled and prayed. Prayed I know not quite what, but I think that she might not be unjust to me. Then *she* took the letter and in words that hurt like swords showed what black mistakes I had made. It did me good; I wanted to suffer for what wrong I had thought of her. She seems nobler, purer, better in all ways than ever she did before. With honesty I plead forgiveness. I pray that I may never so misjudge her again. It was innocent—but from little, as Othello from

Iago's words, I built a great deal. After awhile she came to me and threw herself into my arms, put my hand into her bosom, and said—"Oh, I'm so happy now!" . . .

15 DEC. (FRIDAY), 1882

When I reached home last night after a day of hard work and wearying receiving of visitors I found a most charming & pure letter from Charlotte. . . .

Doll & Richards sent me their check this morning for $25 35/100—all that is left out of the sale of two water colors for $40—after taking out the commission $8—they charged me for the framing of them & the express. I was a deal surprised at the charges but it is best to be patient. At that rate if I had a sale there & sold $1100. worth of things I'd only get $500!! verily, one can not wonder that artists think that they are made for the dealers. But $25 is not to be despised. It represents perhaps two hours' work, *and a year's waiting*.

I must first get me some water color paper with the money. It is too little to my needs.

21ST DEC. 1882. 2 P.M.

I must take the time to . . . record last Sunday's eve with Charlotte. . . . She read me a poem and a prayer.

The poem is very tender, very beautiful in sentiment, and so touching in the manuscript—for one may see by it that her whole soul was in the thought rather than the execution. The prayer is the outcome of her fervent heart. The way in which she gave it [to] me robbed it of whatever of "piousness" it might have had. It was just as if some child had come to me and told me what it wanted. Oh, it is a sad day, when the child goes out of our hearts! Why need we become old and think ourselves so wise because by the juggling of words we can make fine sounding phrases? God be thanked that she is what she is—a noble woman with a child's faith in me. . . .

And here's her prayer, to which I needs must say Amen:—

Father in Heaven! Central Force of Good! Great Power that *is* the Universe! My God—I only know *I am*: this, and a sense that *Thou art Good*! And from the inmost depths of what I call my soul, my spirit cries—*I* cry with voice of passionate desire: Oh God! My God, help me to do Thy will!

Truly Religion, *in esse*, and Love are very closely allied. Often it seems as if the sexual passion—the mere desire for bodily contact—awakes a train of feelings which invariably ends in God. It is good that it is so else there were little difference between pure love and the love of Love. My Charlotte is of that peculiar temperament in which spiritual and material are interchangeable. I myself have it in great measure. She is incandescent, and not finding ease for her passion with me she turns to God, and cries on thine rapt things. It is all very beautiful and lonely: but it is dangerous. The steps are short between her present state and hysteria. God help her.

Last night I was with her. . . . I discovered new symptoms of what I fear—that being in my embrace, being kissed, being as deeply in love as she is there is terrible danger to her health—even as her mother told me. Towards the end of the evening she showed signs of hysteria—a wonderful rapt way of talking—a talking, too, with out knowing just what she wanted to say, and about Duty & Right & God: and she would tremble & leap into my arms ————. Oh how the dear girl needs marriage, even as I do! There is a sin somewhere in two such loving souls, so well mated in intellect, tastes & body would not have to be so long apart. She owned that she wanted me to husband her: yet, she said: "I will be strong & bear it: Oh it is nothing! I will forget it!" and she straightened herself up, but soon the old tender hungering look came back. Help me, God, for her sake!

Ah! but last evening was a delight.

She gave me an india ink drawing, a Christmas token, called "Goodnight." What did I see therein? My Love, standing in a half light to turn out the gas as I leave. She has caught the pose, the action finely and rendering of the effect is very good. How much I prize it, both for the love that prompted it and the evident increase of fine artistic feeling in my Love! She is an *artist*. She showed me a rapid pencil sketch of herself holding a drawing board: an attitude fit for a Salome. It was done in a masterly way, a few strokes to show rotundity, action & all. She grows rapidly in that way.

When we can have years together we shall both do better work. I know I can help her, and she certainly will help me.*

---

*Charlotte had spent part of a year (1878–79) studying at the Rhode Island School of Design. To help her mother with expenses, she gave drawing lessons to younger friends in the community. A number of her sketches and watercolors are in the Gilman manuscript collection, AESL.

CHRISTMAS, 1882

Since I wrote have been busy with . . . business. . . .

Then was the buying of presents: I bought more than I expected to owing to a sudden acquisition of money from a frame I sold. I made one sensible but queer present to Charlotte, accompanied by a rhymed epistle & sonnet. It was some fine linen & cambric, some 30 yards, for underwear. I don't know which pleased her most. . . .

We had a pretty time with the presents, & she liked the verses very much I judge. She showed the lines she had written for those to whom she was going to give things. The "funny" ones were not great successes, but one of a finely serious tone . . . was true, and touching *poetry*. Such as she could not have written a year ago—before Love woke her.

The only thing of the evening which jarred was a *passage d'armes* with Mrs. Perkins. She said, apropos of something, that she thought she should like my mother, but she felt sure that she should fight with father. (I could have told her that she couldn't, for it took two to fight) and that was an excuse for asking why mother had not called on her, at which I calmly told her that she had not been invited. Thereupon she insisted that it was a part & parcel of the disrespect that had been shown her all along, that my mother had not been there, and that Charlotte had been to see my mother. Of course it was the first glimpse I had had of anything of the sort. As mother goes out very seldom it seemed quite natural that Charlotte should go to see her, rather than she to see Charlotte. Mrs. Perkins insisted on the disrespect of it, said that all her friends would think it so etc. I tried faintly to show her, but as she was prejudiced it was useless. I am irritated beyond measure by trying to do as they would have me. Why *can't* people look below the surface of things!

That rather cast a shade over the evening, but Charlotte renewed her sweetness and I felt some of *her* at any rate, and I need not care for anything further, only as it will hurt her: that is, she being with them all the time will have to bear it over & over.

26TH DEC. 1882 P.M.

[After a characteristic description of a moonlight walk with Charlotte the diary continues:] . . . Intermingled with all was talk about the landscape about us: She sees with an artist's eye: perceives the subtle things that *make* the *landscape* and give the expression to it; sees too the delicate gradation of color. I prize most of all her being able to give definition to the sentiment of what she sees: She does it often very aptly. Indeed the atmosphere, the calm water of a mystical purplish grey blue reflecting the moonlit houses was extremely beautiful. . . .

[Stetson then copied a "fine notice" of his painting *May Dance* reviewed in the Boston *Sunday Globe*.]

At Doll & Richards' gallery there is an interesting miscellaneous collection of paintings, of which the one which will quickest attract the attention is, perhaps Mr. Charles Stetson's "May Dance." Mr. Stetson's only appearance in Boston previous to this was at last winter's Art Club ex[hibition], where a single picture showed that here was an artist who had struck a new note of color. The present picture shows such development from this other that it could not be recognized from the same artist, except for the wonderful color that glows in it. It represents two young girls in airy, wind-blown garments dancing upon a green slope, while a third plays upon some wind instrument. The hillside is a deep[,] warm green, the sky and a glimpse of the sea are an intense blue, and there are touches of vivid color about the girls' garments. Altogether, Mr. Stetson shows such feeling for color and such ability [and originality] in the use of it as to set him apart from all our other artists. There are a striking freedom and strength in the figures which are full of airy grace and convey at once the idea of rapid motion. Mr. Stetson is a Providence artist & a young man who has done but little work, but his two pictures mark him as a colorist of unusual originality and feeling, and give evidence of an ability that promises much for the future.*

How pleasant it is to not hear of "lack of reality" and "firm drawing." As nearly as I can judge that is a fair estimate of the work in question. . . .

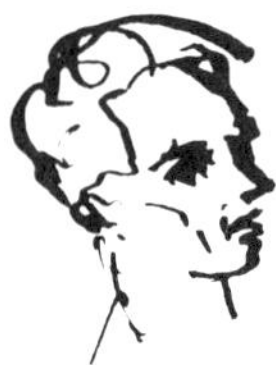

28TH DEC. 1882, MORNING

When I went home, . . . I found that ——[name deleted] had been there. At first I felt almost affronted. . . .

The next feeling that I had was sorrow. Sorrow that I should have been the instrument of pain to one that I loved so much as I did —— [name deleted]. I do love her: how else could it be when our boy & girl days were spent so very intimately together & when all my youth I thought of her as a probable wife? But I could not marry her now. . . . I retraced every step I

---

*With exceptions noted in brackets, Stetson quoted exactly from "Art and Artists," the *Boston Daily Globe*, Dec. 24, 1882.

have taken to see if I had done wrong—any known wrong. I *could* not see that I had. Charlotte is such a love as fills all sides of me. —— [name deleted] only filled two sides—my sensuous and the desire to care for someone. There never was a bit of the intellectual in our intercourse. I never could talk with her about the high things I loved best, though I was ever hoping that I could develope in her a liking & appreciation of them. No! In the very course of natural laws it never could have been. If I had married her, in my best self I should have been untrue to her. No, this moment I love her, not with an approach to love Charlotte has, which includes all loves, but with a love that would shield her from harm, would see her beautiful, pure, aspiring, useful. Never shall I forget all she did to me (unwittingly surely) to develope my character. God bless her, and send her just reward. [Stetson added at the side of the diary page: "No, I think I am wrong. I do *not* love *her*. I am sure I do not. I have the kindliest feeling for her; no more."]

I wrote a letter to Charlotte last evening, told her about the call. Then I came down to the club to talk over the organizing of a sketch class: which we did. . . .

Life is marvellous! One could easily think that there were spirits to plot & counterplot; as if we were the actors in some drama written by them. If it be so—do not my struggles with self, my high desires, my tears for others' sorrow affect them? . . .

A professional model called yesterday (male) and wanted work. It is the first instance of the kind in my "career."

JAN. 1ST 1883 MORNING

Sat. eve. . . . [I] walked a long ways into Olneyville. . . . I saw some beautiful groups of figures & landscape, as it was the time that the mill hands came out & twilight. So I was tired when I was with Charlotte: but oh! how good it was to have her arm in mine again! She told how very glad she was to get back: & gave me a letter which she wrote that day, saying that it would help me to pass Sunday, and it did. It was excellent in its tone of love: a happy strain seems to sing through it all. Let me see, I think I have it with me—Yes.

My own heart's Love, tonight I shall be with you again, see you and hear you speak, and tomorrow night I shall again be in those arms which make my home. Not with the mother who has never known me; not with the family I like so little, nor with any of the friends who more or less admire and love me, not even here with my girlhood's best loved friend; but in the light of your smile, dear heart, where your strong arms wait me, and soul and mind and body turn to me for comfort & companionship.

My dear boy, I'm fairly homesick for you! Every day shows me how near and dear you have grown and how I miss even the outward expression of your love. Tell me, how do widows live? And yet I hope you will die first, and be saved the pain.

I had written her about ——— [name deleted] coming back and how it hurt me to think of the past, tho' I could not see how I had done her wrong. And she writes this:—

I wish you would not grieve so over the heartache of your boyhood. That you have done no wrong I can well believe, and when I think of how the memory hurts you, I long to fold you out of sight in loving arms and kiss the very thought of it away. Dear Love! *Dear* love! I love you, and you love me.—And you believe my every look and touch! O my King! may I deserve that hurt, and live to be the Queen you take me for. Dearest, lean on me ever: and your very faith shall make and keep me strong. I love you more and more.

There it is: she must see that I have faith in her, and that will keep her strong. . . .

It seems strange to me after reading her burning letters to read in reviews that the writing of love letters is no more: that the railroad & telegraph have done away with it; because the one can carry the lover to his love rapidly, and the other exceeds in swiftness. Here are we in the same city, seeing each other weekly, or oftener, that always find some new accent of the old words to send to each other.

Yesterday evening was with her. . . . Our marriage *must* be soon or she, if not I, will suffer. Who could have foreseen a year ago that she would come to so much powerful longing and such absorbing love. God be thanked for her frankness. I know every—nay, but most of the emotions of her heart, and it frightens me (Delicious fear!) to see how whitely aflame with love she is. She is a *perfectly pure* woman. That *I know.* And it is like feeling *sure* that one has a home forever with the Blessed.

PURE! that truth is enough for all life. How do I know she's pure? How do I know the lilies are white or the violet has a sweet smell? *PURE.*

4TH JANUARY, 1883 P.M. THURS.

Tuesday evening Charlotte & I went to "Iolanthe." It was a delight to sit by her side and see the impressions the opera produced on her fresh mind. She never had seen anything of the sort. . . .

. . . Going home Charlotte was very tender, and talkative with all. She gave her opinions of the opera, and said that it seemed strange to her that all playwrights seemed to delight in defamation of character. A very apt characterization, I thought. Said she liked to go to plays with me, in her dear childlike way, with dainty "baby talk." Then we had a chat about *our* home; the costumes we would wear there—and all the thousand delights of cohabitation. . . .

Last night I went to see "Iolanthe" again, with Whitaker. It was acted better than before. . . .

12TH JANUARY, 1883

. . . Sunday was fine with her. She is growing daily more dependent upon me for the bread of her heart's life. I never saw one more humble, more—I know not what, save *in love*. We talked over our marriage, or rather over housekeeping, with her mother near us Charlotte had been reckoning our probable expenses, and the dear girl had figured that one could live nicely, & pay $15 a month house rent, for $500 a year. I took hold of the figures, added $200 studio rent to it, and the amount I should probably have to give towards father's & mother's living and the sum went up to over $1100—quickly. Her face sunk appreciably, but she stoutly maintained that I was planning for luxuries such as she had eschewed in her plan. It was plain to be seen that I could not sell $1100 of pictures a year and she could not make more than $300—I'm certain (would that it were not necessary for her to do that!!). It was a dark picture, though we had a little merriment over the reckoning. I must confess that marriage assumes gigantic proportions of hindrance. She dismissed it all in a truly womanly way, by throwing her arms about me, covering me with kisses, and saying: "We'll *do* it anyhow my love!" And I had not the heart to say I doubted it. . . .

19TH JAN. ''83

. . . Wednesday felt extremely weak but managed to come down & work a little. In the evening felt still better & came to the Ex. Com. [Executive Committee] Meeting & the Clay party at the Club. Clay party a success. Modelled in terra cotta a high relief medallion which is rather pleasing. Think of having it burnt. . . .

[Charlotte] is changed a vast deal. She wants to be treated more as a child now than as a woman. I could scarcely have foreseen so complete a subjugation of self—or abnegation rather. She is willing to do anything, go anywhere, so long as I am with her. She says that she has reached the point where she not only wants to know that I love her continually but to *see* me & touch me. She has felt for some reason that I had diminished my love of her but I have proved to her that it is not so, rather that my love has increased, but work towards becoming able to marry her & my work in club matters has taken so much of my time and energy that I have not been able to give so much expression to it. She has missed my letters most of all. . . .

CHAPTER VIII

. . . *the sickness of hope deferred*

January 27–April 2, 1883

BY JANUARY 1883, Walter was feeling more confident with Charlotte. She was more loving, more childlike, more dependent. "She rests in me as a child might in her father," he wrote; she no longer has

the daring and independent manner of the Charlotte that I first knew. . . . Her heart is melted entirely. She has tamed her effort to doing things for me and that has had a strange effect on her. It has made her more like what is best in other women—more thoughtful, bland, gracious, humble, dependent.

Anticipating a spring marriage, Stetson still had worries, to be sure: how to pay the bills, care for his aging parents, improve his drawing. But at least the problems had been manageable, compared to the strains that followed. In mid-March, Charlotte had another "relapse," another "break in loving," only this time far worse than before. She wanted to postpone the marriage and try a separation, she told him. She felt a "shrinking at confinement," a fear of "restricting possession" and declining self-respect.

Walter was stunned, angry, and miserable. She "stabbed me with a rugged edged knife." Not only was his love "put to shame," his art itself was mocked. After all, his fundamental aspiration as an artist was to "express the loveliness of womanhood & the purity of the sexual relations." And yet what an appalling situation to confront; the woman he had chosen as his Lover felt unwomanly. She claims "she is more [Charlotte Anna Perkins] than a woman. I *don't* believe it. Sex is the paramount thing in every human being: it is first—first—middle—and last." If she is ever to work at all, she must get "into harmony with that 'woman' instead of rebelliously trying to murder it."*

JAN. 27, 1883 A.M.

. . . Have painted some of my best water colors; want to get to work on my more serious canvases: I hate this painting with a hope to sell in mind. I feel my days going—going—ah, how terribly fast, & see clearly that I have done almost none of the work that I care most for. It seems shameful that I needs must spend my time on work which is scarcely my aim & purpose in art. Here I do landscape after landscape while my deepest heart is in passionate humanity. Why? Because less in landscape satisfies the buyer than in figure painting. It is easy to make a fairly pretty landscape—but to paint the soul of man—it takes one's life. I think, I *know* that I have in me the germ of an historic and religious painter. God alone can tell if it ever will fructify.

Charlotte is supreme: she is showing a kind of womanhood well hidden heretofore from all save the eye of Love. I stand aghast when I comprehend how she loves me: that she loves me to the verge of adoration is perfectly clear. I am aghast only because I cannot comprehend why it is so, and can scarce believe the wonderful sweetness & majesty of it.

Having seen that my work & worry is telling upon my body—knowing that I am fearful of failure in May—she proposed—to let herself as governess for a year, save the money so got for *me*—that is towards our future. Oh the dear woman! Ready to sacrifice her dearest sweetest dream of marriage for my sake: willing to give her work to it! I cannot let it be: there must be some way of making marriage possible before long: she has reached the height of desire, and finds herself sadly needy of ease. And I—and I—words fail.

And I am trying to get in tune with death: that death that will come to father, mother, *her*. It is not easy, far from easy. It is her that loves as I love her that prayeth most for immortality.

Meantime I wait and study as best I may: and seek and lay myself open to receive the soul of Beauty, that I may fill the world therewith.

---

*The above quotations are from diary entries of the following dates: March 16, March 22, March 24, March 31, 1883.

JAN. 30, 1883, 2 P.M.

. . . Sunday evening with Charlotte. . . . She can be as childlike in her talk as an ingenuous child. I scarce know which is most dear to me, her womanly high language, or her thrillingly tender girl talk, for each is but a variation of her truly great love of me. And what do I give her for it all?! I know not; she says that I make her wonderfully and strongly happy, and her looks and acts far from belie her speech. She says that she has learned by experience what I meant when I said that she was my centre and circumference of the world. I will not blind myself: I *know* that I make her happy; that she rests in me as a child might in her father; that I fill all her mind with delight and that her whole being body & soul thrills at my presence, my kiss and my touch. I think the knowledge—I *know* it—that I make her happy & better her life is the sweetest part of it all. Her mother has learned to trust me—says that she has not the slightest fear that my care of Charlotte will not be as true & perfect as her own would be.

But oh! it's very hard to live apart. God knows if we can bear it through the Summer if we cannot marry in the Spring. Oh how hard it is! . . .

[Walter posed for a] sketch class in a complete Greek costume—even to sandals and fillet. And I know that I posed well and looked well. It is astonishing how that form of dress makes the most of one's good parts. They all said that I seemed like a living antique. To be sure my face is not that of the Greek statues, but that did not hinder it from being classic. I am aware that it was beautiful in color, for the flesh of legs and arms glimmered through the thin cream color: behind was a terra cotta wall & a couch of oriental hue, olive & deep red & black, & on the floor was a wild cat skin and under that a long rug of plain deep maroon, golden brown & blue following the steps. The warm light of the reflection over all. It showed them the difference between the posing of a hired model and that of one who loves the costume & has some dramatic instinct. Well, what I am coming at is this: Charlotte knew that I did it—I wrote to her about it & others told her. We wanted a lady of proper physique to pose as a Roman tonight. She is to wear the same chiton with a pallium added. Charlotte at once thought she'd like to do it—told Mr. Burleigh so, who was speaking of our need of such a person. She said, "Couldn't *I* do it? I should *like* it." He said in his drawling fashion—"You'd do it better'n anyone else I know—but," and he seemed to intimate it would not be quite the thing. "Well," she said, "I'll ask Walter and see what he says." . . . So she did ask me Sunday evening. Saturday Sydney Burleigh and I had been examining a model—draping her and studying her nude: it "left a bad taste in my mouth" not that there was the slightest thing improper said or done, but there was something about the woman herself so absolutely opposite to my dear Love that it made me feel badly. In short I didn't want Charlotte to pose for the class: and could give no reason. She asked me if she could, and I could say neither yes or no: but she soon found out that I did not wish it and gave it all up as beautifully as if it had been a rosebud she gave to me. She is marvellous in regard to such things. I felt meanly enough: I could give no reason. It seemed so selfish on my part: much as if she were an odalisque and I a pasha, but I *felt* that that was not the reason. I argued with myself and before her that I ought to be as willing to let her pose for other men as I am to have other women pose for me. The latter seems to be a necessity. But I could but think that she was different from other women: was made for me; that it would be a kind of sacrilege to have her taken from her shrine and exposed for the criticism of unloving men. I found that if I could select certain ones from the life class my objections would vanish. . . . She said it was best that she did not after all: that really in her deepest heart she wanted all herself to be for me alone. All I could decide was this: that I *thought* there must be certain women made for such things and certain not; just as some men are made for blacksmiths, some for grocers, some for artists and so forth.* . . .

Father worrying sadly over unpaid rent: and I unable as yet to get him money: he is almost sick. . . . The painting of my water colors drags. I am sure I shall not have a very interesting exhibition, and quite as sure that I shall sell few if any. The B[oston] Art Club pictures have been well spoken of, *very* well I think. This year in which Charlotte has been so wonderful has seen me make a long stride in advance, if I do not flatter myself. But my work is as yet crude, indefinite and just gives promise of good things by and by. . . . There is so much love in my work that someone sometime *must* understand it.

12TH FEB. ''83

[Mary Perkins was planning to go out west to visit her son Thomas, and proposed that Charlotte and Walter get married and live in the lower half of their "tenement" while she was gone.] . . . Charlotte accepted it as a

---

*"This, I'm afraid was a case where logic was at a discount!" GEC to EBK, May 23, 1912, p. 129.

settled thing and was as near wild with happiness as a sensible & strong woman can be. She acted as joyous as a child over it and was lovely to see.*

It certainly is exceeding kind on her mother's part and would lighten the weight of "commencing" very considerably. It will not obviate the necessity of money to get certain things of our own—the which I think Charlotte has not yet thought of. For my part I could not be quite so jubilant over it—and it seemed mean not to be, too,—for there are so many chances that may prevent: but I did feel that it was the most sensible, convenient & practicable plan. The house could be made very pretty indeed: one chamber could have the much coveted fire place, & there are windswept spaces all around, & sunshine enough. It would be well for Charlotte, for she is settled there now & her old friends would be glad to come as usual.

The dear, grand girl said over and over again mid her profuse sweet caresses "Yours—yours—all yours, and so soon! 11th of Feb.—11th of March—11th of April—*May*! And we shall be one flesh!" . . .

P.M.   As I feared our landlord demands his rent. I am responsible for it and as father has not a cent I am to pay, I think $42—at once—that is *if I can*: if not I suppose we must move. I have just 13 cents. . . .

I sometimes shudder as my heart aches at what is and must be—of suffering uneased and certain death—and I wish it were all over with. It is cowardly. I have wondered if my pain is all selfish. I think it is not, for I am sure that if I could see father & mother happy, & out of suffering, all this would pass away. I am sure of it because I am clearly aware that in times when I have seen them less full of trouble & pain my own heart has lightened correspondingly.

It was too much. My poor soul broke before God. Oh agonizing prayers—penitence—humbling of will—but why should whatever sin I

---

* After quoting sections of this entry Grace Channing wrote: "About this time, Charlotte was very buoyant and happy in the prospect of marriage—it was *he* who had all the misgivings, feeling the burden of life he must somehow contrive to carry. He never seems to have lost sight of it for a moment,—and it is characteristic that all through his own anticipation, the constant question is—Of all this happiness—*what fruit*? What more shall we be—do—achieve? Through his whole life—it was achievement, the *thing done*, that counted to him. I remember—I never forgot—one day out West when I had tried to console him for the interruptions of illness to his work, saying nobody under such circumstances could do more than he had done, and he said to me in a tone I can still hear—'Don't you understand that *whatever* the cause, the result is the same—*the work is not done!*' Nothing ever atoned for that to him; no ease of conscience could make up for the sense of loss of the undone thing." GEC to EBK, May 23, 1912, p. 131.

have done be visited on them! There is no cure—no cure! one must simply endure.

Thank God! Charlotte knows nothing of such agony—such heart pain. Oh may she be kept from it, for every happiness however great has the meaning of it in it; it may be sweet for the contrast, much as flowers seem growing over graves, but the skulls and hieroglyphs of agonizing death are just below.

I have hope—but it is only that God will help me to bear even to the end—and "drink the bitterest cup that life(time) can measure out"—. If the bitter drops would come all in a mass 'twere easier to me, but when each must be tasted and the taste remains while the drops accumulate—it is almost too much. And she is happy—so wonderfully happy! Thank God. Father & mother are sorrowful—so deeply sorrowful: I *can't* say thank God: nor "let it be as God wills," they are *my* father and mother.* . . .

FEB. 15 ''83 P.M.

Snows again: very common occurrence this year.

In the nick of time my good friend [George] Whitaker brought me $45– and loaned it to me. $32 of it had to go to father for rent & I let him have $3 more for another purpose. It saved us much pain, & I sincerely feel very grateful to Whitaker. I hope to be able to pay it soon. . . .

. . .

20TH FEB. ''83

Sunday with Charlotte. . . . Her passion grows with the days. She has no doubt about our marriage: she can scarcely wait the time—love constraineth so. She is verily a flame of fire. Poor me! I fear I scarce satisfy her although she seems to be very happy, and indeed says she is so. I do not tell her enough "pretty things," love phrases, in honeyed accents. I know I do not. I can't. Marriage and my love of her seem too serious, too deep for playful words or for many of any sort. . . .

---

*GEC wrote, "Charlotte used to wonder constantly at his not being more cheerful. *I* used to wonder, when I came to know him, that he was ever cheerful a moment; it is too true that the things he suffered all his early life dominated every happiness with their memory; he never spoke of them (or rarely) and never complained, but light-heartedness was forever destroyed in him. Luckily—I understood this; being a little made that way. On the other hand—I don't think anyone ever lived who could more exquisitely *enjoy*—even trifles; and he could be deeply, quietly, divinely happy, even if sad for some things through it all." GEC to EBK, undated letter, p. 133.

I feel that it is my duty to marry notwithstanding the sorrow it may bring [my parents] or the difficulties in the way: for it must be that love is sent to man for some definite purpose, and if so it must be wicked to thrust ourselves from the consummation of it. It cannot be right to love and be even in close communion without utter fulfillment: indeed our bodies tell us that by their sorrow when gratification does not come. It is the law of all living things that in season they shall mate and found a new home. And that season must be when love lays strong irresistible hold of the heart. If such is the law (and what doubt can there be of it?) the pain it will cause parents must be accepted as part of the heritage of sorrow that has come to all human beings. It only is for me to do all I can to make the change less bitter for them. . . .

My heart fills & swells strangely—an indescribable feeling begs for utterance, yet cannot be uttered. On the one hand I see My Love—the woman loveliest, sweetest, simplest, dearest of all women to me—the woman whom I love to the verge of over much if such can be. And with her a more congenial life, a personal home, life long encouraging companionship & medicine to cure much mental & bodily unease, and the joy of having pure children.

Against that I see the possible crippling of me in my Art in a material way: the breaking up of father's & mother's home life (for I am quite sure they will feel as if they had none): giving them the pain of loneliness, and perhaps depriving them of some comforts which they need & I desire to give. O *how much*! Also Charlotte's mother will feel as if her life work is done. She has had much sorrow & lived only for her children. . . . But if marriage does not take place there will be still greater pain, still greater danger. . . .

Charlotte invited mother & father to come over & call some evening soon, yesterday.

22D FEB. 1883

Last evening father, mother & I went over to Charlotte's. It was so that "the parents of the prospective bride & bridegroom could become acquainted." Charlotte & I left them to talk by themselves & came down to see the etchings. . . .

Mother liked Mrs. Perkins much, & I think father was also pleased. Whether Mrs. P. liked them is quite another question. I doubt if she did. They seem to be very pleased at the prospect of my marriage—more so than

I anticipated: they like the plan of our living there. It seems that they talked it all over together.

Mrs. Perkins & Mrs. Robbins are to keep house upstairs. We are to have everything downstairs just as it stands—to add as much to it as we please. We simply take the things and use them. It certainly will be a great help, and it is exceedingly kind on all sides. It rather hurts a remnant of pride which I have, that is all. The rent will be

$15. a month.
  25 a month for groceries, provisions.
  <u>15 for milk & washing</u>
  55

$10 incidentals = $65 a month.

We ought to be able to live for a while at that rate, surely. Then to that I must add $16.33 studio rent & $15 to mother & father; it takes it up to $96.33. I suppose Charlotte will want to put about $15 into the treasury. I wish she need not, though. If she did so that would leave me $81.33 which would be the exponent of an income of nearly a thousand a year, which is more than I ever have made. As we are to marry in the Spring we must surely have enough to carry us through the Summer, say 4 months = $400 say. Now, where is it to come from? God help us.

I am about "run dry" for water colors. And I have only 82 or 3—and they wanted 125! I've got 2 more weeks at longest. To work!

MONDAY MARCH 12TH ''83

Three Sundays have passed since I wrote. It has been a time full of business and happenings. Each Sunday I was with Charlotte, and found her tenderer each time. [Walter then describes a visit to the home of Providence art patron John H. Mason.] . . . I learned how rich people who have refined tastes & love of beautiful things can live if they wish. He has some 600 etchings—selected with good judgment. His wife is very good. He is a pessimist for no reason unless temperament.* . . .

---

*Providence art patron John Mason bought numerous Stetson paintings, but repeatedly insulted Stetson by his niggardly, insensitive style.

. . . Week ago Saturday I sent my water colors to Doll & Richards, 105 of them. Monday I received a letter from them which set me aghast, & showed me how much I had expected something to come of them, however much I flattered myself to the contrary. The letter said that they felt sure that they would not be able to sell them for enough to make an auction sale pay for itself. That the pictures were not of a salable sort, & that their advice would be to give it up. They thought they could take a few of them at private sale & realize more than the whole sold at auction would bring. And they asked if they should send them back at once. I confess I was terribly disappointed, for I did hope that they could find them of value and that I could get enough out of it to square up all accounts & give my darling & me a clean start in life together. And it seemed most too bad that they should encourage me to paint them, as they must have known very nearly what they would be like. I wrote to Charlotte about it & to Mrs. Cresson. I suppose the letters were rather despairing. Charlotte wrote me a most strong reply: she said that it need make no difference to us. We could marry just the same. If we only had $150—to pay rent & so forth through the Summer months. It was one of those letters calculated to give one nerve & courage. But I recognized the impracticability of her plans, and while I felt glad she was so comforting a Love, it did not give me much new hope. Her mother also declares that it need make no difference: if need be she will board with us to help us. I can but feel that her mother is not quite ingenuous in her generosity. I think she would be glad to have to board with us: and I think that after she sees that law has firmly bound me to Charlotte that she will change in her attitude towards me. I shall not stand it long if she does. I think that while she has pretended that she did not want Charlotte to marry that she has been very anxious that she should. So far she has done all the proposing. *She* asked me to marry Charlotte in the Spring. They set the time & gave me hope. I should not have presumed to offer to marry her on my meagre income. But I shall probably be the object of thrust-after-thrust soon after our marriage from her regarding my pecuniary success(?). I hope I am mistaking, but I "feel it in my bones." Charlotte ought to be married. She needs it much, dear girl! She is not the strongly independent creature she was a year ago. With the softening of her heart has also come a softening of physical fibre: a less intensity of physical energy and more of the flame of desire. If she cannot marry soon I fear greatly for her, for passion must have room for itself or injury comes. No human being could be tenderer, sweeter, more willing to be moved as I will. She nestles in me, wants me; wants to be in my arms, lie there, rest there, sleep there. She is beginning to depend, and I doubt not that when marriage comes she will look to me for advice, and make me the ruler of the house. All her strength seems to be turned to loving. Last night she was not quite well, and very humble. She has found, she says, that she has been thinking too much of her own pleasure and delight, and not enough of mine; that she has not been half "good" enough to me. And she began in strange fashion. She's a strange being taken, all in all—but God! How beautiful! And how beloved! . . .

I got no reply from Grandma Cresson, but Mr. Cresson wrote me & enclosed a $50− check. He gave D & R a most severe blow, & said that he could not understand how any respectable firm would deal in that manner. And he said that he had written to John Wanamaker to see if he could help me to dispose of them. Wanamaker said that he could. So Mr. C wanted me to send him on some of them & show him. I've got them packed & shall send them after tonight or tomorrow morning.

That is friendship the most excellent. They are more than kind & good to me. God bless them. They and two or three others redeem all mankind for me.

We have gotten our 4th Annual Ex[hibition] ready to open the 14th: it's the best we've had. Owing to my devoting my time so exclusively to water colors I have but little in it—only the *Burial of a Suicide* & a few w.c.'s. . . .

I find that I am winning a place among artists—slowly, perhaps, but surely. Whether I shall ever sell any pictures no one can tell. It is a dark outlook for Charlotte & father & mother. . . .

16TH MARCH. 83 5 P.M. FRIDAY

Charlotte & I went to the Art Club reception Wednesday eve. We stayed only a short time, caring rather to go back to the house & have each other. She is very gentle and tenderly careful now. She is like an affectionate child that wants to be taken in arms and fondled—so confiding and desirous of being near me is she. One sees little just now of the daring and independent manner of the Charlotte that I first knew. . . . She has tamed her effort to doing things for me and that has had a strange effect on her. It has made her more like what is best in other women—more thoughtful, bland, gracious, humble, dependent. Still flashes of the old fire come once in a while; as she feels herself settling into tenderness she makes struggles against it, but they are weaker & weaker every time. Her only remaining cry is that she is bound to provide her own clothing: and carry her own children—they are not to have baby-carriages, not they. (If they should be *triplets*!)

She is indescribable—not *quite* comprehensible. A *very* long engagement would ruin her health, I am sure. Marriage should come soon.

Mr. Bates bought my sketch of a Boy Reading (8 × 12″), done in the sketch class in little over an hour, for $10−. It is one of my cleverest things. That $10 I'm going to spend on models. I've just written to one, to pose in Greek costume. I shall want her all next week. I'm bound to make studies—I am perishing, artistically for lack of them.

I'm still at my girls jumping rope.* The whole thing does not please me. To be sure, there is some pretty color in it, but it appears to lack solidity and a logical air. The figures on the ground are decent, but those jumping seem out of drawing (as they are) and not perspectively right. And I'm afraid my citron yellow has got the better of me a little. Geo. Whitaker & Fred. Batcheller † commend it, but dear me, I don't like it at all. . . . I acknowledge to any one who wants to know that I don't know how to get at a better knowledge of anatomy & drawing under my circumstances. I must make the semblance at least of pictures, or I shall die of utter poverty. If I spend my time at simple studies of head & arms & legs & breasts and hand, and feet and bellies and thighs and backs and shoulders and hair and eyes & the rest who will pay the bills? That is precisely what I ought to be doing.

I'm going to literally *steal* that $10 for models—for I owe it and the rent at home should be paid. And when models are got I scarce know what to do with them. The one I've just sent for is so modest I suppose she will object to posing with bare arms & feet to say nothing of more. Of course I can draw the folds of the costume & her head, a great deal—but I really *need* most the careful delineation of muscles and joints of the whole figure. Why! boys of fifteen that have been bred in art schools & an art atmosphere can draw with accuracy incomparable to my poor attempts. How to get at the remedy—that's the subject of many of my strangely mixed thoughts. I've got to a place where things are not at all clear to me—either moral or physical things. If I marry I shall be helped I doubt not. If I cannot marry soon—I feel the sickness of hope deferred creeping over me even now.

Oh God! The remedy—the remedy! . . .

---

* By July, Stetson was more enthusiastic about *Girls Jumping Rope* (also called *Rope Skipping Girls*) and planned to send it to Boston. "It seems strangely good in color. On that score it ought to be a success when exhibited." Diaries, July 10, 1883.

† Frederick Stone Batcheller (1835−1899), marble cutter and landscape painter, was one of the original founders of the PAC. George Whitaker wrote that Batcheller's "painting showed honest, conscientious labor if not a vivid imagination." Whitaker, "The Dean of Providence Artists," *Providence Sunday Journal*, Jan. 10, 1915, Stetson Scrapbook.

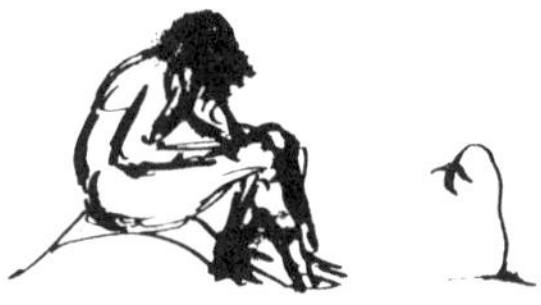

17TH OF MARCH: 4:30 P.M.

. . . I had engaged a little colored maid to pose for me this P. M. She came, but talk with her as gently or persuasively as I might nothing would induce her to take off her modern blue dress and put on a little gown which I have. Such an excess of modesty (?) is rare, I am glad to say. So all I could do was to make a sketch in oil of her head. Luckily she has beautiful eyes, and a clear color: but OH! she gets herself into the stiffest poses—and she could be graceful too were it not for the consciousness. Then she would screw up her lips and let her head drop: and a thousand unwanted things— for which I paid the damsel fifty cents. It was worth that of course, for with a little toning and accessory modeling I can make quite a head of it— though who would care to buy it? One appreciates more and more the pictures of figure painters the more he knows the difficulties one must undergo to get at them. . . .

MARCH 19TH ''83 5:30 P.M.

This has been one of the best days for long, I suppose because I've been doing that which is very dear to me—painting from a lovely model [Maud Forster]. . . . Maud is very lovely & as modest and natural as a flower. Her complexion is ivory with the sweet warm carnations melting into it. Without hesitation, as naturally as if going into her own chamber she went to my "dressing room" (to wit behind a screen) and put on the thin Greek costume. Her arms are very beautiful and her neck is a charming thing. She poses as easily as one could wish, and if I don't get a good picture it certainly will be not because of lack of fit model but some quality in myself. I was happy with her lying on the couch before me, not because it was she, but because I was fitted into my sphere. It surely is the lack of material to work with and facilities for working that has caused my unhappiness. Oh! it was a rare treat to have model and all in harmony. She is coming every day this week—at $1 an afternoon of 2 hours or so.

Last evening to Charlotte's. . . . By & by we went into the parlor & after sitting on my knees a moment she drew up a hassock, sat on it, clasped her hands over her knees and looked up saying: "I've had a relapse!" I knew what she meant. Her love of me had gone for a time in that old mysterious way, and left her full of her old self—the longings after a wholly individual life—her old ambition and all that. I appeared quite indifferent to it, so much so that I fancy she was piqued at it. She would doubtless have liked me to make a grand demonstration of utmost sorrow. But I didn't. I felt inclined to smile—not at her, but at the charming way in which fate seemed to dog my footsteps.

Will finish tomorrow—am *very* tired.

5:30 P.M. 22ND MARCH, 1883

I have had four very lovely days, with much hard work of course, at painting from the model. If it were not so wonderfully fascinating—fascinating with that heavenly charm of true beauty shining through the flesh as a light through a veil—the knowledge that I am learning a great deal each day would make it very sweet. The bare right arm perplexes me more than any other part: in Miss Maud it is so subtlely rounded and so soft that in the light & shade full of reflexions from the [illegible] it is almost impossible to see the planes or curves. All I can do is to examine it in the round as to muscles and then by "feeling" get at the gradations of color which make it seem round. I am improving it and expect to get it quite decently in a few more sittings. She is the acme of what a model should be as to posing—at least for such subjects as this sleeping girl.* Her color is something marvellous and I can scarce hope to render it as it is. But even a faint hint at it in my picture (study) I find to be very beautiful. I think I have caught the weight of the figure—I think she really lies relaxed on the bench. If I can but

---

*The *Sleeping Girl*, signed January 28, 1886, was later sold for $575 to Topeka art patron George Tewksbury. For the next several months, diary entries repeatedly comment on this *Sleeping Girl* study (later called the *Greek Girl*): it "is better in drawing and sweeter in color than any picture I ever did. . . . It seems well modelled and certainly looks like flesh. I spent more time and thought over it than over all the rest. I have shown it to Whitaker and to Mr. Bates—they both like it very much." Diaries, March 24, 1883.

Stetson realized, however, that the large painting (43 × 60 inches) had problems: "I don't seem to get it proportioned rightly—it *will* run off of the canvas in spite of me, and by an optical illusion which I am not Da Vinci enough to explain it looks enormous, while in fact it is less than life-size. I don't know what to do with it so have set it aside for another inspiration(!)" Diaries, April 5, 1883.

Stetson also mentioned a parallel study, *Maud* (12 × 14 inches), signed April 7, 1883: "The sentiment is that of sensuous & pure maidenhood." "Opera" Book, p. 31.

make her breathe—can but draw aright those slightly parted beautifully full lips! Ah this is the way the great painters have learned their secrets—by association with beautiful women—association so delicate & pure at the same time so free that the deepest secret of beauty remained only to be fixed. . . . But the task is tremendous and my means are small. Beauty is haunting me more than ever: it maddens me sometimes until I feel almost as if I could lay myself in the lap of some beautiful being and die, simply because the ultimate beauty is unattainable.

Let me think! I was to write more about Charlotte as she was last Sunday evening. She had one of those spasms of wanting to make a name for herself in the world by doing good work: wanting to have people know her as Charlotte Perkins, not as the wife of me. She drew back with her old time feeling of independence from the prospect of sinking herself in our community. God alone knows how the terrible mood came again to her, for one could scarce find a happier being than she has been for months, or one more desirous of making me happy and of having a home & husband, & children & undying love. And she changed—changed—changed—and who knows how? She has changed her mind often, but I never saw it expressed so hotly & cruelly as this time. I had been lifted away up by her masterful passion & caresses and it brought me low and stabbed me with a rugged edged knife. She could not help it, dear woman! But the hardest part to bear is the insistence with which she asks questions as to what it will be after marriage, what she will be, what I shall demand of her, and if I am sure of this and that. And she brings up most ghastly similes and—all tends to make it seem reckless for me to marry her and—I don't know. I can say nothing. I tried my utmost to be patient & tender: I did not succeed to my desire. The whole thing was honest—most barefaced cruel honesty: and cut and beat me until I fain would have cried for mercy could it have been given.

If I were to attempt to tell of it in detail I should not make it clear. God pity us! She knows it and I know it—and Oh! that is more than enough. I stated simply that if I married her, I *married her*; and she must be my wife and my companion and live with me all the time. She had a wild theory about living in one place—a home of her "own" and having me come and see her when the erotic tendency was at a maximum. Of course I would not do that: and I would not think much of a man who would do it. The sweetest of marriage is cooperation towards advancement: close communion at all times, and the founding of a hearth. I will accept nothing else. At any rate she is not at this time in a fit state to marry: there must be something very morbid in her brain or she could not have said the irrelevant and wild things she did the other night. I have written to her twice since but in no persuading mood. Why should I? She knows the temper of my love: I have given it wholly to her. And in return I have had a bitter struggle, a patience-trying time, then an era of heavenly sweetness—then—then the best of my gifts and her gifts, stained, put to shame, has been flung in my face. But God knows that I will bear it as best I can. I cannot blame her: but I doubt for the first time sincerely if she will give me that deep soul satisfying happiness in life which I hoped for, thought I had attained. These changes are frightful. She knows it—tells of it—bemoans it in a way—at the same time I have a feeling that a great deal of it gives her a kind of pleasure as it gets her apart from other women—it seems a little strategy, some of it. I think her quite honest, but sensitive nerves and ready brain play as strange freaks—and I think hers are running riot with her. She prayed me last night to call her love back—she said she felt as if it would come if I called, but I could not & would not call. She seemed in a great throe of agony of soul, but I could not reach her, for her brain was forming even the while arguments and analogies wherewith to drive me back. I would not call though the acute agony of her wide wet eyes hurt me sorely—I would not, could not call, for my heart cried in me that it had been insulted. She must return—her heart must ache awhile until it shall be glad to call on mine to come and comfort it—until she finds that she needs *me*, and me alone, more than fame or work or freedom. Freedom! She is twice the slave she would be then!

Oh this century is cruel; we are in a transition state: the new industries for women; the talk about them has set their unused minds to work, & they see awry. They must go into the world and buffet. They will come back, I think, and find love better than all. Every one knows that I believe in the utmost freedom for women but that freedom is false which makes them rebel against the ties of love and home. She thinks much of her irregularity comes from her father. It may be: but more comes from ill-digested reading of philosophical works mixed with her imagination & the tradition of what she *ought* to inherit from her parents.

I can but believe that love will reclaim her. I can but believe that she has had so sweet a taste of love that the world bitterness will drive her back to it. God knows these arms are open to her when she can come in simplicity and truth.

This thing could have occurred in no century but this: and I pray it may not occur in those to come. I wait and endure. . . .

24TH MARCH, "83 5:30 P.M. (THEREABOUTS)

. . . Last evening I wrote two sonnets. . . . It is strange how the two—so different in tone—should come at the same time. . . . I wish I could find someone who really knew and whose judgment I could have faith in to tell me if there is any merit in my verses *as poetry*. I write because it eases me—not for fame, God knows. I am not so blind as to not see that my work is not of a sort to give fame even if sought: though I am sure the *ideas* I *intend* to express are not much below a fair standard. I would rather write, however, one elevated perfect sonnet than to paint a thousand good pictures. . . .

I feel a great—a very great enthusiasm for my work. My painting from Maud [the "Sleeping Girl" study] has given me a new & purer interest in life than I have had for long. My aim of late years has been to express the loveliness of womanhood & the purity of the sexual relations. I have done none of it yet. My successes have been chiefly in the way of weird things and strange color effects & sensuous harmonies—all of which I believe in heartily. But *the* thing I am working towards is the beauty of purity in man & woman & the glory of sunlight & transparent shade. And I want to realize that haunting loveliness one feels in the Canticles—the character of the "Beloved" & her steadfast passion. . . .

TUESDAY MORNING MARCH 27TH '83

Sunday evening something went from me—I know not what it was—some subtle unnamed fluid, I should judge, which left me so faint, so powerless, and absolutely speechless. And why—why O my God! thou knowest why—she—she even in my lap and mid her kisses said that she should not marry me at least for another year. She must go into the world and follow the bent of her heart: love, even my love did not seem enough—she must test whether she could be happy & more useful without it. And so she proposes to work here until June—go with Miss [Kate] Bucklin to Maine during July and then go to Boston as some lady's companion for a year.

And it all came to me—how I had prayed with my whole soul and with my hands until I had scarce life left in me to get home to bed—how my first dream of idyllic lovelife had faded, and another, and another, & then another was brought up to take its place. How her mother had urged me to marry her in the spring—how she had urged it & swept away all objection to it and made it seem a veritable surety. How happy she seemed—and how

I had labored as no one knows on my pictures for a sale—which I never would or could have done had it not been for that—and that was a failure: but they said, no matter: it need not hinder. And then to have her tell that—something went from me. I know not how long I sat in the corner of the little room with a heart that scarce beat—and with hands that could not hold the glass of water she brought me. It was long—and I had scarce life in me while I sat in the chair afterwards and saw her unprecedented acute grief. She tried to make it clear that she loved me—as much as she could—tried to make it clear how unworthy she was. . . . "I'm not good enough to *touch* you—Oh why did you love me who am scarce half woman & half beast!" And she plead with me not to leave her until I was sure she *never* could love me enough etc. etc.

I could not blame her for her change and her grief were both undoubtedly genuine: and I pitied her. She wants to go into the world—God keep her! I think the time will come when what I give her so sincerely & wholly will be very desirable, for who knows better than I the world's bitterness and unsatisfying? And she will find the fame she seeks and the ambition that prompts her—worse than ashes—murderous of her soul's peace and crucifiers of the love I give & the sweetness she might have had. I only fear that when world-weary and heart sick she turns to me I shall not be near enough to give her what I would. Fate seems to hold her knife very near me all the time: And I shall be nearly 27 by the time her year is up. . . .

Something has gone from me. . . .

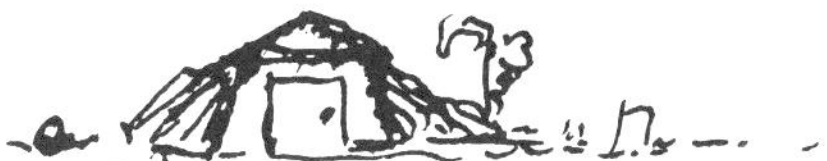

28TH MARCH, ''83.

Last night was wellnigh sleepless—quite so until near morning. My brain and heart ran wildly over the past of Charlotte, and felt the extreme bitterness of the present. Oh how I yearned over her! It seemed to me that I couldn't wait, but must have some authoritative voice to stop her on her road for fame and "freedom"—it seemed as if I *must* find some way to show her for what a miserable mess of pottage she was exchanging her birthright. And I saw clearly how pure and strong and consuming my love of her is— and I drew back with intense heartache as I saw how little it weighed with her—for she as much as says that the praise of the many and the privilege of going or staying as she will is better than the whole heart of a man given with its labor to her.

It is sin—surely sin: anything that takes woman away from the beautifying and sanctifying of home and the bearing of children must be sin. And if I as a man had done what she has done as a woman—I doing it to woman would be accredited with extreme cruelty: but with woman it is prudence—justice to self and many a fine name.

I have learned that I am worthy of her love.

Oh how my heart aches over the days of sorrow she must pass because of it!

She little knows what she does.

And I do not know what I can do. Clearly it must be tried: she must see for herself which is best. But I feel as if I should lose her forever.

31ST MARCH, 1883. MORNING, SATURDAY.

Thursday I received from her a most calm and beautiful letter, in which she stated her position and all the reasons she could find for it. I need not say how my heart ached though outward calm has come again—even with myself—though it never left so that those around me could see that any great pain was being borne. I should say the letter is quite perfect, as a letter, and very just, except in one or two things she implies or says that I require, and those are false only because she has not quite understood what I do want. Her love of me is working hard against her "freedom"—that desire to be a famous woman by doing good deeds. A few paragraphs from the letter will tell it in her own words.

Best loved . . . Let me tell you first what is of most importance, and what you know already by word and sign; that I love you. As far as I, Charlotte A. Perkins, understand the nature of love and the state of my own heart, I love you. (I believe it)

Now as you know, there have been women, (are now perhaps) who would go through blood and fire for the loved one's sake, and who asked nothing more in earth or heaven than to be near him and do for him, living only in his love. Now I am not of that description. Why should I so wildly blame myself for a conformation which I am not responsible for?

(Because, dear heart, your womanhood tells you that you might so love—that the best part of you does so love—and it cries on you to be less selfish and less in love with your own ways. Then she goes on to say:)

I am so made, and probably for some use.

I *cannot* love as such have done. Blame or shame though it be, it is so. But in so far as I can, dear, as far as my nature reaches, I do love you. And wholly. There was no other. I hope there never will be.

Now for a brief retrospect of the time which we have spent together. When I first met you I was—what won your deep respectful love; what you deemed worthy of wifehood and motherhood; what you found worthy of yourself. Or *thought* you found. It is yet barely possible that you were mistaken.

That is all most true. And I still think she is. Then she goes on to state how she showed me just what she was—or thought she was and how I loved her: how glad she was to find a true-faced friend. And then how when I loved her she felt proud at the "coronation" "and all the woman in (her) woke and grew, and still you loved me, and I (she) gradually, and with many sharp regretful struggles rose slowly, unsteadily to my (her) feet, and turned to you."

Aye, all the woman in her—and that woman is in her now, and do what she will, go where she may it will assert itself. Oh that God would show her that her work is to be done if done well and to purpose by getting into harmony with that "woman" instead of rebelliously trying to murder it. She goes on to state how since a year has passed she finds me what she thought me, and that she has no fault to find "with the great sad heart that sought (her) own, save in small matters that could be amended." Then she asks how it is with her, & grants that she's gained in womanliness, tenderness, thoughtfulness & delicacy, and that she finds herself brighter & finer in many ways, but she cannot feel sure (of course) that *some* of this might not have come without me. It is hard for her in these days to give credit for any change in her to anyone but herself for she says "I was trying hard for an unselfish grandeur of soul before you came." Granting that, I must say that it was trying for unselfishness in a most remarkably selfish manner. She did as well as she knew—the finer sides of her had not been awakened to subdue the fierce barbarous onslaught of her awakening mentality. She says further that she has lost as well as gained. "I have lost *power*. I do not feel myself so strong a person as I was before. I seem to have taken a lower seat, to have become less in some way, to have shrunk."

Dear Love! She has not *lost* power: she has only had a chance to test the power she thought she had and found it less: and as she has had a chance to compare what she had with that of others she naturally would find herself of less account in the world, and she would shrink. As one's size seems great beside a great and small beneath the Cologne cathedral. And it is this comparison of self with other, this finding of one's true height & size in the world which she must find in *wander jahre* from me. It will be painful but I can but doubt it will make her more humble and less a believer in the pre-eminence of her own intellect. It is hard for me to write thus, for I love her very sincerely, so sincerely that her selfish pride and heart will cut me sorely & deeply. It will be very sad for me to know how she is cut and pained by the world—but I love her enough to bear it feeling that trial will cure her of her false pride. Have not we all been through that? *I* know what it means: I have had a very similar mental state though love was not mixed in like way with it. I who wanted fame now want simply quiet and chance to do the work that is mine for the world. And she, I cannot doubt, will after fierce pain find that true power is in quiet, unselfish beauty of every day burdens, and in the humble taking of lower seats until the good work done will make our fellows out of sheer gratitude place us in the higher: and even then I am sure we had much rather have remained where we were to do our work. But when our time comes for fame—or to use a pure word—for the reception of the expression of the love & admiration of our fellow laborers it is our duty to accept it—but it is nothing to make a noise over. As soon as she finds her work—she confesses she does not have even a glimpse of it yet—she will stop brandishing her arms and crying out her strength, and creep away and do that work quietly and well, and feel half angry that anyone should call attention to it. I believe her to be a woman of unusual power & steadfastness to what she *knows*, but as yet that power is not directed, not regulated, and has but small effect for that reason. For having no balance it goes irregularly and is as likely to destroy today the effect of yesterday's act as not. When that balance comes she will be of much use in the universe; and I do not hesitate to say that I think that balance will only be acquired by most humbling or-deals, and when it comes it will be in the form of a most serene and lovely womanhood. In actual life she is a mere child. She has ideas of life founded on slight hints from books—and they, very many of them, must fall.

To continue the letter: She continues by saying that I either do not believe or have forgotten what she said to the effect that she is more C. A. P. than a woman. I *don't* believe it. Sex is the paramount thing in every human being: it is first—first—middle—and last. Then she says I ignore her craving for reasons, her way of thinking, her theories & beliefs. The whole of which is false. I ignore neither of them: there are things for which reasons cannot be given—and for such things I think it foolish to demand reasons. Such of her theories as are founded on real life I respect most highly; but her theories that have no foundation but dreams I look upon quietly—do not by any means ignore—but simply wait for them to be displaced by truth. Any one's *beliefs* I reverence, for if there is a sacred thing it is belief. She further says: "You look at me with pitying tenderness and wait for me to outgrow—what?—*myself!*" No, I only wait with that same tenderness the birth of my Anadyomene from the dark sea and froth of inexperience.

She goes on to say that I have felt this lessening of power in her, though she grants that I love her more and more—"that is, you want me more and more and feel more kindly to me every day. But where is the deep respectful admiration you felt at first?" The sweet girl should just remember that a man such as she knows me to be does not desire a woman to bear his children and companion him through life for which he has lost "respectful admiration." I fear she wants above all admiration. And she says: "I think you have come to feel with a patient acceptance of the fact as one of your fates, that I was not after all as grand as you had thought. I think you have struggled against this, and denied the feeling even to yourself, but that it has remained and grown." That comes because she feels and has felt for long that her changing moods and some other things have given me cause for that state of mind. Further she says: "It seems a dear & sweet & desirable thing to you—to marry me— but no such blazing crown as it appeared at first." By & by she says "And I do not for an instant deny that you have good grounds for such feelings: strong as I have been before, strong, brave and single hearted, I freely admit that as a lover I have been far from brave, and as dallying and changeable as any one. You can say too that all this might have come to me if you had not. It *might*. I do not think so." O pitiful! That she should charge my good love with such things! "Since I have been with you I have lost in great measure that strong self-confidence which was my greatest happiness." Yes, yes, that's what hurts her: and she will be hurt all her life, for the knocks of the world are not conducive to one's remaining ignorant that he can't do all things. [The letter continues:]

Perhaps I have been criminally weak in letting myself glide a long as I have done. Perhaps you will think me so. Remember, dear, that change as I might I showed you every change with painful fidelity (that's very true). Never have you held my body in your arms when my heart was not there also.

But of late, when immediate marriage was before me, and when I began to feel a foretaste of approaching restraint, the tide of love which swelled so high in this uncertain heart has sunk and sunk, and I looked eagerly to see what was left under it.

Then she goes on to bring up the case of her love for Martha—how when she stopped loving her, as she often did, she could leave her and in a week or so it would return in greater force than ever. But with me she sees that she cannot leave me in the same way for my loneliness would hold her, and family ties would keep her at her home (where she surely would be-long). "I feel the thousand threads of habit & circumstance winding insensibly around me." Then she says "I think that marriage—wifehood & motherhood would cause those feelings to leave forever. (which I do in a measure.) And that my love & society would make up to her for all else. (which I *don't*. Neither would it be necessary that it should.) She continues: "I am not one to whom love makes up for all else. If I *loved* with the whole souled force of a woman whose whole nature leaned that way, it would be different, but I do not.

"When love comes uppermost in me you are there—none else: but there are times when love so vanishes from out of my life that I scarce remember how it felt. And then I look ahead and see the one dreadful fact that outweighs all else in that direction. *I do not make you happy!*" (Strange, O my God, strange when that upon which a man stakes his whole life seems as shifting as desert sands that he is not happy. As she herself says: "It would be a world wide wonder if I did; I should never have dreamed of it myself, and combatted the idea at its first birth; but to feel that I do not simply terrifies me." (Why if you don't want to marry me—and if your love is so poor?)

"Now if you loved me to that extent that my presence, my society, my goings in and out, my ways and habits and modes of thought and life made you *happy*—that would throw a new light on the subject. To give such delight would be worth a thousand restrictions" (which wouldn't be her modes of thought & life which would have none) "I should know that the joy of my return would cover the pain of absence, and that you would glory in the ever returning warmth of my love more than you suffered from its loss. But it is not so. I without my love am not at all to your mind." (That is untrue) "My ways *jar* on your delicate fibres the more keenly for nearness." (That is surely true in part. There are ways about her that jar, but they surely will be outgrown.) . . .

MONDAY MORNING APRIL 2D ''83.

I am at the studio early, and while I am waiting the departure of the friendly sun from my work I will finish Charlotte's letter & tell of what has happened since. It seems, after all, quite foolish in me to record that letter— but then why not? It is one of those little things which sometimes alter the destiny of two souls forever: one of those effects which point at causes else unseen & undreamed of.

She continues from my last record:—

The moment my love goes, you go, and set me coldly down, saying that you cannot come till I want you. Less than the whole of me you say you will not have;

and I, who am not my own to give, who find a great part of me vanishing and re-appearing at uncertain intervals; can in nowise insure you the whole of me for a month's space. You are like one who would take a fair land on the borders of a shifting river, but insists on its remaining ever fixed.

I *cannot* dear! I cannot assure you what I have no hold on, no control over. Such as I am I am, weak and variable if it be, and I must be true even to such a self. As far as I can judge my life will be ever checkered. There will be times when this frenzy for freedom boils up with force, which, ungratified, would bring misery to myself and those around me; and there will be times when the woman's heart will wake and cry with heartrending loneliness.

Then shall I seek for you like a dream—the tired child that wakes and feels for its mother, and if I do not find you there is nothing but a great blackness and despair, a deep remorseful agony, the unending horror of feeling that I myself have thrust you from me and woven my own shroud. That my love for you is strong you are yourself witness. You have yourself said that it was all you could even ask, more than you had hoped or dreamed. That the other me is strong witness the present trial, when a year's flourishing tenderness has vanished in a week or two; and the delight in your love is lost entirely in the horrified shrinking at confinement, restricting possession.

Now these things are before me: I give myself to you and honorably fulfill all my duties at whatever cost: subduing my deeprooted desires and crushing out this Doppleganger of mine whenever it appears. In due time I should reach content I doubt not; and should only suffer at intervals.

(Ah what man could take to wife a woman who was not *glad* to come—to whom it seemed gain rather than denial? Not I.)

And *if* the glorious sweetness of our love held its own in both of us should know joy enough to overweigh all pain:

Or: I leave you, and strengthen myself at all points, subduing in turn fierce heartache when it rose. In due time I should reach content, I doubt not, and should only suffer at intervals. And *if* my promise of energy and power hold its own, my sense of duty and place fulfilled would counterbalance heartaches (Never!)

Or, if between us two can be arranged some plan by which I can live in force and freedom, and yet when my heart rises turn to you with it and know that sweetness too. (which God knows is all I ever asked. Her "force and freedom" are clearer to me than they are to her.)

That this can be done I scarce hope for you must have all or nothing and would rather go ever without me, and doom me to the same separation, than to take what I can give you and be satisfied.

That I grant, in the sense that *I* mean "all or nothing." It is delicately done, that putting blame on me for it by saying that it "dooms her to like separation."

Now, dearest, (for dearest you are of all the world; and I thank God that I love you even in this poor measure. I thank him from my poor unequal heart, with all my two-faced nature, that he has given me this glimpse of a woman's heaven even though I be not fit to enter! And I thank you, O my Lover! That through you came this love, from God and Heaven; and how dare I demand that you should love me thus and so rather than as you do! *You* and *your* love were sent me, and if I cannot fulfill your needs I must needs go unwed, and do such work as shall leave friends to mourn me if not children. God forbid that I should desecrate the holy shrine of wedlock with this fitful flame that burns so bravely and then goes out.) Now, dearest, to begin again, I will take my year. I will take myself as much as may be from your influence & that of my present surroundings. From the sky & sea I shall learn much, from the sweet woodland and the empty pastures. I shall settle to my true level (if I have one) and shall learn what life is like away from home and friends. If I were asked to decide *now* if I would marry you, in such wise as you desire; if I should *dare* to say yes—too grand and pure is such a House of Love to be entered with thought of leaving.

Amen—amen! Who entereth love's house must enter with whole heart & glad soul and enter forever.

But in this year, away, alone, I may return to you wholehearted; I may have different words to write than these. Let me wait, let me try my wings, give me this year; and then, if I do not turn wholly to you, and if you *can not* take less than all, then must I—ah! I cannot write it! I cannot bear to think of leaving you forever! Oh God! O God who made me! Help me to learn what I am, and to avoid a grievous sin!

C. A. P.

Then she writes a P.S. Thurs. morning, thus:—"It may be if I were once married, and a mother, I should stay so forever in glad content. I cannot tell." The bearing of a lusty pair of twins would weed her of her folly. . . . That last, from "The Princess" I think, to my mind has much truth in it.

In my Saturday's record I called her letter calm: since I have taken it piece by piece, I must say I do not think it calm. It is the letter of one who feels the weakness of the position he takes—the letter of an informed mind battling against a well formed heart. Even the heart cries above the words. "I cannot bear to think of leaving you forever!" That one cry counterbalances a vast deal of theorizing about "freedom." She can't bear to leave— how then is she bound by me—how would she be bound by me? But she'd like to leave and come back—and so she may for her year—but I must not anticipate.

Thurs. evening I determined to go & tell her mother about it. I was sure that Charlotte would not, and I did not want her (perhaps selfishly) to think that it was I [who] had showed the white feather after their aids to the ease of beginning. And as Charlotte would be at the Bible Class that evening I felt that I could tell her uninterruptedly. . . . I asked Mrs. P[erkins] to give me a chance to talk with her. So we went into the front room and [I] told her, in synopsis, our growth in love from the beginning, & told her just how it was at present. And then I saw Mrs. Perkins in her true light, and I respect her. Charlotte had told her nothing of it, or in a way which gave her to understand that it was a mutual agreement because of lack of money. Pretty soon Charlotte came in, came & kissed me & sat down. Mrs. P. said to her that she wanted to know about it, & wanted C. to tell her how it was. Charlotte then appeared the weakest I had ever seen her and upon her saying that we intended to wait because we did not have money enough I think that hurt me quite as much as the mere supposition that she did not love me enough. For either she had lied to me & told me that it was on account of a conviction of duty, when it was lack of money, or else she was lying to her mother, in what was as bad, telling a half truth meant to cover the whole. And I said, That's a new version: I had not heard that before. Then we talked & Charlotte did not show very beautiful sides to us, I confess. It was hard for her.

Then Mrs. P. asked her to leave us to talk. And she did, & I finished my tale. Then we went out to where C. & Mrs. R[obbins] were. Then I took Charlotte in the parlor & talked with her quietly, *very* quietly: thanked her for her letter and made some comments upon it—(must stop now: will finish by & by.)

. . . *how I cling to Art*

April 4–April 25, 1883

ALTHOUGH STETSON FELT there was a "terrible selfishness" in
Charlotte's decision to postpone the marriage, the best policy, he decided,
was to be silent: to "be as tender as possible with her; to not plead my cause
of Love with words; to wait until very love shall drive her to me."

From Charlotte's point of view, however, separation was essential. She
was feeling "unusually well & strong" and "more like myself than I have in a
long time"—"free & strong & courageous." Still, there were painful vacillations. She was rebellious, then suddenly repentant; self-respectful, then
humbled with remorse. "Oh what deep sobs came!" Stetson wrote; "*how* her
pride is in the dust! . . . She felt . . . as if she *should* come back; as if she
should find that she wanted me most." But at least she knows there is a "deep
selfishness in her course," and understands that pain itself shall be en-
nobling: "Blessed dear shall be that pain which burns out false trivial things
and leaves the true."

Meanwhile, Walter struggled with "fierce longings"—for Art and Charlotte both. "What *is* Art but the yearning love of one's soul seeking embodiment? What is an artist but a lover? And what am I but both?"*

APRIL 4TH ''83: EARLY IN THE DAY

. . . I must briefly finish my record of Charlotte. I left off where Charlotte & I were talking about her letter. She was very tender that evening and

---

*The above quotations are from diary entries (including quotations from Charlotte Per-
kins' letters) of the following dates: April 24, April 4, April 24, April 9, April 17, April 21, 1883.

caressed me, and plead[ed] with me to be patient & not leave her until she had learned herself. And told of how she felt certain that her love of me was *there* only some thing hid it from her—and the something was she knew not what. I told her what I thought it was and she said she thought it likely: then she rehearsed again all the feelings of her heart. I told her that she certainly must go out into life and find for herself what it was. . . .

. . . I went away feeling that I had done right—that she loved me—and that if she never came to me fully Love had been honored by me, yea, by her also; for it is because she thinks so highly of wedlock in love that she will not enter it save with a whole soul.

. . . My policy is, and shall be, to be as tender as possible with her; to not plead my cause of love with words; to wait until very love shall drive her to me and she shall be glad to stay.

. . . As I came down to the studio Saturday afternoon I thought—one of those inspirational things—I will get her some violets! And I never stopped to ask if I could afford it: love can and must afford those subtle tokens of itself. So I bought her a big bunch and took them to her house. I knew she would not be there. I knew they would greet her quite as delicately as I could when she came home at half past nine tired out with her work at the Boy's Room [the Bible class she was teaching]. I knew too that they would surround her with *my* presence—for I have always been connected in her thoughts with violets and their odor. It is my favorite odor & favorite flower, and she has inhaled it from me from the first. And I wanted to be near her in that way Sunday. She begged of me not to stay away Sunday evenings—she wanted me: couldn't bear to think of giving up those things. Again her heart spoke in touches & tones & looks more than she knew.

Sunday evening I went to her. She never was more evidently glad to see me. And she had a quiet and contrite spirit and talked of herself in a far from confident and in a most humble and beautiful way. Sitting in my lap with her arms about me she told me of how she had been thinking about it all and trying to imagine herself in any position where she should not want me: and she found that in joy she should want to come to me; if she were sick, none other would be thought of or called first, or if she were hurt or about to die—I were the one to hold her & care for her: so the thought she must be cheating herself and acting in a cowardly manner—trying to grasp the world and me at once, and holding me with every drop of blood in her heart knowing that my arms were ready for her if her life failed else. She began, she said, to see herself more clearly and every glimpse she got of herself she found her confidence going—going—and my love rising in her estimation. She analyzed her moods as I could not—very correctly I think: and there were feelings that just rose for me to see—and then faded which I noted, and which were the real expression of her real self. No, I made no mistake in loving her. She has in her a grand womanhood, which shall stand at Love's altar triumphant and very pure. She just touched upon her repentance—then hastily said, "No, I *must* go into the world: I must be tried, and tempted: and then if I can bear trial and resist temptation I shall be fit for you. But as I am now, I am half formed, and have been boasting of strength that has not been tried." And seeing herself how true that was—and how it was but an echo of what I had told her in her passion she buried her head in her hands on my shoulder and sobbed a little but stifled it. And I told her again how I was sure that was the thin partition that separated us. She must be tried, must be tempted, must be hurt. She would not appreciate love nor understand life until it was so. "Oh, Oh! my dearest—if after it were past I should seek your arms—and *not find you*! Oh the remorse of thinking I had driven you away: *I* had cast to the winds the great love you gave me—!" There was a most terrified expression in her face. "It would but be my just due." Then she went on to tell how she had feelings come over her every little while that she was not honest with herself. Soon she read me a letter which she wrote to Mrs. Smith of Boston in which she gave her to understand that the reason our marriage was not to take place was lack of money. After reading it all through she asked me if there was any thing in it *I* would not wish there. Then I told her what I thought about the hinting about lack of money. Her face fell and she paused & thought. Then characteristically (like all human beings) she attempted to defend it—but I showed her how the *real* cause of the nonmarriage was not that, but her wish for freedom. And she saw the point: and she straightway mercilessly analyzed her motive, and said that clearly it was cowardly: that it was putting a part of the blame of her own deed on me and also would be accepting praise for prudence and worldly wisdom when it was neither. I'm sure she saw a great many things in those few minutes. For she said ". . . Before you I am humble. . . ." And she knelt on the floor & put her hands between mine—the form of Saxon submission. (And I told her incidentally about keeping it from Mrs. Cresson that she was to blame—or rather the cause of this; because I felt bound not to put upon the one I love any stigma—but she wanted to throw it onto me. Also that I gave up my trip to Europe, which might have been brought about so as I could have gone in March, but that I'd rather marry her. That was the first she had heard of that—of course. I had told no one. And she saw how she had deprived me of several cherished things which I had gladly given up—and her cup was about full. There was pain too great for words: and with a white face and trembling body she threw herself upon my neck and sobbed without tears. And there was agony in her eyes, & lips when she told me of her heartache and of how I rose & rose ever in her heart & reverence. Notwithstanding the great pain of that part it was the best evening for long. . . . [On August 15, 1891, Walter added in the margin of the diary: "This was very mean on my part. One learns!"]

APRIL 5TH ''83—AFTERNOON

. . . I must make some further inquiries as to the possibility of getting hack work of some sort to do to eke out my "income"—that is my living money. I can't conceive of a thing that I can do. One can't bore the citizens by beseeching them to have portraits, so-called, painted; and no one wants my water or oil colors enough to pay for them. Behold! . . .

It is decidedly hard disheartening labor. The necessities of the technical part of my profession are surely taxing enough—the study of drawing and color, and light & expression; but when all that is complicated with exasperating problems pecuniary and physical it is almost beyond endurance. My sexual nature is in most powerful rebellion against my will & much of my energy is consumed in trying to subdue the desires thereof—most innocent and sweet desires, in themselves, but most inconvenient and embarrassing when a mate is lacking.

It is a standing sin—that there is not some way provided for men & women that love to marry. I don't see what help there is for me. Every day it will grow worse, for added to the imperative demands of my mind for a wife are the added physical incentives of Spring weather with its insinuating warmth & sense-ensnaring odors & breezes. Alas, that man should make a natural thing so difficult and baleful. My work is not done as well as it would be if I had fond wife for my arms. But let me try to forget it: it grows harder to bear. . . .

. . .

MONDAY, APRIL 9, ''83 9 A.M.

The sunlight that lies on my floor seems to be more sentient & sympathetic than for some time past. It may be because my heart wanting sympathy more goes out to it for it, but I think it is rather that I have put aside my dreams and begun again to live with nature shoulder to shoulder. I have decided, firmly decided to visit Charlotte no more unless some accident or any of those unconsidered things happen. It hurt her and oh God!—it hurt me, but it is best, I feel sure of it.

I went there as usual last evening. They had a blazing woodfire in the fireplace and she drew my chair up to it and as usual seated herself on the hassock at my feet. . . . After that by laws too subtle to be named we drifted into the old channel of discussion—the reasons why she had changed her mind. I tried to turn the conversation into a more palatable channel by asking her point blank what she had learned thus far from history which she could make a part of her own life. At first she resented the question a trifle from a preconception that I had no sympathy with her studies but I found little difficulty in removing that, & we went at it. She gave very good reasons for her desire of such knowledge. I assured her that I thought highly of historical study, but only when it was taken as a means to make this life better; only when it was not memorized as individual facts but when it was reasoned upon and the beauty assimilated & rules for self government gotten from the course of nations & individuals. She retorted by asking my why I studied the sonnet. She couldn't have asked me a better question, and I'm sure I answered her in a full &, for me, unusually clear manner: so much so that she said she was very glad to have learned that much more.

But though the digression kept us from the topic for awhile we at last came upon it & discussion of it was inevitable. She has grown much more lovable, for her knowledge of herself so gotten, and the humility & sorrow that have come with it have given her a more *interior* and subdued air—one that surely is the handmaid of beauty. From what she said I formed a better idea of her position and a surer belief in the utter honesty of her purpose and expression: she has grown calmer about it (but more sorry I'm sure) and can talk with no passionate outbursts of confined "freedom."

In short it is thus: She loves me very much & very truly. Would be glad to marry me. Has reverence & love for me; would like to give me all of her body & should enjoy it. I rest her & make her happier. She can not nor has not dimly, even, wished for any other lover. To think of passing life without me is most deep misery, but—there is that element in her which *must* have its way; that thing which cries on her day and night to be "free" & an "individual." And when that comes she thinks she finds that her love is not equal to it; that that life is dearer to her than I am. She may thank God that her lover can comprehend that thing, & that he can be patient.

While she was sitting in my lap she said, "When I am with you I feel *'little,'* you hurt my pride over & over, I don't feel half so powerful or think that I am of half as much need to the world in general. I shrink from it—my pride cries out. I feel so with no one else." The dear woman's pride *has* been touched: if I mistake not it is the beginning of a womanhood sweet beyond words. I do not know *how* I hurt her pride. Certainly not by deliberation, nor by many words, nor by any boasting in any authoritiveness or any show of intellect. It must be something that emanates from me, a personality which she feels; that is the only way I can account for it.

Our talk was very grave and I need not say earnest, but I must say that my admiration for her grew apace because of it. There is, and she knows it, a deep selfishness in her course; and once when she had a sudden clear view of it she reproved herself for it in a way that my love of her & my natural desire that all persons shall have the chance to follow the instincts of their natures would not have allowed. I know this, that I learned very much last night about right & wrong & their corresponding actions. I saw more clearly then, under the stimulus of *having* to see for her sake than I can now: it came as by inspiration—I cannot remember just *what* I said—but I *know* it was *truth* and know it softened & showed her herself & me more clearly.

She saw the selfishness of feeling sure of me, of knowing that if her plan failed she had me to come back to; and also the selfishness of having me give her all she wanted of myself while I had no hope of any return from her. (Not that *I* care for that: because my love would insist that I gave her all I could without thought or hope of return.) And she finds much comfort in what I give her: my calls upon her make it easier for her to bear—and harder for me—she saw that clearly and denounced herself for making it so. She said she *ought* to suffer for wrongdoing etc etc etc. I can't write it. It was earnest & beautiful & made a deep impression upon me. But as long as I go there she is not getting "from under my influence"; and is gaining nothing in the direction she would go; and there can be no doubt that physically it is hurting me. A man can't caress the woman he loves & longs for all the time & see her often—and know that there is a barrier between him and a proper consummation without injury to himself. Hope deferred is sickening enough, but constant tantalization is worse. For her own sake— for the sake of those for whom I work it *must* be changed. And I told her so. . . . Oh what deep sobs came! Dry sobs of sheer pain. But by some soothing and assurance that my love would ever be for her & all hers the tears came in a flood—*how* her pride is in the dust! Then broken words came and she begged me not to give her over—not to put from me the de- sire & the hope that she should sometime be my wife—she *could* not think of it, she said. She felt—(it *had* to come at last)—as if—as if—she *should* come back; as if she *should* find that she wanted me most. . . .

And so we are in a word apart. . . . It seemed to me as I came home that the pale starlight must know how my heart ached, and how it seemed to me that death had come & the only hope was in a possible resurrection. Oh what a power love is & how terrible! I felt certain of God in that walk home; and by the time I reached my bed, though there was pain and tears I had found myself and my courage; and I found that I *would* live, and work, and try more persistently to be clean in utmost thought, where without boast (ah that I, weak soul, *could* boast!) or hypocrisy I have never been unclean; & try unremittingly to be honest & courageous & faithful in all things. If chastity comes by sorrow, Master, there is hope. And before my eyes closed I found that I should <u>ENDURE</u> and by bearing conquer. . . .

APRIL 12 1883. MORNING

 . . . It does seem to me that there might be some arrangement made whereby each of my brothers & sisters might contribute their share towards father & mother. Well, I guess perhaps they do indirectly. At any rate $30 — a month rent is something of a tax on a young artist—and as could be easily understood I am going behind in a frightful manner.

I am all out of white so cannot go on with my painting until I can get some. I have no money except that $30 — guarded for the coming quarter's rent. I must not break into that.

It is marvelous how one can be intent upon his work & yet be conscious at the same time of feelings & thoughts of another person. I *fool* Charlotte every moment of the day, I *know* that in the midst of most absorbing work I am thinking of her. These three days since I left her have been— ah how long! And has she felt desire to see me in that time? . . .

MONDAY MORNING, APRIL 16TH 1883

Saturday I was full of pain of mind and corresponding lack of physical force, although I painted steadily on my girl asleep. Geo. Whitaker & Mr. [Charles] Hazeltine were in Friday towards evening & in a half joking manner I offered *The Boy with a "Balloon"* & *Sketch of a Loafer* & two other things at any price they pleased.* The fact was I had been pent up so long that I welcomed any change to make a noise. I had no idea that either of

---

* The *Boy with the Balloon* was signed April 9, 1883: "Profile of child, light from behind. He is blowing one of those red rubber things called balloons by the children. It is warm in tone." "Opera" Book, p. 48. *Sketch of a Loafer* is a 9 × 13-inch canvas; "Opera" Book, p. 34.

them would want to buy. But Geo. seized upon the idea & said he'd like to have them. I could set no price, and he would offer none because of Mr. Hazletine's presence, so he said simply that he'd like to have them & that we'd arrange a price. So Saturday P. M. he came & after a little talk took the Boy with a Balloon and the Loafer & two water colors & gave me $35– for them. They were worth more, but as he had loaned me $45– I was glad to pay the largest part of it in that way.

Sunday was a—hard day. The desire to go to Charlotte was almost irresistible. All the past sweetness came to me: life seemed too short & too uncertain to warrant spending any time apart from her. I soon found myself inextricably in morbid introspection: I reviewed my life and every one of its weaknesses rose before me; the light sins of former years—more mistakes of inexperience than sins I can but think—rose up also and they grew to alarming proportions in my disordered fancy. . . .

Yesterday *was* a terrible day. I did my best to forget it. I plunged into Greek grammar and Art Philosophy and at last Chaucer—that last was in the evening when I should have been with her. I succeeded in a measure, but there would come sharp thrusts between that it seemed that I should succumb entirely. At length I forced myself to bed. But I could not get to sleep, for long. Oh if only tears could have come. My grief was deeper and dryer with pain than tears. What senseless reviewing of self I went through and what unmanly, cowardly subterfuges to cheat myself into a comfortable belief in the righteousness of such weakening trial on the part of God. True, if it ends well; if the true love is by this glorified & thoroughly cleansed, why then I can say it is well. But will it end so? . . .

One of the thoughts that came to me last night was that it were best to cease writing in my Journal, and to destroy it all. The first would be too much deprivation—*I* need a confessional. The latter I do not feel ready to do yet, tho' why I should keep it I don't see. Much as the mother preserves the little hose and shoes & dress of her dead babe, I guess: or the lover the lock of hair of his dead Love. Here are all the visible parts of gone joy and sorrow. In my heart it lives ever truly: but man needs some symbol of his life.

Surely what I write of my reverence for Charlotte cannot—could not harm her in the sight of anyone to whom this should come if by accident. God pity whoever reads and misjudges. She is to my mind—and in absolute truth Pure, true to herself as she understands herself. What more could be said in her praise? That I love her is perhaps dispraise.

APRIL 17TH 1883—MORNING.

The air is warm and with the bright sun & blue sky and intimations of leafiness makes my grief, like melancholy, half-sweet. It would not be so had not I found upon going home last night a letter from my Love: a letter precious beyond words. . . .

It begins at 7:15 P. M. Ap. 15th & is headed.

The first Sunday without him.

Dear My Love:

I am upstairs in my own quiet room; with the door locked, the curtain down, the gas lit, and my books & papers on a little white towelled table beside me.

. . . This time is yours, sweetheart, by all sweet consecration, and I want to use it to keep you acquainted with my life and progress.

One week. So long a week I never saw before (that I remember;) (an exquisite touch of honesty—she would not deceive me even in that little) so long it seems hard to realize it is only seven days since I saw you.

Then follows as to how she went to bed on that parting Sunday night "without stopping to think at all." She refused to weep, she says, "and a tired body soon conquered the unhappy mind." O sweet sleep! "As busy a week as I ever had, I think: no time for retrospect or forecast. For the first two days a dull everpresent sense of pain somewhere, pain like a pain in sleep; an undercurrent which almost any line of Rossetti brought to the eyes and over."

(If this exile teaches her naught else it will give her a better understanding of poetry that comes from sorrowing hearts.)

Both Sunday night & Monday night I slept without you, but by Tuesday I could no longer withhold from myself the comfort of prayer & hope; of a short tear-wet glance at a possible future with you beside me again; of rereading your last loving words to me; and then the thought of your dear arms around me as I went to sleep. It did seem unfair for me to so comfort myself, but surely you who never turned from me when I wanted you will not refuse your presence in my dreams.

Thank God—thank God—she feels what I would have her feel—how I am hers ever & ever!

. . . Then follows the account of a strange dream of being beheaded by some female friend and how glad she felt to die honorably.

The first sheet is written in a very cramped hand as if the words came slowly or as if she were in revery. But on the 5th page she has changed pens & has evidently gathered force meanwhile.

5th page.

All the week through I have been busy, very busy; but not very unhappy, for I am looking back at you with your unfailing tenderness, your ever-ready love and sweet caresses; and forward to you as receiving me back again after my self imposed exile with Christlike forgiveness for the pain I have caused you. I, yet not I; for you know that the woman who has held you in her arms as I have done, and longed for you as I have longed, could never have devised this torture of her own will.

Amen, amen my dear Queen! How often have I said so: and how often heretofore have you asserted that your real self was the one that was leaving me—that the other was something I had given birth to. You are learning, thank God!

Then she tells how better it would have been if she could have foreseen & made me realize how "miserably inadequate" she was to meet my wants.

But I could not, my darling. I could tell you and I did, over and over, that my love to yours was like a farthing candle to the sun; but I did not foresee the candle would go out so soon. And it is *not out*! Something has covered it for awhile, but it is there still and still burning. Dear, I think you will live to thank God for this year. . . .

. . . For *should* the candle die, you say yourself that you would rather never have me wife than to have me and lose me; and so it is better to go away now than then. And if the candle burns—better, brighter, higher as life around me is darkened and sunless, why, you can thank him that one year's separation brought a lifetime's union.

And now her inmost soul cries out in this:—

The only cureless terror that I see is—if you should die in the meantime. I am blind with tears as I think of it and have to stop writing. O *God*! not that! It is a horror of great darkness, a dreadful sinking and whirling and—I should live, I should work, but (Oh I can't write for tears!) *Don't*. Oh *Don't* for all Love's sake, my own! If it be sin of mine to treat you as I have, let me suffer even as you have, but Oh *not that!* Just think of it yourself. No misery of mother who had chanced to slay her child or self doomed man who wakes to love too late could equal that: To have *had*— to have had such love as yours in my very arms with marriage but a step away—to leave and then to lose *forever*—Oh I *cannot* deserve it! I never meant you wrong, I never dreamed of this!

And she declared that she had not a woman's nature! How little she knew herself! But she is in a fair way to learn.

It will be very good for me to be away. And do not you write to me, sweet, till I cry to you for it. I want to *starve*; I who have held all in my hand and dropped it; to *starve* till one word of the love I have left shall seem more precious than rubies.

(There's a spirit like that of the women of old who did penance for misdeeds.) But she fears I shall think her too soon ready to repent for she says:

Don't think because my heart is wrong just now that I repent, or would resume the place I could not now reenter even if I would. You can well afford to bear your pain that I may bear mine—alone, uncomforted, away. Blessed & dear shall be that pain which burns out false & trivial things and leaves the true. And don't think I am happy. I am well. I am cheerful and bright, and sing when I think of it. I am busier than ever, and walk as freely and proudly as before.

(The words "freely & proudly" are quite characteristic. Would that they meant truer things to her!)

But the minute I let myself think of it—Sweet, my heart aches and aches and knows no comfort save the knowledge that you love me still. And that makes the pain keener too. And this is only the first Sunday night! And fifty or sixty of them lie before me!

I would do it just the same again, dear. I am not ready to marry you. This suffering, these tears, are only premonitions. I am glad, absolutely glad to go away. Many things I shall enjoy. Better to live alone and die alone than ever to come to your arms, your kisses, and your bed in any wise but as the proudest bride that breathes. . . .

Good night, love. I could not have done otherwise. Why did God make me so? His will be done. It is not for me to criticize his workmanship. Why should I shrink and cringe for fear of pain? There is no pain worth calling such save sin.

(Ah, Love, the pain *I* feel today is not of sin—no no, it is of vast emptiness of life without *you*—*you* who to me art Love & Life incarnate, my earthly, visible temple of the great Holy.

[She writes] "I have *not* sinned!" (Then she stops herself and her conscientiousness makes her detail to me her sins as follows, which I am sure it would be hard to call sins: and which never could bear harsher names than indelicacies or mistakes.)

Save—let me tell you a few things:—When I first met you I was on the offensive (yea, verily) as I always was against new acquaintances. I retailed to admiring relatives one or two of your and my remarks. I rather triumphed in your first call. Your first letter I *began* to read aloud—stopped, and since then have held you sacred more & more. I gloried a little—at first—in your seeming devotion, and let Martha see it. It was only for a little while, you yourself taught me delicacy—I had none as I told you. This was sin.

(O heinous crimes! If those are thy sins dear woman, verily there is no comparison 'twixt thee and the world around. And even those you have no fear for:—)

I can only plead that I neither knew nor meant it to be such. Again. I think that when first you kissed my lips I was not *quite* ready. If it had been left to me to give as I gave the others it would not have been so soon.

(I confess I don't *quite* understand the meaning of "the others.")

Perhaps I am wrong here, and higher forces were at work than my dull senses were aware of, under sky & trees. It is rather supersensitive hairsplitting perhaps, it may have been better for you to give me the kiss of betrothal before I knew what passion meant. I thought it all right at the time, I know.

(And it *was* all right: and God was witness of the utter holiness of it. Oh what a heavenly memory!)

For a third thing, I think I ought to have left you a week or two earlier this spring. I could not bear to think of losing you, and tried to reconcile my opposite wants in a cowardly fashion. I hated to acknowledge my own weakness. Beyond those, and having shown to others some few of my earlier verses to you (the sense to feel the wrong of this *grew from your compansionship;* I never used to have any sense of honor about that sort of exhibition) I am conscious of no wrong doing on my part. *I* feel the meanness of these petty sins you may be sure; and that I can so feel them I may thank you. You have cleared and lifted my mind, enlarged and warmed my heart, and consecrated my body forever by your pure and tender love. And after all that, I——
Good night again love. My eyes are hot & heavy, and my heart cold & heavy. Oh, to feel your arms about me just for a moment! Good night my love. My love. My—Love—!

It seems sacrilegious to comment upon such a letter. . . . I wrote 3 sonnets last night because of that letter. I'm sorry they are not prisons of more of my feeling.

My Journal has become as much a record of her life as of my own. And that truly makes it thrice sacred. . . .

· · ·

19TH APRIL. "83 2 P.M.

Another letter from Grandma Cresson this morning, because in yesterday's she forgot to enclose an article of the N. Y. Times about the Academy Ex. in which the writer speaks of me. I should judge it might be Mr. C. De Kay by what he says of Albert Ryder.* He—strange to say—speaks of me as a possible marine painter: "There is a painter in Providence, a Mr. Charles Walter Stetson, who might be found to excel in marines some day or other. He has exhibited in Boston & Phil. but N. Y. seems to have given him the cold shoulder. The academy or the Society men would do well to look him up."

-----

* Stetson was often compared to contemporary New England artist Albert Pinkham Ryder (1847–1917), who, according to Charles De Kay, was a thoughtful, poetic, and wide-ranging colorist. See De Kay, "A Modern Colorist: Albert Pinkham Ryder," *Century Magazine* 40 (June 1890), pp. 250–259.

I do not know upon what the writer bases his statement as I surely have never shown any marines in public exhibitions, unless the "Shad Nets" at Boston could be called such. That in every respect was a landscape with figures, as the water was far away. If it was C. De Kay that wrote it he may judge from *Early Morning after Rain* which he has. Or what is more likely he may consider that my temperament is one for that sort of thing. And I venture to say he is right. . . .

. . .

SAT. 21ST APRIL. FORENOON.

. . . If I could but go to my Love tomorrow & lay my head on her breast & tell her that her love is better & more desirable to me than the world besides I should be very glad! But her exile is but begun. Oh Love! As thou lovest me rouse thy woman's heart & come! Wherefore should man be so needy of woman? Is not Art enough? Is not gold enough? Is not sight enough? But what is sight, or gold, or Art when love is not? What *is* Art but the yearning love of one's soul seeking embodiment. What is an artist but a lover? And what am I but both? . . .

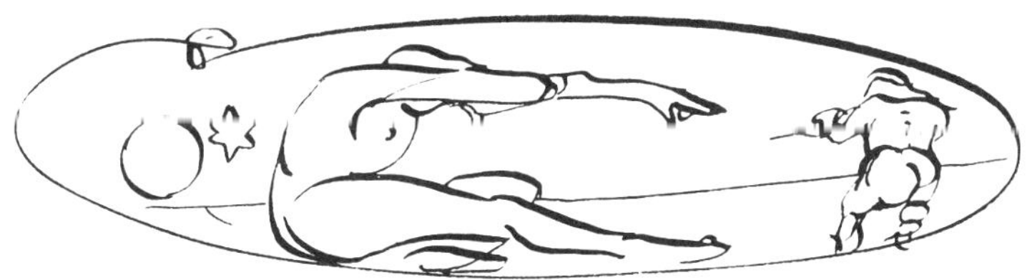

MONDAY 23RD APRIL, "83 1:45 P.M.

Yesterday! What a dreary day it was! I tried hard to subdue my vain desire to go to my darling, and the still vainer desire to live with her near me forever. As twilight came renewed sadness came. The only thing that I could get out of my mouth was "O Sanctissima! O purissima, dulce Virgo Maria!" I think I received a new light on the subject of the adoration of Mary. The fever grew fiercer as the evening went by. The Sunday before I did succeed in reading, and Church did well towards leading my thoughts away; but last night I could not even do that. Every thing urged me to seek her whom my soul loveth, but I could not. What can be more trying to one's heart than this? My last resource was to go to bed. There at least I could get away from mother's watchful eyes and if my grief *would* out it might come unseen. So I went to bed. There were no tears last night. There was a vain reaching out after God & her—and then a certain anger at my own importunity: It seemed so like the child's crying for the moon—but it was not—oh no! My heart tells me it was not. I am satisfied with no bauble in the place of it. But at last with an exceeding dry anguish I went to sleep—a troubled sleep. Near morning I dreamed that she was ill unto death with typhoid fever: that I went to her, that I watched her over a week without sleep and then—and then—she died! Oh what agony I suffered. But I rallied all & I defied God and said she should *live*, and I sent them all from the room and stretched my body on hers and breathed into her. And—oh the delicious sweetness of it! She began to warm and then she sighed & then she put her arms about me and smiled & whispered "At last you've come! Oh, my Love!" and I did not wake then, but the sweetness grew & she bloomed into health & they were all amazed. Then I grew ill; I had given her much of my life, and I became exhausted. And so it went on for weeks, until the next I remember was one day in the woods with her, after our illness, her death & resurrection had made us *one* and most happy and serene as one. The heavenliness of that time awoke me and then from sleep's sweetness I awoke to the *truth*—to the bitterness of not being loved enough by her to be better than the world, and all the rest—it did seem to me that my heart would break. But I had to get up. I have not been happy thus far today: and the leaden sky is in close accord with my heart. I hoped I should find a letter from her when I went home this noon but there was none. There may be one tonight. How long, God—how long? And but two weeks of her exile have passed!

I wrote to Mr. [John] Mason on Saturday to induce him to buy some twenty-five dollars worth of pictures of me. I hated to, certainly, but it seemed necessary as there are only six days to my rent day. He came in this morning. Said he & his wife & another lady went down to Boston almost solely to see some of my pictures at D[oll] & Richard's & the clerk told him he did not know that I had any there; then another clerk told him that he believed I had some there but they were packed away. He thought I ought to know it. And I ought. I think that's a rather mean way to treat me, after they asked for the pictures, too. But the dealers *will* do as they please. I have written for them to be returned at once, when Mr. Mason will take them and look them over & buy whatever he wishes. I hope it will be before rent day. I suppose I shall have to pay the express on them & perhaps other charges. They have wonderful ways of making us pay for things. . . .

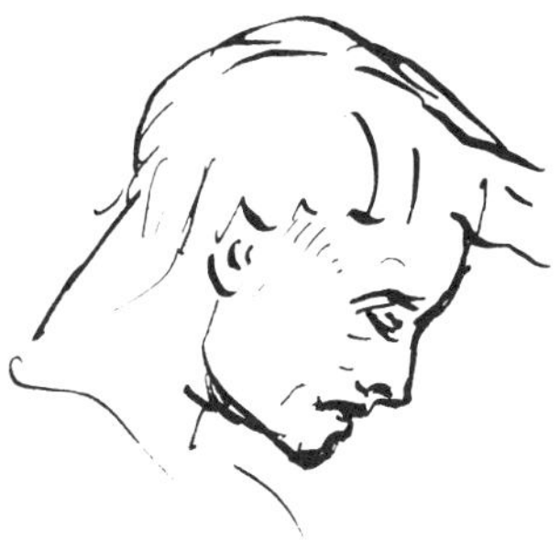

I found the expected letter when I went home last night. There is little to say about it except that there are few terms of endearment and that it is terribly calm. *She* finds it no harder to bear. . . .

Then she says that "Once there stole across me a faint hungry longing for you. It wasn't sharp & I put it by, with a weary smile of self-contempt. *I* want you! I ought to want you all my life."

Once – once—Oh God! and every moment of the dragging days were filled for me with fierce longing. *Once—once* and not sharp! [He quotes her letter:]

Now I mean these letters to be *true* as the laws of nature. I want them to keep you acquainted with my life while I am away from you. I do not want to hide from you one act or thought, that you may judge of my aims and labors while away. . . . Let me tell you then how I am feeling and acting now. I am not positively unhappy. Somehow I have stopped feeling grief or love for the present. I am not looking forward nor laying ambitious plans. Every morning when I get up and do not feel happy, I say to myself—"it makes no difference whether I am happy or not; what I am to do is to fill my place in the world until I die;" I smell the sweet air, look at the young spring growth of leaf & flower and thank God for his beautiful earth. And I pray as I have not before in months—"Help me to do *Right*!" Am unusually well & strong. I feel more like myself than I have in a long time—if I know myself. What I mean is that I feel free & strong & courageous. I never felt more humble, patient and anxious to do right. Whatever I have done wrong I think I am right now. And *you*— O I dare not think of it, I must not, will not think of it. O sweet, I never sought you out to cause this pain! I never tried to win your love, nor felt I deserved its depth & sweetness. May you & God forgive me if I am to blame!

My God *make* her think of it. There is her terrible selfishness. She *shall* think it, she *must* think of it though I be dumb! And thereupon she says "Goodnight. I sleep with your arms around me. My last waking thought is of your cheek pressed against mine."

And then she wrote more the next morning saying over again some of it.

What I most want you to understand is that I am humbly trying to do right every day. I say, "if after a year's exile I come back to my love then it behooves me to keep myself fair & pure for his sake. If I am never to have my love again then it behooves me to keep myself fair & pure for God's sake."

Her only ambition at present is to be *good*, she says.

I think too I shall learn to appreciate more than ever the strength, earnestness & purity of your life. It came over me in church yesterday what a man you were! May I learn to know you! Yours in truth.

C. A. P.

I can stand no more. Her letters are as strong as her presence towards setting my soul aflame, and only added pain can come of that. I must write to her and ask her to stop them. It requires more will power to do that than I thought I had this morning. . . .

Had a letter from Mrs. Cresson this morning. She calls Charlotte very selfish. And she is I know: but I love her—that she is trying to overcome her selfishness.

Now I shall copy what sonnets I have written and send them to Charlotte with a note asking her to stop her letters. She must be brought to do and feel by such means. How can I, God? *I must!*

25 AP. ''83—2:10 P.M.

I am thankful that I had power enough to keep me from sending the letter to Charlotte. It was all written & sealed & post paid, but it came to me just as I was about to mail it how selfish it was: how weak I was not to be able to let her have the comfort of writing—for I believe it to be a comfort to her. And so I am prepared to hear more. God helping I will not lose my patience, and whether it bring her home to me or not I shall have done no violence to the spirit of Love that has taken abode in me. I have no right to question how she can do what she does, nor why she does it. I ought only to concern myself with living more purely and more consistently with the standard my own thought has set. I will make renewed exertions. Oh, wistfully I look for her, and most strongly my desires cry on me to shout to her "Enough! Enough! We are wasting life in foolishness, and cheating youth of all its sweetness. Let us live together!" Perseverance must take me to the goal—but Oh! if that goal should lack her!

I wrote a letter to Mrs. Cresson last night in which I defended Charlotte. A letter from Doll & Richards this morning in which they, satisfactorily to me, explain the matter of Mr. Mason's calling for my water colors. However they return them as I wish, except 6, which they wish to keep and which they think will make no difference to my selling here. . . .

Yes, it does look like me a good deal.

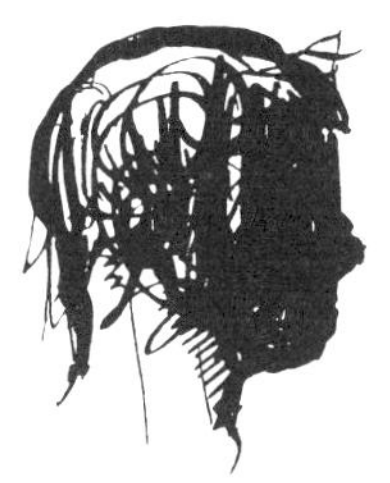 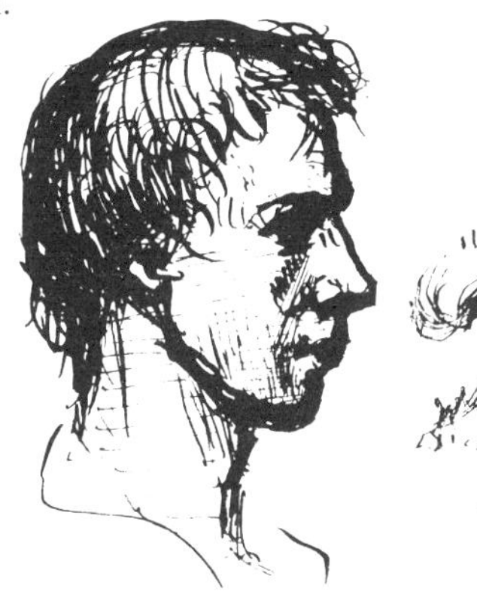

CHAPTER X

. . . *the binding promise*

April 26–June 16, 1883

FOR THE NEXT SEVERAL WEEKS the separation continued, with Stetson miserable, and Charlotte not quite ready to repent. She would "greedily . . . welcome any touch of pain," she wrote him, but her heart thus far was "asleep—numb—gone." In fact, she concluded, she must be a woman who is "not a woman"—"maimed, warped, imperfect" in her loving—and thus must "consecrate" herself to service.

Simultaneously Stetson focused on his own compelling "service" needs.

I feel a tremendous earnestness for Art, and as if everything that I am surrounded with is trifling in the extreme. . . . I must clench my fists and by sheer will power bear up in Art. I have a hard fight before me, for the public will be long in recognizing whatever's of good my work may have, for the good will be for long sadly obscured by the bad qualities.

Ironically, in light of Stetson's persistent insecurities, Charlotte resisted marriage because she felt so "small" with Walter. She was afraid of losing her own work ambitions. She felt threatened by his apparent confidence, by his protective, patronizing stance, by his "masculine" prerogative as compared to the pattern of "feminine" submissiveness to which she was expected to conform. So as long as Walter seemed the "Lord and Master," Charlotte instinctively resisted him. But once he began more fully to expose his vulnerability, to show how much he hurt instead, Charlotte acquiesced.

Although at times Stetson seemed vaguely conscious of the need to change his strategy—"She feels too sure of me"—the "crisis" was hardly planned. The *Atlantic* returned his sonnets, Charles De Kay politely but directly told him that they had no promise; and Walter was crushed. "My painting is of like sort, I suspect. That fact strikes at the root of my whole life. . . . Is my whole life a lie? . . . "Failure on failure came before me pitiably. . . . I told it all to Charlotte . . . it showed me to her as she had never seen me, and it changed all! In my arms with broken voice she told how she loved me—how she had found she *needed* me—how she *could* not live best without me—how she must have me. . . . She promised or vowed rather to marry me. And settled it finally.*

26TH APRIL: 83 1:45 P.M.

Mr. Mason called yesterday P. M. & took all my water colors up to his house, that he & his wife might select two—for $25—the price that D & R get for a single one. Or I told him he might have one water color & an 8 × 10 oil framed for $30–. I expect him in this P. M.† Prof. [John Howard] Appleton called also. He seemed favorably impressed with the Greek Girl.‡ We talked also of the chemistry of colors. He being Prof. of Chemistry ought to know something about them. . . .

I have been longing fiercely for my Love today—uselessly—uselessly— but I *can't* crush it out for long: the sight of some sweet flower—some odor, some sound—some color brings her before me with frightful powers. Yes, I mean frightful, for I am afraid I cannot bear this separation as I should.

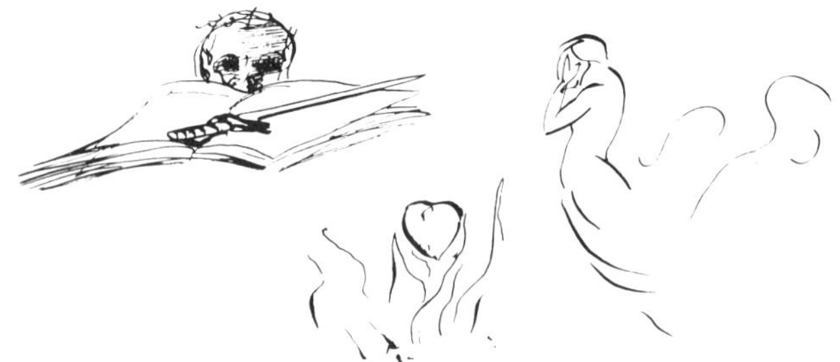

There, there! my brain
went off in revery while
doing those inane things.

---

*The above quotations are from diary entries (including quotations from Charlotte Perkins' letters) of the following dates: April 28, May 12, May 15, May 19, May 22, 1883.

†As it turned out, Mason bought "3 of the water colors. One of them is one of the best, the other two are not by any means. And he offers me $30—for the 3—$30—$10 a piece. I accepted the offer though Doll & Richards had marked them $25– each on the back. Well, that will give me enough to finish out my studio rent for this quarter and $9– besides." Diaries, April 27, 1883.

‡John Howard Appleton, Chairman of the Chemistry Department at Brown University, was also an active Art Club member, elected PAC President in 1883. (The *Sleeping Girl* and the *Greek Girl* are the same painting.)

Now it is back, and I must to work, and try to get a little more "manliness" for the coming Sunday and coming months & years! I wish my Journal was all destroyed, the whole thousand pages of it, through which I droned out my Misereres & Aves and shown myself weak & tender and only half formed for fight with the world. And yet—may be the mission of this Journal was to keep me humble.

27TH AP. ''83

    . . . I know what ails me today: I went to Charlotte's last evening, not to see her, but her mother & Mrs. Robbins: I took a time when I supposed she would [not be at home.] . . . I had such a crying want in me to see her books, the chairs she sat in, the things she daily sees! On the way I thought: Suppose I should meet her at the door instead of her mother! What could I do? Beg pardon and leave at once? Go in and call back her desire of me to new life? I thought I should leave at once. Well, her mother & Mrs. Robbins seemed glad to see me. Mrs. Perkins looked unusually lovely. After some few words we *had* to speak of the subject that concerns us. Mrs. Perkins said it all seemed very strange to her. She could not quite see how Charlotte could act so. She felt sure, and Mrs. Robbins said so too, that she had all ready repented and would be glad if she were back. They said she was much changed—her pride seemed to be quite gone—that is that startling pride that was once so conspicuous etc. Mrs. P. thought I should have done well to stop her writing to me: thought it would do her good. And she urged me to ask her to. So then & there, before my tender heart could overcome my head I wrote her a letter, milder than the one I tore up the other day, but of the same purport, and I enclosed it with the sonnets & left them. It sorrowed me much going, but I think it did me good as well. I told her not to hesitate to write if she really *wanted* me, or if she was to leave the city. But those Sunday letters full of introspection and tantalizing love I shall do better without: and yet I want them. I'm surely contradictory in many respects: I really think in this case the best side says not have them. I think she will soon find out whether or not she wants me.

    [The diary continues with a discussion of money.] . . . How to get it— God only knows. Father took what little he had & put it into some medi- cine—the same sells so slowly that we eat up the proceeds as fast as the sales are made. . . . He is one of those men who with really unusual brains and much physical energy, for some reason that cannot be found out never win a place for themselves in the world. To be sure his children have been a hin- drance to him, but men with half the intellect he has, and with none of the beautiful sentiments, and more children, go up to fame and money rapidly. Father ever since I have known him, has never had money enough to meet our moderate wants. Is it any wonder, I ask myself over & over, that brought up in a family where I have known nothing but impecuniarity & the thousand ills attending it—is it any wonder that I am morbidly sensitive about money matters, and desponding to the last degree about ever having money?

It weighs like a nightmare on me—even that rent at the house—42 dollars—more than the $400 that I owe Mr. Weeden. I do *not* see the escape, but one *must* be made. . . .

28TH APRIL, ''83—10:40 A.M.

. . . When home I found last evening a letter from [Charlotte]—and such a letter as makes me go down on my knees in thanksgiving and in beseechment to be worthy of such praise & such love. I would not lose one word of it. . . . The note I left her seems to have been a good thing. . . . She shall speak.

9:50 P.M. *Ap 26th 83*

I have read your note and your sonnets. I have been pained, and wept. If you could know (how) greedily I welcome any touch of pain, any sense of loss, of want, of remorse, that might hint at return!

There is little such. I suffer at times. Never enough to overcome me, not the fierce agony that shall beat me down in miserable repentance and one long wailing cry for you.

(I wonder if her "shall" is prophetic. God grant it!)

I must feel that before I return. The woman who could leave you as I have left you and *not* suffer; the woman who could lose you as I have lost you and *not* miss you is not your wife. . . .

Explain the horror as you will, the facts are these: that at one time I *loved you*; and that now, in the same sense, I do not. Talk of psychologic phenomena! My own consciousness is simply a *lack*, a loss, a part of me dropped out. Not painfully so, in some ways I feel lighter & freer; but as though a side of my nature was *gone*. You know I told you long ago that I did not and could not love. I meant it. I felt so. You succeeded in convincing me that I could and did. And now it is gone again. *I* can't explain it. This I know, that to marry you in this state were sin; you know it as well as I. I must wait until my heart wakes again. It is yours as you know. Isn't catalepsy something like this? A trance state? My heart is asleep—numb—gone. I don't *feel* much in any way; only think, and pray, & work.

Thoroughly humbled I am. A woman not a woman, the most important part of whose nature as a live being, is as intermittent and unreliable as will-o-the-wisp is not healthy. So I drop that claim. I feel myself maimed, warped, imperfect, cruelly crippled. O God who knows my heart! Help me to mend this crooked life as best I may, to do thy will on earth! Suffer as you may *you* have no blame upon your soul, *you* have not failed nor faltered.

(Oh how little she knows how my poor soul has been beat from side to side—how I have shrunk from pain and faltered in my life work! It hurts to be praised when I know I don't quite deserve it. If she means I have not failed or faltered in my love of her it is true.)

Pain caused by others can be borne by the pure soul; but pain of self condemnation is incurable. . . . And yet what have I done save refuse what I had not at first, give, *give* with glad thanks giving when I had, and show my empty hands when I have not again. For you, God knows there is no blame. For me, for all that I have done, I surely wait my punishment. So let it rest, great heart. You die—I envy you more bitterly than words can say. You live—and by your life make all around you better and more pure.

(Oh that it were so—could be so—my dear dear Love, *does* it seem so to you? To me it seems that I am so very very mean and unuseful!)

I have no fear of your high truth and long self-sacrifice. If I return, some little joy may yet be yours.

And I? Some seventy years at most before me. I consecrate this half-formed being to the service of my kind. With a bitter shame and grief piled high on my dead heart I have no room for pleasure nor for pride. As one of God's creatures, as once your bride, I will purify and elevate myself as far as may be, and O may I be able to make some hearts happy, and some lives the stronger by this poor heart and life of mine! . . .

One thing I wanted to tell you of, dear. That "Reserved" I read you, the "my lips are my Lover's," you know, was written for Retta Clark, that strong good woman soul I told you of; who after years, had learned to love me, *me*! and wondered why I would not kiss her. I really ought not to have showed it you, for it was a letter to her. I am sorry.*

(I confess I don't quite understand this; or her sorrow at it. I think she must be getting morbidly conscientious—if that's a word to express it. But what chastity! Not kiss a *woman* who loves her! I think she meant on the *lips*; and I thank her from the depth of my soul for that noble thought of love which keeps her lover's her lover's due. I reverence that great heart more daily.)

---

* I should note that my earlier study of Gilman mistakenly states that the love poem "Reserved" was written for Walter, when apparently it was originally intended for Providence friend Retta Clark. For further discussion of the poem and of Gilman's attitudes toward female friendships see Mary A. Hill, *Charlotte Perkins Gilman: The Making of a Radical Feminist, 1860–1896* (Philadelphia: Temple University Press, 1980), Chap. IV.

And I wanted to tell you too, that when I put away my green dress the other day, the one I have worn all winter for my best—scarce ever save when you were here—the one you liked; it *hurt* me with a sudden pain, like coming on some toy of a dead child. My heart is dead. Or sleeps. O deep compassionate heart whose depth of pain gives it more wealth of pity, pity *me* when the awakening comes!

Oh my Love—my Love—you read aright. Depth of pain gives wealth of pity: though you slew me I could not but pity you—verily. And I love you—*you*—beyond expression.

I will not send you any more Sunday letters. I will write you when I please and keep them. Do not ask me to go wholly without you! Why I do not wish you to write me so that unquenched hunger may bring me back the sooner.

It is curious to see how complex the feelings & thoughts can be. She is planning all the time for returning to me: tells how her heart aches yet says it's dead. One can see the desire for me flashing out unawares all through this letter.

Send me word I beg of you if you change your address, and I will always give you mine unless there be some reason to the contrary. Now I will go to bed. And, sweet, I will allow myself no more the faint delight of dreaming ere I sleep, that you are next to me. If I must think of you I'll think of your long agony.

O Artist! Poet! Man! To whom, through me, has come such depth on depth of measureless pain! O burden heavier than the weight of worlds—you gave me <u>LOVE</u>—and I can give you nothing!
Goodnight. Goodbye.

Gave me nothing! Oh she has filled me—filled me—for power—forever to tell her—to *make* her see that she is all in all to me and just as she is, if she could but come, could————! but how *can* I tell her.

I never received a letter that thrilled me so. I want to heal her.

This morning I carried to her home a bunch of violets. She will understand. Her mother came to the door, and much to my surprise Charlotte was at home, upstairs in her little room, I surmise, and I hastened away else I should have seen her. May those flowers find words for what I cannot say! . . .

MAY 3D ''83 6 P.M.

Just in from sketching with Whitaker in Cranston:* beautiful day. Sketch has some good aerial qualities—not what it should have of firmness

---

*George Whitaker would later remember, "[Stetson and I] used to go often on sketching trips together. The city suburbs were our favorite haunts. We also liked to stroll along the city

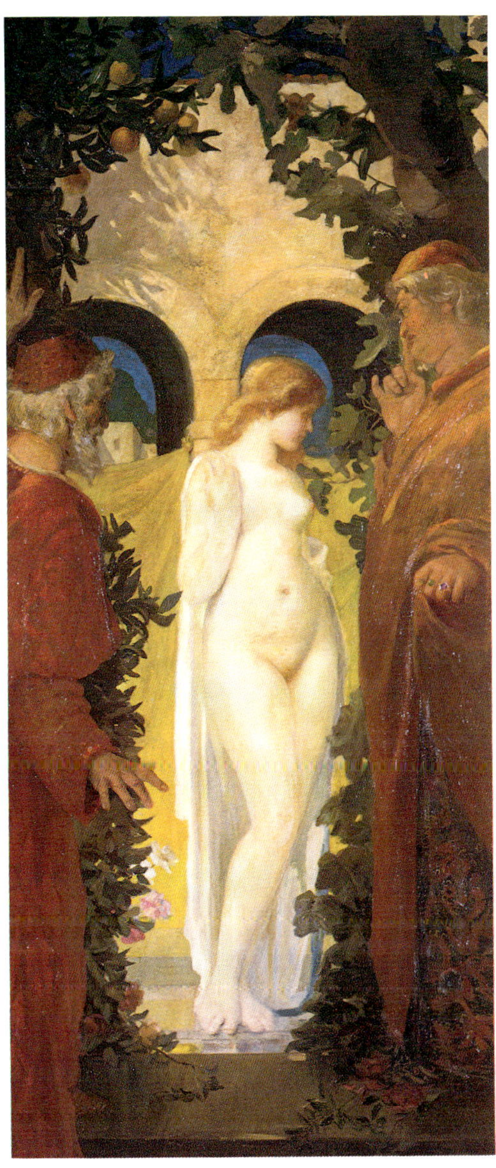

Susanna and the Elders, 1890–1911, oil on canvas (83½ × 36 inches). Courtesy of the Bowater Gallery, Los Angeles.

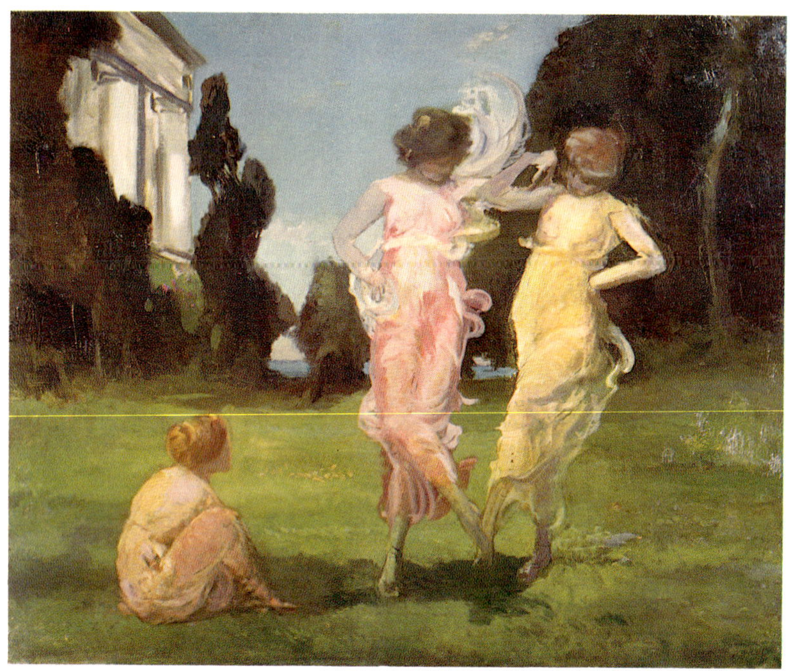

May Dance, 1882, oil on canvas (29½ × 35½ inches). In the collection of Dr. and Mrs. Rodney E. Sanneman, Los Angeles.

Fog Coming at Sunset, Baddeck, Cape Breton, 1882, oil on canvas (16 × 30 inches), Courtesy of Joseph K. Ott, Providence, R.I.

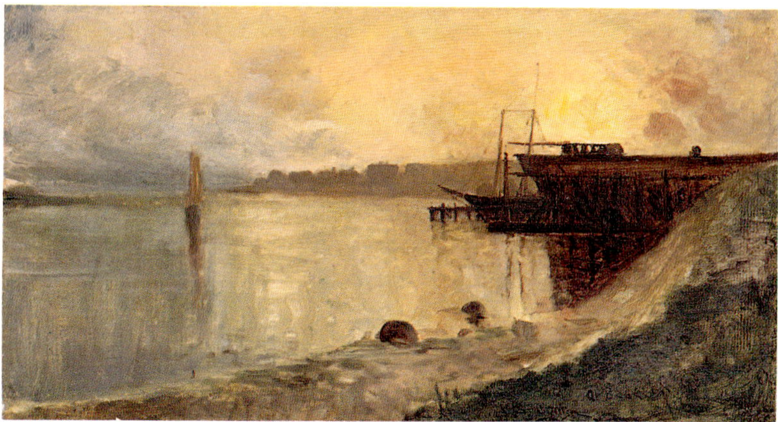

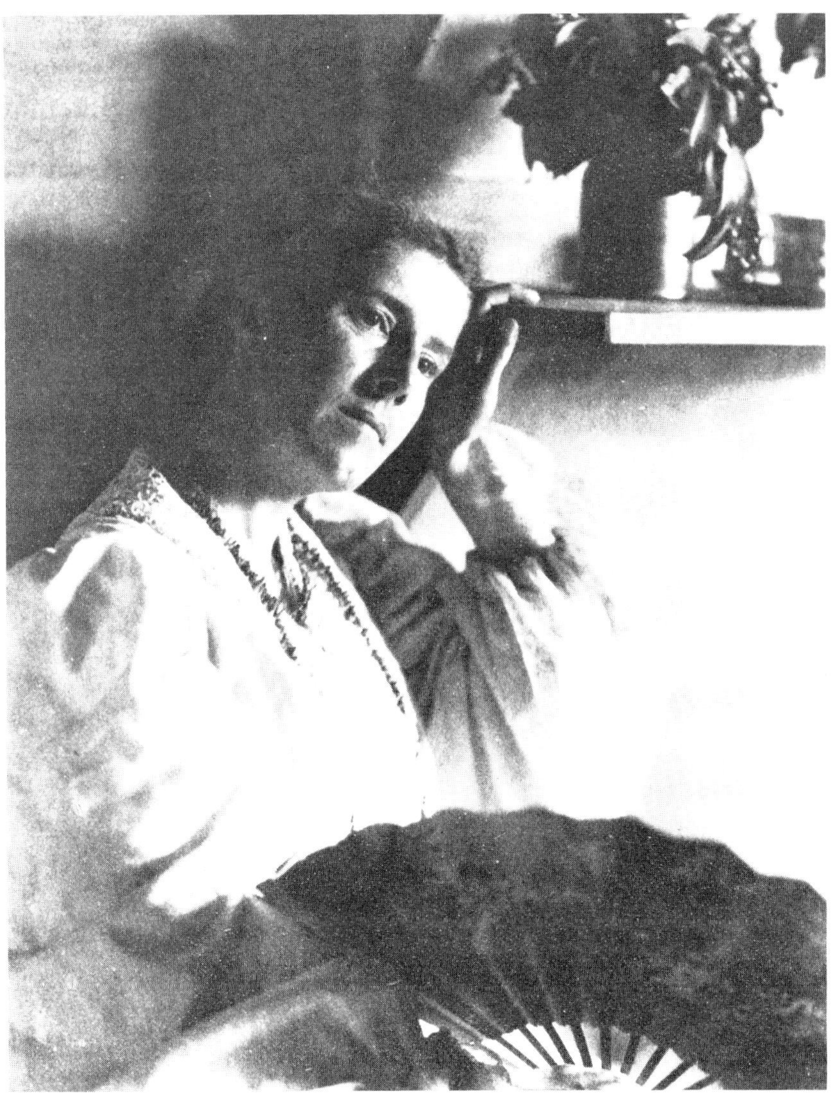

Charlotte Perkins (Stetson) Gilman, 1900, photograph by Eva Watson-Schütze. Courtesy of the Schlesinger Library, Radcliffe College, Cambridge, Mass.

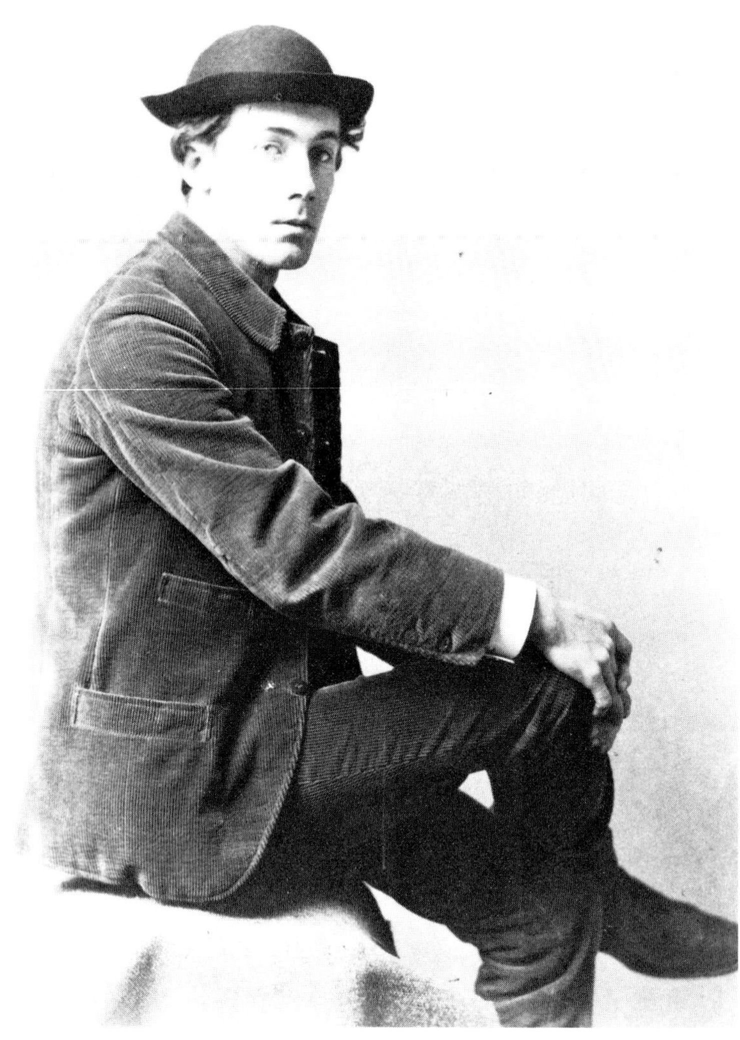

Charles Walter Stetson, 1885, photograph by Hurd. Courtesy of Dorothy and Walter Chamberlin, Pasadena, Cal.

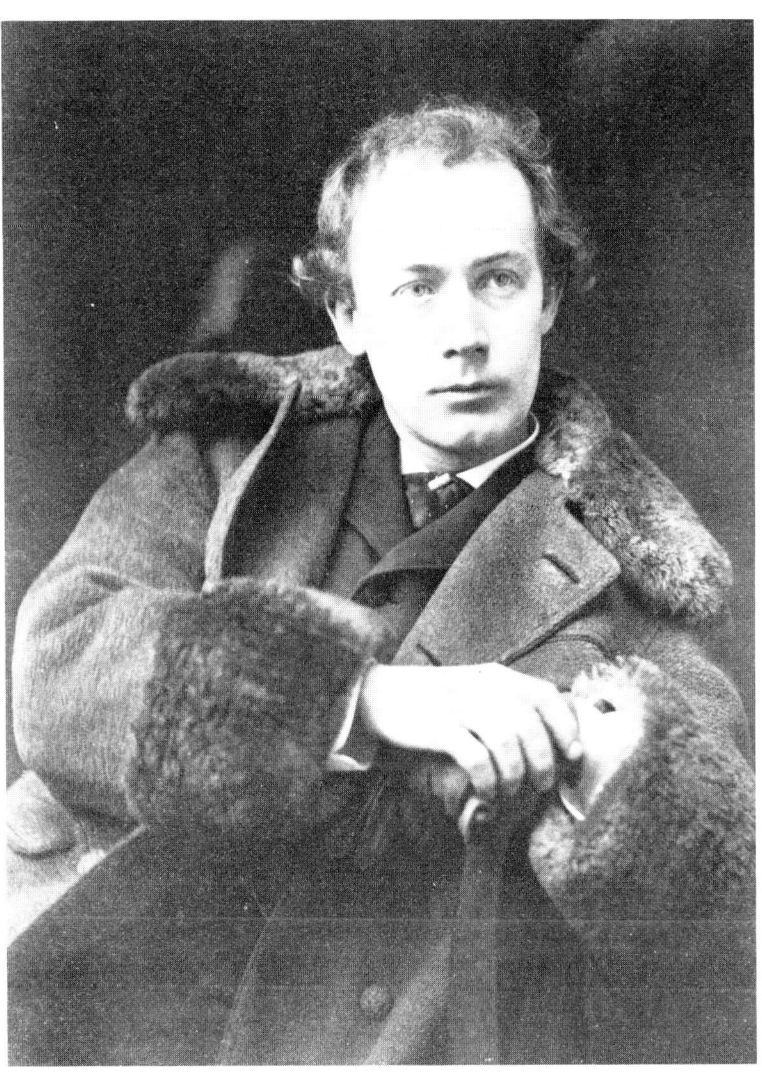

Charles Walter Stetson, ca. 1900, photograph by Hurd. Courtesy of Dorothy and Walter Chamberlin, Pasadena, Cal.

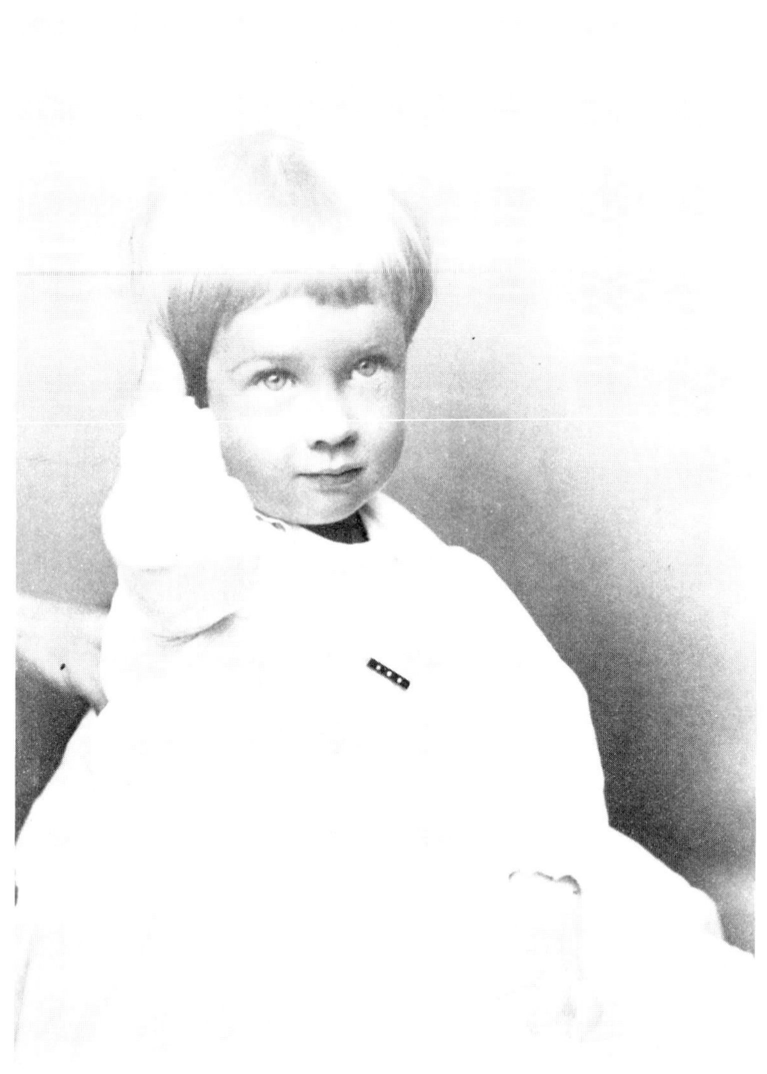

Katharine Beecher Stetson (Chamberlin), ca. 1887, photograph by Hurd. Courtesy of Dorothy and Walter Chamberlin, Pasadena, Cal.

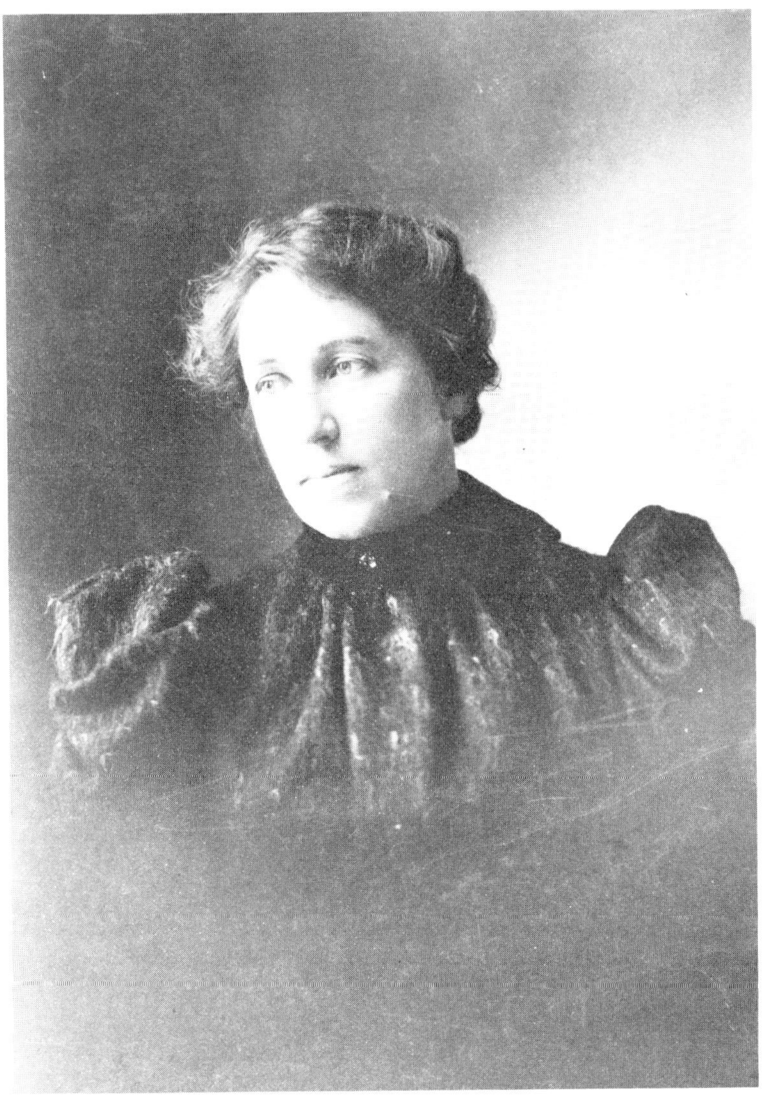

Grace Ellery Channing (Stetson), ca. 1900, photograph. Courtesy of Dorothy and Walter Chamberlin, Pasadena, Cal.

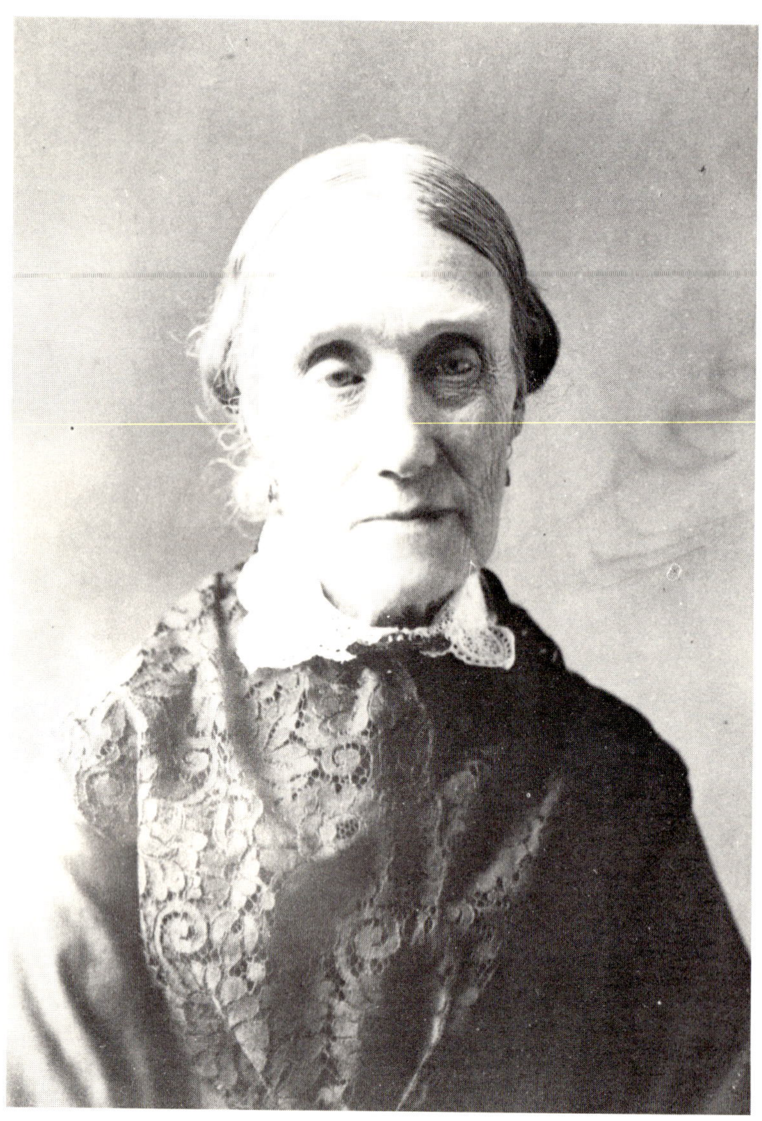

Rebecca Steere Stetson (mother of Charles Walter Stetson), 1884, photograph by Hurd. Courtesy of Dorothy and Walter Chamberlin, Pasadena, Cal.

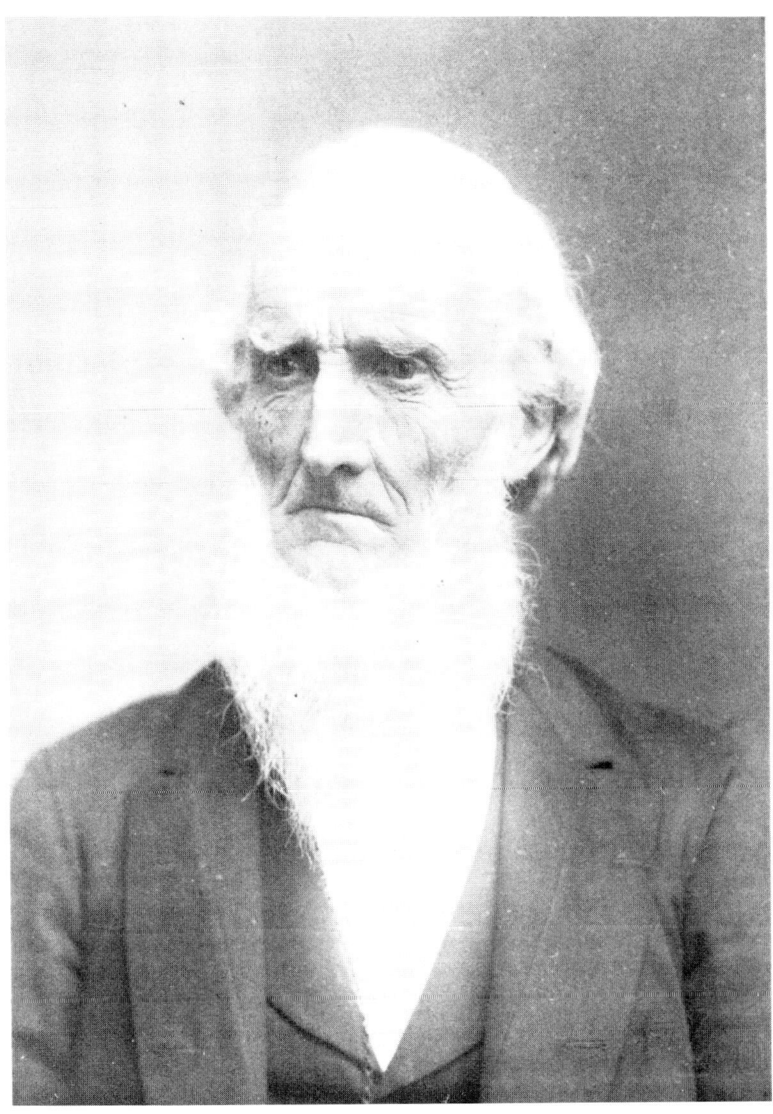

Joshua Augustus Stetson (father of Charles Walter Stetson), 1884, photograph by Hurd. Courtesy of Dorothy and Walter Chamberlin, Pasadena, Cal.

Diary page, July 28, 1888.

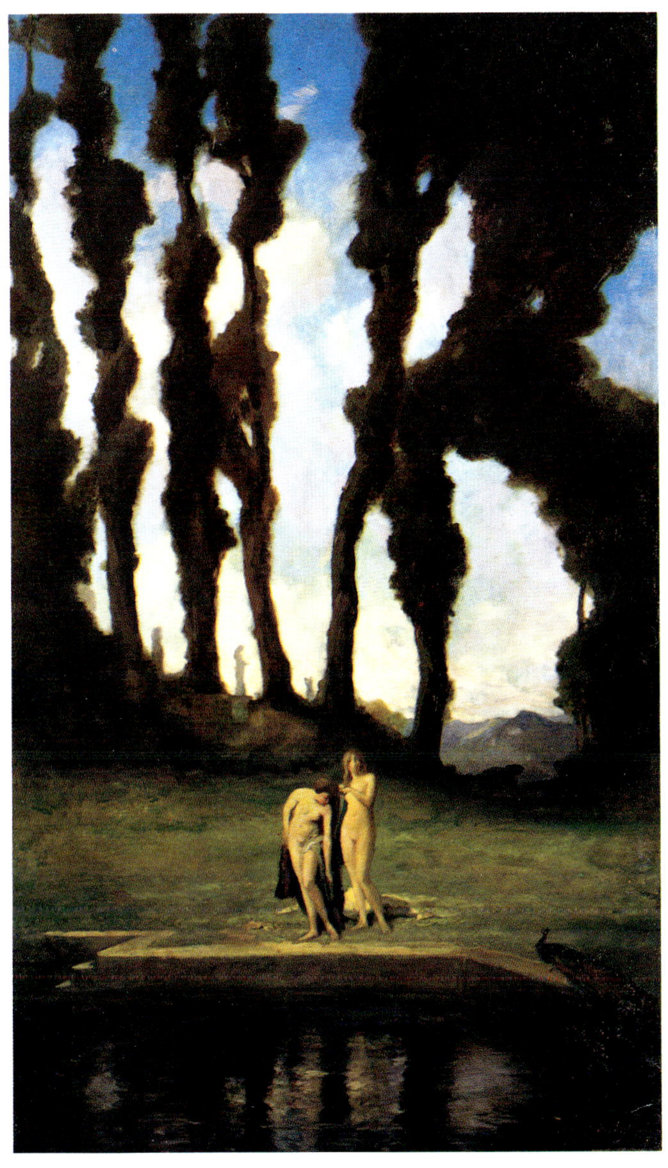

After the Bath, 1910, oil on canvas (67⅞ × 39¾ inches). Courtesy of the National Museum of American Art (formerly National Collection of Fine Arts), Smithsonian Institution, Washington, D.C.

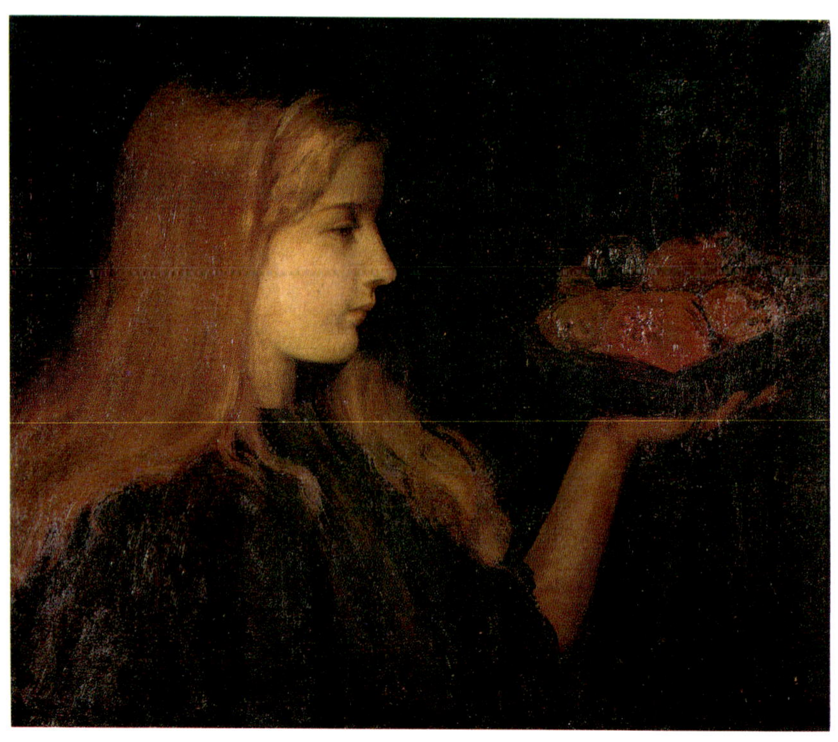

Katharine with Pomegranates, ca. 1900, oil on canvas (20 × 24 inches). Courtesy of Julia C. Goodale, Santa Cruz, Cal.

however. Have been hard at work so far this week. Charlotte has been a dull but heavy ache all this week. I am gradually forcing myself to be strong against my heartsickness—but it comes—oh it comes unawares! Luckily I work & love my work: else I should die—I am sure of it: for oh what a part of my life she had become! And what feels she now? I dare not think. I am very tired: I slept almost none last night. . . .

MAY 4TH ''83 FRIDAY, 2 P.M. ABOUT
   This is indeed the month the anticipation of which was so freighted with sweet dreams of better living: and the reality—!

   I worked to my utmost this forenoon on the Greek girl: trying to reconcile the pose to gracefulness but without success. It all came I know because of the small size of my room & the arrangement for lighting. . . . The chief difficulty is in keeping the figure from seeming of enormous dimensions around the abdomen—in reality it is not, but the perspective & foreshortening are such that it appears so *decidedly.*
   As I came down this noon I stopped at Hugo Bruel's studio. He is a [Munich] man—and has some painting that shames me,—nay, not so, for has not he had years of training in one of the world's first academies, and under [Wilhelm] Lindenschmidt? And he is older. His things are strong, good in color: and one or two of them has some sentiment. If I may judge I do not think him so poetic as myself—but it may be truly that I do not know what is poetry. . . .

TUESDAY, MAY 8TH 1883 2 P.M.
   . . . What have I done since I wrote? Worked much on my Greek girl and to its betterment as far as ease and gracefulness are concerned. The face I have "tinkered" over so much that it lacks firm modelling & looks rather meazly. But I think its outlines better & the rest will come if I mistake not. . . . I find that I begin to attach more and more meaning to the accessories and their symbolism. I do not know what has led to it: but I think it has been the study of the inner meaning of such things combined with the new

---

wharves where picturesque bits are always available. Stetson would occasionally neglect to bring his sketch book. But he would jot down on backs of letters, on any scrap of paper handy the things that appealed. Then in his studio he would work them out, his retentive mind giving him the proper colors." "The Dean of Providence Artists," *Providence Sunday Journal*, Jan. 10, 1915, Stetson Scrapbook.

outburst of my old mysticism that I had subdued in great measure, and which was fanned into life again by the study of Rossetti & his disciples— his disciples, yes, but only of any of them as I have read, for I have never seen their pictures. Within a few days Mr. Mason has brought in a volume which has a few drawings by Burne-Jones & Richmond* & I have seen an engraving or two of Rossetti's but that is all. I found in what was said of them all just the things that I have felt for a long time & I saw how in 8 yrs. painting I am with their aims & loves. I do not think they will influence my work for ill, for already they have given me more faith in my own aims. . . .

Once more I have essayed to have a sonnet published. Why I want to publish I *can't* tell. I have sent something like ten of what I think my best to the "Atlantic." I really do not think it will result in their accepting any of them. One must try—*I* must at any rate. . . .

MAY 10TH "83—5:45 P.M.

A weary day. At work serenely on my Greek: the head looks better; I have taken off lots of width & made the shadows more tender. The drawing of it is a *little* better—but alas! where is the beauty of maidenhood that should be in it? It looks stiff and homely—and as if painted, rather than as a beautiful breathing mystery. But I will persevere: may be it will yet come with study & experiment. . . .

SATURDAY, 12TH MAY, 1883. 2:10 P.M.

. . . I feel that I am in a very peculiar mental condition; cannot hope to explain it or define it. I only know I feel a tremendous earnestness for Art and as if everything that I am surrounded with is trifling in the extreme. The latter must be overcome. I must clench my fists and by sheer will power bear up in Art. I have a hard fight before me, for the public will be long in recognizing whatever's of good my work may have, for the good will be for long sadly obscured by the bad qualities. But if I *can* bear to the end, I do believe that the bad qualities will certainly leave one by one. I fear most that my physical strength will give out before it can be done. I am sure there is no one who guesses at the work my brain is doing—for to be sure, there is little

---

*Edward Coley Burne-Jones (1833–98), British painter and decorative artist, was for a time a follower of Dante Gabriel Rossetti. Sir William Blake Richmond (1842–1921) was also a Rossetti admirer and a Burne-Jones colleague.

fruit of it yet to show. What with literature and painting, and the constant needful thinking about the wherewithal for this and that I am on the rack from morning until midnight. My sleep of late seems not to rest me. And I feel it: for I used to wake fresh and strong for new fights; but now—I am never rested. It is surely true that I am not yet fitted into my place and I have got to fight desperately for power to think clearly and to fix my conceptions and those fleeting glimpses I have of Beauty. Until that is done I really merit nothing from the world but mercy & charity. I must prove to the world first that I *am* a prophet or they will not even stone me honorably.

God help me to still hold out! . . .

I sent Charlotte last evening—a blank sheet of paper. I *could* not write her a letter, and I wanted her to know that I remembered her, and wanted her to think of me enough to surmise why I sent it poor heart! Why *will* I still cling to my love of her. Oh but I do love her with my whole soul!

TUESDAY, MAY 15TH 1883, 1:50 P.M.

I was not surprised last afternoon to find a letter from Charlotte awaiting me at home. I confess to some strange surmise as I saw it, but not for an instant did I allow myself to think it symbol of her heart's return to me.

She says that she must make the blank sheet I sent her the excuse to write me.

The only plausible idea I have hit upon is that you longed unutterably to send me some sign—just to let me know that you were alive & loving still, and would not write because I had asked you not to. . . . My love! My love! (surely you *are* my love, for I have loved you and none other;) if your heart cries so for utterance, write to me as often as you will. . . .

Then she says that it was my own will that has kept me from her these "five long Sunday nights" and that there are yet six more before she leaves the City (for Ogunquit, Me.) "and always Sunday night am I at home & dressed, as though you were to come. Write if you will; I fear my heart is gone too far to turn at Word of yours."

Then she ends with an exhortation:

Live strong, pure, and self sacrificing; because it is right. I do the same, God helping; and happy or not, we live, and the world is better. Our lives have touched and parted for the present, and if they meet again we cannot tell. God direct us!

I have few words. I do not altogether understand my own feelings regarding it. Literally I have but *one* hope—that I may be strong enough to bear whatever comes. The poison, if it be poison began to work in me however, and an overmastering desire to see her came to me. I put on coat & hat & went. She was much surprised to see me, and threw her arms about me and stood at gaze for some minutes. Then she exclaimed how glad she was to see me once more. After going within, she took my hand & looked at me—would not wish me to talk for awhile—wanted to gaze and feast herself after so long a fast. It was rather awkward: I tried to talk about my doings to a slight extent; told her that I felt I ought not to come but really wanted to see her: told her about my plan of getting money enough together so as to go to Europe about the middle of June, as an emigrant—that is to go on passage money & a two weeks board & begin life all over again, & not come back unless father or mother should die & the other need me. She listened and said she was glad I thought of going—it was a faint gladness however. I forgot to say that I did not tell her I intended to give up all here and not come back until later in the evening, when she became a little downcast & said "But, dear, you will give me your address!" And why should I? "So that I could come to you if I should want to." Oh, but I'm not counting on any change in that direction: I've fully made up my mind not to marry—any but you,—and I have no thought that you will find me needful enough. "But how many years will you give me to decide?" said she. It is unnecessary that I should give any. I am not of the retaliating kind. It is not certain that I go. I am trying to make it so; said I. "Oh I hope you may go: it will pay me; I shall welcome any pain that seems as recompense for my giving up," said she. (And yet "it is right"; yet she would be pained for doing "right"!) I fancy that those sayings were the most valient of the evening. She wanted to talk over the whole affair again & argue about it: she was full of prayerful interludes and impulsive *da codas*. She crept into my arms and kissed me over and over and told how more than glad & thankful she was to see me: and how happy it made her. And a thousand other contradictory sayings; incident of two sides of her speaking alternately. It certainly is true that she does not understand herself, and that she is seeking far to defend her position. And she is simulating a certain form of happiness born of "Right doing" until she really believes that she is happy and acting very gloriously. The only thing that will teach her how much she loves me & what my love is—is to *lose* me. She feels too sure of me. If I could die—ah, if I might, then she should know for certainty. I did dream a few nights since that I went to C[ape] Breton alone and went rowing in the strait of Canso. The town's people at Plaster Cove thought me lost, and the report got home here that I had lost my life in the strait. I heard of it. I have a dim remembrance of Charlotte's knowing it—but the air grew a lurid blue-sea-green and I woke. It would require some such episode as that to awake her fully. There is no way of bringing it about honorably. To commit suicide would be to add unnecessary misery to her & rob myself of what I would have it accomplish: and as for any accident's bringing the untrue report about it is not at all probable. She said—"I was just thinking—suppose my physical strength should suddenly give out, that upon which I build so much, & I could not work, but had to lie about almost idle. Oh how the pain would grow, from thinking of what I had lost!" It was apropos to my asking her to send for me if she were ever very sick. And she said she most certainly would. It is certain that some great pain or great calamity to one of us must come before she is made to see love in his nakedness. Oh Lord God, let it be *to me*, and let it come soon!

I confess the evening was painful & to me unprofitable: I confess her caresses did not move me although they were beautiful in the extreme: I confess her prayers seemed unhealthy and apologetic rather than the fervent desire of one who wants the Right. *She* wants to be shown that life *from* me is right, because prejudiced that way: for it is easy to see that any inclination she may have to come back is crushed out. It is very strange to see how she clung to me & caressed me and gave every honest evidence of love and then, or meanwhile even, sought to prove that she was doing a nobler & wiser thing to give me up.

There is falsity some where in it. And I shall be shown what it is. When I see it I beseech that I may have enunciatic ability given me to show it to her. . . .

9 A.M. MAY 16TH ''83

The sonnets—all of them were returned by the "Atlantic" editor. It is what I expected; am not at all disappointed; nevertheless I would like to know why. It is clear enough that they are not excellent else they *would* have retained some of them; but wherein their lack of excellence lies puzzles me. Is it in rhythm—is it in obscurity, is it in lack of concise presentation of the subject? I do not know. Oh well, it matters little! I will keep them and in a dozen years or so may be able to see the truth. Would that I for one short hour could see myself & my work as others see them! It is the blindness of the fight that makes one distrust self. If one knew just what he had to overcome the battle were half won. I feel *now* that this will be the last time for long if not forever that I shall try to have a manuscript published. And in these cases it was not wish for fame at all or "to see myself in print" but to try to find out if my work had merits. That the idea which I sought to convey was good & true I have not the slightest doubt. . . .

A lovely morning for our Auction—and if gold is as plenty there as sunshine in my room we shall be rich indeed therefrom. . . .

2:10 P.M. 16TH MAY

Well, our sale is done: & it was not an overpowering success. Few, very surprisingly few assembled and the bidding was far from lively. The whole 50 pictures sold for $500–, my share of which is the largest, say $125–; out of that comes the expenses—so that I shall probably get $100 clear. It is a little consoling to know, 1st that my things averaged as much as the others & 2d that they were bought by good people, notably Mr. James H. Coggeshall, Dr. [Edward S.] Allen and Lawyer Miner, and I think Dr. Kingman. It is very surprising that they sold at all considering the number present. Mr. Miner bought certainly half of them.

But above that when home I found a letter from my Love the key note of which is "I suffer." Oh, it was good to know it, not that the suffering is pleasant to contemplate, but that her "torpid heart" awakens. I must copy most of it for I would not lose it.

"May 15th" 83

I have an odd fancy that it will comfort you a little to know how sad I am.

O my dear love! I thank you for coming, for you have awaked me to a pain I had not felt before. Not remorse nor pity, but a genuine selfish pain, a sense of loss, a hungry ache.

How greedily I drank in the pleasure of your presence! I could feel the happiness pouring in at my eyes in a great continuous wave as I sat and looked and looked at you. And in the touch of your dear hands and the pressure of your face to mine I realized as I have never done before that there is no other in the whole wide world who can so touch and comfort me.

O I am *glad* you came! This is what I should feel, alone, uncomforted, bereft. I wish you would find and read over again that little poem which was one of the first I wrote you, ending

> "And I think of the hours of hopeless grief
> Which I know I shall have to see,
> Till I long to turn from my journey wild
> And throw myself like a tired child
> In the arms that are waiting me."

I have been thinking of that this morning with saddest foretaste. Go my darling. It is right you should. I am glad you are going. I am *glad, glad* to be assured that I *shall* have my share of the pain. It is not often that I feel weak. And then I cry for you with every voice that is in me—O I *want* you!

Well is it that wide ocean and foreign land lie between us in that day. *Let* me ache, I well deserve it. I am to see you once more. O let nothing hinder it! Tell me when you are coming! And my darling—O be true to me for a year or two yet! O do not let me come and find you gone. Forgive me this please. It is not a "Sunday letter." You should know of my weakness who hear so much of my strength. Give me one year's grace before you shut your heart. Love, I suffer.

Strange cry is that "Be true to me!" It seems very like as if my longing, my pleading with Love in daily strife were to be heard and the object granted. I *dare* not hope it yet. . . .

SATURDAY, MORNING: MAY 19TH ''83

Much to write and no spirit to write it. If ever man was humbled—if one who was not very proud could be so humbled—I am. It came in this way: The vexing question why are my sonnets not good? overcame me. Would Mr. [Charles] De Kay tell me? Did I want him to know that I had written? And I concluded to send to him all that I sent to the Atlantic and ask him. Send them as the work of a "dear friend" whose age I described & his puzzle as to their lack. They were returned this morning with a most kindly letter: I have learned what I wanted to know. His merely private opinion is: "to advise my friend to consider sonnets the amusement of vacant hours, not a serious matter for publication. I have marked a few technical errors of the kind that give offense to magazine editors, but the work is so slight, so little above the ordinary run of verse, that perhaps no criticism were better. I am sorry to give such a verdict on someone whom you doubtless prize very highly—and would be glad to be converted. But I see no promise in these lines. It may console him to know that many people see quite as little in my own!"

The rest of the letter is talk of art & friends.

Now without *his* knowing it, I see myself as I am seen by those who have seen my rhymes. Oh blind fatuity! I wanted them to be good, for I love good work. I wanted them to be full of deep feeling, for God knows how deeply I felt, how pitiable it is that any so miserable a veil as grammar and sound should keep one burning soul from another. And it was grammar and sound:—no, he saw *no promise in them*. I am most thankful for his words— most thankful. I have asked myself over and over why I seek to write and have had no reason but that "I feel like it." That makes it clear that I have no reason at all. And doubtless he softened it some, supposing that I loved "my friend." What then is the truth? They are good for nothing! Better burn them—better rid myself of them. Poor cripples—I love them a little—what are they good for—let them go. All I can do is to color—I "give *promise* as a colorist"—how barren a life were that where only color gave the lie to insane things!

Yes, I'm glad I sent them. Any dreams of making good sonnets will now die at the first breath. I must get them back from Charlotte & Mrs. Cresson. My poor heart-aches shall not be laughed at by chance seers because of bad grammar and rickety metre. They must be sacrificed.

My painting is of like sort, I suspect. That fact strikes at the root of my whole life: if these things into which I put my utmost feeling and honest work are hollow—what can be all else which I have thought I felt so deeply and loved so well? Is my whole life a lie? I'm in sad state *that* is sure.

I can do no better than to strive on.*

Thursday another letter came from her telling that they were not coming that night: that her eyes were red and heavy even after a night's sleep, and her heart heavier: that even the clear sunshine did not comfort. "O for a smile of yours, or even the tender sadness in your eyes! Would not a year of this prove that I needed you?" I had sent her a letter that noon, but that decided me to go to her at once. So I spent the evening. We said scarcely a dozen words: she was unutterably sad, and gave her wealth of love all back. She was glad she was suffering: said she deserved it. She needs me. But what am I to be needed! Oh miserable!

I am almost decided to give up keeping this Journal. Life is so fickle, and I of so little use that it seems silly. I am reaching nearly to the time when

---

* Grace Channing summarized this entry: "Now occurred a thing which was for Walter of the utmost seriousness, and which has angered *me* for years. He was absolutely driven to 'know' what his sonnets were worth, critically viewed, and had the unlucky inspiration of sending them to Mr. Charles De Kay, as the work of 'a friend,' for which he asked a frank opinion. I dare say Mr. De Kay pierced that ingenuous disguise. He wrote back a kind and courteous letter—which fairly prostrated Walter, out of all proportion it would seem to the importance of the event. But his heart was much in poetry, and he thought Mr. De Kay knew. He himself wondered at his blind faith in later years, when he could see for himself how very poor is Mr. De Kay's own verse. At the moment he accepted the verdict as final and without appeal. . . .

"The gravity of the thing lay not in the discouragement to Walter as a poet, but that he was already in a state of depression and at the end of all hope, so that it reacted to make him doubt himself all through, and amounted to being one of the terrible crises of his life; he never, in after years, regarded it as less than so. He at once concluded his verse was useless, destroyed most of it, and planned never to write again." GEC to EBK, undated letter, p. 161.

I shall not need it as confessor: a time to which I have been brought by painful stages, and in which settled bitter bearing of things in reticence is my only hope. But oh! my heart is here—*can* I destroy all. I think I can: I think I must. I will ask her if she would like to have me destroy all, for it is as much [a] record of her as of me. If she says yes—it shall be done.

My model came yesterday. She is, I know not what, but I think an octoroon of Spanish or Italian mixture. At any rate she has a lovely face.

22D MAY, ''83. TUESDAY, 9 A.M.

Very rainy with thunder and while I try to use myself to the dim light (or I may say *pale darkness*) I will write. The days of last week after my last entry—indeed there was only Saturday—were terrible. I cannot remember many days in my life when I had been so weak as I was Sat. The sonnet matter seemed to waken all of my sleeping pain and caused a retrospection & introspection that were the forerunners of an utter breaking down Saturday evening. I could not conceive that I had done one good thing—not with the spirit of the "convicted" ones in prayer meetings, but in sober truth. I only saw that what pleased of that I had done was because my thoughts had been dressed in a way to deceive the pleased persons. *Color* had blinded them to the truth. Failure on failure came before me pitiably—but I must not write of it: I told it all to Charlotte in Sunday's letter, told her about the sonnets; asked her to burn them; told her of how it seemed to strike at the foundation of my art, as I had believed most sincerely that deep feeling would communicate itself to work even if the material part was not perfect; and I told her how I had to begin life over again in many ways, and how hopeless it seemed since what I failed to do was most certainly the result of a wrong training, of habit and environment and only in the way dictated by training, habit, and environment could I try to get out of my state, and it was like traveling in a circle although each turn seemed to twist the bonds tighter & tighter.

Well, Sat. eve. I wrote a letter to Mrs. C. asking her to burn what she has of verses. *Sunday I burned my old journal*, 939 pages of foolscap. Oh how hard it was to do! Therein was a most minute record of all my life from the simplest thought to my speculations on God & man and art. It began when I cared nothing for human beings, when all the entries were innocent delight about the flowers and fields and birds; about the colors of the sunset, the shape of the clouds, and how the shadows came from the east and the stars too—I always watched them from my window. Then these were naive accounts of hunting for minerals and what I had seen in those walks. Almost nothing about companions and nothing about games & romps, or even gymnastics of which I was exceeding fond—and proficient, too, in them. Then as I entered higher grades in school notes crept in about plants, (of a botanical nature) regarding male & female flowers, the exact way the lips of the corolla of this or that turned over—and a host of other would-be scientific observations, although all the notes closed with some thought as to why the flower was beautiful and sweet or poison or mild. Then chemistry & physiology came—and with the latter a love of human things, of men and women. How I loved those two studies! They seemed to put me into vital connection with the whole breathing world. But it was plainly to be seen that it was *life* itself that ———.

I don't feel like writing about it—I told all to Charlotte in my letter. And I carried it to her Sunday evening. Oh, how loving she was! She read it while I was there—and—oh how *can* I say it—it showed me to her as she had never seen me, and it changed all! In my arms with broken voice she told how she loved me—how she had found that she *needed* me—how she *could* not live best without me—how she must have me. And I must not try to tell what she said: nor could he who had seen the gods describe them for the glory. She promised or vowed rather to marry me. And settled it finally.*

No, I can say no more now. I am completely humbled: *but she loves me.*

I find I am not well this morning—I can't write.

25TH MAY: MORNING—1883

Wednesday eve with Her. She could not do enough to show me how she loved and desired me. Her state now surpasses any of previous months. That day I had received a letter from her—one that seemed almost divine in its love and eloquence—and it was one long passionate cry for me, and a plea that she might keep my poor verses. She argued well for it. She told how they had affected her—how she seemed to have my heart in her hand while she had them. So pointedly did she plead that I was forced to consent. I am so tired that I have not the spirit to write much. I am sick and want to flee all my work.

------

*Charlotte Gilman later wrote, "I demanded a year's complete separation, to recover clear judgment, but could not secure it. . . . Then, at one time when he had met a keen personal disappointment, I agreed to marry him. After that, in spite of reactions and misgivings, I kept my word, but the period of courtship was by no means a happy one." CPG, *The Living of Charlotte Perkins Gilman: An Autobiography* (New York: Harper & Row, 1975), p. 83.

I have spent a week daily drawing from Ella. It has done some good I think, notwithstanding the pain it is. One must win by pain. The Dr. [Edward S. Allen] was in yesterday and told me a little of the good Thos. Robinson had said of me—to the effect that he thinks I have more ability than any of the artists here.*

I slept little last night—very little.

SATURDAY P.M. MAY 26TH "83

Very unwell today: a subduing weakness—lack of tone—I know not what in all parts of me. Throbbing headache such as usual comes after great grief and love. I just sent away my model as I could not draw. (She has been of much use to me.)

Mrs. Coleman & her daughter—a delight, called this morning. Also Miss Carter, artist, and Mr. Bates.† Mrs. Coleman seems to be very fond of my Greek Girl—says she is, in fact, and in her soft mild way says she is surprised that a Prov. artist has painted anything so "lovely.". . .

. . . To believe one's self to be an artist in very soul is to be very *very* humble. He that knows that it is duty by God's gift to make apparent some part, great or small, of the Loveliness and Holiness that is unseen of most men, and who knows that he has but hands and eyes and brain and heart wherewith to do it must tremble and bow low. Who ever laughs at Wm Blake for saying that the artist must approach his work with fear and trembling only reveals his own ignorance and insensibility to what Art really is.

The praise that comes in words while it may serve to force one to strive more earnestly is of little real value. If one could see involuntary tears in the eyes, in a new rapture in the face of him who looked at his work one could be surer of progress and feel that after all he had not labored quite in vain.‡ Or if he knew that any were helped to live more beautiful lives, or to make their bodies more cleanly and sweet it were a precious thing. . . .

---

*Thomas Harris Robinson (1834–1888) was a member of the Providence and Boston Art Clubs, a student of Courbet in Europe, an associate of the Vose Gallery in Providence, and a life-long friend of Dr. Edward S. Allen. In Allen's view, Robinson was noted for his "rough and rugged landscape" paintings, for his use of "rude and homely material" to express his "artistic emotion." See Dr. E. S. Allen's *Memoirs of Thomas H. Robinson* (printed privately for the Providence A. E. Club, pp. 14–16), which contains an etching of Robinson by Stetson.

†Oil and water-color landscapes of Anna Coleman were exhibited at PAC in the 1880s. Elizabeth Carter, a teacher of watercolor at the Rhode Island School of Design, exhibited at PAC in the 1880s.

‡Following this passage, Grace Channing wrote: "It was given him to see both—many times, in later years, and in many faces and eyes." GEC to EBK, undated letter, p. 164.

[Charlotte] is going to accept about the middle of July the position of private tutor to Mr. J[ackson's] boy. She will live with them. It will be good for her, I think. She ought to get away from home. It is a good chance, and as usual has her mother's entire disapproval. The compensation in money is not large, some $210 a year, but the chance to be by herself, and among moderately refined & cultured people is a great thing. I fancy it will do much to reconcile her to "home life" if she has any remaining thoughts that war against it. She supposes I can call there ("if I want to") but if not we can write to each other as if she were in Washington or I in Europe. She seems to be much pleased over it. I think I am too.

She cautions me to work as well as I can to *save* all I can towards our "Home." That "save" is very pathetically read by me! What *can* I save. Ah God! what shall pay for coal & heat & clothing? And the rent!

But surely I shall do to utmost.

She is sorry I would not go to Europe, as she wanted the pain of being without me. She takes it as a sort of omen that I am to work out an original manner of my own. Who knows? It was a sad day that the deities were forced by us to flee the things of nature and we had no faith left in the workings for or against us of the gods. *I* do believe in destiny & unchangeable fate: and for me spirits are not all flown, though I may call them by other names than they of old time. But I cannot read omens. . . .

MONDAY, MAY 28TH ''83

Yesterday with her—that is, last evening. Love filled us and towards ultimate union I think we made advance. She was very beautiful, and her intense eyes had even greater depth than usual. . . .

She said a good deal in one way or another about my dying—tried to make me promise not to for long—until she had shown me how much she loved me and how she respected me. It is strange to see how things which she has despised before are coming to her as almost the chief. Surely her short exile of 5 weeks taught her more of life & love and her own heart than months of my companionship. And I think her time of teaching in Mr. J[ackson]'s family will do still more. . . .

Well, last night was sweet and profitable. Her mother is evidently turned against me again. She *will* not understand us and *will* believe the worst of us. She clearly thinks that while we are striving to be and do better and better each day that we are indulging ourselves in unmentionable lust. . . .

Mr. Bates had [John Selinger's] copy of Ruben's nasty "Shepherd &

Shepherdess" sent over. It is fine in color, one need not say it, I have set up some of my things near it to try the effect. I do not, humbly I say it, think that my color is tremendously inferior to it. It is not quite so clear perhaps—not quite so dashing. It is equally strong, and *I* feel it to be more mellow—softer in tone—less tiring.

I should feel ashamed to paint so obscene a thing. The nude! Ah God knows that is my goal, so to speak, but this thing is filthy in intent and the clothing but makes it worse. Such coarse types and lascivious gestures are unpleasant to say the least and certainly *not beautiful.* If all of Ruben's work is like this, and I fear much of it is notwithstanding the sonority of the color, I shall say gladly, goodbye Mr. Rubens. Let us turn to Titian and question him. Oh to see a Titian! Should I be disappointed and find only clever brush work and luxuriant composition. I can scarce believe it. There must be some painter whose works express that heavenliness which I feel could be in color.*

MAY 31ST "83 5:45 P.M.

This has been an exasperating day if such ever was. I have not heard a pleasant phrase today. At home things were all at "sixes and sevens" and at studio my work would not be done as I desired. I worked on the hand of my Greek but dear me! it is dreadful and as lacking in grace or intimation of a soul within it as a sea lion's paw. Then Mr. Hazletine called a short time ago & he was very hypochodriacal and swore at poverty and his fate. I do not blame him. In his case it is clearly fate. But how dismal he was! And I—I did what I could to cheer him, but it was a sorry effort for I too partook of his disease. . . .

Money *is* going; and I find myself in need of new clothing and *rest.* Nothing can be done without money. The price of a harlot is the price of a wife, and rest is an alien, and comes but rarely to these coasts inasmuch as but little gold is here. . . .

I need comforting. I too am human and lonesome and homesick. She

---

* Grace Channing wrote, "Rubens was a pleasant surprise to him; he wondered that his great, serious pictures were so much overlooked in favour of the 'carnal' ones; he admired him too more and more as a *painter* pure and simple. . . . Titian was a good deal of a disappointment. No one, anywhere, coloured *so* beautifully as he had hoped and dreamed. Of all the painters, I think his heart turned oftenest to Quentin Massys and a few such men. He loved above most things Massys' 'Entombment' in the Antwerp Gallery." GEC to EBK, undated letter, p. 166.

loves me I know: but I want her nearer. She belongs with me. What right has ill fortune and custom to keep my own from me!

God help me to endure with more patience.

JUNE 6TH, 1883. WEDNESDAY, 5:30 P.M.

I have had no spirit to write before. Things grew from bad to worse. Sunday I was with her. Oh how she showed her love. I wrote her a letter during the day and she read it then and it gave a tone to our whole evening. It was about myself. How I was growing weaker daily and my hair was becoming unsound. I ought to marry and have the rest from struggle with desire that it would give me. . . .

One thing she said warmed me a great deal. We were talking about my lack of cheerfulness; suddenly she threw her arms about my neck, and said with thrilling softness: "*I* know—I know what would cure you, what would make you cheerful: *a little child*. And I'll bear you one—you'll *have* to be cheerful then." And she was not far wrong. She is most precious and glorious and every fair quality in her has become intensified. She *is* wonderful.

This week she is in Boston. She was so unhappy about our talk that evening that she went the first thing to Dr. Keller (a lady) and asked her about it. She is her friend. The Dr. told her things which showed her that I was right. I'm *very* glad she went. I learned it from a dear letter I got today. Have written to her.

Monday I was very ill in mind and consequently half dead in body. I could neither eat nor sleep nor work. My friends wondered at my haggardness. And Tuesday it was still worse. I have rarely been as ill: I think I have been very near insanity. I have not been able to reconcile my ideas of what life should be with what it is. . . .

JUNE 7TH 1883 4:30 P.M.

This is another day of great depression. My work seems empty and useless. The heat worries me (although my room is cooler than anywhere else I go). Food at home is distasteful, unless it is a rare meal. . . . My digestion seems good, so I think I am not deceived in referring the disorder to the mind. In fact, I know it to be in the mind. . . .

This P. M. Mrs. Burt called.* She is now the art-note-woman of the

---

* Annie T. Burt showed her work in the 1883 PAC Exhibit, and was for a time an art critic for one of the Providence papers.

"Press" in Mrs. Selinger's absence. She had never been in my studio before. I showed her a few things. She waxed enthusiastic over my sleeping Greek; called the face "lovely" over & over with emphasis. . . .

If I can but get back my lost hope,—that which made me feel that my mission was to wed purity and sensuous loveliness, and shed glory on motherhood and that time & power to do the same would be given me, and that I should conquer all obstacles & enemies—I think I may do good things after all.

I scarcely touch now the hem of the garment of Beauty—I who have prayed to clasp her to my heart and kiss her lips with long kisses & fathom her deepest eyes. On my very knees I woo her, and if God has care of my prayers I shall win.

My dear Love will help me. She *will* marry me, she has promised it, and she wants to do it: there is no barrier now but *money*.

P.S. How many times of late I've found myself beginning a sonnet or some verses! I have not conquered that passion yet. May be with time it will die out.

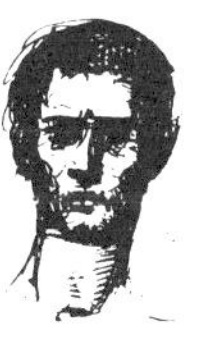 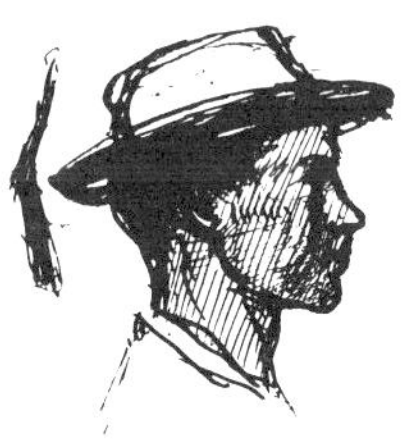

SAT. A.M. JUNE 9TH 1883

My soul is full of great perplexity but I feel above it all a most passionate longing to do good things, a most intense aspiration Godward, and desire to work for my fellows. It is all allayed by selfishness that is sure; by doubt of the possibility of my attaining in any degree. I feel that the clear longing for sensuous delightfulness that I used to have, and for which I am so fitted by nature, is wellnigh crucified in me. Gladly now would I choose renunciation of pleasure and all the joys God plainly intended man to have were all as it should be, for the help I might be to sorrowing humanity—! Yet it seems to me, judged by the light I have, that I am intended to work on Art. My shortcomings and fears caused thereby pour in upon me until hope is drowned. There *must* be a way out of my distress. . . .

IITH JUNE . . . 1:30 P.M.

. . . Charlotte showed me a drawing she made in the Museum of Fine Arts, Boston, done in a very few minutes. It was of the Venus Milo and the proportions were noted and the modelling suggested by the outline in a fine style. It was much better than I could have done it. She seems to have a natural talent for correct lines. I must do all I can to help her cultivate it. She would make an exceptional draughtsman that is sure to me. She draws, I guess, quite as well as I do—that is saying much, when the relative experience is considered and the time devoted to it. Whether she has a poetical inventiveness is to be shown in the future—I mean of a plastic nature. . . .

WED'S—13TH JUNE: 9 A.M.,1883

. . . Dorrance & Mason & Burleigh and Bates were all here in the early afternoon & Geo. Whitaker & Hazletine in the late afternoon. Geo. has a fever again for going to Nova Scotia. Particularly to Grand Pre and Horton's Landing where he could stay two or three weeks and find plenty to paint & study. Ah! how my heart beats at thinking of going, and how these enervating days my longing is for those breezes, meadows, and quiet hills: and for the glorious Bras d'Or. But I can see no possibility of going. . . .

10:10 A.M. JUNE 15TH 1883

Yesterday morning Charlotte & Miss Grace Channing called. It was delightful. I don't know when I have enjoyed anything of the kind so fully. Miss C. is a very sensible but graceful young woman; one who is refined and kind and very earnest: a good companion for my darling—one which makes me at rest. Showed them my pictures. Miss C. seemed to think my coloring interesting; wanted to bring her mother. I took my rope skipping girl upstairs where they could see it in a strong light. They really seemed sorry to go. Ah, how tender in a good way my love was! She made me feel new strength and helped my hope to grow a bit. . . .*

---

*Grace Channing wrote, "He indulges in a few comments upon me—all very polite and *one* funny, as that I was 'sensible *but* graceful,' as if there were an incompatibility. The important thing is that he decided I was a good companion for Charlotte—'one who makes me at rest.' If I made him at rest about *anything*, on that first visit, I consider myself excused for having been born!

"And there was no one to tell us that ten years almost to a day (four days out) was to be our extraordinary marriage. Truly we could not 'read omens'—either one of us." GEC to EBK, undated letter, p. 169.

I have done no work in three days, no painting, I mean. . . .

Mr. Cresson has sent home my water colors, having sold none. . . .

SAT. JUNE 16TH ''83 10 A.M.

At the 5:10 car I joined Charlotte at Trinity Square and we went to Pawtuxet. The ride down was quite instructive, revealing to me her tender treatment of children and showing me how strong and clean she was compared with other women, for those on the car were a fair sample of the multitude.

We took boat at 6 o'c and rowed up the river; I rowing most of the time but she joyously relieving me. And she *can* row too, quite as well as I; pulls a more steady stroke I should think and seems almost tireless. It was exhilarating to watch her strong, supple waist and shoulders sway back and forth and the muscles of neck and legs swell out firmly. I was proud of her, albeit it made my puny body seem still more meagre and weak. It would be very difficult I fancy to find her peer as regards physical things among women of her age. And I have cause to be sure that her purity is even as her bodily strength. We went almost to the old bridge, made fast the boat and went ashore and lay on her shawl awhile under an oak; barring the mosquitoes it was pleasant. She talked of her love of me, and of certain other things to my admiration. It grew dark though the "lady moon" shone clear. We found that we had not much time left so got aboard and floated down stream lying side by side in the stern touching an oar once in a while to keep us in the center of the stream. It was beautiful and full of a most exquisite idyllic poetry. We two together floating in the soft light towards port!

She looked at her watch & found that we had but fifteen minutes in which to reach the landing & get the 9:04 car for home, and we felt as if we must get that. So she took one oar and I one and we pulled. It would have been a charming sight, I'm sure, if there had been any to see. She pulled with great steadiness and energy and we reached the step triumphantly. She sprang ashore & ran full speed to stop the car while I paid Mr. Gardener then ran after her. Few, very few women could have done it, *surely*. . . .

. . . Our talk from the car to her house through the moonlight and the festive appearance of the colleges was of those ever deepening mysteries, life & love. . . .

She would like to marry me *now*, I know.

She is fearful lest I may be dead before it, she has a presentiment that somewhat terrible will take me from her, not that she has found me so needful to her, in some sort as a punishment for her former uncertainty. But she has done nothing that deserves punishment and if I die, it will be because my life could not find rest and hope enough to keep it alive. . . .

In glancing over foregoing pages it seem to me that the words *love* and *glorious* are the two of my vocabulary most used. They have been the most needed since she came. And I notice an ever recurring set of expressions for my feelings which if this were meant to be read would be terribly monotonous.

It is all iteration & reiteration of the staples of my life,—"I love" "she loves me" "I suffer" "I want" "I desire" "I pray" "I long to be worthier" "I would that I could do better work." There is the concentration of 472 pages of my journal. Yet with my habit fast upon me and with no sufficing reason for seeming to destroy it I shall probably continue to repeat the old words for long. They may have new meanings in them as my life deepens.

It does seem egotistical to keep a journal. How innocently I began it! At any rate it is an outlet of silence for those things which I should probably have to tell my friends and which would bore them. It is a system of drainage or sewage for this microcosm: an anodyne for over excited organs.

I have not painted this whole week. My utmost art work has been a design for Love singing a lullaby to Death and a few pencil sketches of children in action. I think my idleness will give me more energy for next week.

CHAPTER XI

. . . the curse of poverty

June 18 – July 28, 1883

"MONEY! I *hate* IT. But it must be had." "It is a sin that man's best qualities should be degraded by poverty and almost obliterated by having to give way to the cry for bread." But how to earn it? Should he give up Art—"even for a year or two"? Was this to be his "test of love"? The choice enraged him. "I feel my whole essence tremble at it," the "unwise economy" of a man sacrificing either of his basic needs—for creative expression in his work, and for human warmth and love.

From Walter's point of view, Charlotte's problems were quite different. Her responsibilities—to curb ambition and learn the gentle ways of loving—were so unlike his struggles—for self-definition, for economic independence, for professional integrity. In fact, he decided, "women do not seem to understand what a man's life is. Even woman's earnestness seems half play." "When one sees how much influence the man has over the maiden's life," he continued,

how his love reciprocated changes all her manners, thoughts, aspirations, and influences the creation of her ideal, one must shudder in fear that the man may choose to influence her for evil. For, I firmly believe, a lover has power in a great degree to make the loved one do as he wills. Of course it will depend much upon the character of the woman, but what will she not do to please her lover?

Whatever the price in conflict and depression, Charlotte *seemed* to learn her lessons well. She agreed not to read Walt Whitman (Stetson wanted her to learn that men could be "delicate and tender before she read of such slaughter-house rankness"). She repeatedly acknowledged her sinfulness. And she offered him appropriate respect—"as though you stood high and white upon a shrine and I lay at the foot, bringing as smallest offering all I had." Only occasionally was Charlotte somewhat self-assertive; she suggested, for instance, that he should be more cheerful. But for the most part, she emphasized the "elevated purpose" he inspired. "You have made me what I am. . . . *Your* love has conquered, as Good always does at last."*

JUNE 18TH 1883, 10 A.M.

. . . It is important for my own sake that I should record that I am the joyful possessor of just *one cent*. I should probably believe myself (in future years) to have been rolling in riches at this time if I did not fix it thus (??!).

JUNE 19TH "83—MORNING

Yesterday P. M. a letter from Mrs. Cresson inviting me to the Pier immediately, as her first visitor, chiding, or wondering why I had not written. I cannot go as I spent my last cent this morning to complete the postage on a letter to Charlotte. I wrote Mrs. C. last evening.

Have been destroying a lot of old sketches & subjects for pictures this morning. They increase rapidly. I cannot believe they will ever be of any value, so—away they go.

Very dark owing to heavy rain clouds and the full-leaved horse chestnut just without. Almost impossible to know what tints one is using. . . .

. . .

JUNE 21ST "83. 2:10 P.M.

. . . It would be a great and interesting study, that of tracing the development of a girl into womanhood and in love. He who does it must prepare himself for keenest pain and live purely & prayerfully. When one sees how much influence the man has over the maiden's life, how his love reciprocated changes all her manners, thoughts, aspirations, and influences the creation of her ideal, one must shudder in fear that the man may choose to influence her for evil. For, I firmly believe, a lover has power in a great degree to make the loved one do as he wills. Of course it will depend much upon the character of the woman, but what will she not do to please her lover?

Given a handsome man with wit and nervous energy and I think he can subdue any woman and win of her a certain kind of love.

---

*The above quotations are from diary entries (including quotations from Charlotte Perkins' letters) of the following dates: July 21, June 21, June 23, June 26, July 28, 1883.

With my love it is clear that she loves me and wishes to please me and make me happy. She reiterates how happy I make her, and I can see that she is delighted if she sees some gleam of joy in my face caused by her. And oh— what a longing and ardor has come to her! I tremble. My God, if, we cannot marry soon—pity us—pity us!

The desire to stay with her, to be ever near her was so strong last night that when I left a strange struggle was ready for me. All the way home I wrestled with the unseen some what that kept us apart; and I looked ahead frightened at what I saw—years going in ever increasing need and painfulness with no hope of fulfillment. I could see no chance of winning money enough to keep her & me. I could see no chance of painting some good thing which would take men's hearts and give me fame and money. It was dark, intangible, terrible. . . .

JUNE 23 83 SATURDAY, A.M.

. . . This morning while taking my bath I was struck with the softness of my skin, its fairness and the litheness of me; and it recalled Walt. Whitman's poems by contrast. And I remembered how I had asked her not to read them, as I did not want her to think all men such animals as Whitman describes them.* I wanted her to find love and the sexual relations something so holy and lovely that it goes into some hidden place to enjoy its holiness rather than stands in the market places and cries up the odor of its perspiration, the action of its phallus, the hairiness of sweating breasts—and all the Whitman delicacies. I remembered how I wanted her to have learned that man could be delicate and tender before she read of such slaughter-house rankness. But, said I to myself, surely she should have a chance. She is pure and honest. Let her read it free of all entreaty to the contrary. May be it is just the book to help her. May be I am all wrong; that I am too delicate— that concretions of bodily exudations are to be preferred to the sweet odor of newly washed limbs. Let her try it.

She has learned a little of the quality of my love. If Whitman's tales of harlots and dithyrambic explanations of generation can make her believe my

---

* About this time Charlotte's diary notes that a friend gave her a new copy of Whitman's *Leaves of Grass*. "I am obliged to decline as I had promised Walter I would not read it." CAP Diary, April 5, 1883, AESL. Years later, Whitman would become one of Gilman's favorite authors. In fact, there were only two volumes—Olive Schreiner's *Dreams* and Walt Whitman's *Leaves of Grass*—she carried with her when she travelled. "Having them," she wrote, "I had with me mountains and sunlight." CPG, *The Forerunner* 3, no. 7 (July 1911), p. 197.

love to be weak and ill—so be it. So I wrote her before coming down that my entreaty was at an end.

They may say all things are pure to the pure. It may be: I don't believe it. All things are pure to the *ignorant*. If I thought that I objected to Whitman because my own mind is filthy I would hang myself. It is *not* so. I do not object to the utmost nudity in art: I advocate it. I would have every child taught the principles of generation and the hygiene of the organs pertaining thereto. I would have love made as pure and natural and easy as the mating of birds *seems* to be, or the copulation of flowers. It will not, never *can* be done by such books as Whitman's. They must be wholesome, direct expressions of the truths, not filled with gore and gangrene and the odor of semen. That gore is, that gangrene and semen have odor none will deny, but any child could find that out without being told: but the child must be told that penis and semen and clitoris and womb are the sacred instruments by which God peoples his earth and that the divine sensations connected therewith are but to endear the labor connected therewith and to make us gladly accept it. The world might call me prurient and evilminded, but I object to Whitman, wholly.

But she may read now if she will. Her brain & heart are made of stuff too good, I think, to embrace his rankness.

25TH JUNE, EVENING

. . . Apropos of the letter I wrote about Whitman, she said that now she'd rather not read him. There was no need of it; that she was intent upon cleansing herself entirely of any such things. A characteric thing she told: She was reading in her Persian History that the Greeks took the vice of— some word I had never heard—into Persia. Her first impulse, she said, was to get the dictionary and find out what that vice was. But it came to her that she need not know: it was only a prurient curiosity that she would gratify and she need not tell it to any one. What good would it do to know the vices? So she *didn't*. And she don't know now, and won't willfully. She has been doing that sort of thing some time.

She wouldn't go to the "Museum of Anatomy," that vile show of monstrosities and sin, because she thought about it, and deemed I would not want her to, and that it was not in the cause of science. She wanted to at first—some of her friends went. Well, we learned much of each other.

I am tired—will write more later.

26TH JUNE ''83 MORNING

I see that I left the last entry unfinished, for no words of mine could tell of what we saw in each other, or how nearer together we came. But I went home feeling *surer* than ever; feeling a calm such as I had not felt, feeling that at last I was resting on *facts*. Though she told her little sins it made me feel that I was black indeed when I considered all my waverings and desires for things really foreign to purity and my real nature—desires that came of fleshly uneasiness rather than willful choice of them.

I went to my room at home, undressed, took my usual bath and quite naked—how else ought man to approach his God?—prayed—ah no words must tell how God knows that; enough. The burden of the prayer was that I might be less selfish; that I might live closer to my ideal of manhood, which is founded on the facts of life and must be true. . . .

I was reading in [Edward] Dowden's "Shakespeare—His Mind & Art" yesterday and was very much struck by his analysis of the character of Isabella in "Measure for Measure." It is almost a perfect description of my love's character. And so much so that I thought she'd be pleased to see it, so I copied it and sent it in the afternoon. . . .

I intend going to the Pier Thursday P. M. at 2:40 to stay—I don't know how long. My darling will go to Ogunquit [Maine] Saturday morning to stay two weeks. May my God keep her, even as I would. . . .

P.S. 26TH II A.M.

She has just left here! Came to bring a most dear letter, sweet as the morning, fresh as her face with its roses, soft as her lips in her kisses. . . .

And the letter: it is a paean, a threnody, a eulogy, a love song all in one. It begins by telling that she is "happy beyond words": that she is just beginning to feel the happiness.

Fear, Doubt, Shame stand near enough to enhance the radiance by darkest contrast: fear lest it fail of realization or fail in realization; doubt, horrible doubt of my fitness and capacity for taking or giving such joy; and shame at what I have been and am still beside what I *should* be to be your wife.

[Stetson adds:] Ah, beautiful—beautiful—

But Fear, Doubt and Shame fade like night shadows before the sun when I do feel what lies before us—what every month brings nearer.

I saw this morning a bit of a picture, just a glimpse of the bye-and-bye. You and I reading some book together and I dropping the book as the *consciousness* of it all rushed over me, dropping the book and burying myself in your arms. I seemed to feel a foretaste of that deep flowing peace of possession which you so need. Oh my dear love!

Then she waits a moment. Is it not holy to me, my heart? Hear her pulses throb and her sweet breath come faster!

I am reading your yesterday's letter. Reading it till sobs come, and tears. And as I read comes a feeling as though you stood high and white upon a shrine and I lay at the foot, bringing as smallest offering all I had.

I dare not write what comes next. It would stamp itself on me, I fear, and make me feel myself better than I am. It is too great praise for my poor efforts to be good and grow wiser & purer. But she says:

It humbles and raises me. I rise and stand with eyes on heaven and whole soul upstretched towards that divinest strength and loveliness I seek. To be a woman worthy of you!

Worthy of me! I feel like kissing the hem of her garment. Worthy of me—God, cleanse me, cleanse me—cleanse me! Worthy of me—of weak changeful me—striving and failing me—worthy! O my great Love, how you humble *me*! but it *will* help me to be better.

After a little about her endeavoring to do right, about her doing what she has *thought* right, and how if one does not that he must either do nothing at all or do wrong. She says:

And who but grows with trial, and learns with doing what they should not do? I half wish I could escape this haunting terror of your death. Only half; for I really would not seek escape from one smallest pain or grief that comes with you—*I* who have caused you so much! . . .

Your Isabella letter this morning. Only another proof of your great love. It is like (your love) the music of the spheres—too *large* to be heard. It is only as I grow to it that I can feel it. I can only say that your belief of what I am is in itself the greatest help to be that thing. Knowing as you know what my life has been, still I accept your trust—I *will* be all you think me.

My love, I want you. I want to be with you. I miss you. I feel an empty place that you alone can fill. . . .

I—I *had* to copy it! I would double the chance of its being saved to me: for in such words, blazing with ardent love, is my safety when the life-buffeting grows almost unbearable. . . .

JUNE 27TH ''83 9:30 A.M.

. . . [George Whitaker called.] Whitaker was quite critical of my Greek Girl.* He can't "stand" the color in the face. Evidently thinks the whole picture one of my inferior ones. George cares almost nothing for the subject of a picture: he wants "color." Now I do aver that I have as good feeling for color as any artist in Providence, aver it in my Journal, that is: and I insist that the color of the face is not wrong. Geo. says it's too natural: follows some of his theories. Others praise the color of the face and all the rest. Some think it is my best picture. . . . It bothered me some, but the denouement was that I was left where I have been all along—to depend upon my own criticisms of my work. Did one but change his picture to suit the fancies of his critics he would never finish one canvas—indeed, he'd "finish" all of them. One *must* paint just as he feels a thing ought to be—as nearly as his mechanical skill will permit. One who *wants* to paint rightly is apt to pay too much heed to his critics especially if they be artists.† But my! I find that my likes are incomparably more broad than any artists that I know. They are bound to a creed, to a theory—how can they progress when they insist on making every picture conform to some preconceived and unchanging model. Every subject has its own treatment—every subject makes a law for itself: and as for the subject being of no account, it is the subject that ought to determine the mechanical workmanship. An artist must have poor feeling who paints Jesus and Aphrodite with the same colors and same touch: or a storm and a calm with the same sort of brush work. . . .

JUNE 28TH—THURS. 1883. 8:30 A.M.

Today I must bid goodbye to my little book and this room with its poor evidence of my life. I go to visit the Cressons.

---

*George Whitaker later said that the *Greek Girl* (or *Sleeping Girl*) did not "agree with his theoretical idea of color. . . . He proposed alterations in the color scheme, which in themselves might be desirable but which would alter completely the sentiment of the picture and the meaning of the figure. I don't think Geo. has very keen sensibilities as regards the figure." Diaries, Nov. 21, 1883.

†Although Stetson frequently received favorable reviews, he bitterly resented the majority of critics. In an A. E. Club lecture, he called them "stupid," "ordinary," and often "mercenary to the last degree." They dash off their opinions and in "one short hour a whole year's work, perhaps the work of a whole life time, is judged, and all that is beautiful or true or helpful, or suggestive in it, is obscured perhaps to the public by a flippant phrase, a smart allusion, or a bright bit of vulgarity." The helpful critic, Stetson continued, "should be like the expounder of holy scriptures seeking meanings, not inconsistencies." CWS, "Criticism," A. E. Club Lectures, April 23, 1891, Club Papers no. 143, pp. 4–5, 9–10, RIHS.

I went to her, after dining with Putnam last evening. . . . Oh, heart, name the loveliest thing you know—she surpassed it even as the archtype the type. Such a wonderful minglement of passion and purity, such a full yielding, nay, *giving* of her every beauty that I am feeling this morning that it must have been a magnificent and lovely dream. . . .

I shall once more seal this Journal and leave it directed to her. If I come no more back————.

If I come no more back it shall be hers: this picture of my strength and weakness, my love and sorrow shall be hers. . . .

She gave me the letters she wrote during "her exile," the Sunday letters. They are *so* honest, so painful, so strange! We cannot wholly understand it yet. She mourns that it could be. I am glad she has seen in time, that she has known that I am hers—and the world is as nothing beside. . . .

JULY 9TH 1883. A.M.

Back once more: back from the best of friends, from clouds and waters which are mockers of my own deep coloring—intensest blues and purples and gold—rocks that are rich with browns and flesh tints and blacks & greens, and pastures full of lush vegetation of living green. Back from the rural quiet of farm life and the sound of the ever moving waters. Back from the kind words of my friends to poverty & dismalness. Ah, *such* a change! No one knows—no one knows. Everything there was delightfulness. Everything here is sadness and misery. Out of the refreshing coolness of salt air into the burning dusty heat of the city; home to find mother very sick, father miserably unwell and sorrowing at lack of money; and yesterday morning Caroline [his sister] was brought home—that is, to our house—sick. It was a great change. Home to small quantities of unvarying food, cooked not to my taste, but done with the listlessness of illness. There was not *one* pleasant thing to welcome me, although indeed I am thankful to see them all alive once more. . . .

. . . [Mrs. Cresson] said that she did not have one cent that was her own—if she had—ah, if she had it would not be long before I was in some other land and with my darling to wife. No, she had nothing; she was dependent upon Mr. C. . . . If she could but get him to do that desirable thing—let me have a few thousands and take pictures in payment, how glad she would be to do it. . . . She said that when she saw me so miserable and my way so hard she felt like taking me right into her arms, and comforting me: like giving me all her jewels to save me. But she could not. Mr. C. would buy for her diamonds to the amount of thousands but he would not give her the *money*. She said, also, that often she had felt guilty at putting on a costly jewel or dress, knowing how in want I was: and often she said she had said to herself: "Would he not despise me for wearing these costly things knowing as I do how he and his family suffer for want of money?" And she said once or twice she had taken off her jewels for that reason—they hurt her. But she could not help it. She could have money for those things—but for what she wanted it most—none at all. And yet Mr. C. is very very kind, in his way. Kind to her, and kind to me.

He and I also had a talk: a well meant talk on his side; but impracticable, very impracticable was the advice. He *was* very kind, but it did not advance me a bit; though he did not help me I liked him better for it. . . .

JULY 9TH AFTERNOON

A letter from my darling. [Charlotte was staying with Martha Luther Lane and her family in Ogunquit, Maine.] It is exquisitely beautiful to me. The substance of it is that she is discontent with the people she is with & wants me. . . .

JULY 10TH ''83 3 P.M.

. . . Painted on the girls jumping rope this morning. . . . It seems to me strangely good in color. On that score it ought to be a success when exhibited, I think. Hope I can get some one to make a frame for it—and trust me: I would that I had money enough wherewith to buy one outright.

JULY, 11TH 1883 2 P.M.

[The secretary of a local Woman's Temperance Association,] . . . a lady named Wilkes . . . came to get lessons in chalk drawing. Wants to illustrate her lectures, picturing the wicked wine glasses and lusty beer barrels that amorous maids and inexperienced youth may flee them affrighted at their fearsome forms. She was perhaps aged 50. Never had drawn; didn't know anything about it. A hard case! I concluded to try her at 75 cents a lesson: I felt peculiarly generous after I found that she had not come to try to turn me from my fondness for Nieosteiner & Claret. . . .

Dorrance came in and talked so much about dress & that sort of thing that it made me feel very shabby even in my good new gray suit that fits so admirably, and set me about anxious to shake him. . . .

12 JULY ''83 FORENOON

I am so weak today that painting, or indeed anything, seems next to impossible. The truth is—and a truth that few of my acquaintance would believe, I suppose—that I do not have enough to eat. Our breakfast this morning consisted of bread and oatmeal porridge. Both were good, but of the latter there was not enough, and of the former too much. My breakfast consisted of about two tablespoonfuls of oatmeal and a half cup of coffee. When we do have plenty as to quantity, it is not such as suits me, my wants, and I have no appetite for it. The result is that I am weak and hungry half the time, or more. It was such a change to live at the Cressons. And it was a violent contrast with home fare. I cannot complain: I should earn more money for father, then we could live better, although mother seems too tired of cooking to make efforts towards nicety and nourishment. It is a great mistake, and I do believe that a good deal of my lack of power to *do* in art is to be laid at that door. It breeds hopelessness & produces a low state of the system not at all an incentive to nobler work. I do believe that such living is degrading. And then to have to eat in the room where cooking is done takes away all relish for even good things. I see no way out of it just at present, though surely it has gone far enough.*

I *can't* paint this morning. I've tried.

Wrote to my darling last night.

13TH JULY—MORNING FRIDAY.

. . . My darling's letter was very loving, . . . albeit she hurt a bit by what she said of my sadness. Ah, she does not, and indeed cannot, yet understand why I have any reason to be sad. [He quotes her letter:]

How a man, young, pure, and wise; with noble work to do, an art which makes his work a long delight, and a selected wife who gives him all her heart *can* furnish with its growing love, can be so sad is more than I can see. Think of the things you *have*, not what you want and can*not* have as yet.

---

* Following this entry, Grace Channing wrote: "This was a serious matter; how often we discussed it in after years. Our modest table was always a delight to him—the tiniest of eaters— as he always was. . . . But I made a perfect study of that one department, and do honestly believe it helped to prolong his life by years. He used to say that he never knew what it was to be comfortable 'digestively' until he married. Charlotte was an admirable cook, you know; they say all 'literary' women are so, and so far as I am aware, it is the case. . . . But how awful that under-nourishment of *such* a system, just during those years of youth." GEC to EBK, undated letter, p. 178.

Sweet, I should love you *more*, honor you more, respect and trust you more, lean on you with more confidence and peace if you were different in this.

That is the only thing in a tenderly beautiful letter of 11 pages which hurts. And that does: not with any doubt of her, not with the slightest resentment, but wholly because it shows that as yet she does not wholly understand me, and as much as she might if I were different. It is a strange way to make one less sad—that of telling how she dislikes it (for I *can't* be less sad until I have changed many things) and how she loves me less for it. And I who know the reason for my sadness, can see that it arises from a good quality rather than an evil. She, God willing, shall live to see the day when I shall be set right in her mind.

I wrote her a hasty letter upon it, which I am sorry for now: I ought to have said nothing, only waited until she has grown still more, when I am sure she will see more clearly. And it does seem very mean that I noticed what I didn't like and wrote of it rather than that world of beautiful tenderness that surrounded it.

After all, I fear I need these shocks and pains to keep me nearer and in more living appreciation of my dependence upon the *Over All*. When I have put my desires into tangible shape *then* I shall not be misjudged for long. Oh for more patience, for more hope. It would be better if I could put my desire for companionship, my love, and all that I so brood over far from me until I have made money enough to make the most important step possible. And yet, I doubt if mortal man could do it. Love, as I feel it, penetrates every atom of being. It cannot be laid away like a garment to be worn Sunday nights and feast days only. . . .

Though she is so brave and says things so cheerfully and hopefully I sometimes catch a stray sound of longing and sadness in her letters. Yes, she says not ten words after that little sermon about my sadness, that she *must* put *her own* sadness from her—that she has no right to feel so while she has me. . . .

Truly did Rossetti write about kisses that in each we should remember the first and forebode the last. If we could always keep that in mind there would be less foolish talk (foolish only *relatively* I mean) about trifles compared with the grand truth that Love, divinest of all things vouchsafed our lives, had taken sanctuary in our hearts.*

God, be merciful!

———————

* Following this entry Grace Channing wrote, "Another of his favorite sayings, . . . if he built a home of his own he would grave above the door—was—'Remember Love; Forget not Death!'" GEC to EBK, undated letter, p. 179.

Mrs. C's letter was full of a wrung heart. She feels very pained that she cannot help me. . . . She is going to wait until a propitious moment and then read [Mr. Cresson] my "pathetic" letter, as she calls it. Now I did not write that letter so as to be pathetic, did not think of it, nor did I write it to be read to him; and I can't say that I want her to read it to him. What pathos there may be in it I'm sure he will think weakness of will or intellect: and after all it will do no good, for though he is considerably kind to me, I'm sure he is too good a business man to risk $1500 or so on a fellow like me. I told her that the *real* [help] would be for him to show me some man who would advance that amount of money & let me pay it in pictures to be consigned to some dealer for say five years at 10 pictures a year, I always retaining the privilege of paying it in cash if I should happen to have success. It was not written with the expectation of her telling him but as a sort of formula of what I felt would be the best thing. . . .

Read last evening in Schiller's "Aesthetical Letters." Very instructive! . . .

SAT. JULY 14TH 1883. FORENOON

. . . [Charlotte] goes today to the Jacksons' to begin the governing of their boy. It will do her good and be a school for her in the governing of our children—of which she talks so fondly. . . .

TUESDAY, JULY 17TH ''83 LATE P.M.

. . . Dr. Allen called. . . . He showed me an instrument used in cases of reversion of the womb, ingenious in the extreme. And we talked some of women and more of diseases. Now, though I believe Dr. A. to be a good man, a reverent man, and one who strives to be chaste in thought, I should not want him to attend my wife in child birth, nor yet any man else. He set me to thinking with new force upon that matter of male midwives and male physicians for uterine diseases, and I must say that my reason and my feelings pronounce strongly against them. I believe to be right the feeling that men have that they want the young girl who is to be their wife to be inviolate of man.

I shuddered to think of any physician (male) using an instrument of any sort in my love's holy place. No, God willing it shall not be so. There are women physicians: Why don't women employ them? I'm afraid they *like* to go to "the doctor." My love is so pure, so full of honor, and so just to me, I know that she would do nothing of that sort. Did she not go to see a lady,

Dr. Keller of Boston to be *examined* for my sake? For my sake examined, I mean, not to *a lady* for my sake. No, strong and free and pure is she, and she has a sense of beauty—and a feeling for the beautiful shudders at the thought of a man not a lover manipulating parts that have to do with the fashioning of new life.

If it were a matter of life or death it were different. In 99 cases of a hundred, if not more, it is useless to call a physician. Physicians themselves say so: and smile at the credulity of the poor women who suppose them necessary. Alas! some of them do too much, and childbed deaths occur too often. A physician is a noble thing—but a physician ignoble is the vilest of earth's mortals.

After Dr. went I went to dinner. Came back and finished my letter, telling of my thought apropos of the Dr.'s talk and quoting a deal from Schiller's "Aesthetical Letters" about the calling of an artist, for I believe her to be an artist. . . .

Am reduced to just 1 cent! Oh richness!

WEDNESDAY: JULY 18TH ''83 2 P.M. (THEREABOUTS)
. . . The Jacksons are going to Moosehead Lake the middle of August to stay until the middle of October. They will take Charlotte with them. As she says, that will be the longest time we have ever been apart. God keep us true to each other during it. And he will. Yes, we love each other truly enough to be true.

Painted on jumping girls this morning. . . .

THURSDAY, 19TH JULY, 1883 A.M.
I expect that my darling is lonesome, if not just a little homesick, for in a letter from her written yesterday morning, I think I feel traces of it. . . . [She] says frankly: "Dr. J. I confess I do not like. Mrs. J. I do. But what I miss in them, as in nearly all I meet, is the outlook—the aim and purpose and interest in life that we share with some others. And they have it not. . . ."

Ah, yes: how many have outlook and high purposes! She will find it so all the days of her life, unless it may be that she and I can find some little colony of similar men and women and spend our lives therein. The outlook? Increase of wealth and ease. The purpose? To have a quiet life and fill the small place in "society" well. That is about all that people care for. No wonder that she feels lonesome—even as I. . . .

She ends by begging me to write to her to tell her that I love her and am glad she is so pleasantly situated in many ways. I may judge wrongly but I do judge that she is not "pleasantly situated in many ways" and that she is characteristically trying to force herself to believe so. Ah, what a school for her! This is her first experience in not being her own master. She may think that they are to treat her as a daughter, but I'll assert now that they will never permit her to feel for long that she is any more than "only a governess" and poor Charlotte Perkins with a future. Oh what a school for her! . . . If I may hazard so much I will say that this will be the hardest year she has ever known. It is hard to feel one's self a servant, when one knows that in heart he is more fit to be served than to serve. But verily the good servant has his reward. . . .

P. S. Read or *studied*, last eve. Schiller's "Aesthetical Letters"* and some in [John Addington] Symonds' "Renaissance in Italy." My old fever for study and philosophy has returned in full force. It is because I feel vastly more settled in my love-life. I can *feel* what life, at its hardest even, will be with my darling. And I pray that it may come very soon. . . .

.   .   .

SATURDAY, P.M. JULY 21ST ''83

I had a good and strong letter from her this morning. It pleased me much. She is to have Sunday evenings for me to call, she says. I will try to go over tomorrow eve, but unless I grow better from a sickness I feel coming on I fear I can't. But oh, I want to see her very much.

She says:

Don't you fret about money. Why *do* you! If it seems right for me to marry you I will if you have any money or not. I hope to have some myself at any rate. There seems to me no sense in your feeling badly over that. *I* am here, and I love you, and I will marry you on as little as you dare ask—perhaps less. At *worst* you could stop painting for a year or two, and we could go out west and teach. Pity if you and I could not support ourselves. Fear not, sweetheart. So long as I love you and you love me there will be a way.

Bravely said, and out of a courageous heart, too. It is very strengthening to believe that she would do that thing: but she makes a distinction

---

* Stetson often said that Schiller captured his own perspectives on the purposes of art. In an A. E. Club lecture Stetson wrote, "Schiller says in one of his aesthetical letters: 'Humanity has lost its dignity, but art has saved it, and presents it in marble full of meaning: truth continues to live in illusion and the copy will serve to reestablish the model.'" CWS, "The Nude in Art," A. E. Club Lectures, Feb. 19, 1886, Club Papers no. 19, p. 5, RIHS.

justly in adding that little—"perhaps less." How *dare* I ask her to join her daily life with mine unless I can see *clearly* a way to support us decently. And I do not quite *fret*. It concerns me, and concerns her—this getting of money; more, it concerns father and mother. And to be indifferent to it would picture a strange heart and a sterner one than I have.

Money! I *hate* it. But it must be had. (Commonplaces most terrific.) She certainly is disposed to bear a deal of privation and I think she would do it with a certain sense of pleasure for love of me. Yet I am not so heartless that I could see her ill-cared for bearing it.

As to giving up my art—even for a year or two—oh I could do it, for her sake—but—is this the test of love I've wanted. If so I will do it. My *love is* equal to it: but I feel my whole essence tremble at it. Give it up? Two years? I doubt if I could go back to it. In some ways it would be most unwise. . . .

Oh the terrible lie it all is! The curse and thralldom of loving and having to give up the purest and best efforts of your life to win the favor. It should not be; it is incongruous, unbeautiful, false. Let me pierce this vile show and see the reality. Love is best of all. My love of her is true and steadfast. My art is the expression of my love of God and his beauty. Are the two incompatible? *They are not.* . . .

Oh that man should have to ask! That such cruelty should be, such unwise economy! Is it not plain that the two combined would produce great work and calm holy poetry. It is plain, to me. It is truth. And these things asundered! Things that I have sought to mate so earnestly. Keep art, give up her—Take her, give up art. I prayed & pray to marry the two. . . .

Women do not seem to understand what a man's life is. Even woman's earnestness seems half play. Why! things are tangible and must be put down, conquered, not compromised with.*

I must endure. . . .

It is a sin that a man's best qualities should be degraded by poverty and almost obliterated by having to give way to the cry for bread. But it hatches a desire to call things by their right names. No gloss of the *beauty* of poverty to one who wants to manifest the loveliness, the eternal.

---

*Grace Channing commented: "He never did compromise—never did yield to one temptation which threatened his art-life. On that side he was absolutely, triumphantly, a conqueror. And I am satisfied that he, to whom love was a necessity of existence, would have renounced all of us—Charlotte, myself, every love he ever experienced, put together,—before he would deliberately have give[n] up his high vocation,—*the* thing he knew himself to have been sent into the world to do." GEC to EBK, undated letter, pp. 181–182.

Poverty is damnable and degrading, even as great riches are to one who is vile. Born in it, bred in it, suffering from it, debarred by it from being my best self in every act, and hindered by it in my art, how can it be lovely and grand to me. I say that poverty to genius is *damnable* and nothing else.* A spur to exertion! It is a millstone hung about the neck of every noble thought and every delicate beautiful emotion.

25 JULY 1883. 3 P.M.

A letter from Mrs. Cresson this P. M. which wants me to come to Narrangansett this P. M. So I am going, as she thoughtfully sent me the money to do it with.

I was with my darling last night. Ah! God knows the glory of her love & the beauty that I deem it. I have much to write about her, but must leave it until I return. I shall come back Thursday.

JULY 28TH 1883 A.M.

Thursday night I came back from the Pier. . . .

Yesterday I worked all day long at ink drawings of the pictures (2 of them) I'm going to send to the Institute Fair.† They are *Allegro, Over the Dorrent Meadow* (30 × 40), and *Girls at Play*, (which is the chosen name for my girls skipping rope. The Blomidon I think I succeeded in doing well; but the *Girls at Play* must be done over. It lacks in color—that is in suggesting the rich harmonies of the painting.‡. . .

My darling's letter sent to the Pier is more than loving—it is enthusiastically loving, as many of her letters now are. She says: "I knew I was right in what I told you: coming here has brought me nearer to you instead of separating us at all.". . .

Farther on she says:

---

*Grace Channing wrote, "About the only time I ever knew him to use the word 'genius' in even indirect connection with himself. He *must* have had the consciousness of it." GEC to EBK, undated letter, p. 182.

†The New England Manufacturers and Mechanics Institute, *Exposition of American Painting* (Boston: The Institute, 1883).

‡Stetson later described *Girls at Play* (43 × 60 inches, canvas): "The figures are not drawn well, but I think they convey an idea of freedom & action. I am told it is a daring composition as to color. . . . I have worked especially to keep it from being heavy, yet to make it rich; to keep it from being glaring yet keep it brilliant." "Opera" Book, p. 33.

Sweetheart, please don't call me "Mrs. Stetson" even if a sister & governess & child are present. If I must have title instead of name let it be wife. But it strikes me that that is higher than Charlotte after all, and should be better kept. Let it be Charlotte when we must, "darling" when we may, and "wife" in low breathed ardor when I am in your arms. I wish I were there now.

Then she tells that it has taken her a long time to be able to say things like that.

Because with the wish comes thought that in present circumstances it could not be without unpleasant consequences, & that I do not honestly wish it. Many's the time I have not said "I want you" for that reason that in that place and time I did not want you. Often I would have wished for you at night, and then would say "no, I do *not* wish him here; for if he were I should be maid no more, and that were hardly worth one night's delight." But of late I have come to see and hope you will understand, that the wish ignores circumstances; that when I long for you as I did on Sunday night I mean that I wish I was out of all this and in your arms forever. It is with me now, that Wish, but I will look at it no more, (not often at least); I will work until the months fly like weeks and the weeks like days; and the time comes when heaven and earth shall melt away and we be conscious of nothing but that we two are One.

[Walter adds] That is very Stetsonian.

O may that One, one love, one power, one will and high endeavor, help the world! "If you can prove to me that we two together can do more than we two alone, I will marry you!" Strange wooing was yours; strange answer from a girl of the nature you now know me to have, to make to a lover. Ah! but I had not this nature then. You have made me what I am. *Your love*—unaided by art, unstrengthened by any alluring prospect of power, wealth, and ease, hindered by every force of my resistant nature and by opposition everywhere, and by poverty and fear of want—*Your love* has conquered, as Good always does at last; and by its steady pouring flood of gentle light and tenderest fire has won its one desire. Think of it, darling: that your nature has brought to you what no other force could have.

As I look back upon the fight I've been through, fierce fight with my selfish will and silent contest of my love with all her preconceived notions of life, I wonder—yes, I *wonder* that my love with no collateral help has won her. And I thank God. . . .

CHAPTER XII

. . . etchings and exhibitions

July 30, 1883 – March 13, 1884

ALTHOUGH STETSON still faced some major worries—about his drawing, his parents, his heavily depressing romance—the next few months showed some marked improvements. Several of his paintings were shown at regional but prestigious art exhibits; repeatedly he was attracting favorable reviews; and occasionally he even found money for hiring a model (Miss Annie Jeffrey was currently posing for a painting he would later call the *Sleeping Girl*.) Moreover, by January 1884, Stetson had organized a one-man art show: some 83 oil paintings, 77 water colors, his accomplishments of the last six years. In the "Preface" to the exhibition catalogue he bluntly stated that his work still had some problems. But if anyone "accuses me of . . . [having] no real love of nature and reverence for her beautiful laws," he wrote, "no earnest search for the meaning of her adorable mysteries, he accuses me falsely." *

Meanwhile, Stetson was also gradually developing a professional relationship with Beriah Wall, a Providence patron, who asked him to do a series of etchings for a catalogue of his art collection. For Stetson this was yet

---

*Charles Walter Stetson, "Preface," *A Catalogue of the Pictures and Sketches Exhibited by Charles Walter Stetson*, Providence Art Club, 1884.

another strikingly important opportunity: not only to bring him closer to the work of such artists as Corot, Daubigny, Couture, and Marilhat, but also to expand his reputation, to provide him with a larger studio, and to secure a steady source of pay.

Although Stetson was elated by these prospects, he still was troubled by Charlotte's alternating moods. At times she seemed enthusiastic about the marriage. "*She wants* now: wants as I dared never hope she would." But then again she would have a "relapse" in her loving, one of her "apathetic" times. Occasionally, at least in her more assertive moods, Charlotte argued that the relationship with Walter was the reason for her growing "weakness." But in Stetson's opinion, too often in her own as well, she suffered from "a form of insanity" instead: "It is all her old ambitious 'freedom' loving nature rising in rebellion against the 'weakness' of tenderness and love."

Whatever the reasons for the violent ambivalence, both Charlotte and Walter continued with the marriage plans. Perhaps it was because economic burdens had lightened so dramatically; or because both accepted Stetson's view of Charlotte's needs: that her "strange spirit" was "caused by physical things," by the delayed marriage, and "by restraint of sexual power." *

MONDAY, 9 A.M. JULY 30, ''83

Lovely atmosphere, soft blue and pale gold sunlight. Maybe the result of the aurora borealis of last night, which I saw when I came from seeing my Darling. Of course I did go to see her and right glad was she that I came.

She wants now: wants as I dared never hope she would: wants until I fear for the consequences. . . .

. . . Thank God for her! . . . If her need of me and my need of her increase in the remaining ten months as they have in the past two or three it will indeed be far better to marry if we only have enough to pay the minister and our board for a week. It will be safer, wiser; Sapere Aude! It takes some courage to be wise—but I *will* dare it. . . .

We were speaking about children. "I have heard of a child's being loved after it was conceived but never of children being *named* and *loved* before *marriage*. Ah, our Sigmund and Katharine!"

And it is strange, how that sweet dream of children has possessed us, even to the naming of them, and how she looks forward to their birth and rearing with longing and gladness. Rare woman! And *my* love!

---

*With the exception noted, the above quotations are from diary entries of July 30 and Nov. 26, 1883.

And if it should be—if it should be—we live all our lives childless! A son I will be to her as well as a lover and husband. . . .

*   *   *

JULY 31ST ''83 P.M.
. . . Charlotte's letter is written at 10:45 Sunday evening after I had left her. Among other things is this:

My darling! truly we need no more words; and there is nothing for it now but to wait with what patience we can until we rest at last. I don't want to talk to you. I want to lie with my cheek on your breast and let your heart speak to me in its own voice. I want to listen to that quick beating and answer it with mine and have no words. Sleep as I might I can imagine myself awaking and reawaking for very contentment—not knowing what at first, and then to remember—to touch you at will—ah! love, I am ashamed to be so impatient. The very glory of it should make the time as nothing. . . .
I can put all my heart in six words—
I wish I were your wife. . . .

. . . I feel more courage than for a long time. I *will* succeed sooner or later. I beseech the good God that it may not be too late to take my Love to bed and to have years of heavenliest habitation with her. She is beyond all words of praise, and my love of her is a steady glorious growth. . . .

.   .   .

MONDAY MORNING, AUG. 6TH 1883.
. . . Saturday evening, being full of joy, I wrote to Mrs. Cresson. It was the only joyous thing I ever did for her. Strangely enough, it occurred to me that my Love might not like to have another woman call me her boy, or me call her "my grandma"—Wishing to do all in my power to make Charlotte feel that I *am hers* I thought the truest way would be to write to Charlotte and enclose the letter to Mrs. C. and have her tell me if there was anything in it disagreeable to her. That I did. I took them both to her last night. My ride over in the car was rather harsh, but a perfect prelude to my darling's pure self; for on the front seat beside me were four harlots; and they talked loudly, and coarsely, and laughed forced hellish laughter. When I entered and saw the utter cleanliness of my Love, heard her love-filled soft tones and touched my lips to hers: Ah! The rest of the world vanished. . . .

After a while I asked her if she would have the letter then. She would. So, with a pretty gesture, she looked at the one superscribed Cresson, and took the other. She was pleased. "My dear love, you may call her grandma all you please!" said she. But she read on and when she had finished kissed the letter, again & again as a child might if it knew enough to feel the full meaning of it. Then as I desired she read the letter to Mrs. C. Suddenly she looked up and with a laughing face, but serious intent she said: "Why, I didn't know you could be funny!" I laughed in spite of myself. I knew long ago that the truest way would be to let *love* win her in utmost seriousness and dignity; and indeed I could not say funny things to her while love filled me. So she conceived the idea long ago that I could not understand fun as fun. I knew she would find it out in time. That letter, I fancy, taught her a great many things regarding me. She said herself that it seemed strange to read a letter of mine to someone else: but she was very glad of it, it made me more *tangible*, she could see another side of me, she said also. And her face showed more pleasure than any word she said. Words *are not* needed now. . . .

AFTERNOON AUG. 6TH

[The diary continues with a discussion of an argument with Dorrance regarding modern midwifery as practiced by males.] . . . Mr. D. was a warm champion for the accoucheur, while I of course, was rabid against it. And I told him that if I had money enough I would found an institution for the education of young women, or old women in the practice of midwifery. He conceded that *that* would be a good plan, and before we parted I had got him so far softened that he agreed that it would be quite as well if not better to employ women and call in a surgeon only in very complicated cases, where a surgical operation or death would be inevitable. . . . It is a most fortunate thing that my Darling thinks in this subject as I do, otherwise there would be a painful, very painful struggle on my part. Of course if she did not believe as I, out of love I must yield to her view. As it is she shall have me to deliver her or a woman.

I have engaged a copy of Dalton's physiology of Mr. Gregory. There are many points in physiology that I want to study more thoroughly and Dalton looked to me like a good one. Carpenter I think very much of,* and have studied considerably first & last but there is nothing like owning books to have them by for particular words. I shall purchase certain works on theoretical & practical midwifery just as soon as I can get the money. I will learn all that books can tell me & await my time to put it into practice.

---

*John Dalton, *Treatise on Human Physiology* (1859) or *Treatise on Physiology and Hygiene* (1868), and William B. Carpenter, *Principles of Mental Physiology* (1887).

Surely I am not so stupid as not to be able to do what any physician does; I *know* I'm not so stupid as *some* physicians, and from my boyhood's days I've always delighted in such things. . . .

AUG 7TH ''83 2:30 P.M.

Dorrance came in this morning and startled me by asking if I had heard that Sidney Putnam was drowned. It does not seem possible, but the report seems well founded, and his uncle Scott A. Smith has gone up to the Adirondacks to see about it. My first thought was—He has committed suicide! I hope not—I hope not. He was so despondent when last here, life seemed so tangled and useless to him, and his loved one so utterly apart from him that I could not blame him if he had done the deed.

He was a very generous friend—one of my best & truest friends, and it will hurt to part with him. And his mother! God pity her. . . .

Dorrance has been in again and says that it is indeed true that Sidney has been drowned. I can't quite make it seem so yet. Ah, he was very very kind to me! It seems to undo me completely for the present. . . .

. . .

AUG. 9TH. 1883 P.M.

. . . The latest accounts show that the drowning of Sidney is only sup-posed from a boat adrift containing a rubber coat & a coat found on shore belonging to him. They know he went out in the boat. That is all. They are searching for his body. I yet think he will come out alive. And I still think that if he was drowned he committed suicide. . . .

10TH AUG. ''83 FORENOON

. . . To my shame I find that in my struggle for material things—bread and home and skill—I have lost an appreciable spiritual nearness to the un-seen and strength giving Eternal. Life has gone hard to my heart, notwith-standing the marvellous blessedness of knowing Her, and of having her only love: and the doubts bred of conflict and darkness have made me less actively trustful.

God pardon me! I do feel thee in all.

I need new strength to bear with what comes daily more deep & strong.

I find that my struggles for bread & skill have shut out from my sight the great Heart of the universe. The fretfulness of ill health & unease have made life's purest and sweetest alloyed. . . .

Day unto day proves to me more and more how earnest and terrible life is. Also I get frequent glimpses of how grandly calm and lovely it ought to be, and might be. Help! . . .

11TH AUG. 83. 8:30 A.M.

Sidney Putnam's funeral is to be tomorrow. Then he *is* dead.—Not yet do I realize it, though why it should be hard I cannot tell, since he so longed to be rid of life's terrible strain. Good friend to me was he. Ever to be depended upon for charitable deed or sympathy. *He* introduced me to Charlotte. Should I not weep these tears for him then? However fickle the others might call him, however erratic and without foundation, I can vouch for the warmth, the tenderness, the sincere affection of his heart. . . .

Yet in my heart of hearts my grief at his death is not great. I feel sure he wanted it; I feel sure life's weight had become too much for him; and the ardor of fruitless love of one who could not respond with like passion was wearing out his life. Merciful death! Do thou even so to me when my life becomes as his seemed to be.

I shall miss him. . . . Through him I met the Cressons.—Oh, friend, friend! If thou canst see now from thy new place my heart see its gratitude, inexpressible, though it may be, that thou broughtst to me the two great things, and the sweetest of my life—the Cressons and my maiden-wife. God grant thou the fullness of what is beyond for those two deeds. . . .

13TH AUG. MONDAY P.M.

Yesterday Sidney's funeral. Quiet, heliotropes, tuberoses, darkness of the house, and cloud filtered sunshine of the cemetery. It seemed strange to stand at the head of that dead body and think of him. So shall it be with all of us. . . .

· · ·

22 AUG 83.

. . . I spent the time in studying midwifery, and feel that as regards the description I am better posted: I think I could officiate now with certainty at a natural labour. More and more I become convinced that it should be wrested from the hands of male practitioner and I would like to have the means of founding an institution for the education of midwives. Ah, I hope my darling may escape them all. No *man* shall touch her while I live, unless it is the *very extremity* of danger to her life. I will have the courage of my convictions. If we live in a city at the time a female physician can be called for service: if in the country midwives can surely be found to supplement my knowledge. She is very strong, never sick, is well formed, athletic and uses no stimulants, whether tea or coffee, knows no dissipation and is pure: with such qualifications child bearing ought to be easy. And I'm sure it will. Ah, I'm sure she ought to be thankful that her husband is not ignorant of those things and wants to shield her body from all men. . . .

.   .   .

25TH AUG. ''83 3 P.M.

. . . Yesterday P. M. Hazeltine—. . . we were talking of marriage and kisses, I maintaining that utter purity was right and practicable; and he, that if the world were different it would be right but that it was *not* practicable. . . . He said I was old fashioned, because I still believed there was such a thing as adultery. He said it was only found now in the Bible and law courts, which is too true in one sense. But—she, my pure Love, reigned over all and I *knew* what I said was true, having experienced it. How hard it is to make those who are brought up in the world's way amid luxury realize that there *is* such a thing as true marriage founded on the intellect and pure love.

[Several weeks earlier Stetson had written that Mr. John Mason "was in high glee because his wife had just given birth to a girl. I surely can congratulate Mr. Mason" (Aug. 6, 1883).] I'm so sorry for Mr. Mason! He's lost his infant girl and his wife is not expected to live. I'm afraid Dr. M. has been doing what he is noted for, Dr. Allen tells me,—"quick deliveries" and sad effects. It makes my blood grow hot with indignation. Charlotte says I'm inclined to be supercilious. I think I have been, yes, and am now in less degree. I shall be cured. One can't be haughty long without paying the penalty. Indeed, my penance has been done over and over. I deserved it, in a way, although I knew no better, or rather followed an instinct. I could have been an autocrat, *never* a subject. Inherited too from father. He will bend to nothing; and it has hurt him financially. Candidly, I admire it in him. It has helped keep him up against adversity. When I say he would not bend, I mean to rulers, church king-makers, politicans, and creed-vaunters. To God he bends most humbly, and to all virtue likewise.

I spent last evening in trying to define a list of words taken at random from [John Addington Symonds'] "The Renaissance in Italy." I was inspired to see how difficult I found it to give exact definitions, which shows that I do not—how can I?—use words with strict propriety. I propose continuing the study. I learned a deal by it. I like to study the dictionary—especially for etymology.

I used to hear greybeards say: "The older one grows the less he thinks he knows." *I am proving it*. It *is true*. I seem to learn slowly. I used to learn quickly. My schooling did all it could to ruin me. Ah, what a mistake it was!

*　　*　　*

MON. 27TH AUG. ''83 A.M.

Yesterday I read nearly all day. The evening with her. . . . She said last night, that the only consolation she had for all the pain she had given me was the fact that *never once* had she written or said an untrue word to me: always she said the truth as she knew it at the time. It was a precious, rapturous evening such as all husbands & wives, in theory, might feel, by having no secrets. . . . She had a new name for one of our girls: Hildegarde; much to my liking too. Let me see: now we have, Sigurd, Katharine, Gottfried, Hildegarde—four that is a good beginning. I should like four children. And she told how she had noticed in the children she had met an absolute lack of ambition. None were going to "be" anything. Why, she said, in her girlhood she wanted to be the greatest poet, author, painter, sculptor, actress and the most beautiful woman in the world, all combined. And out of her little pupil and his associates she could get no ideas of life nor any wants of a greater one. Then she stopped and her eyes shone but gazed afar off, and she said slowly: "Our children, dear love, . . . will be ambitious to *do*.". . .

TUES. 28TH AUG. P.M.

. . . A letter this morning from Mrs. Cresson bemoaning her inability to do for me what she wants to, because she has no money of her own: "I feel like a slave with hands tied behind me. . . . Dainties are given me to eat, fine apparel clothes me and I see those I care for suffering for my superfluities and I cannot aid." Ah, we little know what pain lies in the hearts of the rich! I have learned a great deal by knowing her. She is not to be envied. She says she told Mr. C. to send me a check for $50— to tide me over for a while, and he promised to do so but she did not think he had, and did not want to urge him too hard for fear he would not do it at all. It is a very tender and sad, faithful letter. . . .

MID-AFTERNOON, AUG. 29, 1883

Hamilton MacDougall has just been here. It was good of him to come this early after his return. He came home this morning. His European trip has improved him much. Ah, it was good to grasp his hearty hand once more. He has lost none of his simplicity, but has gained a certain polish of manners that is quite charming. I'm glad he is home.

Today I have worked on the maid with the lute, and upon an 8 × 12″ head which looks a little like Charlotte.

Hamilton has revived those deep longings to go out into the world. They are not fierce now. They give an autumnal tone to my life. Oh, *I* want to be a painter, and see the beauties of the world! But I am quiet even in my heart. I will wait. I will be as faithful as I can over a few things, not alone to be ruler over many, but because it is best. I feel keen premonitions of a state of mastership. I do believe that I shall be a great painter. At all events I shall be a worthier man.

Hamilton, with much delicacy, talked almost less of himself than of me. He told of what he had seen in the papers about me, and spoke of the pictures I had here. And even when talking of London, it was London in relation to me. Yes, he has acquired much grace of manner. I admire it. . . .

AUG. 31ST ''83. 11:40 A.M.

She came about 10:30 to bid me a last goodbye. They go at 1:20. She left not more than 10 minutes ago. It was a holy morning. It was beautiful of her to come. . . . [Charlotte was leaving for Moosehead Lake with the Jackson family, still serving as governess for their son.]

1ST SEPTEMBER, ''83 P.M.

. . . Worked on the Greek girl—her face, her pillow, etc. I find this room is responsible for many of my faults. It is too small, also the light does not strike a "decent sized" canvas evenly. It will be strong at the bottom and almost a shadow at the top. As for being able to get a light on a full length figure, & on my easel at the same time, it is impossible. And when I have models the dressing & undressing is very inconvenient. I ought certainly to have two rooms, the one extra, however small, for a dressing room I have worked thus far under strains and affecting disadvantages. My next move I hope will be a betterment. The lack of money is a root of many evils, quite as much so as too much of it. . . .

SEPT. 4TH 1883 9:30 A.M.

. . . Monday's post brought a tender letter from Mrs. Cresson, enclosing a check for fifty dollars. Ah, what a relief! . . .

8TH SEPT. 1883 SAT.

Wednesday last Geo. & I went to the 2 Fairs at Boston [the Exposition of European Painting and the Exposition of American Painting]. I spent the day. Saw my first Titian, Rembrandt, Correggio, Duner, S. Rosa, Tintoretto . . .—the [James Jackson] Jarves collection. My pulses throbbed at the influence of those men. They had souls, and the modern paintings of the French & Italians we had just left seemed like clay. I felt that if I had been born in their times I too would have been among them. I could sympathize with them truly & deeply.*

At the American Ex. there was tameness & sameness. My three canvases had very good places & looked better than I thought they would: but the faults stood out glaringly in the large room, though not all seen in my studio.

We also went to Noyes & Blakeslee's, Doll & Richards, where we were well attended by Mr. Hatfield & shown a [illegible], a Millet, a Monticelli and the finest Corot I have yet seen. It was consummate poetry of the idyllic sort. . . .

MON MORNING. 10TH SEPT. 1883

Cool & clear. A letter from Her, full of love & longing & trust and hope. They were still in camp [at Moosehead Lake] but intended leaving that day, if I understand her letter aright. She is lonesome, that is evident. Her descriptions of natural scenery are lovely, beautiful, and fresh as her

---

*The Exposition of European Painting and the Exposition of American Painting were both sponsored by the New England Charitable Manufacturers and Mechanics Institute. Stetson's negative response to the French Impressionists was typical of his contemporaries. One reviewer spoke for many when he said that Manet was "the least objectionable of the lot," and that Renoir and Courbet were "the craziest and most utterly valueless association of painters the feverishness of the present day has produced." "The Fine Arts," *Boston Journal Supplement*, Sept. 8, 1883, p. 1.

Three of Stetson's paintings—*Fog Coming at Sunset, Baddeck*; *Allegro*; and *Girls at Play*— were shown at the American Exposition. See *Boston Globe*, Sunday, Sept. 10, 1883; see also "The Fine Arts," *Boston Journal Supplement*, Sept. 8, 1883, p. 1.

own heart. She takes great interest in lichens, mosses, insects and the like. . . .

The "Globe" yesterday gave my pictures a very kind notice*—those at the Exposition. It said that they possessed that "brilliant, intense" coloring which is my specialty, if so young an artist who has exhibited scarcely a half dozen(!?) pictures could be said to have a specialty. The *Allegro* they characterize as being "a bit of glowing poetry" which it is. "The Girls at Play" they consider not quite so successful. The theme is "too commonplace" "to fit into my treatment." I require some subject which will give full scope to my imagination, and at the same time not try the imagination of the spectator. I'm afraid those conditions can only hardly be filled. However, the notice was better than a young artist could expect, especially one who by his nature has been obliged to break new paths across the ruts of predecessors. . . .

SEPT. 11. 9:30 A.M.

. . . Mr. [John] Mason asked me last night to get a price on the damsel plucking apples (?). I purpose setting $28– as the very lowest. That would be equal to $35– as sold by a dealer. It is as good a picture—and the same size as the one sold to Mr. De Kay for $50– and the one to Mrs. C. for $35–. Mr. M. wants me to take a book "L'Artistes Contemporaines" worth $5 or so in part payment. I doubt if he is willing to give so much. In which case I will keep it unless perhaps he offers me $20– which will give me a good chance to show him that 2 dollars is not of so much account to poor me as to monied him.

It's odd, how barter & bicker comes into poetry. And also how rich men will rant over a dollar or two, and yet want to be a real patron of art. They are all willing to take advantage of our necessities.

4 P.M.   It has come up dark and chill. I am shivering in my summer clothing. Have been trying to draw. It is discouraging. I make no headway. I can't draw better today than a year ago, it seems to me. Is there any hope? I fear not. I can color—oh yes, the papers all say so, and my fellows also: but to draw—the best part of art's expression! I am afraid. Why *can't* I have models. Others do, with time & money. But I who am suffering for them— I have none. . . .

---

*Stetson's summary is from "Art at the Exposition," *Boston Daily Globe*, Sept. 9, 1883, p. 14.

SEPT 12TH ''83 2 P.M. THEREABOUTS.

. . . [Bannister] showed me a Boston Journal which had a notice of the Fair's pictures. They said of me: Mr. Stetson has an original feeling for color which he uses in producing two extravagancies which are shown. If they were done in stained glass they would merit favorable mention, but on canvas they are staring and not even decorative.* Those are nearly the words. It did not impress me deeply. Why should it? They are not masterpieces, and are *not* staring. If he don't like the quality of color, I'm not to blame. Some persons do, besides me. They called Rossetti's color like stained glass. I am not better than him. I can bear it *surely*. I want time. They shall see. I have only gone a little way as a colorist, and no appreciable distance as a draughtsman. I must expect very bad rubs. They have been unusually lenient this far. . . .

13TH SEPT. 1883 MORNING.

. . . Dismal again today, with rain. . . . Called on [Fred] Batcheller at his new room. He was glad to see me. We talked of art & love, and marriage. He is 46, he feels he made a mistake in not marrying, also that he never will be much of a painter with all his hard work. . . .

It is tragic. To have reached that age & found one has made a mistake in his vocation. And yet, the humblest, the poorest of us have a place. God help me!

LATE P.M. 13TH

. . . This P. M. been painting on two twilights. One a bridge near a salt marsh, the other at the edge of an orchard with dark buildings in the centre. The latter I think very decent. The former—well it is rather botchy. Glazings & repaintings may give it health. I fancy a little gain in my command of brush, but none as to seeing and translating proportions. . . .

14TH SEPT. ''83 LATE P.M.

. . . Yesterday P. M. after entry Geo. called. He liked the two things I had just done very much and we had a long talk about my work etc. It gave me a clearer knowledge of myself, and so helped me. I felt stronger for it.

---

* Stetson's summary is from "The Fine Arts," *Boston Journal Supplement*, Sept. 8, 1883, p. 1.

I have an indistinct feeling that Geo. thinks I'm getting ahead in color too fast. I sometimes fancy he is a little—a *very* little, however,—jealous. But no, he is too generous, too much my friend. He has always been kind & helped me in many ways—usually pecuniarily. . . .

15TH SEPTEMBER 1883. 10 A.M.

The letter which came yesterday shows her in a lovely light. . . . The calm of nature seems to have settled upon her, and is surely doing a good work in her. There is a beautiful thing in this letter, showing how true she is to me, and how no thing however small that can possibly affect me is kept secret.

I did a thing this morning which I questioned a little as to whether you would be pleased or displeased. . . . When we got on the steamer there was a fine black setter chained to a rope on the forward deck. He had been in the water, was wet, could not exercise or change his place, and was cringing and shivering with cold as the boat started in the fresh morning air. (Remember it's a little boat, with only our party on board, and the captain and fireman) I sat down by this poor doggey, stroked and comforted him, put my big shawl around him and let him sit close to me with my arm around him. After awhile the spasmodic shiver grew quieter and quieter and ceased: he crossed his brown paws over my knees and went to sleep. I remembered that you did not like me to kiss Belinda [her cat], and thought perhaps you would object to this. But I see no harm in my shedding love and tenderness as far and wide as I can, so that I rob you not of what is all your own. How could I, for what I give you springs only towards you, is drawn forth by you, *is* yours and no other's. O that you were here now, and my husband in very deed!

Her child's heart lives yet in her grand womanhood. . . .

20TH SEPT. "83

. . . Letters from Her daily. They were full of what she felt. Tenderly loving—passionately fond—full also of revelations of all her deep thoughts regarding truth & life. She has found that she cannot teach the boy. I felt how hard it was for her—it came out in her letters once in a while, besides there was a something about them that told me she was in trouble. Yet she said nothing directly to me fearing to have me hurt because I could not relieve her pain. She had almost made up her mind to tell the Jacksons that she must give up when one of my letters gave her new courage and she determined to stay the appointed time. But Mrs. J. herself relieved her, telling her that she had seen that the boy *would* not study and that it was no use to try to teach him in that way. But she would like to have Charlotte stay with them, taking her board & room in pay for amusing the boy evenings. But how glad my darling was to get out of it all so honorably. It was a fairly jubilant letter, and in it she confessed how hard it had been, how lonely and homesick she was, and how she greatly needed to be with me. . . .

A letter yesterday from Wellesley College, asking for information regarding myself as they have a picture of mine called "At Johnson[?]"—I can't remember it. It must be a very poor early affair. How funny! How *did* they get it, and why? And to have them want to know about me! It is certainly novel.*. . .

· · ·

29TH SEPT 1883 P.M.

I came from the Pier last night [after visiting the Cressons]. A pleasant stay full of kindly attention, and glimpses of the most entrancing colors in sea and landscape. One ride that we took near nightfall up Boston Neck is never to be forgotten. It was one long picture of the most marvellous *tone*. Beautiful! Strangely beautiful. And one day—it was last Tuesday—was grand for sea studies. I made a few sketches. . . .

A letter while at the Pier from Mr. Robinson† of the Fair saying that it will be impossible at present to give a catalogue to every contributor. That breaks one of the promises. He asked permission to publish one of my drawings in the N. Y. "Studio": says it will be a fine advertisement. I have given my permission. That and the Wellesley College affair marks a gain in my reputation. Charlotte will be glad. She endorsed upon the Wellesley note "My famous husband! with biography in demand!". . .

To the sketch exhibition in N. Y. I shall send the *Study of a Page in Red & A Swamp of Pocassett* 10 × 14″ and 9 × 11″. . . .

OCT. IST ''83

. . . "Studios" came. Read them and found out why I had not received one of the "grand catalogues" of the Fair. Simple enough. They had not seen fit to publish either of my drawings therein, as I saw by the list of names. That is why they asked permission to publish in the "Studio" I suppose a sort of "Sop to Cerberus." I found out later that Mr. Burleigh had received

---

* Wellesley College seems to have no record of this painting.

† Edwin Robinson was later Curator of the Boston Museum of Fine Arts.

his—and he had a drawing published. Only a white lie on the part of the Art Director—and life is so full of black lies that one must not be over mindful of them. I hate to be fooled though. I have written to him telling him that it had just dawned upon me why it was and begging his pardon for asking about it previously. It would really have been too much out of the usual course of my affairs to have it done. But my time is coming. *I feel it.* Now, I, ingenuous creature, *gave* them my drawings for the benefit of the catalogue—so I am "out" in all ways. I believe that my drawings were as *good* as many that were published. Sydney [Burleigh] says they are the usual things—if so I am sure of it.

I will try it again, by making one for the Penna. Academy Cat. . . .

OCT. 2D "83 3 P.M.

She came this morning [from her stay with the Jacksons]: could not wait until she had been home to take off the carsmoked garments. She wanted me so. It seemed about unreal to be with her again. But she soon made it real! . . .

. . . I shall not be willing to have her gone again so among people who care nothing for her. A hard lesson she has learned. It makes her value my tender love higher. I think it makes her more anxious for her own home—*our* home. How shall it be made? God alone knows.

Last evening at the Club. 4th quarterly meeting. Refreshments after it. Mr. Bannister and I stood on the sidewalk talking of art—particularly the "impressionists" which he dislikes as much as I. . . .

Have nearly finished a drawing of my "Girls, Hills, and the Sea" for the Penna. Acad. Catalogue. It will be my usual fate if they should not publish it. It may not be good enough. But I think it as good as many they have published.*. . .

OCT. 5TH 1883 FRIDAY A.M.

. . . Mrs. Diman† wants [Charlotte] to take charge of a class of girls in gymnastics, the class to meet at some place hired by themselves. Also she is

---

*The Secretary of the Pennsylvania Academy later said that Stetson's drawing of *Girls, Trees, and the Sea* (20 × 24 inches) was "very effective." Diaries, Oct. 12, 1883. Stetson later wrote, "I consider it one of my very best landscapes; especially in tone. Usual palette." "Opera" Book, p. 35.

†May Diman, daughter of Brown University History Professor J. Lewis Diman, had

going to teach Miss Carpenter for her board and lodging. (She wants me to paint Miss Carpenter. I expect to do so.) And she can get pupils outside. Also her Christmas work as a decorator will be in some demand. She is going to advertise for work.

I'll wager that she gets more money out of her winter than I.

What a dear girl! [Two lines are crossed out.] And she went on to show that she had $15– which she should not want to use and that I ought to take some of it, as it would be too bad to lose the chance of securing a model etc. She argued so sweetly that I let my pride give way and took five dollars of her. I know it pleased her. That represents her pay for a week's work. Of course I shall not use it unless forced to; but I did use some yesterday, of necessity, in sending off my things, and suppose I must use more in getting the Philadelphia picture off today. . . .

6TH OCT. ''83 A.M.

A weary day yesterday. Did art club work—receiving pictures and the like. Went home at 6 o'c., found two letters. One, short, from my Love. One long, from Mrs. Cresson. The latter made me ache. It was a report of what Mr. Cresson had to say about me. How I had not right to so expensive a studio: how I ought to give it up & do something else if I made no sales. And much more. Then there was something about my marrying. It was kind—yes—and practical. But—oh what was hurt? Pride? I don't know. It may have been my natural combativeness arising to defend self. It hurt. And what also hurt, was that he said he'd send me a check for $100–. I felt it almost as an insult. He said I was doing wrong to go on in this way, yet would send money to help me go on. In haste, I sat down at [sister] Caroline's, whence I had gone to tea, and wrote a note, saying that I declined the check with thanks. I'm afraid that it would hurt.

After tea I had to hurry back to the meeting of the [Art Club] jury. On the way down I thought it all over and concluded to take the money pay all my rent to Nov. 1st and give up my room. To try to find business to do. It seems foolhardy for it will set me away back in some ways, but I can see no other way. If some strange thing should occur, such as unlooked for sales, I should still keep it on condition of a reduction of rent. I sat down at the club

---

been one of Charlotte's closest friends prior to her death in 1881. Mrs. Diman, May's mother, continued to be supportive and affectionate toward Charlotte.

and wrote a second letter, acknowledging the haste of the first. I talked plainly to her.

One who understood the art feeling, the instinct, could imagine how I felt at the prospect of giving up my work, perhaps forever. Ah, I am all in a whirl. I see nothing clearly. God help me!

I have written to my love about it.

[Charlotte] had her first picture taken by the jury last night. It is a very tenderly felt bit of water color. . . .

.   .   .

WEDNESDAY 10TH OCT. "83 A.M.

Yesterday a letter from Mr. Cresson, in which he seeks to prove to me that I have misunderstood him, that he would have me give up art on no consideration whatever. That undoubtedly I shall succeed, but not unless I "stick to it" unflinchingly. That he has started to see me through and intends to do it—(what that means I can't say for certain). He also told of a man from a place he calls "P" who has a son in London who sells all he paints but who could not make a living even before he went there. The gist of the matter was that I ought to leave Providence. [But] *how?* . . . He also wants "a good square practical talk" with me. I hope he may have it, also that it may differ from previous "practical" talks in being really practical. It was a very kind strong letter. I brought it down here at noon and proceeded to reply to it. Half through when Charlotte and her new pupil Miss Carpenter called.

Charlotte seemed very lovely beside Miss Car[penter]. And she wants me to paint Miss Carpenter's portrait. I didn't fancy her much, and failed to find the prettiness Charlotte had told me of, and too, I didn't like the damsel a bit. But I made an appointment for a first sitting for next Tuesday. She was much surprised when I told her I should not paint her in any way but as I thought best, apropos of her asking Charlotte what kind of a background she ought to have. I told of course that I should make a background such as I thought proper. She evidently imagined that I painted backgrounds, dresses etc. to order. Of course her only experience had been with photographers. Also she was very surprised that I told her I thought a ⅔ or full face was better than a profile. Photographers had told her to the contrary. I see clearly that it will be a very irksome job, and if Charlotte had not asked it I would in no wise attempt it. I dislike her mouth exceedingly. There is no clear character in it. It is neither childlike nor mature, nor beautiful. And she has "baggy" under eyelids, which give a dissipated look to her, albeit it adds to the force of a smile.

I shall not suit them, I feel confident. They have no art-feeling I'll warrant, and no respect for art.

Charlotte is going to study French with her at the Berlitz school. Glad and sorry. . . .

THURSDAY 11TH OCT. "83 A.M.

Yesterday P. M. Charlotte called. . . . She has been grieving over my affairs. Also her own are not so roseate as she thought they would be. She is not going to live at the Carpenter's after all, but they will hire her for $3– a week to teach the girl. So she will have to live at her mother's. A most deplorable thing as we both think. . . .

We talked about all the things we have to talk of on our way down. She told me about going to see [Bronson Howard's] "Young Mrs. Winthrop" and how she hated it and what a shame it was that the types portrayed therein were true. "Its truth is its shame," said she. She was all excited about it and has written a hot critique upon it. She is beginning to hate the world deeply—just as I have, for its shams and sins and uncleanness. It draws us nearer together and makes us love the bright things of God's loveliness better & better—a compensation, as she says.

Well, she gave me great pleasure last evening [at the Art Club Reception]. She could not stay long though as she wanted to get home so that her mother might go to bed as she had a headache. But I came back. Was feeling in a rarely conversational mood. Was introduced to a Miss Brown; a handsome young woman about whom Dorrance, Prof. Appleton, and Mr. Mason were raving! I went at her immediately, took her away from them & received her quick assent to posing for me. She was willing if not eager to do so. She *seems* childlike, is easily flattered, is soft and yielding. She would make a superb model. Has a rich face and *a very* fine form, full but supple and strong. . . .

FRIDAY 12TH OCT. "83 LATE P.M.

. . . Dr. Allen came in and paid for the water color he bought last week for the wedding $10– and also bought the Flower Girl sketched from Miss Briggs in sketch class last Fall. I let him have it for $10– although I know it to be worth more. If sales would only go on now!

Also I wrote a little letter to Her this P. M., to cheer her and quoted some of [William] Morris' "Love is Enough.". . .

Would I were with her!

SAT. P.M. 13TH OCT. ''83

. . . Have been painting a landscape this afternoon for a rest. 9 × 12 upright. It seems very soft & good in tone now.

Mother is downcast today. She cleaned house two days last week. I think it was too much for her; yet it may be that the barrel of flour I bought last May having gone, and there being neither eggs nor sugar in the house she felt sorrow for that. I let her have a dollar to get eggs and sugar with.

The winter is going to be very hard. I clearly see it. God grant strength for it.

MONDAY, 15TH OCT. 83

As I wished she came Saturday towards dark. . . . . She wanted to rest—was sad—and mostly because of the world's sin, but with it there was the pain of our being kept apart by only one thing—kept apart—that was pain. . . .

Yesterday read [William Morris'] "Lovers of Gudrun." Went to her in the evening. She had not quite got into tune, tho she was tender and strongly earnest. She read me her brief of "Young Mrs. Winthrop." I was proud of her thoughts. Also she read me two or three poems. . . .

1:15 P. M. Mr. Beriah Wall called this A. M.—father of George. They wanted to find out if I would attempt to etch 10 or 12 plates from some of his pictures by Daubigny, Corot and that class of men. I fancy they are going to get up a fine catalogue of his pictures, perhaps for a sale. I talked with him frankly about it, telling him that some of them I could not etch satisfactorily, I thought, and some I could. I will go there tonight and look at them and talk it over more carefully. It would be a fine thing for me if I could do it well for I can see that it would give me a new field of reputation. I think he does not want to pay more than $25 a piece for them. Some will be very *very* difficult for *me* to do. But if I see a chance of getting $250 out of it I will attempt it. It was kind of him to come to me.

He said that Geo. said my pictures at the fair were receiving very favorable comment from "critics and connoisseurs."

TUESDAY 16TH OCT. 1883 2:15 P.M.

. . . I went to call on [Beriah Wall] last evening & he showed me some of the things which he wanted etched [for the catalogue of his collection.]* I think I could do all he showed me unless it were Richter's "Judith." I suggested to him that a part of them be phototypes of pen drawings which I could make. He seemed to like the idea but I'm afraid Geo. [Wall] will not. Probably they will want to pay me little for them but the "advertisement" as they say, would indeed be worth a great deal provided the etchings were well done. . . .

17TH OCT. 83 A.M.

. . . Mr. B. Wall been in. Wants me to take the Marilhat & etch it *in tone*. God help me! It is a task indeed for a fledgeling in etching. I cannot foresee the end. And it may be well that I cannot. Upon this depends a great deal. I feel it.

Just written to Charlotte to tell her about it. Also to Mrs. Cresson. . . .

19TH OCT. 1883 A.M.

. . . This morning: a letter from Mrs. Cresson saying she was glad to hear again from me and that it was possible she might be in Providence to-morrow, if so she would try to call. Also that Mr. C. would send me a check by the 1st. With it came a pair of tickets from the Museum of Fine Arts which showed me that my 3 water colors were accepted. Here I saw too Mr. Manchester's Boston Herald that they were mentioned as among the "interesting" things. There's a gain. My way is opened there hereafter. Also a card from the Am. Galleries, their sketch exhibit, private view. So now I have pictures at the Fair in Boston, also [the Boston] Museum of Fine Arts, at the

---

*Wall's illustrated catalogue of his oil painting collection would eventually include the following Stetson etchings: Eugène Fromentin (1820–1876), *The Arab Falconer*; Prosper Marilhat (1811–1847), *Feeding the Camel*; Jean Baptiste Camille Corot (1796–1875), *Bayou of the Seine*; Alexandre Decamps (1803–1860), *The Good Samaritan*; Thomas Couture (1815–1879), *Gamin*; Charles F. Daubigny (1817–1878), *After the Storm*. Several pen drawings are also included in the catalogue: E. V. Luminais (1821–1896), *Teuton's Crossing the Rhine*; Jean Pierre Antigna (1818–1878), *Fisher Girl*; Constant Troyan (1810–1865), *Sheep in Pasture*; and Johann Barthold Jongkind (1819–1891), *American Ship 'Canada' at Harfleur*. In George Whitaker's view, "These etchings and pen drawings show great force and vigor and interpret the paintings in an original and clear style." George Whitaker, "Charles Walter Stetson," A. E. Club Lectures, Nov. 21, 1895, Club Papers no. 263, p. 13, RIHS.

Penna. Academy. At Doll & Richards. At Sketch Exhibit. At [illegible] & Kennedy's, San Francisco. It would seem that out of *all* those enough should sell to keep me from starving. I forgot to mention the 5 I have in our own [Providence] exhibit. Now to work.

SATURDAY, 20TH OCT. ''83 9:30 A.M.

Yesterday morning finished my water color after making Journal entry. About noon the new application for position of model called—a Miss A[nnie] S. Jeffrey. I found her very refined, elegant, sympathetic and I doubt not full of dramatic feeling. She is brunette, with large black eyes, and a very Oriental cast of features, but with more soul than most Orientals are supposed to have. She is studying for the stage,—"Tragedy but I may find myself only a soubrette after all," said she. Her teacher advised her to take up posing for artists for practice as well as the income it might give her. We had a pleasant talk and I "took to her." Sydney [Burleigh] came in while she was here. He informed her that she was just my style, said he should like to use her himself. The trouble is she is employed during the day so we can only use her evenings, unless we can find her employment enough to make it pay her to give up her place. I doubt if we could do that. I wish I had the money, I would hire her outright for 3 months. Well, we shall see. . . .

22D OCT. ''83 MONDAY A.M.

. . . Went to Geo. Wall's. Learned something new about the etchings. He showed me some newspaper cuttings which spoke of my pictures. I think the best one that which he himself wrote to the Phil. *Times*. I did not care so much for them as I should if greater men had written them, albeit they were true and kindly. We don't think there is any chance of selling things at the Fair.

From his house to Charlotte's. She was very glad to see me. Our evening was spent in love—which was in & over all—in conversation about pictures and poems. In reading a letter which I wrote for her Saturday night: in talking over some pictures she was making—one a very queer conception, but full of good feeling of a "literary" sort, in which a reptile swarming swamp, a pure lily and a deep pine wood with a red light behind it made the form of a cross with interlaced branches. She also showed me some chimerical animals which would have done DaVinci's heart good. She is going to copy me one of them. . . .

The *Globe* of yesterday informed its readers, *apropos* of my museum water colors that my methods of coloring in water colors were not nearly so successful as in oil. It is strange that people are so narrow. Why could not that critic see further, and perceive that I had in no wise attempted deep tones and brilliant color. The first being scarcely possible in aquarelle & the second not suited to the subjects I had treated. They gave Syd. Burleigh rather a hard rub for his picture which did not illustrate certain lines from Morris. As far as I have seen Sydney's pictures are not noteworthy for any poetry beyond a certain delight in daintiness.

My etching is much delayed by Calder who failed to order my materials as I desired.

TUESDAY A.M. OCTOBER 23RD 1883

Painted yesterday P. M. on a large twilight water color. Am afraid I have got it too muddy to please the philistines and dilettantes. . . .

. . . [Charlotte] has outgrown the Simmonses [Sam and Jim Simmons].*. . . They have not changed: it is *she*. I am glad. For good as they are I want her to be with more ideal living. I want her to be with me. I am—I *do* make her happy in the best way. It is so strange: she cares nothing for what most women care most—fine clothing & jewelry & establishment. She wants our one little room and—Sigurd. . . .

WEDNESDAY, 24TH OCTOBER ''83 MID AFTERNOON

. . . A letter from Miss Jeffrey yesterday thanking me for my note of introduction to Bannister. Also she proposed very kindly to "come to" me on Sundays to pose—if I did not think it "wicked." She would be glad to do it, and hopes she may have a favorable answer. Indeed, it is kind. . . . I just now read the letter to [Charlotte]. She made no comments, only said: "Tell her simply the truth about models—it is no kindness to conceal it."—in which I differ a trifle with her. That was apropos of Miss Jeffrey's question as the "uprightness" of models. . . .

---

* Although Stetson always regarded Brown University students Sam and Jim Simmons as annoying competitors, Charlotte liked them—as whist players, as fun-loving debaters, as supportive confidants. One of her diary entries reads: "Mr. Stetson arrives. Very unhappy to find me engaged [with Jim Simmons], and won't stay to tea. . . . Why can't they all be friends like the Simmonses?" CAP, Diary, Feb. 19, 1882, Gilman manuscript collection, AESL.

Catalogue today from the Museum of Fine Arts. First time pictures of mine have been recorded therein. . . .

SATURDAY 27TH OCTOBER 1883 A.M.

The drawing of the Marilhat is finished in the plate. I must now wait until Dr. Allen pays me for the last picture before I can bite it, as I must buy a new tray, my old one not being large enough for this plate. I am prepared for a failure, but will "doctor" it as well as I can before giving it up. I shall also get leave to try another plate.

Been painting steadily on my water colors; doing between whiles a little to my paintings. Yesterday morning I made a hurried charcoal sketch for a picture. A fool & a maiden are in the foreground, the fool discourses to her about death, because of a dismal funeral procession of a Romanist sort going up the steep hill which they have just descended. She is full of pain & wonder; it may be that the one on the bier was an old lover, albeit he had a wife who follows the coffin supported by two sisters of mercy (or monks). The tone of the painting I purpose to have autumnal with lowering gray sky.*

I will make the water color sketch of it next. The composition came to me without conscious effort as I was going to bed a few nights since—why I can't say. I feel now that it is as complete as anything I ever conceived.

A good letter from my Love yesterday morning, in which she advances the idea of marrying sooner than Spring, and shows how she thinks it may be brought about by Christmas. She only needs a hundred dollars now to make all a success; that hundred is to assure us of one month's living. Her mother offers her the furniture of the room she now occupies. We should need little else she says. She wants me to be looking out for a room. No woman could be more content with little. . . .

I sell nothing. The only prospect of sale that I see is that Miss [Sarah] Eddy may buy my "Shadowed Path" for a few dollars.† Noble prospect

---

* Stetson later gave a slightly different description of the *Fool's Sermon on Death* (30 × 40 inches, canvas): "A Fool meets a maid of whom he knows that she was mistress of the dead man who is being carried up the hill, by monks, and followed by his wife. The Fool is subtly dwelling upon it, somewhat maliciously. Maybe he loves her himself. I think the composition as good as any I ever did, & I believe it is quite as well painted." "Opera" Book, pp. 37–39. It was sold in 1885 to Mrs. George Tewksbury of Topeka, Kansas.

† Sarah J. Eddy, PAC member, painted still-lifes and religious subjects.

surely! I believe Raphael would be unknown even, in a town like this, and in those days. I do not overrate myself in saying that: it is only a comparison to show the fault. . . .

SUNDAY: 2 P.M. OCT. 28TH ''83

I came down today to see if the worthy Brechs [the landlord] pleased to supply me with steam on Sundays. To my sorrow they do not, so Miss Jeffrey will not be able to pose for me until mid-winter when I'm confident they keep [it] heated to preserve the water pipes in good condition. . . .

I wish the world cared more for what I do so that I might do what I feel I could do. I am by no means buoyant today: I see no shadow of turning in regard to my affairs. I thought a good deal last night after going to bed about my exhibition. I must prevent any failure if possible. I think the best way will be to hire the Club gallery for a week, opening the show by a reception in the evening to the members of the Club and such others as I see fit to invite. Then state in circulars frankly that I am going to offer these things hoping to get enough by it to enable me to stay here and continue my studies. I may be able to get Henry Tilden Jr. to be a salesman for me.* I fear that *I* should make less than a brave one. Now, I think I can hire the Club room a week for $25– with gas one evening; they surely ought to let it for that considering all I have done for the Club in the way of work: indeed, I am sure they ought to tender me the use of it gratuitously for that length of time, but they will not on account of precedent—*not* the President. My catalogues will cost me $15–. I shall have to hire frames etc. I fancy I could get out of it short of $100. to name the least. And a city of 16,500 inhabitants that can't patronize an artist to cover that amount better be sunken by a Javanese earthquake. We are getting into a tight place, our family. Rents due and due! no coal for winter; flour gone; clothing to a large amount to be bought—ah! every thing seems to come at once.

MONDAY A.M. OCT. 29TH 83

Last eve. with her. . . . I took over a letter & [Eugène] Muntz's "Raphael," thinking the latter might be good for her to study, as I'm sure it would have an influence for good on her style of drawing. . . .

———

* Unidentified.

30TH OCTOBER. ''83 A.M.

Yesterday A. M. (about noon tho) Miss Jeffrey called. She talked to me as if she had known me a year. Said she liked me much, and I fancied she would like to have a chance to like me more. . . . I must say that her 40 minutes' chat was very pleasant. In the afternoon John Mason, in response to a note I had sent him asking him to let me have fifteen dollars for the Fruit & a Maiden,* which I had offered for 22–, because I was brought up sharp with my etching, needing a tray, etc. While he was here my Love came, clad in waterproof gossamer and surmounted by a tiny cap which made her look like a girl of the Italian Renaissance. . . . In the hall she opened a heart full of gladness, the burden of which was that we *could* marry by the New Year— so she went on to show how she deemed it possible and easy. It seemed almost wicked in me not to join in her enthusiasm, but I could not. . . .

Mr. Mason offered to let me have the money without taking a picture, tho he would like the Fruit & Maiden. He took 3 things—2 oils and one w.c. home to show Mrs. Mason. He will take some of them. He let me have the money. After sketch class I went out in the pouring rain to buy my porcelain tray. I hastened home, and after supper began to bite the plate. And I *did*— alas! I over-bit the foreground amazingly. The result: I shall have to make a new plate or spend many weary hours in getting out the creme; I prefer getting a new plate, and have just ordered one. Delay! delay! . . .

SAT. NOV. 3D ''83 A.M.

I might write pages of what has happened since I wrote but time is not plenty.

Thurs. evening, as the steam would be on owing to an art club show, I had Miss Jeffrey come here that I might make studies of her. I illuminated the place with candles and Japanese lanterns, so that it seemed "very romantic," as she said. She came at half past seven and stayed until quarter past ten. I had her put on the Greek costume. She was—wonderfully beautiful. Her form is charmingly symmetrical and her bosom as firm and pure in contour as any antique statue I have seen. It was a vision of beauty in this warm, dimly lighted room. I asked her to be natural, to lie on the lounge, to walk, to stand, to do what she pleased, as I felt certain I should learn more of grace

---

* *Fruit and a Maiden* or *Girl Plucking Fruit* (7 × 11 inches, mahogany panel), was sold to Isaac Bates, November 1884.

by watching her instinctive poses than by trying to force my duller conceptions upon her. Graceful! Strangely so. She was like a breathing picture in every attitude. She seems very fond of me in a quiet undemonstrative way. She seemed grateful that she had met a man who could appreciate her and look at her without amorous approaches. She said she *felt* that I understood her—"queer" as she is—and I was the first who had made her feel so. She could trust me implicitly—she enjoyed posing for me—she said all those things, and more of an untranscribable nature, so subtle were they. But it all made me feel how different I *am* from most men. I can see myself as I never did before what Mrs. Cresson once said—that I could have much influence over refined women because of tenderness, and a respectful treatment of their natures. Miss Jeffrey felt that I knew. There was one pose that she took—a man who could paint it and make it *real* would be immortal and a great benefactor. Oh it was lovely!

There was nothing done which my Love might not have seen.

As Miss J. was ready to go, the outside door being locked, I said to her experimentally, suppose I could not find my key? She should have to stay here all night—you'd have to be alone with me. She turned gently and looked into my eyes saying, "Well,—I should not be afraid." It made my heart leap, that she trusted me so.

I asked her how much I might pay her. She looked at me and said—"Please pay me—nothing—I—I can't take money of you. It has been too much of a help to me—besides you have drawn none—and it would destroy the charm of it. I don't like to feel that I was hired. What I showed you I showed because I knew you would understand, and because—it did me good to feel that there is a man who is—like you." After a little hesitancy I accepted her gift. Then home with her. I could but say, as we were going, how grateful I felt and how I was indebted. She replied: "If you are what I think you, and will be my friend; there is no indebtedness whatever. You do me good."

I learned a deal of grace. But the worst effect it had was to force upon me the brusqueness of my Love. I had no *amorous* desire for Miss J.—no, but she was so graceful, so restful, so in the region of my artist contemplation, that it made me feel how my dear wife lacked those things, or if not lacked, how she subdued them to her activity. The comparison ceased there; I should not have cared to say that her body or her mind was lovelier than my Love's. I don't know what her mind really is, though it is plainly uncommon. . . .

[Stetson later wrote in the margin of the diary: "This was outrageous! I can't understand or remember it. C. W. S. 19th Aug. "91."]

I was ashamed of my feelings, since I know how truly & deeply I love Charlotte, and since I am certain that she loves me. She is so true & good and earnest and single that I am ashamed. Well, the feeling followed me through yesterday, though I fought with it, and when she came with Miss Carpenter to the sitting her laugh and her aggressiveness grated on me painfully. But when she returned late in the afternoon it was made known to her by my lack of ardor or some subtle something. And she was frightened and pained—ah God! and clung in wonderment. I told as much as I could—.

. . . It was a painful night. She seemed half insane, though not because of incoherence. *She was not well.* A painful walk home. . . .

TUESDAY NOV. 6TH 1883 A.M.

. . . Sunday evening with her. She was unwell and we had a painful, though loving time. It may do us both good. Yesterday. . . . As I went home about 6:15, I found in Breck's a letter from Mr. Weeden which made my heart ache. It was only 3 lines: "Dear Mr. Stetson; I think it about time a payment be made on your note. Always yours, W. B. Weeden." Short? Ah, but what a depth of meaning it had! How to pay him! Last night I wrote a letter to Charlotte & one to him, telling him in substance that I knew it to be time to pay & I was trying to do so, and would do so as soon as I could, thanked him for his patience etc. And—How?

. . .

8TH NOV. "83 A.M.

Charlotte yesterday A. M. She was happier. Feeling better. Brought me a letter to the same effect & telling of her success in selling her water color & some cards to Miss H[azard]. She wanted me: so I stopped for her. I showed her Miss Jeffrey's last letter. I *felt* that she was a *little* jealous of Miss J. & I thought the letter might cure it. I don't know as it did. She acknowledged that she *was* just a little jealous—as I might like to have her be, she said, and yet she knew there was no reason. She was glad I had learned that one might *like* another and yet remain true to the loved one. She wanted to go to see Miss Jeffrey, as she (Miss J.) was lovely. I discouraged it, not that it was anything but a good sentiment, but knowing how my darling lacks tact I was afraid her virtue might miscarry & she become suddenly disagreeable to Miss J. Besides I knew that Miss J. would feel that she was looking after me.

Charlotte suggested that herself. So she did not go. She asked if I had any objections to her selling the land she owns in Hartford and taking the money to pay my debts & set up housekeeping. I told her I had no counsel for her. Then we both laughed—I grimly—at the attitude Dame Grundy would assume thereat:—the men would think me not such an idiot as they thought, and the women would think her more of one.

She walked home with me, seeming more buoyant than for over a week. . . .

SAT. 10TH NOV, "83 3:30 P.M.

. . . When I went home last evening I was simply undone. I could scarcely walk. It is a nervous prostration I suppose. At any rate I'm almost afraid to work on anything I don't want to spoil, as I think I *should* spoil it. . . . While getting ready to stop for dinner—a knock. It was Miss Jeffrey. She wanted to see me, felt homesick; wanted encouragement. She seems very fond of me and desirous of aiding me. Said she liked my letters. . . .

12TH NOV. "83 A.M.

Yesterday wrote a letter to Miss J. In evening went to my Love. She was very very sad. Showed me a picture of a wan creature who had traversed a desert and came, worn out, to an insurmountable wall which extended around the earth. It was powerful, albeit the doing of it was not so artistic as might be. It *was* powerful. If she keeps on like that she will do great things. I know it was a literal transcript of her mind. I had pained her: she magnified her feelings, or my feelings, until everything had dropped from life. . . . Because I told her of one remediable fault—behold! there was no reason that she could make me happy, no reason that she could be anything but what she is. What she is is better to me than all others, so if she is nothing I've small matter. I only wanted her to acquire a little more softened manner. . . . I'll predict that two years from now her manners will be much different.

Home at 10:45 in the rain—started at 10. This a. m. invitation for Phil[adelphia] So[ciety of] Artists to exhibit my sketches with them—those now in N. Y. Allow it. Also Cat.—Penna Acad. came to the Club. It contains my drawing, which reproduced pretty well, though the values are a good deal confused. First time I ever have had a drawing published. . . .

. . .

14TH NOV. "83 BY CANDLELIGHT

This A. M. worked at home on the plate of Marilhat, which came last night. Grounded it last evening; made drawing this A. M. and shall bite it this evening. Worked last night until 12 o'clock. Tired! . . .

. . .

MONDAY NOV. 19TH 1883 11 A.M.

Yesterday painted some proofs from plate. I have hopes of it. Needs some corrections and additions. In the evening called at Mr. Wall's and showed him proof. He seemed much pleased with the progress. After that went to Charlotte's. Passed a painful evening on account of a letter I wrote in which I unwisely said something about harlotry, which easily enough made her think I should resort to it, on account of long waiting for her. She was rightly indignant and her whole being blazed with chastity. I had said in the letter that I had reached a point where I was not sure it was totally unjustifiable under some circumstances. She showed me that at least in *my* case it *would* be unjustifiable. I acknowledged it, and her trust, which has been extraordinarily perfect, came back. She made me promise to marry her January 1st if Mr. Weeden was paid. . . .

This morning call from Geo. Wall, who wanted to talk about the etchings. Wants me to go to his father's & look over the pictures to pick out such ones as I think will etch well. . . .

. . .

THURSDAY. NOV. 22D 1883 2 P.M.

. . . Last evening went to Miss Channing's & met Charlotte there. Like Miss Grace very much. . . . It was a very good evening as there was no gossip, Miss Grace being intellectual and inclined to talk of best things. I'm glad she is Charlotte's friend. Then to Charlotte's she being full of love all the way; but when we were there she seemed to recoil somewhat & shrink from being so loving, and said so that it hurt, "I hate to feel myself doing all the loving." Strange how one forgets past things in a moment of strong feeling. Why could she not remember my weary months of loving while it seemed as if she never would be mine! and those two years of longing—ah she should remember!

I wrote her a letter before I went to sleep, from my bed.

Miserable day. . . .

. . .

MONDAY A.M. 26TH NOV. 1883

. . . In the evening . . . I went to Charlotte. Right off I saw she had one of her "relapses" in loving—one of her apathetic times. It seems almost like a form of insanity. It is all her old ambitious "freedom"-loving nature rising in rebellion against the "weakness" of tenderness and love. Ah, how my heart ached! These are black times—black times, indeed. One must have much courage to marry her knowing of these things. I want to marry her, and I trust, perhaps foolishly, that marriage will cure her, or that life with me will ease her of her strange spirit. I think her literary instincts are half to blame. I think that she feels a little undesirous, and straightway takes that as a theme, enlarges upon it, traces to the uttermost limit all its possibilities of horror and pain, until she loses control of herself, and the possibility becomes the reality. I have watched her carefully and I can but feel that a great deal of it is caused by imagination, and a great deal by restraint of sexual power. Though she sat & derided herself, condemned herself, and said cruel things of me, to the exemplification that *I* was the one cause of all this present weakness, that before *I* came she was strong and self-reliant, and not the "woman" she is now: though it would have seemed to another that she hated me for loving her, yet when I asked her if she wished not to marry me she said no. She still wanted to marry me: but to my question could reply with no reasons why. I tried to soften her by calling up the past joyous days when we were in the fresh landscape and so full of power, and as I called them up—I was appalled to see the change that had come. And she said the saddest day of my life was the day I knew love of her.

Good God, it ought not to be. I love her. . . .

. . . If this sort of thing should continue through our married life, I should be miserably unhappy: but I love her, and love gives patience. . . .

If I thought she would be happier, better, the doer of better work if I were no more as hers—I would bear the ignominy of severing our "engagement" and formally giving back her "freedom." Oh would that I could give her back her child's heart untouched by love & me! Would that I could. I shudder at the pain she must bear—shudder—oh—God knows how—.

These are black days.

·   ·   ·

NOV. 28TH 1883 ABOUT 4 P.M.

. . . Charlotte felt better. Said she could make a very good dinner for 10 cents—what the one she was eating cost her. Also said that she & I could live for 5 dollars a week. Whether she meant rent & all I don't know. She is so practically impractical that I have to smile sometimes. I know well enough how her hearty appetite would crave more solid fare than cookies & apples, and how each week would find her a little more ready to spend more for food. Still, we might be able to get along on that until we *could* spend more.

She was as assured today regarding marriage as I have known her to be. She does not seem to be willing to give it up. I still cling tenaciously to the idea that she will be all right when she *is* married. Of course I shall have to bear many of her quaint ideas, but I in my turn have just as much which will test her patience. . . .

. . . I know our own "thanksgiving," at the house, will be meagre, and less the customary turkey & its fellows. We have no money. My day will probably be spent here as usual: my dinner will probably be the usual bread & milk with a few dates. What matter? To be sure a little cheer now and then would be pleasant; and I have often wished there were more of the old days of feasting in our halls— . . . not in our case of carousal & drunkenness, but of good food and delicate wine and a smiling countenance. Ah God! how utterly empty of such things my life has been. A little taste at the Cresson's—the rest a monotony of privation. . . .

It *is* belittling. It reacts upon one's mind; I'm sure of it. The noblest enterprise is nipped in the bud. Generosity becomes a pain because with every desire to do generous things comes the knowledge that more than every cent must be spent on ourselves just to keep us comfortable. Here am I going chilly with the thinnest cotton drawers and gauze undershirt—and I generous! But it is sweeter to give than to receive. Oh yes—yes! . . .

THANKSGIVING DAY, NOV. 29TH 1883

To our surprise we have a turkey from Henry [Linsey, Walter's brother-in-law], and more. . . .

And do I give thanks? God knows aye God knows. And it is him that I would thank.

And Mr. Weeden is enjoying himself and perhaps has forgotten that I owe him $400–. *But I have not. . . .*

. . .

MONDAY 3D DEC. 1883 1:40 P.M.

Yesterday, read most of the day. In evening went to Charlotte. My dear Love! She is unwell, and strangely unhappy. There is no limit to her self denunciation, and a great spasm of self abnegation seems to have come over her. She talked of dying until my heart ached—ached, and tears came. She thought everyone should make a will—and what would I rather she left to me—her pretty amber bracelet? her lace neckerchief? or her tiny red slippers? All asked in so deep and earnest a way, with a touch of childishness that—oh my God! Cover that dying day from my sight! Cover it—cover it! She was evidently sick—I fear for her. Ah, that we could have married months ago. She thinks she will bring me pain & discomfort instead of strength and joy. And I fear she broods over it so much that she *is* making herself to be the instrument of pain & discomfort. It is very, very strange how she has changed in 6 months. She was so confident of her powers, of her physical vigor and her ability to make me happy: and now—she says she is weaker in every way physically, and sees that she is only a pain to me. Those feelings must be the result of morbidity brought about by the effect her work and waiting & worry have had upon her body. If I could take her now and had money enough and go with her to some pleasant place for a while all would be quickly remedied, I feel certain.

Oh it does make my heart ache! . . .

DECEMBER 8TH 1883 A.M.

During five days much may happen. A part—and a goodly part of my time was given to arranging the water color exhibit. I had calls meanwhile. Mr. & Mrs. Cresson were here Wednesday. And weren't we glad to see each other! He stayed awhile then left her here while he went to attend some business. So we talked. She was as kind and comforting as ever. . . .

. . . In the morning I had received a poem and a few words from my Love. It was utterly sad and without courage. . . .

My water colors in this exhibition are generally liked, strange to say: besides it is evident they rank among the best of those here, and those here are supposed to represent the N.Y. and Boston and Phil. men. . . .

. . .

WEDNESDAY 12TH DEC. 1883 10 A.M.

Well, the proofs came back yesterday. . . . Mr. Wall senior . . . seemed much pleased with them, and saw by the variation in the looks of the proofs how a printer could spoil a very fine plate even. Then we went up to his little gallery & looked over other pictures to etch. . . . I told Geo. I should have to charge $30– for the plate. As I have spent about ten on it, and—well, I feel that I shall not be too well paid for my services. They can have a dozen proofs taken & sell them for at least $2– a piece, which will nearly pay for it, besides they will have the plate to use indefinitely. Also I told him I must have some money before going on. . . .

MONDAY, A.M. DEC. 17TH 1883

. . . I sold my "Going to the Shad Nets after Leaving the Cart" & "Sunset: Motive at Narragansett Pier" to Dr. Ely. He made me an offer of $75– for the two—about ½ what I should have gotten. Money was needed so badly I could not afford to lose that much. 10% must come out for commission. To be sure it took not more than 3 days to paint them, but God knows the weary days of work and waiting which should have some recompense. . . .

. . . Last eve. with my Love. She was feeling *much* better physically & mentally. Her face was ruddy & creamy & clear and bright; her caresses what they always are—indeed she was fascinating, charming, tender, lovely. She showed me some of her latest work. Her "In Duty-Bound" has been accepted by the *Woman's Journal*. She feels as if it was a start, and it is. We talked of what lovers love and about Home & children & work. . . .

WEDNESDAY 10 A.M. DEC. 19TH 1883

Monday afternoon Charlotte called while I was at sketch class, but I left & we went shopping together. I bought some Canton china for her, but she wanted me to keep it on account of her family; so took it yesterday noon to the house. Then we went to several stores, she buying many little things for Xmas fun. Unbeknown to her, while she was standing near I bought her Geo. Eliot's poems, which I knew she wanted. I believe that I have now bought all my gifts except Gussie's (that is my nephew), and I have bought 3 times as much as I had any idea I could, for I was paid yesterday morning for my water colors. Gave father 2 months' rent also. Got him pair of shoes and a coveted blank book. . . .

Just met Mr. B. Wall, who says the proofs are satisfactory (Marilhat) and that Tom Robinson praises the plate much and says he did not know I could do so well. That is pleasant. My plates have not yet come. He is in a great hurry! . . .

. . .

24 DEC. 83 NOON

. . . Been bitter cold for a few days. My underclothing came just in time. I don't know how I could have borne it with my gauze affairs.

This is a time of very hard work with me. Harder because so hurried & tremblingly uncertain. I *cannot* etch them as well as I might had I the leisure to obey my impulses. One can hurry anything better than an etching, it seems to me. . . .

27TH DEC. ''83—NOON

. . . Christmas passed pleasantly—though I worked on the Corot until about 4 o'clock. . . . The truth is, it is a poor etching. I have not got the softness & tender sentiment of Corot. If it were not promised I would not let it go at all. I quite hope he will not like it, so that it may not be published. I found that for my time the process which would best translate the tenderness would be too long, so I boldly interpreted—that is I made a lot of scrawly lines do for the charming indefiniteness. That is all right. But—I fear I for once became Philistine and tried to soften them with delicate shading. It gave the plate a better tone, but it left it neither interpretation nor imitation. A few square inches of it do very well, but the rest!

I took it to him yesterday with a note, as much explanation as I was able to make. It is a *stinking* plate, I think.

I took the Decamp "The Good Samaritan." It will try me, but I *feel* it. It is grand & solemn. I find it as I study it full of the most fascinating and studied lines. There are some grand oppositions, which always make an effective etching. I am trying to make a careful drawing of the lines.

They are difficult *for me*. . . .

Last evening I determined to rest. So I wrote a letter to my Love, to Miss Morse (regrets), to Grandma Cresson, and a small note to Miss Jeffrey. Then I read [Philip Gilbert Hamerton's] Etching and Etchers, looked over my proofs of Corot and shed mental tears at the defects. . . .

28TH DEC. 1883 1:40 P.M.

I have been at home working on the Decamps all morning. My heart is sick, for mother is no better, rather worse *I* think. All that *may* be rises before me, and I realize how tender hearted I am, and how much in need of comfort from something higher than myself. I am calm yet, but it is rather the calmness of one who knows a thing *must* be, than that of one who is glad to trust God. My religion seems to resolve itself into a belief in a God, of whom I know nothing, to whom I cry vainly, it seems, believing that he could help if he would. I believe him the voice of all Good, Truth & Beauty.

But I fancy that is far less comfortable than to believe like the Romanist. And mother's sickness, as is usual, emphasizes all death. If our prayers are answered often even, and our loved ones spared to us, there must come a *last* time when our prayer is useless: for indeed all must die. . . .

SAT. DEC. 29TH 83, 10:15 A.M.

Came down to get Dr. Allen to go up to see mother in consultation with Dr. Knapp, for she is dangerously sick. It takes all energy of an artistic sort out of me. I fear Wall's plates will fare badly. . . .

MON. 31ST DEC. 1883. 11 A.M.

. . . Sat. about 5 o'c. I came down to see if letters were here. Found one from the New Ex. Co. saying a paid package awaited me. I went after it. Found it to be a very beautiful copy of Shakespeare's Sonnets edited by Dowden & bound by Sutterby of London in black russia. It is a fit dress for the contents. It was from Mrs. Cresson, my Xmas gift. How good of her! . . .

. . . Geo. [Wall] says that he shall be satisfied with my work he knows—tells me not to worry, for I shall do my best under the circumstances & what more could one do? But somehow that is no cure for the self knowledge that they are not as good as they might be. The best part, though, is that often he asks me to attempt the "Arab Falconer" of *Fromentin*, saying that he will give me $75– to do it. I think if I have time I will attempt it. . . .

JANUARY 1ST 1884 3:30 P.M.

This is a new year. There does not seem now to be much prospect of "A Happy New Year"'s being anything but ironical. Yet what may be ours I dare not try to foresee. It is best that we keep our hearts ever in the temper of prayer. . . .

. . .

SUNDAY A.M. JAN. 7TH 1884

Time for only a word. Mother's chances for life being less & less each day, according to the Drs., and seeming indeed so, caused us—because it seemed that the medicines she was taking was hurting rather than bettering her because of their violence; and also because Dr. Knapp was manly and true, and dared say that the medicine of the old school could not reach her case and that she should be treated homeopathically. He withdrew, and, though it would if known cause his discharge from the Medical Society (For shame!), advised us to employ E. B. Knight, a homeopathist. Dr. Allen, though my much prized friend, was not treating her properly, I feel certain, and was evidently mixed up in his ideas of it. We had to telephone to him that we wanted him no more. It will make it awkward for me, but that is nothing if it betters mother.

Well, Dr. Knight came, and made a thorough examination, and thought the quinine they had given her had produced her shocking mental condition.* He naturally could not agree with their method of treatment, and said, what we thought, that the rum they gave her tended to produce the very disease they were trying to cure. . . . Dr. Knight wanted her to drink cider, which she wanted to do, and truly I think the first glass of it did her more good than all the calomel & quinine she had taken. . . . She passed the best night last night of any since she was sick, and seems brighter and better this morning. Whether it is anything permanent who can say? She may be dead when I go home. . . .

Geo. Wall is very much pleased with the Corot plate. In his forcible lingo he says it's "a buster." The second Decamps came out very well; the dry paint and scraper will finish it. I think it the best of them, so far. The Couture is next. That will be hard, for it is a rich head, painted with much *verve*.

Then came Daubigny (which I can do) then—the Fromentin, and all in 5 weeks(!!!) besides some pen drawings. . . .

10TH JAN. 84 11 A.M.

. . . [Mr. Wall] broached a new plan—that of having me make 12 large etchings after some pictures—1 a month which would take a year. It would be very desirable indeed. I am ready to try it.

------

*Dr. Edward Balch Knight was the Stetsons' physician and also one of Walter's closest friends. An important art patron of Providence, he served as PAC President from 1902 to 1904, and was the man to whom Grace Channing wrote as she edited and annotated Walter's diaries.

There are a number of entries that stress Stetson's close relationship with Knight. "I am quite in love with [him]. I should miss him more than any man I ever met. He *is* such an honest lovable clean minded man—and—so firmly gentle." Diaries, June 30, 1888. Or again: "We spent the evening in the Dr.'s library discussing social questions, especially the "Social Evil" and its relation to the underpaying of work girls. Dr. Knight is a thoroughly *good* man: the best I know. We agreed that the patriarchal system of wives and concubines seemed to us nearer the truth than modern monogamous marriage." Diaries, June 20, 1888.

I have not had a chance to finish the Decamps yet. To be sure there is little to do to it.

15TH [JAN.] 1884. TUESDAY A.M.

Five days has made great change in mother. She is greatly improved though still unable to move about, only in the most limited way, in bed. The Dr. came Sunday and found her on the lounge, whither we had taken her so as to remake her bed; and he said he saw that his services were no further needed; that father could care for her now as well as he, and that he should come no more. There was a thrill of joy running through us all I'm sure.

I went to my Love Sunday. There are no words for her loving & her loveliness—but I must go back to last Friday evening when I went to Geo. Wall's at his request; and there in secret he & his father and I talked over a plan, "a great Plan." It was this: Mr. Wall has decided to put off the sale of his pictures another year, and to make some money out of them in strange wise; namely, he wants me to etch twelve large plates, the smallest not less than 18 inches, of a dozen of the pictures. It is to be kept a profound secret until they are published, and it is to take a year—1 a month. To insure the secrecy of it he offers me two rooms, larger than my present studio, in one of his own buildings; one of them to be used for a printing room and laboratory, the other for a painting room. Further, he is to buy all the materials, get a big press and so forth. They are to be sent to Boston first, so that no one shall know their real destination. Then I am to have some excuse for changing my studio.

I told him I would do it for $1200. Little enough surely for the possible results. But then it will be sure to pay—*and my Love and I can marry!!!!* Further, when they are to be printed for the market he is to send to N. Y. for a printer to come here, instead of sending the plates there. It is a fascinating scheme & I sincerely hope it may be carried out, although I begrudge the time taken from my painting. I shall try to get out of it two weeks to take my Love to N[ova] S[cotia] & to make some sketches. Meanwhile the small etchings are to go on just the same, for when he has his sale he will want them to use in the catalogue.

Well, I told my darling about it—and she was very glad, but said she should be just as happy, if it should not be. And heaven knows she seemed supremely happy that evening. We talked about what we should need and about rooms and————. . . .

17TH JAN. "84 P.M.

. . . This A. M. I bought a Jongkind [illegible] and an Appian & a Lalanne.* I felt I *wanted* them for study. Those 3 men I admire as much as almost
any moderns. Jongkind is surely not appreciated. Appian's things leave an in-
sidious charm. One finds himself thinking of them almost unconsciously. . . .

This P. M. I have painted on two landscapes, put a figure in one of my
N[ova] S[cotia] studies. I am looking forward to my private, and public exhibition. I do hope—for her sake, it may be a success. . . .

24TH JAN. "84 6 P.M.

Rains very hard: am down only to see if there were letters. Yesterday
was in Boston with Geo. Whitaker. Went to Art Club. To Dolls', to Blakeslee's where we saw Whistler's "Etching & Drypoints" and got his unique
catalogue. I must say that I think just such a catalogue was needed, and the
arrangement in white & yellow did not displease me a bit. As for the etchings, I liked them much. They are so sensitive, and full of delicate decision.

Also we went to the Art Museum to Faneuil Hall and to dinner at the
Old Elm, and met Geo. Wall & Mr. E. Robinson. The latter I liked much.
We talked some about my coming exhibition, & they wanted me to have it
in Boston.

We have decided to do the big plates, and I am hunting up a big press
for them now. It is as before $1200– and materials. . . .

FEB. 9TH 84. 5:30 P.M.

I have been too hurried to write. Exhibition is coming on all right.
Have been to Boston twice. Ordered Mr. Wall's big press 24 × 36. $220– and
been getting price lists etc. about other things connected with etching. Have
finished all the small plates but the Fromentin that is promised for the 15th
and is not yet begun!

Have written innumerable letters; and received many, among others
very dear ones from my Love, and Mrs. Cresson. Charlotte *seems* very happy
and expects with all her heart to be married in May. God make it possible!
My money has to be spent as fast as earned. A great deal depends upon that
show of mine. I do not really expect to sell anything.

------

* Stetson purchased prints by Johann Jongkind, Adolphe Appian, and Maxime Lalanne.

Charlotte has found a house for us that seems to be just the thing and has the refusal of it. . . .

*   *   *

16TH FEB. 84 5 OR SO P.M.

Yesterday I about finished the Fromentin plate in which means that I finished the lines of etching for Mr. Wall in the time agreed upon. I do not think them technical marvels (!) but they give one an idea of the paintings. . . .

I can't help feeling how little Charlotte cares for my pictures, or seems to care; and I wonder if I shall ever have the technical mastery to *make* her care.

Am happy as I can be getting my show organized: and *I'm so very tired*.

*   *   *

MARCH 13TH 1884 A.M.

Nearly a month since I wrote! And so much has happened! I cannot hope to record in detail. To summarize:—The press has been set up and everything nearly ready to begin work with. My exhibition has been finished, beginning with a perfect social success in the way of a reception, at which all were surprised at my work both as to quality and quantity; it continued for five days, during which many visited it, and I sold some 14 pictures, for no great sums it is true, but still for more than enough to pay my expenses. Besides I met many people, made new friends; had Boston visitors, notably Mr. [Louis] Prang & Mr. [Edward] Noyes;* got fine newspaper notices and won several hearts. Altogether it *was* a decided success.†

This morning I paid Mr. Weeden $100— on my note. And I feel that

---

*Louis Prang, print publisher of Boston, bought a number of Stetson paintings over the next several years. Edward Noyes was an owner of the Noyes and Blakeslee Art Gallery of Boston.

†In the "Preface" for this 1884 Exhibition (the first complete review of his efforts thus far), Stetson tried to anticipate comments of reviewers. On the one hand, he attacked them; they lacked a "native feeling for art" and failed to understand "original or unusual expression." But on the other, he admitted his limitations, his "dearth of those enviable trade-marks of mastery which long experience gives." "Without contradiction or mistake," Stetson concluded, "my critic may write of all those, and should those prove insufficient, I can tell him more faults. But if he accuses me of no respectful emulation of perfect draughtsmanship—as some obtuse critics have done,—no real love of nature and reverence for her beautiful laws; no earnest search for the meaning of her adorable mysteries, he accuses me falsely." CWS, "Preface," *A Catalogue of the Pictures and Sketches Exhibited by Charles Walter Stetson* (Providence, R.I.: PAC, 1884). The catalogue lists 83 Stetson oil paintings and 77 water colors.

much happier. He was very pleasant: a little advisory perhaps, but yet pleasant.

Mr. De Kay wants me to show my pictures in N. Y. and has sent $25 to Miss Anne Morse that she may select for him a picture. *That* is evident appreciation. I sold six to one man (Ellsworth Yomey).

Our house is hired, to be possessed April 15th. I traded a $45 picture . . . for Cookery.

In payment of the rent of the Art Club I hung the Annual Ex. I am tired out. That's a fact. But I do not expect an hour's rest for months yet.

My love is sad: she has been very happy; and now correspondingly depressed. *I* think she is unwell. I think a cure will come with marriage and *home*.

. . . *petty exactions of a domestic sort*

August 18, 1884 – September 8, 1885

ON MAY 2ND, 1884, Charlotte and Walter were married. "How I love her," he exclaimed. "She is *everything* a perfect wife should be"— "dainty and exquisitely gentle now as a woodland flower," and yet also joyously content, "quite like her old time buoyant self." She was "proud of doing the housework." She was reading widely, attending lectures, and holding her own in political debates. "She thinks with astonishing clearness, and logic that paralyzes me. . . . It is great fun to have men call here and engage with her in discussions of politics or morals or most anything. She invariably puts them at their wits' ends."

Predictably, however, when Charlotte became pregnant, she felt despondent. She was afraid that all her dreams "of great usefulness, may be past or beyond her reach." From Walter's point of view, however, she was becoming "better fitted for usefulness," and learning those much needed "lessons of humility and self-sacrifice and patience."

Yet diary entries become increasingly sparse during this period: as though he decided not to mention fears or disappointments, as though he were simply waiting, hoping for a change. When Katharine Beecher Stetson was born, March 23, 1885, he wrote: "Motherhood such as hers is the divinest thing life has yet shown me, equal to love itself—the love of lovers." But then again five months later, Charlotte finally "broke down entirely." She manifested "violent hysterical symptoms, and long periods of taciturnity, melancholy and utter loss of the desire or power to will." She was now "a nervous invalid requiring the utmost care and tender treatment, lest it should settle itself into an incurable mind disease." "I have no doubt in my own mind that the whole trouble is some uterine irritation and until that is cured she will be no better."

Walter responded to the crisis by helping in every way he could—by arranging for a maid, and by doing many of the household chores himself. But there were double-standard expectations of which he was starkly unaware: for a man, family life should enhance career ambitions, whereas for a woman, domestic obligations should replace them. "For the first time . . . I felt . . . sorry that I had married. . . . I would not marry if I had the chance again, knowing what I do now."*

WAYLAND ST. AUG 18, 1884

It is a task to take up my recording after five months of silence. And yet I want to. I feel the weight of what has happened, know well that I can't write one hundredth of it, and so I shrink from doing any of it. Yet, supposing I should live to be the average age of my kinfolk, I feel sure I should be glad of even what I can do. So I have in sheer desperation, my Love being in Boston and I very lonely, decided to begin.

The dates are flown and I confess to too great laziness to try to find them. I think Charlotte has them in her Journal.

After my show here in Providence, at Mr. Noyes' solicitation, he having taken great liking to my work and sold four of my best things, I sent all my pictures (with the exception of a few poorest things) to him [at Noyes & Blakeslee's in Boston]. He offered to arrange the sale and bear the expense if I failed to sell any. May 20 last, at 8 in the morning I sent them by freight. . . . Up to that time I had worked no one knows how hard on my etchings, my paintings, and the house furnishing. Such glorious hours as she and I filled with continuing the things for this house—the painting & papering, the carpeting & chair buying, the selection of all the things needful. I lived in a happy clime. And she seemed to expand, growing and growing in the loveliest qualities. I was not harrassed by money matters. My Providence sale, the sale of those four in Boston gave me all the cash needful, to say nothing of what my etchings brought me. Instead of having one bare room as we thought we must, we found we could have as cozy and beautiful a home as need be. Charlotte had many presents of cash and so forth so that she got a lot of beautiful things. The irritations caused by the almost inevitably stupid

---

*The above quotations are from diary entries of the following dates: Aug. 18, Nov. 17, 1884; Jan. 21, Jan. 18, 1885; Sept. 15, 1884; May 2, Aug. 24, Aug. 27, 1885.

tradesmen were so much spice. And when I found that my painters had painted dining rooms and parlor beautifully in colors that would *not wash*, I straightway with small ado made them do it over: it became a pleasant family incident.

Well, our home made beautiful chiefly by the love working in our hearts showing itself in what one bought and in the arrangement of our goods, was already for us, and I gave it up to my darling. Thursday May 1 & Friday May 2nd to do with it as she pleased. And what did she do! Oh my heart! All was ready then, and on the evening of May 2nd we were wed.—We—were—wed—. My darling, pure and true, fought for, prayed-for, longed-for, loved with a love I wonder at myself, though she merits more than I can possibly give her—*we were wed*—. Oh where were the bitter days and the toilsome waiting and corroding doubts when, after my dear father had said the simple ceremony with our mothers near and her aunt Caroline, and the fine supper Mrs. Perkins made for us, we took our basket with some late gifts and a few clothes and came arm in arm through the windy night to this beautiful home full of color & pictures and fair sweet flowers. On the way the Phelons lifted a window to wish us joy.* Oh the hush of our hearts! The stillness—it had come! It had *come*! Waited for, ached for—and come in all the fullness we could ask—came attended by all the fortune we could wish and quite luxury where we had been willing to expect privation. Come. Come.

Here then, in from the blowing wind & storm outside—also from the blowing wind & storm of our lives—to this color-filled candle-lighted warm room,—the logs burning on the hearth, the flowers thrilling the air with their [illegible] aromas. How happy I was. How very happy. And she—. God knows.

Leaving me in this parlor she took the bedroom which is sacred always with us. I put on the wedding garment she had made for me, a stainless chiton, and took the ring she had never worn in which *Ich liebe Dich* is engraved as she wished, and waited. There was a gliding sound and a hush of new light and she She SHE was there. Oh radiance! Oh divine loveliness! How love illumines! Clad in the thinnest white, fairer than I had ever seen her, her intensely dark eyes, and exquisite mouth sweeter than any thought, bearing a crown of roses, wherewith I was to crown her. When we had the true ceremony, an offering to God, as the other had been a sacrifice to civil

---

*Mr. and Mrs. Ray Phelon, Providence neighbors.

law. Simple right, unutterable, beautiful, and imperishable long as my soul lives! Oh my Love, my more than Love! . . .

Each day gives me new cause for loving her; each day I love her more and she grows more wonderfully tender and "beautiful" in all her ways. A marvelous impalpable change has come over her. She is as dainty and exquisitely gentle now as a woodland flower might be if it had a clear brain and quick senses. . . .

She has gone to Boston, to Mrs. [Martha Luther] Lane's. It is our first parting. I am very lonesome. I have cried in what is supposed to be unmanly fashion, but to be without her—I think it is a foreshadowing of a final parting, the feeling of how uncertain life is, that perhaps we have already—Oh God God! no no!

I could not sit at our table at supper tonight and look at her empty chair; I brought my baked apple and milk in here—and wept with every mouthful. . . .

Right in the midst of our joy came the wonderful news from Boston that my Exhibition was something great as a success. And newspaper articles abounded, one from James Boyle O'Reilly full of ardor and candor, in which I was put down as a new power in art, a genius, and poet and so forth. All that did not affect Charlotte & me much, her more than me, though. We were too full of our happiness in each other & the peace of our home to have that more than a ripple of pleasure. But I did feel . . . pleased, deeply, that it all came *for my work*, that none of them knew me personally, that notice was not sought. What pleased me the most was that it gave Charlotte more respect. She was not thought to be a fool, any more, for marrying me—me, Stetson, but rather she was made the object of almost fatiguing congratulations. . . . Besides the checks that came were surety. They sold about $2500. worth & I got $2058. from it.

Meanwhile I went about my work, my large etchings for Mr. Wall. It has been verily labor. The large Corot is done, the Couture, a Daubigny, and the small Corot with a bridge is nearly done. He is much pleased with them all. . . . No one knows, unless it be my love, how much of a *devoir* they are. I am grateful, for the commission, and for the chance to practice etching (about which I feel I have learned a deal) but my artist-heart is with creation not reproduction. . . .

The hundred-dollars that come in at the end of each plate are very agreeable. It keeps us feeling very comfortable. I've paid all my debts, Waterman's, Weeden's, all. It is glorious. And I've been able to help father and mother, considerably, a thing that has been one of my chief hopes for long. . . .

We should have gone to Europe if it had not been for the etchings. Charlotte takes deep interest in my work now and helps me much. She is *everything* a perfect wife should be. . . .

And now how could I write tenderly enough to tell how in my love's clean womb lies a two months' old babe—either Sigurd or Katharine—a longed for, already loved child? What joy she felt when she knew it! I never saw such a heavenly face. Her face very often since I've lived with her has seemed divine, but that time she felt sure our child had come to her fair well-kept house from the unseen wide world her face was ineffably heavenly. Such hours as we have passed!!

And when I knew it—God knows of those secret hours spent with him. Why tell what I felt? Save that it was joy and a fervent prayer that I might become worthy, and that the babe might be moulded to love: that it might be a beautiful, true, good-doing, great soul, and that its mother might be kept as holily as if she were a chief angel of heaven.

How gladly will I work for it and its mother that it may be more than its father ever may be!

Our first night apart. How I hate to go to our bed alone! Oh it frightens me to see how I love her, how I am so hers that I should die if she were taken, or worse, much worse, live uselessly to grieve and have one thought. These partings are terrible because they make clear the instability of our relation since Death comes ever, and recalls the inevitable final—Oh God! God cover my eyes! *I love her.* . . .

19TH AUG. 1884, 8:20 P.M.

. . . I saw a sight which fascinated me. The Gano St. beach was covered with women, girls & youths, in the water, on land, naked, half-clothed, screeching in fright or glee. First I thought someone was drowned, but soon I saw it was clear sport. Down below not far, were 4 girls & a woman, generously showing their white limbs. I was so tired that I was glad of this diversion: so I watched them. Presently the delight of my eye, the artists' passion for seeing & enjoying action, overcame me & I came in for hat & boots to go there to see them nearby. . . . It was a sight. I should say there were a hundred persons quite. Boys & girls alike naked, young women whose whole bodies could be seen among the high sweet scented clover & in the water. Passionate girls with flushed cheeks & baring bosoms sat about with scarcely a rag on gazing at the sexuality of the downy youths nearby. It astounded me truly that there could be such license in the city. They did not seem to mind me at all. So I saw a great deal, not stopping to moralize. I'm certain the youths & maidens were fired by each other, but I do not dare to say it was wrong. Many of their mothers were near & some of them were participating, thinking it proper to clothe themselves, but so thinly that the hair of the pubis showed clearly. I could not moralize. I enjoyed it all & was glad I had found something to distract my weary feelings. But since I've wondered how it should be considered. Personally I should feel ill to have my wife, or daughters of mine, so boldly naked. But I dare not judge.

Some of the girls were very beautiful, one little 5 year old especially, who was bewitching when she kicked the waves with her plump pink legs & laughed through her dripping hair. . . .

21ST AUG. 84. 9:30 A.M.

Overslept. Am waiting for the water to boil for my coffee. Slept well (!) A fine, loving letter from my Love yesterday morning while I was washing dishes. She is better. And Dr. Keller pronounces "prognosis favorable." Indeed I'm intensely glad, albeit I felt that I knew it to be so myself! . . .

Oh! before that I stopped at Gregory's and ordered [Pierre] Cazeaux's Obstetrics which Charlotte thought we'd better buy. Dr. Keller advised it. Also Harpers Monthly for Sept.

AUG. 26TH "84. 5 P.M.

Journal-keeping seems to flag again. But I've been amazingly busy what with etching, painting, and housework, for owing to Charlotte's unwellness, caused by the early stage of pregnancy, I have had a good deal of such work to do. She came home Thursday last, having had a fine time at her friend's, being better, in good spirits; but the nausea soon came on again. It is by no means severe and I think in her heart of hearts she is very happy and greatly pleased to feel that about my next birthday, if all goes well, she will bring forth a child. Oh the dear noble woman.

. . . *Fool's Sermon on Death* I finished today. I believe it to be as good as most of my work, if not the most thoughtful of any I have done. Mr. Whitaker came to look at it today & he liked it very much. He is especially pleased with the landscape part of it, and most especially with the sky. *That* he fairly gloated over. The fool is pretty good in action and expression, I think, but the girl does not satisfy me—nor does any of it of course— I speak relatively. The fact is, I don't know how it does look, having had it round for 2 or 3 months.

Met Mr. Bates this morning.* He spoke of the head I let Mr. Tilden have—that little boy, a sketch of whom I made from my studio window. He liked it much. Said he was trying to get it of Mr. T. Thought he should. If I have any thing similar at anytime he'd like to have it.

Say what one may, it is pleasing to have people like one's things, and, however mildly, strive for them. . . .

How beautiful the river & sky are after the storm. The clouds are a sweet orange brown, pale, against a mild bluish sky. How fresh the salt-laden air, and the greens of the foliage. We live in a lovely place, a very lovely place. I know of few so much so. How blest we are! After my bitter fight to sit here at ease with money for every decent want and luxuries, with beautiful nature out our very windows, and the supreme knowledge that I am loved truly by one of the noblest of women, is almost too much for any thing but tears. . . .

*   *   *

SEPT. 3D—84 8 A.M.

For a few days I have felt discouragement about my etching. It is clear to me that I was not made a reproductive etcher and that whatever I may do in it will be by sheer force of some sense and will. There is little love in it truly. To strive day after day to express another man's thought when I have burning thoughts of my own to say is not cheerful by any means. . . .

Here at home, all is well. My Love is happier. Less "sick," and we watch the growth of our little one with many tender thoughts. If ever a child should be lovely in all ways because of its parents' loving thoughts and mu-

---

* Grace Channing noted: "He speaks too so warmly of Bates, 'a guardian friend' to him in those early, dreadful days. And I feel more warmly to Whitaker, reading of his real and constant kindness. If those Providence men knew what careful studies—or better, sketches—exist of them in words! It is just as well they don't know too much. But he likes them—nearly all, and I am struck with the position so mere a youth evidently early attained in that circle of older, richer, more fortunately placed artists. It is very much to their credit, I think that they quickly felt his power and personality, and I shall begin to revise my impressions of my native city, in this light. True—he could have starved there (and no one knows how near he often was to it,)—but the men of his immediate circle were most kind; I think they *all* felt rather 'big brotherly' to the ardent and gifted boy. It warms my heart toward a certain circle in Providence." GEC to EBK, April 30, 1912, p. 17.

tual love this coming child should be. In the very ecstasies of bodily marriage I have been conscious of prayers that the child that might come—of intense longings that the child that might come should be noble, beautiful in soul & body and a grand helper of the world. We shall see.

Charlotte was unhappy a few days ago—not deeply—but some—and she read this journal, some of the entries during our early love days. Seeing that I loved her so, and having it all brought to her freshly made her quickly happy again. She got up one morning & brought the book back to bed with her & there read it with increasing joy. . . .

SEPT. 15TH 1884. 8 P.M.

I have been so occupied or so tired when unoccupied, that my record has been neglected. However, perhaps a summary will be useful to me sometime.

My Love has been, on the whole, better this month. That hidden child has grown. She bears it patiently, though she is more sensitive and easily fatigued both physically & mentally & at times despondent, especially when she has fears that all that dreamed of life of great usefulness, may be past or beyond her reach. Truly, I think, she is becoming better fitted for usefulness. She has learned some lessons of humility and self-sacrifice and patience. She wants me with her all the time, wants what comfort I can give her—and Oh she loves me! Why should I not leave my work and be near her? I love her and would do the utmost to give her joy & ease. Sometimes when I am very tired myself it is a burden to do housework & all the things she asks, yet I feel glad to bear the weight & do. It is not for me to ask if it is right for me to give art less attention while she needs me. God will bring all about rightly. It is my right to do all I can for her. And I will do it.

She has been absent a deal helping her mother off to Utah. She goes Thursday.*. . .

Perhaps one of the most notable things that has happened is that a young man, named Geo. Tewksbury, of Topeka, Kansas, came here last Thursday after spending two days in fruitless search for me. . . . He proved himself to be a "raving" enthusiast, in a sensible way, however, regarding my work, only a few specimens of which he saw in Boston, among others the "Fool's Sermon on Death."

---

*Thomas Perkins, Charlotte's brother, asked Mary Perkins to come to Ogden, Utah, to help him with his family. Although anxious about Charlotte's pregnancy, she felt obliged to take the trip, and did not return until several months after Katharine Stetson was born.

He determined thereupon to see me & get something to take home. So down he came. He certainly was indefatigable. I like him. He seemed modest, earnest, energetic, & well read. He is tall & dark by the way. We made an appointment which he kept by coming to the studio Friday morning at 11. Then we had a long talk in which he told me interesting things of himself. And said he had $25 a month which he wanted to devote to buying my pictures. Asked me if I could find it in my heart to want to receive $25 monthly for a while, I to send him pictures in return. I agreed to it willingly. Also he selected 4 things, some early studies, which I let him have for $80—. He took them with him and is to send a check on his return. Everything about him led me to trust him. He told me about his call at Noyes & Blakeslee's. He said the first day he was in there they charged him $800— for the Fool's Sermon, but the next day they said they'd had a letter from me which said let it go for $500—. Which, if he told the truth, is false. They set the price themselves at $500. I did nothing, but give my consent. He said he bought two small landscapes of them. It is clear that he is truly in love with my work. When I came home however & told Charlotte that I had let him take $80— of pictures away she began to distrust him although she had liked him. Somehow what she said made me suspect him. So I am awaiting a letter from him with small patience, not that I should hate to lose the pictures— for I cared little for them—but I hate to be cheated. I can't help feeling, however, that he is all right. . . .

My darling has found in the Sept. "Art Amateur" notice of my Boston show—only 3 months (!) behind time!—I can't see what anyone could wish better than it. It praises & tells truly my faults. Whether it praised too highly I cannot judge. I must confess that it pleased me.*

That A. M., E. M. Kilvert that sent me her MS. about my show—a

---

*According to the review, Stetson's pictures "stirred" the "whole community of connoisseurs" in Boston: "The rumor of them soon spread. The town came flocking. They stood the test of the highest art—that is they satisfied the popular enthusiasm for story-telling pictures and excited agonizing admiration among the aesthetes. They had, indeed, something of Vedder's cleverness of subject and a great deal of La Farge's poetry of color. One aesthete remarked that the color was as passionate as Swinburne's verse. . . . In short the young man went home to Providence after hanging his pictures with prices like $50.00 and $30.00 marked upon them, and in a few days awoke famous, with the great guns of a fervor over his little things booming in the Boston newspapers. To speak in calmness at this distance from the event, which apparently has not been thought worthy of mention in the New York Journal hitherto, young Stetson gave proof of a natural productive genius. . . . Nevertheless he needs to study drawing. His anatomy is generally uncertain and indefinite, and sometimes ridiculous. All the same, he makes it clear what effect he is trying to produce, and often times produces it in a way to take one's breath away with his audacity, his crude strength, and his success withal." *Art Amateur*, Sept. 1884, transcribed by David Goodale, Stetson Scrapbook.

critic on the "Transcript" wrote me again a few days ago to re-invite me to call on her. It is an odd letter of the florid school. It amused me.*

Charlotte & I had a fine sail to Newport last week. . . .

19TH SEPT. "84 ABOUT 9 P.M.

My Love has just gone to bed after a full day's work. She has been better of late (I think, too, that she grows better daily)—and felt strength for a deal of housework, "settling" the things her mother sent over. She is tired, but healthily, I think. . . .

. . . The painting that I'm at work upon, the nude girls & elves & a temple and nine dancers—is about done. One to see it would not guess how much I've worked over it. The fact is, I've been seeking for a tone I only felt. I've not quite got it, but it is nearer than usual.† I feel full of subjects. Little things daily suggest what might be large (in an intellectual sense) pictures. Never before did living human beings, especially young boys & girls in their teens seem so lovely and wonderful. I can scarce wait to paint them. Perhaps my having learned so much of late of the depths of the pain & misdoing of men & women is the reason for seeing so much more in young people. The trees, too, have grown dearer to me. My Charlotte has led me nearer than ever to them. I never knew of a person who was so intimate with them as she is. She seems to feel their very growth, the minutest variation of their lines of growth, and the meaning of their forms. She talks of them as if they were human. . . .

---

*This is the first of a series of diary citations about a "hot correspondence" with Mrs. E. M. Kilvert, art critic for the *Boston Transcript*. For the next several years she kept up a "steady fire of letters" which were both "interesting" and "entertaining." And although she helped him professionally (introducing him to art collector James Jackson Jarves, for instance), Stetson clearly did not like her. "Such an odd, rather gaudy woman!" he wrote. "Per Buccho! I shrug my shoulders. I am glad she lives no nearer and comes not every day." Diaries, Dec. 6, 1886.

Although occasionally Stetson enjoyed the "vivacity and sustained power" of Mrs. Kilvert's letters (Aug. 4, 1888), he nonetheless remained suspicious. Her letters "are interesting 'and all that,' but dear me—I don't want to know her much better" (May 5, 1886). Or again several years later: "Mrs. Kilvert has been almost as effusive as ever writing letters that might be interpreted as amorous in the extreme. She is either an absolutely pure woman who does not realize what she does or one who loves to play with love. I incline to believe the latter. She surely has made almost no progress with me in three years." Diaries, Jan. 30, 1888.

†*A Joyous Place* (18 × 24 inches) was shown at the 1884 Providence exhibit and at Noyes and Blakeslee's in Boston. Stetson wrote, "whether the result be good or bad, it has been carefully & lovingly thought. The only purely technical feat sought after was that of making powerful pure colors keep a distance & to take so called 'foreground colors' & make them aerial. I believe I have succeeded." "Opera" Book, p. 39.

She is sleeping. Quietly I will go to her. I feel as if I were an unmarried lover whose loving mistress awaited him. God grant that this beautiful "romantic" sentiment may not wear away! It is laid waste enough throughout the world without being frost-bitten in our hearts. Keep warm, my heart!

*   *   *

SUNDAY, OCT. 5TH ''84 ABOUT 6:30 P.M.

What a misnomer—journal! May be it is better after all that I condense, rather than jot down the little happenings. I have finished the picture spoken of in the last entry. I call it "A Joyous Place," which I think apt. It goes to the inaugural Ex. of the Am. Art Association tomorrow. . . . I've worked a deal on the picture and it seems to me one of my most happy tonic subjects. I really think there is an approach to suppleness in the tiny nude girl in the foreground. The one in the grass is rather lumpish to be sure. Mr. Whitaker thinks it good. Well, go my child, and smile even on your critics. They may snarl and misunderstand, but be sure you shall outlive them.

Our cash has been embarrassingly low. . . . We depended upon a check from Mr. Noyes, (N. & B.) he promised it at two different times. At last we got so low in exchequer that I decided to ask an advance on my half-done "René Menard" plate, when a draft from Mr. Tewksbury for $85– put us at rest. That was Friday. It was immediately cashed & my Love & I went shopping. Partly in search of a thin overcoat, & we failed to find it.

It was extremely pleasant to hear from the Kansas man, and [it] made us a little ashamed that we had doubted his honesty, even in the small measure we did. He said he was going to send another letter soon which he thought would be as acceptable as the present one. It may be he is to send the 1st installment of his monthly payments for pictures which if I remember rightly, or understood rightly, was to be $25– a month. It is a romantic proceeding surely. And I judge him to be an extraordinary man any way.

That Mrs. Kilvert has sent two letters of entreaty lately. She is either daft or else a most "peculiar" person. Charlotte & I think that she must write with rolling eyes and gasping mouth. . . .

As for Mr. Noyes, a letter from him yesterday disclosed that he had no money for me; had left the city expecting checks to be sent in, & had left a check signed to be filled and sent to me during his absence. That is why I did not hear from him—the checks were not sent & he did not know of it. It strikes me he had about long enough to raise the money. To be sure he offers interest from Sept. 1st. I have written him today telling him that I want some by the 20th & a note for the balance for 20 or 30 days.

Have also written to Mr. Tewksbury.

My darling has, on the whole, been better, than since I last wrote. She has often told ecstatically of how happy she is. She can scarce wait to see that child she is fashioning. God grant all may be well and that she may see it happy & gloriously proud of her labor! But today she has not been very strong, so I washed the lot of dishes for her & have done all I might to make her light housework lighter. . . .

OCTOBER 31ST 1884. 8:20 P.M.

Not from indolence has my record been neglected, but from lack of time partly, and from weariness when time was mine. These occasional entries will have use to me I fancy.

My Love has been better & very happy. She seems full of reverent & sweet expectancy since she has felt the movement of that new life in her fair clean body. A lingering holy memory, that of her face beaming with goodness & love when for the first time our child made itself sensible to her touch by its "quickening." All the intense motherliness of her nature seems in flower.

Oh those poor people who said stale things about the shortness of our honeymoon! If they could but know how greater is our happiness, how much fuller the satisfaction we feel of each other, how intense our love for each other, I think they'd be ashamed. Life together is quite what I thought it would be—even better!

Since she has been better—I mean stronger in body—I have been more at peace. And since it is certain that a lady physician will attend her—that no man need enter our chamber I feel better yet. . . .

On the 10th I received a letter and his draft for $25– from Mr. Tewksbury. He confirmed my memory by saying that he intended sending the same each month so long as it was mutually agreeable. I am to send him such pictures as I may choose. . . .

About the 10th I finished the "René Menard" plate. It is the most pleasing so far. I did not resort to dry point work but got my most delicate passages by bitten Lines. I feel it to be an advance. But—I am oppressed by my work. I feel that I am not doing what I can best do. That as my heart is not in it, I am unjust both to myself and my employer. . . .

On the 13th we went to Narragansett Pier, to the Cressons at their Stone Lea. Charlotte & Mrs. Cresson fell in love at once. It was beautiful to see. I had my fears set at rest. . . .

. . . Oh we *are* so happy, so full of what we sought! My wife seemed flooded with her great joy. She is happy, happy, happy! And I—I—I, from painter that I am have made her so! Dear God O thank thee!

*   *   *

NOV. 17TH 1884 7:40 P.M.

My Love has gone with the Westcotts, our neighbors, to hear a lecture on political economy at the 1st. Cong.[regational] Church. She is greatly interested now in the free trade & all that sort of thing, studies the tariff lists & Fawcett & Cobden, etc. so that our unborn child bids fair to have a leaning towards affairs of state. I don't know whether to be pleased or not. Truly, I would rather it had been a subject more esthetic, but what the world most needs I know not. That is God's affair. Let it be done. If our child inherits our disposition at all he'll have love enough of the beautiful & fair. I fear nothing for it—her or him. (I was too tired and indisposed to go with her, so she would not have me.)

She has been well of late, say for two weeks. And we think she grows stronger all the time. She is quite like her old time buoyant self, but infinitely tenderer & happier. I can but see that she is happy, very happy. I can but see that she loves me beyond any power of expression, oh so deeply, so intensely & fondly! . . .

So she being gone, I have been making a list of pictures to send to Mr. Tewksbury. Mr. T has become a firm friend and no less an admirer. His letters are not infrequent, and are always enjoyable. He seems a genuine man. Strange too, as if suppressed in some way. He seems to be a crust beneath which molten matter rages, ready to break out at anytime.

We have agreed upon the sale of the *Sleeping Girl*. He is to have it in payment for these monthly $25 drafts that he sends. I have agreed to let him have it for $575–. Not satisfied with that he wants more, so at his request I am about to send some 15 or so of the best things that I now have to him. He wants the *May Dance*. He is to pay freight charges etc. It is all very strange. Today a box came from him with 8 pieces of Pueblo & old Mexican pottery in it. One piece is extremely beautiful in color. It was very kind of him.

I have nearly finished the Antigna. I think it will be successful in a mediocre manner. Mr. Wall likes the early trial proofs so there is little doubt he will the final state. . . .

He now wants them done by Feb. 1st. Great Caesar! He *is* an American. But I never worked for a man who treated me better & was fairer. . . .

Perhaps I have been extravagant since marriage. I *can't* regret it if I have; for neither of us could buy before but very very little that we wanted. It has been so sweet to know my darling could have just all she wanted. To be sure her wants were few indeed compared with those of most women, but no man, unless the outcome of similar circumstances could know the supreme delight of making her so happy that she fairly ached, so completely satisfied that she could not think of a thing she wanted enough to buy. Dear girl! She never had had clothing suitable, and I have gradually got her to buy, until now she is fairly clad. I even got her to buy an ermine-lined silk circular, as good as could be bought. God knows it's a great change. I can't believe it will always last. There must be hard, very hard places financially, yet for me to go though. Well?

I too have bought an overcoat, a fine one with beaver cuffs & collar. I felt that I wanted one—a family coat as it were—one that would last years. It is very warm and so grand that it seems incongruous to put it over anything but one's best clothes. We have much sport over our "pride" over these things. She is infinitely playful and tender. . . .

SUNDAY, JANUARY 18TH 1885 QUARTER OF 3 P.M.

I have read over the last entry to find out just where my happenings had come to, as it were. I am surprised that two months have gone by without a word written here. Therefore only the main things can be said. So much the better.

The paintings were received by Mr. Tewksbury. He has been enjoying them much, I judge from his frequent letters. He likes especially, as heretofore, the "May Dance," also the "Blomidon over the Great Meadow," which he calls an appealing landscape, and with the other wants to own. He speaks highly of "The Potion,"* and some others. The fact is, he sympathetically gets at my motives at once; at any rate he seems to. . . .

His last letter contained an invitation which is very tempting:—to visit him. He offers great inducements. But it can hardly be, with my wife with child.

At last my affairs in Boston are settled. It took long to squeeze out of Noyes & Blakeslees my dues. But I have them with interest; not without writing them a very plain letter however. . . .

I have delivered to Mr. Mason one of the pictures he purchased before

---

*The *Potion* (24 × 36 inches, canvas), earlier called the *Cure of Love*, was shown in the 1884 Providence Exhibit, and sold to G. E. Tewksbury in 1885.

it was finished—the "Place of Sighs." I have been to his house since. It holds an honorable place near a Corot the tone of which is no wise a detriment to mine. They are greatly pleased with it. Naturally that pleases me. He is rather anxious to see the other completed (Memento Mori).* But it requires time and I've been completely occupied.

The "Troyan" is done—done before Christmas. It pleases Mr. Wall: and I think it decent. I am now working on the Luminais and Daubigny. The former is delayed by the painting going to the Art Club Loan Ex. The latter I shall bite for the first time tomorrow. I believe Mr. Wall has about decided not to have his sale in March, if so, I shall have until April to complete my plates. . . .

As a matter of money I did well last year. Would that I had done as well as a matter of art! I find that from last Feb. to the 1st of this year I received not less than $3683.59. There is a hundred unpaid which as to sales should be added to it. A great change indeed from the year before and all the years before that. I have spent nearly all of it, paying debts (I owe next to nothing now) helping father and buying for the house and our persons.

It is not at all likely that I shall do as well this year. There will be no "sale." There will be no etchings at $100 a month. Tewksbury's checks will come; I have an order for a portrait, and there is a ready market for one or two other small pictures. But I am not afraid. I feel stronger than I ever did. More certain of my own artistic power. More confident that but time is needed to develop that which burns within. My dear Love is strong. She will be patient if I am not pecuniarily very successful. God bless her!

Christmas was the most joyful of any I ever passed. We began our buying a month before, partly so that Charlotte would have less difficulty in getting about. How she did enjoy it! She spent about $150— I think. Spent it well. It did the others good and gratified us. We sent Mrs. Cresson a vellum bound hand-made paper edition of Keats. Charlotte painted some lovely flowers & things in it. How pleased my dear Grandma was! Such an odd thing too! I gave Charlotte the same edition. Charlotte gave me the same edition. Mrs. Cresson sent me Lord Houghton's edition in blue calf. And Jennie gave Charlotte, an edition, and *her* friend Retta Clarke gave her

---

* *A Place of Sighs* (8 × 10 inches, canvas), signed December 1884, was sold to John Mason for $30. *Memento Mori* (10 × 16 inches, mahogany panel), signed March 1885, was sold to John Mason for $45. Occasionally it was called the *Early Millet*: "A sarcophagus by the sea. A grove at night, trees in distance at the left. On the left of sarcophagus a naked woman, seated, holding a skull across the sarcophagus to a merry young man playing a mandolin. Tone golden. I consider it one of my best works thus far." "Opera" Book, pp. 41–43.

Rossetti's edition.—So, lo! five volumes of Keats. Well, why not? If in his upper world Keats could know, did know, how he would have smiled pleasedly.

We all went to Caroline's. Had a fine time. 189 presents distributed. I sent a carriage for mother & father. It stormed. Same carriage brought us home. . . .

My Darling has been far more "well" right along. . . . With . . . the glad, deep, new light in her eyes, the knowledge that the work that has fallen to my share, the getting of breakfast and this and that seems as nothing. It *is* nothing, though I have not been able to do my special work as well. Only two months more does she have to bear her precious burden. God—ah, I must not even let a suspicion of what might happen lodge in my mind. It has done so at times, and I have found myself in absolute agony and utter paralysis of working power. . . .

She thinks with astonishing clearness, and logic that paralyses me, as it were. It is great fun to have men call here and engage with her in discussions of politics or morals or most anything. She invariably puts them at their wits' ends. My friend Mr. P[urinton?] took it into his head a week or so ago to tell me (which was a well meant kindness) what certain of my "friends" was saying about me: How I had become very secluded, uncommunicative, how I was slighting my work, and other untrue things—a state the outcome of my secret etching of course. Well, I thanked him, and invited him here. He came, and as well as I could without revealing Mr. Wall's secret, I told him just how matters were. He saw what an ass he came near making of himself and how asinine his friend—the mutual friend had been. Then Charlotte and he had a tilt on morals etc. It was great. Since that he has written both of us astounding letters and sent to her many papers with articles marked. . . .

Father & mother have been photographed by Hurd.* The photographs are very fine. Mother is more cheerful of late than I ever knew her to be. I can but feel in my inmost heart that it is in some measure due to me. Oh for the blessed knowledge that I had added some pleasantness to all her bitter! There is such a sweet, patient breaking [?] smile in these photographs! The very sadness is a noble monument to a true heart. . . .

Father's face tells me what I already knew—that he is fitted by nature for a greater sphere than his has been. His nature has been overgrown with the weeds of small cares, and his road to honorable large place blocked by

---

* See photographs of Stetson's parents reproduced in this volume.

adherence to what is undoubtedly duty to his family. I see it all. That man who in N. Eng. forty years ago gave his life to the ministry took upon himself such sacrificial honors as men of these days cannot experience. Literally they gave their lives "for Christ's sake.". . .

Probably one of the most important events in my art-life (since I wrote, surely so.) was the seeing of Watts' pictures at the Metropolitan Museum.*

6:35 P.M. . . . To return to the Watts pictures. . . . Geo. Whitaker decided to go with me, so very reluctant to leave my darling, we started Monday at 7:10 P. M. I never felt so badly about leaving anyone before. . . . But, on the other hand, it seemed almost a duty to see them. I felt from what I had read that truly his work must be the outcome of a very great soul; also I had seen a few reproductions in black and white of some of his work. They appealed to me, and make me feel that despite the difference in our ages, countries, and skill we were closely akin. At any rate, I felt I needed the inspiration, the change, and the chance to judge for myself.

I was not disappointed. They are the noblest pictures I have ever seen. They are nearer like what I have dreams of doing than any I have seen. In some of them the color was not all I could hope for, and in some I felt the drawing to be needlessly loose, but a mighty spirit was dominant in them all; it called me on. It called me up. And while there before them, in sympathy with them, I felt as deeply as ever that I could, should do great work, and I felt too with reverence rather than presumption, that in the same field I could do work as good as true, as beautiful.

The portraits were simply living souls. With the exception of a Rembrandt in the same museum I never felt the force of a portrait so strongly. They are, I feel certain, superlatively good.

I took a long step onwards that day. I was confirmed in my judgment of my vocation; in my ability to paint the essence of human life. Oh amazing cheap, pasteboard things the work of some of the French and German etc. painters in the other galleries was after coming from Watts! So very superficial and purposeless, so nothing but a trick. Geo. Whitaker said he would not have believed there could be so much difference. . . .

That was a noble time we spent there. In the other galleries we saw a

---

*Charles Eldredge argues that the "mysticism and imagination" that Stetson admired in Rossetti also "subsequently drew him to George F. Watts, Rossetti's successor among the subjectively oriented English school." Years later, in the International Exhibition in Rome (1905), Stetson's works were acclaimed for their "aristocratic and classic charm [which] breathes of Böcklin and Watts without imitating either of them." Charles Eldredge, *Charles Walter Stetson: Color and Fantasy* (Lawrence, Kan.: Spencer Museum of Art, 1982), pp. 35, 92.

few good old masters. They did not seem very superior to Watts! The fact is we did not enjoy any other pictures much that day. . . .

We went to St. Patrick's Church. It impressed me. I saw a very touching Florentine entombment (?) on Deposition. The expression of the faces fairly brought tears. All honor to the church, despite her bad qualities; that recognizes the power of art towards good. . . .

19TH JAN. 85 6:55 P.M.

Up little earlier than usual. Hurried down to work room so as to be there when expressman came with the 1st "Couture" plate which I have been having replaned in N. Y. While fire was coming up I got my things ready to do the 1st biting on the Daubigny and painted some on Mr. Mason's picture—"Memento Mori.". . .

Found a letter from Mr. Noyes. My "Fool's Sermon" was rejected by the Boston Art Club. He says: "100 accepted out of 600 sent." Munich & Paris men are rampant this season. All right. Care less and less about such things. Means nothing against my work, except that it was not done in Paris or Munich. All right. . . .

. . .

21ST JANUARY, 1885 8:40 P.M.

My darling has gone to bed, being tired and rather uneasy. Oh she *is* so loving & patient; she has grown so very thoughtful of my likes & wants & needs! Almost too much so for my comfort:—I mean that she does so much and is so very tender that I fear for her own health, fear that she will do more than she ought. She is simply anxious to work. She is very proud of doing the housework, that that I do not do—the more she relieves me of it the better pleased she. I think it is good for her, and believe it will be better for the little one than total idleness. I try to see that she does not over do, a thing that in her ambition & energy she is very apt to approach into. *I* think, as women are, she has been *very* well thus far in her pregnancy. *Very* well indeed. . . .

Owing to the stopping of Charlotte's watch and the deceiving cloudiness of the morning we were up later than usual. I got her a nice breakfast, which she pronounced delicious. I believe I am much prouder of my cooking than anything else I do.

Lunched at mother's. Father tired. Mother-would-be-cheerful. In afternoon went at the Daubigny. Am increasing the character of the sky & opening the underbitten passages in the rest of the composition. I believe, if my acid does not play me false next time, that it will be interesting. . . .

I have felt uneasy all day, have for a week indeed. I don't know what it is about. I fancy—or I *think* the cause is indigestion partly, secondarily: primarily it is a mixture of anxiety about Charlotte's travail and the pressure of my own work. Oh well, one must keep a brave heart for who knows how long one may live? and one must needs have a brave heart to do good work, and one must work hard to make life however long or short of some value to others & himself.

It is strange, I thought I knew years ago of the petty and great jealousies, envys, meannesses of all sorts in the world, but I find I knew almost nothing of them: each day reveals new & startling ones. Much believing must be my heart that it does not wholly condemn my fellows and even God. I stand aghast at the mere thought of some things, but I dare not judge. I see nothing better in this world than to be honest with oneself and do as best one can that which comes to him to be done, enduring pain, ignominy, false accusation and indifference—all things unpleasant and damaging to one's peace and health with courage, and groan less. Love and happiness seem too good to be true. Too good to be true! Ah mighty God, what agony, what countless pains and disappointments had been endured, suffered before that saying became a true thing, Too good to be true!

My wife is happy! Oh blessed sweet motherling! happy! Your dear pure soul has been so unharmed so good, so clean & honest with all & itself that happiness with you is a reality, a blessed reward, not a thing to shrink from & tremble at as a portent of some direr disaster. I have unawares come upon myself when I have been happy—and started back with trembling and unbelief. Yet I *have* been happy, and the Being of my heart *is* happy—happy— O so happy now!

The wood fire burns brightly. It is blustering & wet without.

Love has made for me here a sweet haven of refuge.

The most I can tonight is: I will endure and try to make all I know as happy as I can.

To bed. To her.

Sunday, Jan. 25th 1885 10:10 p.m.

Yesterday was an unprofitable day. I was miserable with dyspepsia and a headache, and as my Love was ill also I stayed at home all day. We were a miserable pair. She is sick of indigestion or rather constipation. It makes her restless and very sensitive to everything. There is housework to do and though she does what she can, I find enough to tire me, and make me feel sometimes that I am wasting my energy, power that should be applied to my art. Yet it plainly is my duty and I do it as cheerfully as I can. For love's sake one must bear all things. I fancy I shall be stronger for it after it is over. But I feel certain that my other work is not so well done because of it. I cannot let my mind roam in sweet fancy's field now. It is utterly impossible. I find so much to do here at home. Well, that must be done. But if it seems to last very long I must hire help, move into a larger house, for I cannot afford, nor would it be right for me, to give up all my time and strength to such things.

Sickness makes Charlotte clinging, dependent in disposition. I dare do nothing contrary to her request lest she take it as a signal of vanishing love. I want this child to be made by her under circumstances, as favorable as we can make them. I have sought for its sake as well as her own to make life as easy and pleasant as I could for her, to present her with as cheerful and beautiful things as I could. I confess I should be surprised if the little one proved itself to be ugly and a dullard.

I feel that the next two months, these two months that remain before its birth will be hard for me. Necessarily so; for there will be, naturally, an increasing uneasiness on her part, and though she is brave and very glad there *must* be an increasing perturbation, knowing as she does the *possibilities* of danger, and a physical unrest. . . .

. . . Perhaps I have too much fear that her love as it grows will grow in demand until it dwarfs my art life, which must not be. That would be wrong, yet I cannot see how it could be stopped without pain to us both. Possibly the little child will be the very being to loose me for my art's sake yet preserve our intensest love. When I stop to think of it it seems marvelous that we love each other so. And it is fearful—for a shadow stays ever nigh me, but I pray love to cover my eyes. . . .

This evening have been Charlotte's amanuensis for a letter to her mother. Also have done the bed-making, as usual, and the putting up of the weekly wash, besides the many little "chores" of the household. . . .

. . .

28TH JAN. 1885. 8:35 P.M.
This has been one of the stormiest days of the season: cold, very, snowy, and haily, with a high wind. I noticed in the river the violet, dull and weird, of the channel which wound through a festering obscure yellow (composed of fields of sleet and the dingy water of low tide evidently.) . . .

MAY 2D 1885. 10 P.M.

I have waited all day for a chance to write in this. This night could not pass without record—this night of all others, for a year ago tonight in this room, in lovely guise stood my wife, the Bride of a few hours. Before my eyes now, as I think of it rises vividly the perfectly loveliness of that hour. None of the loveliness has departed. If I loved her then—and Oh! I did— I love her more now. The loveliness has taken new forms, perhaps, but it is about as always. Our honeymoon yet hangs glowing in meridian.

What a year, and what changes it has brought!

A year ago tonight we two stood alone among our new household goods; *alone*. Tonight by our bed stands a crib and in it a fair blossom of our making—our little Katharine who came at five minutes before nine on the morning of the 23rd of March. Before that were months of apprehension and dismal forecast, and I verily believe that I suffered fully as much pain as her mother, for oh, to see the dear woman suffer, even what she did (a small part of what some women are brought to) made me ache in every atom. Oh if I could have borne it all—if I could have had the pain and she nothing but the joy! It was a heavenly look that filled her face when first she heard in rapture the cry of that new being. Would to God, I could perpetuate that look! Motherhood such as hers is the divinest thing life has yet shown me, equal to love itself—the love of lovers.

During those latter months I could not write here—I had no heart to write—I had no time to write, for when I was not working at etching or painting I had housework to do. I was quite sick after it for a week. The reaction was great. The glorious knowledge that my own heart's Love was safe—safe to me yet and that I was the father of a lovely violet-eyed girl was too much and I broke down. But I've recovered and am doing pretty well *I* think as a father.

The dear mother gets along well, tired of course sometimes, a little fearful sometimes, but never "cross" never wearing. Her mother is coming to us next week, which will be a relief to both of us.

I have a great deal to write, but am so very tired tonight I must leave it till tomorrow; I felt I *must* on this anniversary of our joy say that love has not waned but rather waxed; that she is not worse, but better; that I am not sorry I married, but rather glad.

And now she sleeps beside our babe, and I must go to gladly sleep beside her.

There are roses in the house now as then, and there is much love here, even as then, and please God both shall be here ever.

*   *   *

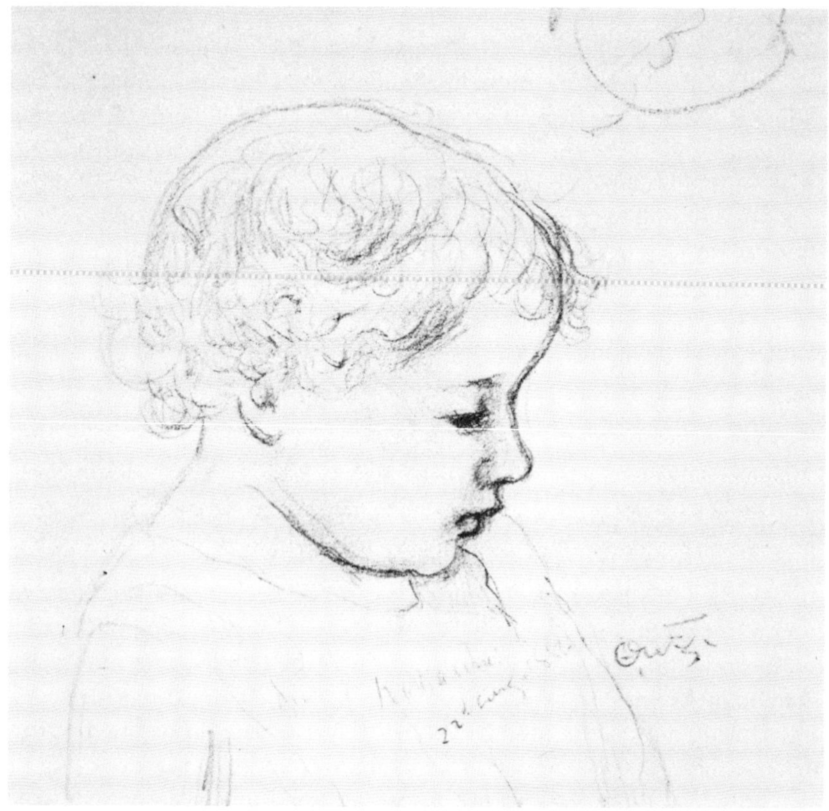

Katharine. From Sketchbooks.

24TH AUGUST 1885 STUDIO 12 P.M.

The entry that I must make now I find will be in sad contrast to the last one which I have just read over. Ah God; what changes may come in a few days, even in a few hours. My dear Love, happy in the possession of a perfectly made child bore well the low state of her strength for some time, but as Katharine had symptoms of diarrhea which frightened her she grew very nervous and weak. As I wrote in my last we had to send for her mother. I have lost all count of just dates, I have had so sad a time for a few months. (Katharine was 5 months old yesterday). Her mother came, but was a week later than Charlotte expected her so that the dear girl grew apprehensive, very weak, and fretful. I had a hard time. I hope she'll never know how hard. But she came at last, and none too soon. Charlotte kept up for a few days by means of the excitement of novelty, I suppose then as her mother took all care of the baby from her she broke down entirely, and has been since—a nervous invalid requiring the utmost care and tender treatment, lest it should settle itself into an incurable mind disease.

I dare not recall all the steps of its growth. There have been violent hysterical symptoms, and long periods of taciturnity, melancholy and utter loss of the desire or power to will. I sent for Dr. Keller, who came, and examined her. She cheered her a bit & left some slight medicine just before we went with the baby to the Pier. But neither words nor medicine availed much, for her illness brought back all the thoughts of how strong she was before marriage, how much she wanted to do, the remembrance of "her mission" and a fierce rebellion at the existing state of things. Poor dear wife! Since that subject has taken the form of a monomania—a terrible thing that crushes all joy, all enthusiasm and sweetness out of my life. No body even guesses how terrible it is.

Well, we simply had to move out of our little dove cote soon after coming back from the Pier, for it became necessary that Mrs. Perkins should care for the child nights so that Charlotte could sleep. We found a cottage on Humboldt Avenue—rent $25– per month. It cost me $100– to get into it and some besides for new articles of furniture. Money became scarce. Mr. Tewksbury came to the rescue with a partial payment of his debt.

We took all care of it from Charlotte and for a few days the change seemed to benefit her. Her condition however soon became terrible. What nights I've spent with her! Ah God, why, *why* need she be afflicted thus?

Well, she grew worse, became so wholly unlike herself that (against her wish) I sent Dr. Knight to see her. She told him how she felt, that her whole usefulness & real life was crushed out of her by marriage and the care of the baby—that she was useless and a wasted soul. Then he came to see me. I told him the whole case from the beginning. He thinks he can cure her, and goes twice a week to talk with her, having resorted to moral measures more than to medication. There has been some improvement I think. Or at least the nature of her complaints is different. Whether there is any *real* gain I can't say. It is still almost unendurable. It calls for tremendous patience and tact. She still rushes in her mind from all our sweet life to try to go out into the world to rid it at one fell swoop of all evil, pain and the like. Strange and terrible how such ideas can take possession of one's brain. She forgets that she could do good right at hand, even in our family. Of what account is that to her! She would convert the whole world. Even worse than all that she has grown very dissatisfied with me. I think at times she feels hatred of me. But at times on the contrary she will express the most tender love and regret for all her paining. The true Charlotte is in a dreadful mist—oh, for recovery soon! I *can't* bear it much longer! I have no doubt in my own mind that the whole trouble is some uterine irritation and until that is cured she will be no better.

I can't write more now—I myself have grown too "nervous."

WEDNESDAY A.M. 26TH AUGUST 1885

After a severe rain this day is lovely. It was cold last night: it is cool this morning, but it sends one's blood with new life from the heart. All around our new home one can see beauty—beautiful trees, beautiful meadows, beautiful hillsides dotted with beautifully colored cattle. There are far stretches to look across, and a large stone house on a hill with a dark wood, which one might well take for a bit of England, I love to fancy.

Since Monday morning Charlotte has been much better. After I made the last entry I felt that I ought to go home to her. I did so, and was glad that I did. I found her at table lunching with a "Century" at her side. She seemed pleased to see me. . . .

. . . Since that time Charlotte has been brave and charming. Avers that she will recover and yet make me happy again. She is in love once more, even to enthusiasm, with the baby. She now sees herself that her brain is not diseased in itself but that the trouble is purely local. She purposes going to see Dr. Keller as soon as she can. Dr. K. can examine her & "treat" her if necessary.

I do not flatter myself that there will be no relapse to her melancholy. There must be as long as the cause remains. But she feels herself really better, because now she can write even when she is very miserable, which she could not do a few weeks ago.

Yesterday Geo. Whitaker came over. . . . [He] liked my *The Approach of the Centaur very* much. And also the *Morning Measure.** He approved of the

---

*The *Approach of a Centaur* (20 × 30 inches, canvas), signed September 22, 1885, and sold to Isaac Bates. "Tone rather golden. Centaur coming across a hillock. Two girls in foreground; surprised motion. Sympathetic dark mass of trees in hillock." "Opera" Book, p. 45. *Morning Measure* (33 × 40 inches, canvas), signed September 23, 1885: "Two girls dancing (white & yellow) one at the front on a tree playing a mandolin, she in purple. Daffodils in foreground,

slight glaze I had put over the two principal figures in the *Fool's Sermon*. I believe that in George I have an honest and intelligent admirer. It is so good to have someone able to give a reason for *not* liking a thing. I fancy that our criticisms have helped us both a good deal. I know that his have often aided me.

I have sold nothing recently. I have about $200– to pay, and nothing wherewith to pay it. I wonder where Col. A. S. Johnson is.* I've forgotten whether I mentioned him herein before. He is an uncle of Mr. Tewksbury's and wants to meet me, because he has liked the pictures Mr. T. has. He spends the summer at Cape Ann, although he lives in Topeka. He said he was coming here last week, and Mr. T. said he was going to buy something or give me a commission. I foolishly felt that he would buy something in time to help me over my present embarrassment. . . .

Today infant Katharine was for the first time arrayed in short clothes. The wee shoes were to her unutterable delight. She is a fair Katharine, so sage looking and so unchangeably good humored. Not a sick day—not a touch of colic since her birth. No wonder she's goodnatured.

THURSDAY, 27TH AUGUST, 1885 1 P.M.

. . . Last evening, after a little difference in regard to building a fire in our parlour, wherein I meekly withdrew to the library, I read to Charlotte the finishing "Vigils" of *The Golden Pot*. It is an exceeding strange story in which one can grasp quite nothing but Herren Paulmann and Hellbrand: and yet I feel that [E. T. A.] Hoffman had some definite idea in mind which he sought to express allegorically. It is so unreal that one cannot feel the slightest sympathy with any of the characters.

Then we went to bed, say at half-past nine. It was amazingly chilly for this time of year. Charlotte told me this morning that she cried herself to sleep regarding her old woe. It could not have been very violent for I heard none of it. This morning while awaiting the postman we read together the concluding chapters of Marion Harland "Eve's Daughters."† It is a noble

---

sea at right." It was sold in 1885 to Mrs. G. E. Tewksbury for $250—"a discount made because of her taking the 'Fool's Sermon [on Death].'" "Opera" Book, p. 47.

* This is Stetson's first mention of art collector Col. A. S. Johnson, who, together with his nephew George E. Tewksbury, would purchase some of Stetson's most important works (see *In Grief*, for instance, the cover illustration for this volume).

† Marion Harland, *Eve's Daughters; or Common Sense for Maid, Wife, and Mother* (New York: Scribners, 1885).

wholesome book. But somehow it set Charlotte to thinking in a way that made me very dismal. I felt that I was sorry that I had married, for the first time distinctly. I would not marry if I had the chance again, knowing what I do now. Something in the culture, or half culture of the time has set our teeth on edge, as it were. I can't tell exactly what it is but it seems to make us or at least me unfruitful in an intellectual way: possibly I lay at the door of marriage things that are caused by something else. Possibly, too, the parts of us whereof we would bear fruit are no more noble, if as much so, as those parts that deal with the petty exactions of domestic economy. Charlotte's physical weakness has made her faultfinding & very difficult to please. She focuses her microscope upon every one of my acts about house—not to my exultation by any means. The nobler part is for me to hear it all as patiently as I can. She is in nowise to blame, nor am I. I have striven to make a home for her that should be pleasant, also to have her relieved of all household responsibility so that she might work. I have done more than I ought, for I am again burdened with debt. So far it has counted for little in her favor— too little it seems to me. On account of all this I have lost the power I used to have so strongly, to conceive of colors & forms and pictures clearly, if not correctly. I feel that I am becoming degraded to a mere instrument of money getting. God forbid! God forbid! But how can it be otherwise if I do duty by wife & child & mother, & father?

$25—	a month for house rent
15	about " " studio "
12	" " " girl's wages
4	" " " gas
<u>6.30</u>	a month for milk
62.30	

aside from fuel, clothing, and food, incidentals of studio & house. I dare not reckon exactly for fear. . . .

Yesterday afternoon I re-read some of my sonnets & verses. I tore up some, changed a few words in some of the others. It was rather sickening. But, inconsistent that I am, I conceived again the idea of sending 3 or 4 of the best to some magazine. I could give no good reason for doing it, could not even tell why I wanted to, but I was and am very sure it was not for a desire of what is called fame. I wisely perhaps, bethought me of C. De Kay's letter, & got it out, and re-read. I did not send the sonnets. However, since I have read De Kay's poems, I confess to a less faith in his opinion of mine.

I see neither merit nor promise in the poems by him that I've read. He said that even of mine. But I did not send them.

I feel so cramped & twisted, so out of place, so undeveloped & unexpressed that I am becoming either more & more sick at heart or more and more apathetic & uncaring. Nature does not wear the colors it did for me. God grant there may be a revival, a restoration in my heart.

It is true, I was in the excess of delight in being able to buy for *our* house, for my darling, for mother & father, rather extravagant with the money from my sale. If I had reckoned more closely, been a trifle niggardly, I could even now be out of debt and hiring models & things I need for my work. But as it is I *cannot*. Nobody but an artist would understand the poignancy (however well concealed) of that fact. . . .

31ST AUGUST 1885 4:30 P.M. MONDAY

I had a letter a few days ago announcing that Col. Johnson, with Mrs. J. & Mrs. Tewksbury (G. E.'s mother I suppose) are to come here next Wednesday from Boston. I am hurrying, as it were, on the *Morning Measure* & *Approach of a Centaur*. If one knew my financial condition he could understand how I pray that they may like some of these things so much that they *must* buy them. Here it is the last day of the month. I ought to pay rent for this room tomorrow. I simply can't. . . .

Our charming maidservant, Daphne, has filed an intention of leaving next Saturday. . . . Wherefore we are vext as to the finding of a substitute. I think Charlotte intends calling on the Swedish clergyman to inquire if he knows of some desirable Swede. . . .

Charlotte and I are reading Dickens aloud to each other. I have not yet made the acquaintance of a number of Dickens' best stories. I don't know's I'm to be pitied, for I think myself better able to appreciate them than I should have been some time ago. What would certain ones say if they knew I had never read more than two of the Waverly Novels? Well, I like Scott— but I never used to care much for the novels.

3D SEPTEMBER 1885. 3:30 P.M.

Well, Col. & Mrs. Johnson with Mrs. Tewksbury came yesterday about noon. I was charmed by them. Col. J. seems all that Mr. Tewksbury said he was. Mrs. T. seems a woman of unusual mentality & rather haughty charity.

They stayed about two hours, in which I'm certain we began very happily an enduring friendship. They are anxious to have Charlotte, Katharine, & me with them in Topeka, and almost persuaded me to promise that they should. Mrs. Tewksbury bought that little golden haired crimson coated, high ruffled [illegible] young woman 7 × 9 inches for $25– and Col. Johnson took with him that 6 × 10 study of a grieving girl, begun in sketch class, & colored in studio. I got $20– for that.* So they left $45– with me (which is a help indeed) and purpose sending for more things. I shouldn't be surprised if Mrs. Tewksbury took the "Morning Measure" for $300.

Later in the day Charlotte came down & walked home with me. For 3 days she has felt like her old self, bright, hopeful, *well*. God knows what it is to me to see again her incomparable smile and brilliant eyes. It gives me courage and renewed hope of yet being great in art. Wide, beautiful vistas of usefulness & power, and ability to make Beauty open before me. . . .

And what have I done today? A piece of folly, may be. Yet it is not of vanity, nor desire for ignoble fame or any fellow of those things. I ache to know if I can write a decent sonnet. So what have I done but send six of my best to the Century. There is no doubt but that they will all be declined with thanks. Hearty thanks, very hearty thanks of course. After all it costs but five cents. Therefore the trial is not amiss. I can but feel how proud my little girl would be if she saw by way of surprise one of my things in the Century. Ah it *would* be sweet, let who will ridicule. I feel certain that they are as good even in form and workmanship as many they have published.

Mr. Gregory got for me a lovely large paper edition of "The Book of the Sonnet." What a gentle soul Leigh Hunt seems to have been! And he's so encouraging too!†

I meant to have dined with mother today but I feared to miss a certain German Mädchen who was to come to see about doing our housework in place of the gentle Daphne.

8TH SEPT. 1885. 12 M[IDNIGHT]

The best thing I have to write is that Charlotte—dear dear wife—is much better, and, I think, continually improving. . . . Only once have I felt

---

* *In Grief* (9 15/16 × 6 inches, oil on wood panel) is currently owned by the Topeka Public Gallery of Fine Arts, Topeka, Kansas (see cover illustration for this volume).

† Leigh Hunt, *The Book of the Sonnet* (Boston: Roberts Brothers, 1867).

truly that I was sorry that I had married and then not that I had married her. . . .

Our new studio building is getting fairly on its legs.* It is encouraging, making me feel that I shall do good work in the near future. . . .

Mr. Tewksbury's draft yesterday ($25–) and two letters from him the two days before. It looks as if our friendship were becoming colossal.

A letter from my dear Grandma Cresson yesterday. She seems to be extremely depressed & melancholic. She wishes she had the reason for extreme happiness that Charlotte has—wishes she could be loved as Charlotte is loved. Ah, my Grandma has never been satisfied with the love she has had. She has never had sympathy and fond delight. She is a so passionately loving soul that she feels always repressed. I pity her, I'm so very sorry for her. I

---

*Since Stetson would soon have to give up the studio Beriah Wall had financed during the etching commission, in 1885 he began to work with Sydney Burleigh designing and constructing the "Fleur de Lys." It was a "unique and mysterious domain of art," Stetson later wrote, "a building misunderstood by the people, disliked by the perfectly modern and neat, and beloved by us who harbor there." CWS, "The Studio: Sydney Richmond Burleigh," unidentified clipping from the Providence press, ca. 1892, Stetson Scrapbook. Inspired and designed primarily by Sydney Burleigh, it "was a novel intrusion among the colonial and Federalist homes on the city's prosperous College Hill," wrote Charles Eldredge. "In style the building was 'like the mendicant's pennies—obtained from many sources,' with reminiscences of Nuremberg, Holland, and medieval England." Eldredge, *Charles Walter Stetson*, p. 37. According to the description of contemporary writer Frank T. Robinson, it was "a unique cozy-looking structure which time will mellow and fashion dignify. . . . The exterior is certainly medieval-looking, with its half timber and plaster, figures in relief and color, and scrolls and shrine. . . . Mr. Stetson's studio, overhead [of Burleigh's], is mellow with light. The dado is treated with a sort of Japanese red tint, which seems to change color with the varying degrees of daylight. The floor is stained grape-green tint, which, by oiling, will in time grow deep and rich in hues. Great spruce beams and rafters, stained brown, form the roof. Rugs, screens and pictures show up their colors for full value in this room. The fireplace is simple, yet effective. Here is a high mantel for ornaments, little shelves and niches set in just the right places, with mysterious shadows here and there. Both [Burleigh's and Stetson's] studios are agreeable in atmosphere, and not the least affected." Robinson, "The Sign of the Fleur de Lis," *Art and Decoration* 3, no. 1 (May 1886), p. 6.

Historian Edgar Kaufman offers still another enthusiastic appraisal of the Fleur de Lys: "Certainly the unity of the arts is incorporated here in an example probably unparalleled in American architecture for the fusion of the useful and the ornamental arts. Vernacularism governs not only the use and detailing of half-timber work and rough, grainy plaster, but also much of the thematic expression based on folk tales and legends. The poetry of everyday life is revealed in the do-it-yourself building program; in the many contemporary portraits; in the common animals, domestic or wild, used emblematically; and finally in the empathetic intensity of the underwater ornament." "There are few, if any, American precedents for such an ornamented facade." Edgar Kaufmann, Jr. "Some American Architectural Ornament of the Arts and Crafts Era," *Journal of the Society of Architectural Historians* 24, no. 4 (Dec. 1965), pp. 290–291.

could almost wish myself two that I might righteously give her one to love her & to love. . . .

Eddmann & Schanz of London sent me some photographs taken from nude figures for artists' use—a packet to select from. I kept a few. Possibly may be useful. At any rate when I am painting from memory a glance over them (or *at* them?) will keep me more to life likeness. It must be a great convenience to live in so large a city as London where models may be had in quantity. Well, we poor chaps here have made a certain supply. I think I shall yet come across one that will be *just* right sometime—and then she'll go and die! That's always the way. Or marry, which is even worse for my purpose.

Let's see what will happen when we get into our new studio.

8TH [SEPT.] 4:30 P.M.

I finished the Boy Sketch by Antigna, the series of 13 plates for Mr. Wall. I put the finishing touches on it this afternoon. It is satisfactory to Mr. Wall and expresses what I tried to realize sufficiently.

Mr. Wall has been a most excellent man to work for. In no wise hyper-critical, but respectful of my opinions,—almost too much so. I can imagine the cry that will go up when he publishes them. I doubt not that they will be considered innovations and possibly impertinences. Though I tried to re-produce the feeling of the painter of each picture at the same time I'm sure that each one is bristling with Stetsonisms, if I may say so. They are unconscious personality. I did them with one exception out of my heart, as far as I could get and the man's work first into my heart.

If I get the same price for the Antigna as for the others they will have brought into my treasurey $1300–. That is a goodly commission from one Providence man. I must say I have been verily happily disappointed in Mr. Wall. I've found him a very much *larger* man than I thought him. He is very generous in his judgments and very willing to help rather than hinder. I have found that he has a strong sense of justice. Altogether I like him very much.

I feel as if I had fulfilled a very difficult (considering my experience & talent) commission satisfactorily, at least to the giver of the commission! In no single plate did I fully satisfy myself, which was to be expected. When I have seen them happily through the printer's hands I shall have a heavy load removed from my mind. . . .

. . . *and she shall someday preach*

September 10, 1885 – October 27, 1886

DURING THE DREARY, sometimes hellish months that followed, Stetson's worries mounted, financially as well as emotionally. The Cressons helped him (buying over $2000 worth of pictures within a year and a half); but now that the Beriah Wall commission was over, he always needed money—for models, for his parents, for creditors, for daily bills. Moreover, Charlotte was still seriously depressed. "I go home tired & tried and she wants to talk of some insolvable moral problem." "I feel the futility of human endeavor more than I ought. I feel incapable of doing the work I *must* do."

To make matters worse, Charlotte decided to visit friends and family in the West: her brother in Utah, her father in San Francisco, and the Channing family in Pasadena, California. Momentarily Walter resisted her travel plan: it "will embarrass me; it will cut me off on my models that I intended to hire; it will deprive me of helping mother & father as I intended. But if it will help her to regain strength, or if not strength, cheerfulness, oh gladly gladly would I undergo much more."

There are very few diary entries from November 1885 through April 1886. Charlotte was in California, Walter worked, and both hoped travel would effect a cure. Temporarily it seemed to do so. For the "first few days [after her return] she took hold of her duties here strongly." She has "regained health and gladness; learned a great deal about the world: got humility in large measure; wrote a more or less successful play." But far too quickly, she was "painfully unhappy." "I did fondly hope to have *one month* at least of unalloyed joy. Alas, I had scarcely a week." "I left her this morning crouched on the floor with her head on the lounge in a most dejected condition. The picture has been with me all day."

Without question, Walter desperately wanted Charlotte to be happy, and helped in every way he knew. He did housework chores, financed her travels, arranged for outings when he could. He even supported her career-oriented efforts; when she was painting greeting cards and water colors, for instance, or writing articles for *The Woman's Journal*, or composing plays with Grace. But despite all supportive efforts, irritations persisted. There was competition about who would publish first and in the better journals, about who would earn the higher pay. And there were differences of values—Walter's aesthetic preferences versus Charlotte's "didactic preaching" on "affairs of state." But most importantly, both faced the core assumption that work commitment for a woman meant sacrificing family life.

My darling wife thinks now that she shall some day preach—sermons about health, morality and the like—from the pulpit on what you will. Ah well, my dearest love, if you have anything to say that will help us, and real solution to offer for moral problems and the destruction of moral miasma, for God's sake preach! And may you have power beyond all the preachers of all time! Leave me—Leave mother—Leave child—leave all and preach! We need some one to tell us what of all these "truths" *is* truth. Go. God help you!

Despite Walter's love and generosity, Charlotte developed an uncontrollable resentment, a seething anger in fact, which only later she would come to "preach" about in "moral" terms. She was learning "truths" about nineteenth-century sex-role standards, for one thing, and unconscious habits, and patterned inequalities which most people thought were fair. Ineffectively, indirectly, even "hysterically" at times, she nonetheless confronted some important questions: whether as a woman her work was "naturally" more home-based and domestic, whether as a man Walter had exclusive needs for professional expression and support. The assumption was that Charlotte's ambitions were less significant and even selfish, whereas Walter professionally must push ahead. He was working with Sydney Burleigh on the ornamental and artistically unusual Fleur de Lys studio building on Thomas Street. He was setting up a cooperative Art Workers Guild with Burleigh and John Aldrich. Compared to Charlotte, understandably he enjoyed more professional support, most recently from distinguished art collector James Jackson Jarves, who praised the "color & glow," the "touching and powerful" effect of several Stetson paintings. "I feel it, am proud of it, and have been so weakly human as to want other people to know it."

Although Walter, like Charlotte, found that marriage interfered with outside work, the major difference was in social expectations: that Walter should continue painting; that Charlotte should be supportive, loving, and generously "reconciled" at home. If only she would "aid me by cheerful conversation and willing life," he wrote. Instead, she must be suffering from "a disease of some sort," and "has not the temperament to make light of it and throw it off."

Charlotte *was*, of course, suffering from a "disease," a "nervous break-down" which she would later explore in countless essays, in an autobiography, in some fifteen or more potent theory books, and most grimly and starkly in an autobiographical short story, "The Yellow Wall-paper." But for the moment, Walter's central problem was to find a way to cope. For him the contrasts seemed so striking: loving an "ideal" wife who was "hysterically" complaining, painting from models who were often "damsels of the demi-monde." It was almost as though the circumstances now compelled a different subject for his paintings, as though the sheer toughness of the situation intensified his search for the ideal. He would try to paint a Venus Aphrodite, he wrote, the "mother of all delight and love—the pure, tender foam born mother. . . . Ah Aphrodite! Thou art not dead. In one heart thou livest on. Comfort and help me: reveal thyself to my mind that I may paint thee truly."*

. . .

10TH SEPTEMBER 1885 11 A.M.

Mr. John H. Mason has just gone from here. I don't know whether to pity or despise or laugh at him. I wanted money for father, I thought I would see if Mr. Mason would buy the picture he calls "Early Millet" say for $15–. I concluded to let it go for that although I should think it ought to bring easily $25.

Well, I restored a few places on his miserable little Corot, for which he thanked me decently; and indeed offered to pay for it, which of course I couldn't allow as it took not over five minutes & was not my business. As he was looking at the little picture (7 × 9) I said: I've got a little bit of charity to do. I want some more money to do it with. What will you give for the picture? Thereupon he discovered that it had a very unfinished look—that he liked it only a little. I said no more but at length he examined it again and said with apparent effort at magnanimity "I shouldn't go higher than five dollars for it."

No, thank you, said I—not even for charity.

I calmly took the panel and turned its face to the wall.

Can it be that the work of my brains for some time, for it has been painted slowly, is only worth the price of—5 dollars worth of fine groceries? Bah! He'll have to wait a long while before I offer him another picture. $5–! and he taxed for well nigh two hundred thousand! . . .

---

*The above quotations are from diary entries of the following dates: Oct. 9, 1885; April 27, May 5, 1886; Sept. 11, 1885; April 27, May 13, May 18, April 27, May 28, 1886.

11 SEPTEMBER 1885. A.M. FRIDAY

. . . I found the sad news in this morning's paper that my old beloved playfellow Fred. Rider had followed the example of his father & committed suicide in N.O.[?] What a blow to his widowed mother! Good God, how can human hearts stand such terrible strain! He was her darling, the pride of the family—a suicide, a murderer of all our hopes of his steady rise to the heights of his profession. I will not, dare not blame. How do we know what is in the hearts of those who do those deeds? I have many a time felt the impulse, tasted by anticipation the sweets of having life done with. Yet—I thought of mother, of father, of the art that [illegible] would I felt I had a call to do—and I *endured*. How many times have I cried out that watchword in the dark tear watered nights! I say it with no thought of merit. It only shows that the fibre of my brain was more resisting than that of my poor friend. . . .

My darling wife thinks now that she shall some day preach—sermons about health, morality and the like—from the pulpit on what you will. Ah well, my dearest love, if you have anything to say that will help us, and real solution to offer for moral problems and the destruction of moral miasma, for God's sake preach! And may you have power beyond all the preachers of all time! Leave me—Leave mother—Leave child—leave all and preach! We need some one to tell us what of all these "truths" *is* truth. Go. God help you!—

SAT. 12TH SEPT. 1885. 4 P.M.

Last night Charlotte was doleful & hysterical again. It is the time of month in which such could be expected. It was a hard night for me. When she first awoke in the morning, she said she didn't love me, but by ten o'clock she said she did *some*. I hope that she does a great deal by this time. I should not be surprised if she were very unhappy tonight, but I expect that by the 16–17–18 she will feel very much better. The Dr. said she'd better take Elixir Coca once in a while if she felt dismal & growing more & more tired, so we got some this morning.* It was so lovely a morning that she was tempted to sally forth with me. She did on her pongee dress, fine bonnet &

---

*Elixir Coca, a medical preparation from coca (the South American bush whose leaves contain cocaine), was described in 1877 as having a "gently excitant effect," especially on the circulatory and nervous systems. Syrup from the plant was also commonly used in making Coca-Cola. George B. Wood and Franklin Bache, *The Dispensatory of the United States of America* (14th ed.; Philadelphia: J. B. Lippincott and Co., 1880), pp. 1643–1644.

goodly gloves, bore her fair parasol & came forth. We went briskly through lovely Angell St., down Thomas St. to see the progress of the studios, then after shopping at the market went to Greene's drugstore for soda. After that took car to Pharmacy for Coca, thence to the stone man's to look at stone for dining room. . . .

MONDAY MORNING, 14TH SEPTEMBER, 1885

My dear wife feels badly again this morning. I could scarcely prevail upon myself to leave her but I really felt that it would be better for her if I did. She is mourning her lot, but not to the extent of last month at this date. I think that tomorrow she will feel better. Our so inefficient servant seems to be a weight upon her, and we are thankful that she goes next Saturday night and that a German comes Sunday morning to take her place—a certain Elise Gärtner. . . .

Charlotte's illness takes all desire of activity out of me: yet—not exactly. It seems to paralyze all power. I do have desire enough but I can't bring myself to the *doing*.

But I *must*. Courage! Endure!

*   *   *

15TH SEPTEMBER, 1885. A.M.

. . . I found my sonnets sent to the "Century" awaiting me this morning, but it was the most encouraging refusal I've ever had, as it was subscribed:

"These are pleasing, but our crowded condition makes it impossible to accept them." I suppose that was put on as a salve—which it appears to be for I don't feel very badly about it. With the hardihood of youthful combativeness I have enclosed these in a new envelope and purpose sending them at once to Harpers Mo. with a like result of course—but then I must give them all a chance(!)

I'm glad to be able to say that upon going home I found Charlotte much more cheerful & active. She had been writing on an article called "The Homogeneity of Evil" and a letter and the first verse of a rather didactic poem. I confess I wish she'd strive more for beauty in poetry than for didactics, for when she does let herself forget to preach she writes very very tender & lovely things. To my mind beauty is as much needed as preaching. What we want most is a poet who feels strongly & can stir us with hopeful measures. I lack it severely. It may come by & by who knows. . . .

.   .   .

18TH SEPT. 1885. MORNING

About noon yesterday George Whitaker came in & wanted me to go sketching with him to [illegible]. . . . Ride delightful. Also the sunny spot in the woods under an ancient quaint sweet apple tree where the sun was warm & the ground dry making my nose feel much comfort after its week of influenza. The goldenrod blazed, and a few bunches of vivid crimson sumac enlivened the russets & quivering dark greens. It was a glorious day. After leaving that place we went still further, to a place called the "Crystal Spring Bleachery," Geo. said, but which was a perfect picture, a veritable poem of light & color. I've seen nothing for long so completely satisfying. Our way to it led by a barn overgrown with grapevines, and mounted by a rustic who showered the Bacchic fruit upon us. We ate the same gladly as we went down hill. . . .

. . .

22D SEPTEMBER, 1885 A.M.

This is my mother's 70th birthday. God grant there may be many more in store for her—happier, calmer than all gone before. I must dine with her today and take some slight offering. . . .

Well, yesterday Mrs. Tewksbury came, but not until nearly two o'clock. I liked her even better than I did when she came before. We talked of George, of her family, of Manchester, and of my pictures. She warmly pressed me to take Charlotte & baby to come to Manchester for a visit.

Well (again) after an hour or so she frightened me by saying that she wanted to buy the "Fool's Sermon" & the "Morning Measure,"—and I decided for various reasons to let her have the two for $650 instead of $700, which was my price. 1st I'm glad to have them go to George. 2d our fortune for almost four months would be assured by that sum. 3d I knew that they had been very kind to me, 4th I felt that Charlotte would be easier in her mind if I could make it certain. So I let them go. I do not get my pay much before January 1st. But—that is far better than nothing.

I did *feel well* to have the sale really made. That makes over $2000. worth of my pictures that family has bought within a year and a half. They certainly prove faith in my work. . . .

FRIDAY 25TH SEPT 1885 A.M.

Day before yesterday I began my "Remorse" in the afternoon at 2 o'clock and got the whole canvas covered with a very strong resemblance to what I want by 4 o'clock. It is the strongest two hours work I ever did.

The canvas is 43 × 60 inches. The conception came to me one evening just after the babe was born. I was thinking how very very terrible it would be if my darling had died in child bed, and what terrible remorse, groundless of course, I should feel if it had been so. Straightaway in my mind came a windswept hillside with two tall poplars bending before the wind a low moon making all the rest seem more desolate, and in the foreground a bier grounded by four huge candles with flames glaring in the wind. On the bier a carved mother & child. At the foot with head buried between the mother's feet a kneeling figure with hand clasped over her legs.*

That is *Remorse*. It is a very terrible picture. . . .

. . . The Dr. said yesterday that he thought [Charlotte had] better wean the bairn. It goes sorely against her heart to do it; but for all our sakes, her own most of all, it seems to me she should do it if there is any chance whatever that she will grow stronger. God—God knows what it is to me to see her so low. I see more and more clearly, *too* clearly, what my life would be without—her. I must be strong and *gay* without her, for it may have to come. It may. God forbid. God forbid.

Little Katharine is perfectly well, & thrives, vampire like on her mother's blood. Oh she is the dearest child!

The mother-in-law worries my love, my mother-in-law. She *is* very aggravating with nothing but very kind intention. A strange woman, hard to bear with. My dear dear Love, my sweet wife! Oh if I could only say Be whole! and have it be!

It shall be! . . .

MONDAY P.M. 28TH SEPT 1885

. . . Dr. Knight came to see me Saturday afternoon while I was at the new building. He came back here with me & we had a talk regarding Charlotte. He thinks her much better.

There was a very pleasant article about the artists in yesterday's Journal in which my work was spoken very highly of. Sydney Burleigh & I are of course much interested in our new studios. I certainly am going to have a

---

* *Remorse* (43 × 60 inches, canvas), signed November 6, 1885. "First exhibited in the Autumn Ex. '85 of the Prov. Art Club, where the light proved insufficient to accentuate the values. The darkness of the picture a great drawback certainly; but I know no other way to express my meaning." "Opera" Book, pp. 47–49. In later years, Stetson's reaction to depression apparently changed. In 1897 he wrote, "Whenever I feel gruesomest and most dismal myself I usually paint my jolliest pictures." Quoted in Charles Eldredge, *Charles Walter Stetson: Color and Fantasy* (Lawrence, Kan.: Spencer Museum of Art, 1982), p. 109, n. 27.

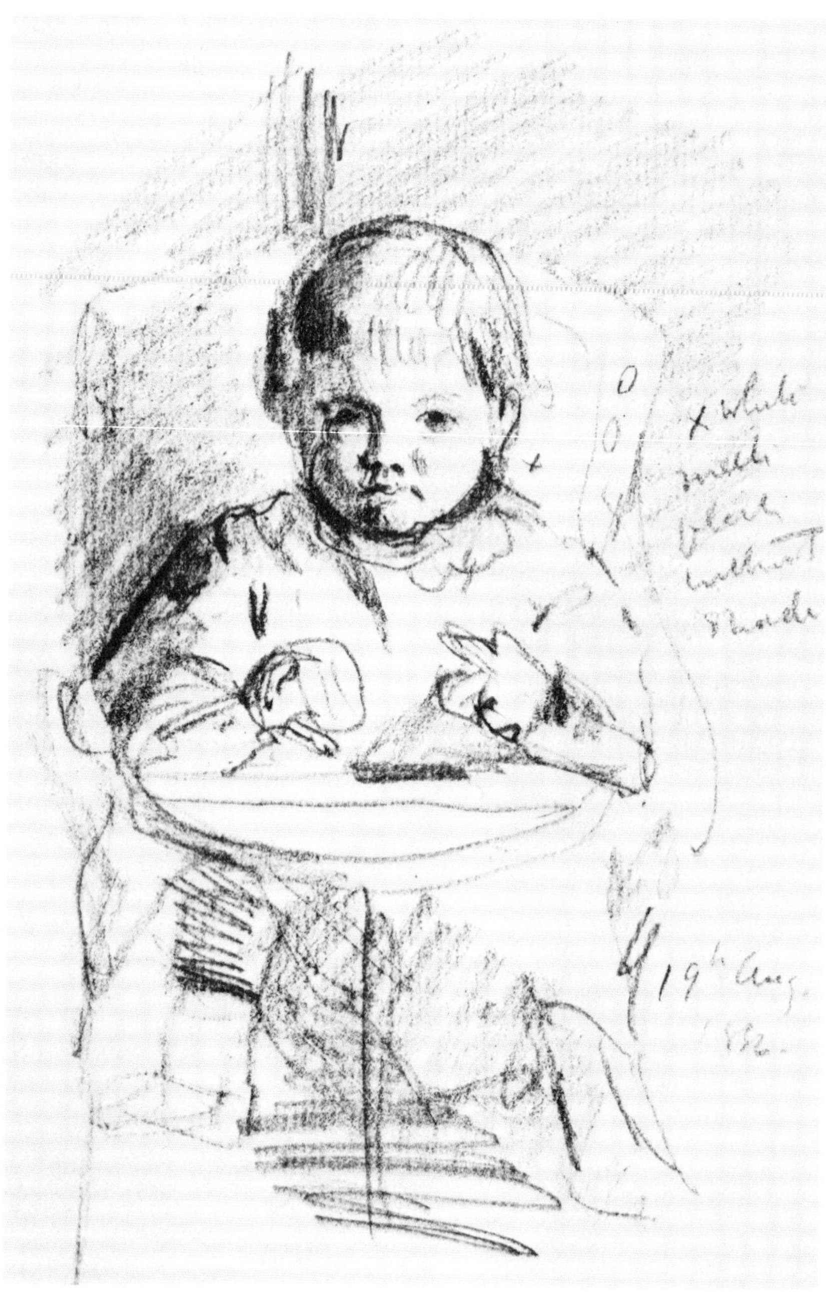

Drawing of Katharine in high chair. From Sketchbooks.

charming workroom. With a certain cozy solemnity about it, if I may so express myself.

MONDAY 5TH OCTOBER, 1885

. . . I've been working mostly on the carving of the beam ends of the new studio building. New work to me, but I fancy I have done it as effectively as Sydney or young Aldrich.* Terribly grotesque, both.† Now we've got to wrestle with the outside plaster. We dined at Caroline's & called at mother's yesterday.

The Masons want me to paint them a 7 ft. picture of the Ascension. So I'm awaiting an inspiration.

I had to borrow $100— of Mr. Bates Saturday to be paid by Nov. 28th. Bought coal & wood.

I feel much unsettled on account of the new studio, but I guess it will do me good.

TUESDAY 6TH OCTOBER 1885 P.M.

. . . I've traced the lifesize figures on the studio building front yesterday & should have begun coloring them today if it had not been so wet. . . .‡

Am wondering *why* my sonnets are not returned. It *can't* be they're going to keep them for publication. They've been gone nearly three weeks. I've written to N & B [Noyes and Blakeslee] to see if they would like to have

---

*John Aldrich (1864–1952), a successful Providence industrialist (President of the New England Butt Company), was an active Art Club member and also an arts and crafts enthusiast. forming the Art Workers Guild.

†Edgar Kaufmann's description of the design of the Fleur de Lys explains why Stetson used the word "grotesque": the beams were "boldly carved" with "grotesque masks" representing "the Wise Old Owl, the Frog King, and similar fabulous creatures. In the center the Frog King mouths a great, twisted, iron ring for hoisting fuel, and maybe pianos." Edgar Kaufmann, Jr. "Some American Architectural Ornament of the Arts and Crafts Era," *Journal of the Society of Architectural Historians* 24, no. 4 (Dec. 1965), pp. 288–289.

‡Kaufmann describes the facade of the Fleur de Lys: It "looks like two loosely angled folding-screens placed one above the other in front of the basically rectangular building. The decoration culminates in large figures of the academic trio, Painting, Sculpture, and Architecture modelled in place in fresh plaster and then colored. The pre-Raphaelite style of these is evident. Each figure is named in informal lettering; each stands on a simple molding and is surrounded by a geometric pattern as by a frame." Kaufmann, "Some American Architectural Ornament," p. 287.

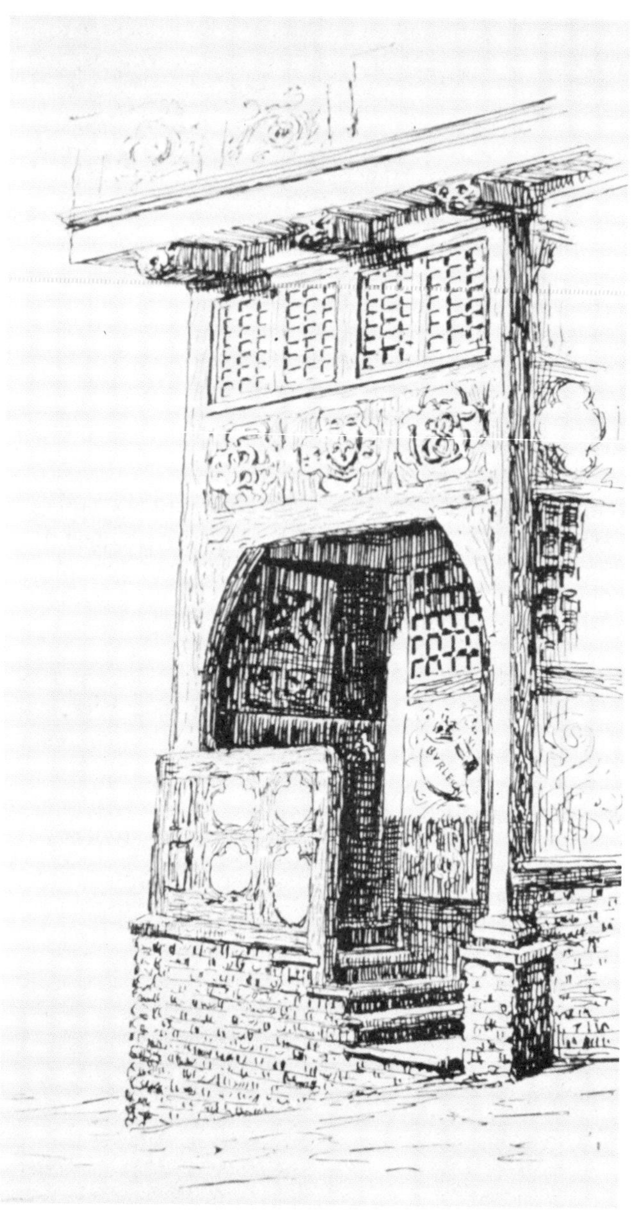

Drawing of Fleur de Lys Building, Thomas Street, Providence, R.I. From *Art and Decoration* 3, no. 1 (May 1886), p. 6.

the "Approach of a Centaur" & "Procession to a Temple," also "A Game at Sunset."*. . .

9TH OCTOBER, 1885 12:30 P.M.

I thought I had outgrown the need of this old friend, but I find I have not. Somehow I'm all out of condition, or rather, I am in a condition familiar enough a few years ago. There is a great weight of the need of a large number of dollars weighing upon me. I feel the futility of human endeavor more than I ought. I feel incapable of doing the work I *must* do. I feel so tired and—mentally haggard. My dear Love tries me terribly. Poor dear Love she don't know it and if she could help it wouldn't do it at the price of her own life. But her depressed state, her weakened nerves & brain have made her restless, peevish, and inconsolable. I go home tired & tried and she wants to talk of some insolvable moral problem, or else I must remain cheerful & patient under her fretfulness when I myself am almost as fretful.

Now she has a new project which I am trying my best to hear her out with. She has conceived of the idea of going to her brother in Ogden City, staying there awhile, and then going to Santa Barbara for a longer stay, after which to Pasadena, Los Angeles, Ca. to the Channings—the stay to be indefinite. It is only a matter of about $400. I am to try to furnish it immediately, and of course it must come out of the sale to Mrs. Tewksbury. Gladly will I borrow it if I can. Already I have tried to get it of Mr. Mason (350) until the middle of January at 10 percent interest. It will embarrass me; it will cut me off on my models that I intended to hire; it will deprive me of helping mother & father as I intended. But if it will help her regain strength, or if not strength, cheerfulness, oh gladly gladly would I undergo much more for it. I really think it will benefit her. I know she'll be lonely, but perhaps that will call self-reliance & will into action again. At any rate, the new sights & long journey will take her mind off her trouble to a great extent, and it will enforce her to rest from thinking she might *do* things. . . .

The baby is successfully in the process of weaning. Mrs. Perkins will take care of her while Charlotte is away. . . .

A Procession to a Temple (22 × 24 inches, canvas), signed August 15, 1885, "Opera" Book, p. 45. *A Game at Sunset* (cherry panel about 8 × 14 inches), signed August 21, 1885. "Girls on a slope by the Sea at Sunset. One is in vermillion, one in greenish blue, chasing the one in red; and one in purple who stands with one in emerald holding a scarf of yellow. Tone amber (yellow)." "Opera" Book, p. 45.

13TH OCTOBER 1885. 2:45 P.M.

Very gloomy. Rains.

Charlotte's journey is assured. I borrowed the money of Mr. Mason, or literally of his mother through him, as he said he really had no cash himself. Charlotte seems very glad, and benefited by it already. She expects to start next week Wednesday. Naturally I feel grateful that she can have her wish, for truly I believe it will do her a great amount of good. We shall be very lonesome without her, I know that, but the thought that she is seeing some worthy sights & gaining strength will fully compensate. She *is* such a lovely and loving soul! . . .

19TH OCTOBER 1885 A.M. MONDAY

Well, my darling goes west this week. Her preparations are nearly complete. I fancy she feels a little hesitancy at this last moment.

People with whom she has talked wonder how she can leave baby & husband for so long. But it is I who should complain if any should, and I do not: I understand how she can go, and I am truly glad she can. The folk pity me. They should not. . . .

I shall live without her to my best limit—God granting that she may come back to my arms and her real home again. It is a long and somewhat dangerous journey but strengths of heart and love of right would carry one through far more dangerous places. . . .

23RD OCT. 1885 A.M.

Well, my dear Love left last night at 5:45. She said she had *every*thing that she wanted, and that I should be glad that I gave it her. And I am. It is not for me to say how how terribly my heart clutched at itself at the parting, but I held it in check, for I was *glad* for her sake that she could go—glad that I could give her this chance to gain new life, new thought, new ideas. I am glad I had this opportunity to do this small thing as an attempt to return to her what marriage seems to have taken away. But after I left her, and got where I knew she could not see me, the restrained sobs & tears came, and came at intervals all the way home. It was long before I could control myself enough to face Mrs. Perkins & eat my supper. But I did at last and lavished upon the fair Katharine what her mother could not take with her. . . .

I noticed when I reached home that Mrs. Perkins had kindly got the wood to blazing brightly, the gas more pleasantly lighted than usual, some fine coffee and flowers on the table. It was very kind, for the poor woman will be very lonely I'm afraid. . . .

Undoubtedly Charlotte is amazingly lovable. She seems to fill a very large place where ever she is, and we shall miss her greatly.

The dear girl wrote me a letter on the cars last night & I got it this morning. It was so kind & tender of her. She tells her love. Says she feels "pretty well—not badly in any way." and "O how lovely to be with you again, *well,* and with such lots to tell about. Such a large new current in my life. And you give it to me darling."

God keep her! . . .

SAT. 24TH OCT. 1885 4 P.M.

I have worked rather hard today on "Remorse," which I've carried pretty well along, on the Bathing Nymphs, which I improved.*. . .

30TH OCTOBER, 10 A.M.

My darling reached Ogden Tuesday night. Every day now I receive from her messages along the way. The last came yesterday. It was near Lincoln, Nebraska that 'twas written. She felt a little lonesome that morning, perhaps for the first time. I'm afraid she is going to be lonesomer. . . .

---

* *Bathing Nymphs* is an early version of the "bather-by-the-water" subject which Stetson later perfected in *After the Bath* (see reproduction in this volume). (Possibly it was first inspired as Stetson watched the bathers at Gano Beach. See Diaries, Aug. 19, 1884.) Charles Eldredge suggests that the "formula" was first influenced by Corot, but was given a "new vitality" in Stetson's "grandest essay along those lines," *After the Bath* (1910): "Instead of the academic figure study which such a title might indicate, the large painting is predominantly landscape, featuring traceries of slender trees against sky. Those silhouettes are echoed in the standing nudes by the reflective surface of the foreground pool. The human subject, in a state of classical nudity, immersed in richly pigmented nature, is painted with a full authority which marks the mature artist. In works such as *After the Bath*, Stetson finally achieved the reconciliation of the humanist, the pagan, and the colorist which Italy inspired." Eldredge, *Charles Walter Stetson*, p. 102.

Moreover, Stetson's "selection of bathers as subject" was, at least among American artists, relatively "avant-garde." According to one reviewer, a similar painting, *Water Play* (1895), "anticipates other such American scenes by a decade." "Stetson's involvement with female bathers would seem to be totally without precedent in American painting. One thinks, rather, of contemporary French paintings of the Moulin Rouge dancers, such as George Seurat's *Le Chahut*, 1889–90." "Selection VII: American Paintings from the Museum's Collection, c. 1800–1930," *Bulletin of the Rhode Island School of Design, Museum Notes* 63, no. 5 (April 1977), p. 220.

Mr. Whitaker, a Mr. Bartlett* & I went to Boston yesterday to see the English water colors. Rather enjoyable, but I don't believe it is a collection representative of English water color works. . . .

I'm glad to find that I enjoyed the antique room at the Museum more than I did the water colors and more than I ever did before. However little my work may show it I'm sure that I am in deepest sympathy with the real Greek Art, not modern classicism but the living breathing idealized Greek *life*. And the nude, I love it *passionately*. No one knows how much. The day shall come please God, when I shall have opportunities to study it as I should. Meantime I love it, and shall make tentative essays in it.

27TH APRIL 1886 AT THE FLEUR DE LYS

Once again, after six months of silence, I turn to my old Journal, with so much done that I have no hope to write it, and so much felt—Ah that is the hardest part!

But I must summarize. Why? Because heart is heavy: because this as in other days is my one refuge, my one place of outpouring that replies nothing, can be as all and not murmur. It is for comfort that I turn to my book again. Here I am in my new studio, where I have been since the 1st of the year, surrounded by very little of my work, and such luxury of light and space as I have never had before. But today it seems mockery, for it avails nothing to ease hunger of heart & mind in me and help me pay my debts, which weigh heavily on me.

My dear wife stayed in Pasadena until the 22d March. She regained health and gladness; learned a great deal about the world: got humility in large measure; wrote a more or less successful play in company with Miss Channing, and came home on the 29th with her sister-in-law [Julia Perkins],† something of an invalid. My pictures had not sold as I anticipated. The money I borrowed of Mr. Mason had not been paid: the money I expected to get out of the Ascension‡ which I had been at work on since Charlotte went away, had not come to me as they had not got ready for the picture. She wanted to come home so I borrowed $150 of Mr. Bates & sent

---

* Sculptor T. H. Bartlett exhibited at the PAC in the 1880s and modelled "owl panels" in terra cotta for the club building in 1887.

† Julia Perkins, the wife of Thomas Perkins, Charlotte's brother, who was living in Ogden, Utah.

‡ The *Ascension* or the *Ascending Jesus* (48 × 84 inches, canvas), signed March 4, 1886. It was at the Berkshire Athenaeum, September 23, 1886, and at the Providence Art Club, January 4, 1887.

$125 of it to her. In order to have her sister-in-law I had to furnish another room expending about $100 on it. She could not have come in a more inopportune time. If it had not been for the drafts of Mr. Tewksbury, I cannot see how we could have got through the winter. But this not being able to meet one's notes is terribly trying.

Well after a variety of adventures which were amusing enough, they came. Charlotte seemed glad to get back & I was—naturally—glad to have her. But things were not as they might have been. She had taken a fearful cold on reaching Denver and she is not quite over it yet. The first few days she took hold of her duties here strongly, but since she has been growing troubled & very melancholy again, so that now it is pretty hard to see what real good her winter's sojourn did her. It is rather discouraging. I did fondly hope to have *one month* at least of unalloyed joy. Alas, I had scarcely a week. Dear wife, it is not her fault. It is a disease of some sort: she has not the temperament to make light of it and throw it off. It is all the harder now as my debts have been piling up and almost no money coming in. I owe about $800. . . . Summer is at hand—no pictures sell! The outlook is darker than it has been for two years at least. It does seem to me that Charlotte might have been permitted to aid me by cheerful conversation and willing life. But one must bear whatever comes as best he can. She is trying to sell her share in the property at Hartford, but it seems unavailing.

Oh my dear Love! God knows what it is to my heart to see you unhappy from day to day. . . .

I had an excellent model, a Miss M. from N. Y. I painted a profile of her. Perhaps the best thing technically that I have done, unless it be the recently finished portrait of Mr. Pegram,* now being shown at the Art Club. She posed for me nude—in *any* way I would have her. She had one of the most beautifully modelled mouths I ever saw, but very insincere. Her color was wonderful.

Then I had Miss J[effrey] nude also. And Miss Phethpeare nude. I did a good deal of work from the model. . . .

My Ascension was completed in the middle of March. It was shown here evenings to the Free Masons and the A. E. Club. It was very generally liked & highly commended. But the Free Masons refused to buy it, much to

---

* *Portrait of John C. Pegram, Esquire* (4 × 7 feet, canvas), signed April 1886. John Combe Pegram, lawyer, and also President of the Art Club from 1885 to 1891, bought the painting for a "nominal sum" in 1886. "Opera" Book, p. 55. Stetson did at least two other portraits of Mr. Pegram: one in May 1886, a 20 × 24-inch "life size head" ("Opera" Book, p. 74); and the other, now owned by the Providence Art Club, in 1893.

my hurt & the Committee's chagrin. So it is now on my hands and I am near pecuniary ruin. . . .

WEDNESDAY, 28TH AP. 1886 A.M.

My wife went with her sister-in-law to see the "Mikado" last night. Came home about 12 P. M. The opera seemed to make very little impression upon her, nor break her melancholy. When she awoke this morning the old haunting look was in her eyes, and I shuddered. I dare not even write it: though I thought of it all the way down this morning till my throat was swollen & parched and life almost too much to bear. To paint today would be impossible, at any rate this morning. Her condition worries me exceedingly. I cannot forget it an instant. That with my pecuniary embarrassment is making havoc in me. I have not by nature the *insouciance* necessary to tide me over. I must simply rely on my "grit," clench hands and *will* to bear it— not for my own sake, God knows, but for the good of my Darling and my lovely child. I see before me months and months of deepest torture. To see her ill in mind and not be able to reach the disease—!! God—God why thus? But my duty is clear. I must keep my grief locked up; never letting it out at home surely. I know this room must feel it & repression will be terrible. The next part of my duty is to be as patient & tender as possibly can be; to be firm if need be, but always tender: for it is far from willfulness with her. It is disease. God come through with some form of comfort, lest I fail them until it is past. If I should succumb, die, now my child would be in a bad dilemma, and my precious mate would be alone verily. No, I must bear for their sakes and drink the bitterest cup that can be measured out.

I am in worse condition today than I ever was in my whole life. The misery I have lived through seems as nothing to the misery that seems about to be mine.

Ten minutes ago I saw Hamilton MacDougall. He is recently back from his second tour to England. He is robust, cheerful, spirited, successful. I could not help feeling the contrast as I stood beside him. I don't think that I envied him. I'm quite sure I didn't. But oh, how I would that my wife seemed as strong as he seemed! . . .

30TH APRIL 1886 A.M.

I am so utterly undone this morning that I can't fix my attention on any sort of work. Fortunately, my Love had a very much improved day yesterday & seems more cheerful this morning; otherwise I fear I should be quite distracted. Tomorrow I ought to pay at least $800—and I am possessor of 26 cents. I have not even enough to pay Elise her wages. Coal nearly gone; wood quite gone. I don't know how patient my creditors will be. I don't know either what they can do further than seize my pictures—and heaven knows they are welcome to those. The worst is my largest debts are to my friends who would not seize my goods. That is where the sting lies mostly. . . .

Then Miss Jeffrey was in yesterday A. M. Came to see if she could get posing to do. Heavens! how blue she was also. Talked wildly of suicide & all that sort of thing. I bluer than she I'll wager, tried to cheer her! . . . Miss J. needs clothing: any body can see that. She needs a Physician, I know. And, I can't even give her employment Take from me all manner of fine living but give me power to spend somewhat on those in distress! . . .

Mrs. Perkins took her goods and chattel from my house yesterday. She was eminently faithful to our Kate in Charlotte's absence, and I cannot be too grateful for it. But she has a very deadly effect on Charlotte. I think Charlotte's spirits rose as soon as she left the house. She is a woman who sucks the life out of one, I scarce know how. I marvel that I got through the winter with her as well as I did. But I find I am so strongly an individual, so wholly selfish and self sustained mentally, that other folk have very small effect on ME. She used to aggravate me unconsciously but it did not go very deeply. I am ungrateful in thinking of her bad qualities when she is so intentionally kind and loving. But her love is like that of a porcupine. The nearer it gets to you, the more sharply the quills intrude.

Is there any help coming? Desire should bring it.

WEDNESDAY 5TH MAY, 1886 ABOUT 2 P.M.
. . . My Love had two days of genuine cheerfulness, but yesterday she was downcast again, and this morning found her completely subject to it. It paralyzes my thoughts of beautiful things. I am irresistibly absorbed in endeavors to imagine something that will cure her. It is clear enough that her temperament unfits her for caring for Katharine and the house. I don't know as she would be any better if she did not have the cares, though. My duty is clear at any rate.

As soon as I can I shall make an effort to find a suitable person to attend the baby, and try to draw Charlotte into a more active life. It is an extremely difficult case to deal with. I can see that if I were rich many of the obstacles would vanish. God knows that for her sake, I crave riches. Oh if I might but have enough to give her rides and trips here & there, for theaters

& fine clothes, and parties at home! Oh if I might! Instead of that there are debts, and she knows it. The knowledge does not help cure her by any means. I feel the weight of her day & night. There is a constant desire to know what I ought to do for her and how to do it.

I left her this morning crouched on the floor with her head on the lounge in a most dejected condition. The picture has been with me all day. I do not complain because it unfits me for work; I only *ache* because it unfits her for work and life at its best. It makes a solitude of what might be a song. . . .

I could not pay my Art Club assessment so they, rightly, posted me with the others. Pres. Pegram was incensed that a member of the Board of Managers had failed to pay his dues & was very kind in what he said. He wanted me to send an excuse to the Board. He said it wasn't the cash they cared for but it set a poor example to the other members of the Club. I told him that I could not pay without injuring my family. This morning a receipted bill came from the treasurer. I suppose someone paid my tax, probably Mr. Pegram or Mr. Bates but I was too proud to let it go, so returned it to the Treas. with a note stating that there must be some mistake, as I had not paid & was therefore not entitled to a receipt. I told him that I should pay whether they expelled me or not. . . .

Yesterday afternoon Smyth & Whitaker called at the house & went sketching with me in our region. My Love was much disappointed not to go. But I could not ask her because I *knew* the men would think it an intrusion & not feel so free. It seemed to hurt her disproportionately.

It all upsets me. I feel no more like painting than like a balloon ascension. I *want* to work. I am dragged out, weak, heartsick and altogether deplorable.

People that I owe are remarkably kind. Some people even seem to think well of me.

Well, I'll hang on a little longer & see if something don't change for the better. Ah, but I love her!!

13TH MAY 1886 10 A.M.

Yesterday was a marked day. In the morning Charlotte, Julia [Perkins] & I went to Miss Wheeler's studio to see the portraits that Herkomer left.*

---

*Mary C. Wheeler, an early PAC member, was founder and later President of the Wheeler Art School in Providence. She studied in Paris, and had a studio in France as well as Providence. Hubert Herkomer, portrait painter and Oxford University professor, gave an eve-

He painted four in two weeks and a half ($10,000.00). As he had left the city I wanted much to see them. We were very cordially received by Miss Wheeler. We saw the portraits. I am glad we saw them. Dr. Grosvenor's is silly. Judge [Charles H.] Bradley's pretty good. Mrs. Goddard's a poorly drawn sketch for which he had the insolence to charge $2500. It is a fraud downright. He calmly told Miss Wheeler that it should be finished more but "he hadn't time." Bah! Well, I wouldn't be afraid to put my portrait of Mr. Pegram beside either of them. . . .

I went to Young's to lunch, as a telegram from Mrs. Kilvert told me that Mr. James Jackson Jarves was coming to call on me that afternoon.* I got my things into "spectacular" order, so that he might not be embarrassed in seeing. He came promptly at 2 o'clock. He is a ruddy, white bearded, blue-eyed quiet little man, with a great reserve force. One feels almost immediately that there is power behind his quiet.

He came expressly to see me, and naturally, I feel honored.

He talked of my pictures very appreciatively. He said the Ascension would make a glorious stained glass window, and he was very glad an American had chosen to paint it. It was so unusual. He said the Pegram was a noble, powerful and finely serious work. It showed great strength. The unfinished portrait of Dr. Knight, he admired much, and said it was very like the work of the old painters. (I could not ask for a greater compliment than that.)

He noticed the color & glow of my other pictures. He said that my work reminded him strongly of Vedder as he was twenty years ago combined with color somewhat like Babcock's.† He said that what I needed most to study was design—including I suppose drawing in large measure.

---

ning lecture on portrait painting at the PAC in 1886. A number of his paintings are owned by Brown University.

*James Jackson Jarves (1818–1888), voluminous writer and distinguished art collector, owned one of the largest and most important collections of early Italian masters in America.

‡Stetson's senior by 22 years, often referred to as the "dean of American artists in Rome," Symbolist painter Elihu Vedder (1836–1923) was frequently exhibited in Boston and New York, where Stetson almost certainly encountered him. Years later, when Stetson moved to Italy, he and Vedder found they had a lot in common: a love of Italian scenery, of imaginative imagery, of literature and poetry. Charles Eldredge writes that Stetson's "spirited" portrait of Vedder itself suggests the warmth of friendship (it was far more lively and less rigid than his Providence portrait work), as does the fact that Vedder dedicated his autobiography (*The Digressions of V.*) to Grace Channing. He was expressing "appreciation," Vedder wrote, "for all the patience she had displayed in typing the pages, in advising him where a 'link' was needed to keep the 'bits' together, and in giving some shape to the manuscript." Quoted in Regina Soria, *Elihu Vedder: American Visionary Artist in Rome* (Rutherford, N.J.: Fairleigh Dickinson University Press, 1970), p. 243. See also Eldredge, *Charles Walter Stetson*, pp. 94–95.

He wanted to see "Remorse" very much so we fished [it] out of the cellar & brought it upstairs. He pronounced upon it very forcibly: said he did not wonder the Boston critics did not know what to make of it. But the truth was they never saw anything, anything like it. He said it was "full of Doré's best qualities; an extremely touching and powerful piece of painting of the impressionist type."

We talked of his books; of his collections, of Mrs. Kilvert & our ancestors. His grandmother was a Stetson.

Altogether the visit was extremely agreeable. He is very unpretentious and kind in his criticism.

He gave me courage, because I *know* that his opinion is founded upon reality & a profound study of art and its products.

Later Mr. Pegram called.

My Darling seems a little more cheerful and more nearly reconciled to life. In hopes that it would cheer her I bought tickets to the Comedy of Errors for tonight, & for her & Julia seats for Othello, with Booth & Salvini in Boston Saturday.

She is a dear good girl & altogether too much to me.

I am expecting Dr. Knight every minute for another sitting.

10 A.M. TUES. 18TH MAY 1886

My love has been cheerful for nearly a week now, and I have hopes of a steady gain. I can see that lack of money in the household irritated her. . . .

Mrs. Kilvert wrote to me regarding what Mr. James [Jarves] said of my work. It scarcely coincided with what he said to me, and I told her so. Thereupon she sent me a very warm & tender letter telling me that I misunderstood hers and that he really said the same things to her. She pointed out how great an honor it was for him who "had acres of art & could give a great bounty to the Met. Museum" to want to possess my "Path of Duty" as he did. And it *is* an honor surely. I feel it, am proud of it, and have been so weakly human as to want other people to know it. . . .

William P. Babcock (1826–1899) was a figure painter, particularly of Biblical and classical scenes. Born in Boston, he studied with Thomas Couture in Paris, and subsequently moved to Barbizon, the small French town so popular among romantic landscape and figure painters. According to one writer, his works "have a strong poetic strain and what may be described as a Venetian feeling for form, color, and light, in a manner reflecting Couture and Titian, but also akin to the fine studies of the nude that Millet painted in the 1840s. . . . Although Babcock lived most of his professional life in France, . . . his work was appreciated in his native Boston." Matthew Baigell, *Dictionary of American Art* (New York: Harper & Row, 1979), p. 22.

I have had another sitting from Dr. Knight. The portrait is growing much to my liking. I think I am better pleased with that than anything I've done for very long. He comes again this afternoon. I hope I shall finish the head then. I have nearly finished the "Path of Duty."*. . .

FRIDAY 21ST MAY, 1886, 2 P.M.

Am just back from mother's where I dined. Sydney [Burleigh] & his wife met me at the door. . . . He says that in "Art & Decoration" this month are facsimile of our drawings of the studio. . . .†

FRIDAY MAY 28TH 1886 9:45 A.M.

Another week gone. Well.

Charlotte has seemed more cheerful and willing to bear her share of the burden that comes to us. Katharine has the chicken pox, mildly. She is a most dear patient girl. She makes no trouble at all beyond caring for her necessary wants. . . .

A charming letter from Mr. Tewksbury came. He sends very interesting letters—strong, manly, cultured. Among the rest he says:

Now then, what do you say to a Venus Aphrodite? You must not argue me out of this notion. Painters and poets only have seen her rise out of the water. There shall be no meaner critics. Tell me what you think of this, and do not say it is impossible, since he achieves most who strives most.

What *do* I think of it? It thrills me. What would I rather paint worthily than the mother of all delight and love—the pure, tender foam born mother? She stands side by side in my mind with Mary, mother of Jesus. Not the lascivious companion in lewd revels and tipsy orgies, but the uncorrupt giver of love and beauty. Ah Aphrodite! Thou art not dead. In one heart

---

* *Portrait of Ed. B. Knight, M.D.* (20 × 24 inches, canvas), signed May 1886. "This is undoubtedly an excellent likeness and truly characteristic in pose & facial expression. I have presented it to him." "Opera" Book, p. 57. *Path of Duty* (6⅛ × 11 inches, cherry panel), signed May 19, 1886. "A youthful artist starts out to work, and is tempted from it by two women, one at his left, in red, one at his right in yellow. Artist in greenish black. Mountain & temple in background. Trees in middle distance & at right of picture. Tulips in foreground. Promised by James Jackson Jarves, who expressed a desire to buy it." In the margin of this entry Stetson later wrote, "Sold on 19th March 1888 to Hon. Geo. M. Carpenter. $50.00." "Opera" Book, p. 57.

† Frank Robinson, "The Sign of the Fleur de Lis," *Art and Decoration* 3, no. 1 (May 1886), p. 6.

thou livest on. Comfort and help me: reveal thyself to my mind that I may paint thee truly.

But *how* to paint her! My store bill is very large. My rents are due very soon, milk, gas, clothing, and all the rest. I could not get the models for Venus for less than $100. Probably the sum would be much larger than that for besides her, I suppose I should introduce other figures. I have written my friend and told him *just* how I am situated.

And besides my dear Grandma Cresson is sick. A letter came by an amanuensis which touched me. In her sickness she thought of me. God grant that she may be well again.

I ought to be working but I am unsettled, *anxious* and that really upsets me. I can work in bodily pain, but that peculiar perturbation called anxiety does for me thoroughly.

2D JUNE 1886. 9:35 A.M.

I left Charlotte in tears this morning, as I have almost ever since she came home. She goes to bed crying, or at least deeply melancholy, inconsolable. I am not sure that she does not weep all night. The poor dear lovely woman! Oh how my heart aches for her! This constant grief of hers is wearing her out and wearing me out. I feel utterly dragged. My knees are weak, my head thick and heavy, and a peculiar sense of not getting air enough to breathe constantly. There must be some change or it will either kill me or craze me. Combined with lack of money and a burden of debt—!

I don't know that she can help it. It has become a disease, a sort of monomania. I can only see one cure for it which lies outside herself, and that is an entire change of residence. If I had money enough I would pack up, store all my goods and emigrate to Europe, to London, or Paris or Florence, or Antwerp—anywhere, so that it would give her a new circle of thoughts and oblige her to think of something beside her own trouble. I would even move to Pasadena, a thing she would dearly like, I doubt not. But how, O my God, can this or any other thing be done without money and ridden by debt? But that there must be some change is absolutely certain, for I've got, I feel pitifully, almost to the length of my patience. I dread every day lest I lose control and say some harsh word that will make her ache the harder. Sudden [illegible] unexpected pains are hard enough, but this dragging, anticipated—agony! I will bear it as best I may. God help me.

There is no one to whom I can tell these things. They must be borne alone.

Endure! Endure!

Charlotte's mother has another hemorrhage.

I am almost ashamed to meet my grocer. I am almost ashamed to meet the furniture man. I am quite ashamed to meet Mr. Mason and Mr. Bates, though God knows I am guiltless on that score. The money if I had it would go to all of them instantly. . . .

2 JUNE ''86 AFTERNOON

. . . It occurred to me that my darling might be benefited by a gentle surprise, to wit, by my going home to lunch at noon, instead of to mother's or Caroline's as usual. . . . She really seemed pleased to see me. The tears had abated but her smile was mournful truly. She was resigned, or nearly so but quite unhappy still. We talked of the possibility of another child etc. Little Katharine awoke soon after my coming. . . .

I am in a beastly condition of bovine laziness—perhaps—and surely utterly unable to do good work. Money   money   money!!! That would work a cure of a certain kind. Ah, why can I not have it? The "Ascension," the three portraits and other minor works surely ought to show that I am not inherently lazy; and make me think that I deserve some pay for them. $50.00 is all I have gotten out of them so far this year. But I sold a few other things. The Pegram portrait ought to have given me at least $500. and the "Ascension" certainly as much.

Well—one can bear perhaps. I will try.

18TH JUNE 1886. 4:45 P.M.

Here one over two weeks gone and I have made no entry. Probably it is quite as well. I would have written for the most part rather melancholy things. My dear love was painfully unhappy and hypochondriac. Then last week she has been better, even quite cheerful. I am looking for a return of her distemper in a few days. May God avert it! it is terrible! It seemed to me for a day or two that I simply could not stand it another hour. But I did. Possibly I am the stronger for it. I doubt it, but I do not feel sure of my doubts.

I think I helped my love by theatre and excursions. Mr. Tewksbury sent me $100 towards the Aphrodite—to be expended for models. Well—there was a large grocery bill. I paid $25 of that. The girl had to have a swing $5 more went for that. I gave Charlotte ten for little things. I bought theatre tickets and so forth, so that towards the Aphrodite I have spent only $16.00. $11.50 of that for casts. There are perhaps ten dollars left. That will have to be spent for the servants' wages. It could scarce be helped, and since the change in my Love for the better was worth very very much more even if it be but temporary.

Wednesday we went up the Pawtuxet as far as the Pumping Station. Charlotte rowed with me clear there with a pair of oars—did it truly & strongly. I rowed back. It seemed to do her good. It was a fair six or seven miles steady exertion for her.

The only drawing I have made toward the Aphrodite I have been doing this week from Miss J[effrey]. I have been very careful with it. I spent four sittings on the outline, and began to model it this morning. I think it the most accurate drawing I ever did. I can't see the expression I hoped to get in it. Indeed I fail as yet to quite conceive of the pose of the Aphrodite I dream of—the pose that will express all I want—this is a trifle too affected, too bashful, and *limp*. Yet it is not bad, I think. . . .

Ah it is such a comfort to have the Venus Milo before me daily. And this sweet pensive Faun that stands on my desk—these things are inspiration, and give a touch of eternity to the ephemeral present. One can dream and feel large with such old time wonders before the eyes and appealing to the heart.

What a woman, this mighty Venus! Oh to be able to create at this late day fit mates to such! I could die feeling my day not empty if it were granted to me to do such things. How can I hope it? I dare not expect it. Yet—God help me!

17TH AUGUST 1886 A.M.

Over two months since I wrote. The truth is I was too languid as regards my affairs to write. I confess that I have forgotten for the time many things I should be glad to embalm here, but perhaps the very forgetting is a sign that they should not be embalmed.

Briefly: Julia went home long ago. Charlotte had another rather prolonged attack. Dr. Keller came down to perform an operation and succeeded. Then Charlotte had a violent time & went to see Dr. Keller in great haste. Stayed over night at her house. The Dr. told her that she was suffering from a disease of the nerves, that her brain was all right. It is a form of nervous prostration. She came back rather disgusted for I secretly think she expected to hear that her brain was organically injured. Just before this I had written to Miss [Grace] Channing to ask her what she thought of the probability of Charlotte's being able to get employment in Pasadena: for Charlotte thought that if she could be away somewhere where she was unknown, and could get work to do she should be all right. Miss Channing's reply was kind in the extreme, and quite just. She, like any sensible person, said that the best thing would be for us to separate, but she could not advise Pasadena as the people there knew Charlotte & would not understand how she could leave her family a second time. That is clear to see and it would doubtless cause a sort of ostracism for her there.

Charlotte & I had a long, detailed, & serious talk about it. We decided that as soon as possible, meaning by that as soon as we could get money enough, we would migrate to some other city—say to London: or in that failing she should go and we would hire someone to care for Katharine. Meantime she was to live in hope & try to do all she could here.

The result has been very happy so far. She took hold of her work. She wrote poems & a story, the former the best she has done. She sent [it] to "The Journal" & the Editor took one of the poems & assured her that he would accept others.* She has been sending her water color work about in hope of commission and altogether has acquired a great deal of new life & cheerfulness.

About three weeks ago my dear Grandma Cresson came to see me, &

---

*Charlotte's poems and short stories at this time reflect a growing resentment about "brainless" wife/mother roles. Her poem "The Answer," to which Stetson refers, won first prize in the *Woman's Journal*, edited by Alice Stone Blackwell. It reads in part:

> A maid was asked in marriage. Wise as fair,
> She gave her answer with deep thought and prayer,
>
> Expecting, in the holy name of wife,
> Great work, great pain, and greater joy in life.
>
> She found such work as brainless slaves might do,
> By day and night, long labor, never through;
>
> Such pain—no language can her pain reveal;
> It had no limit but her power to feel;
>
> Such joy—life left in her sad soul's employ
> Neither the hope nor memory of joy.
> Helpless, she died, with one despairing cry,—
> "I thought it good; How could I tell the lie?"
>
> And answered Nature, merciful and stern,
> "I teach by killing; let the others learn."

Quoted in CPG, *In This Our World* (Boston: Small, Maynard, & Company, 1898), p. 4.

she wanted us to come to Stone Lea at once to stay week or so. She sent me $25—so I could not have lack of cash as a plea; we went two weeks ago Saturday taking Elise to care for the baby. Our stay was one long delight. Charlotte enjoyed it very much as there was tennis & much amusement. Mrs. Cresson gave Charlotte $35 for her gymnasium fees, much to C.'s delight. We stayed two weeks and have nothing to regret.

But I am the most impecunious devil imaginable, for I owe nearly a thousand dollars and see no way to pay it. . . .

27TH AUGUST, 1886

I have painted on Mr. Purinton's portrait, the "Knight & Girl," & the "Eve's giving fruit to Eros," quite steadily and I think effectively.*

16TH SEPT. 1886 P.M.

Well, once more a breathing spell for this. It rains dismally. I have almost got my pictures ready to send to Pittsfield where my show opens on the 23rd in the Berkshire Athaneum[?]. Rev. W. W. Newton has been very kind in helping me there and in securing the Athaneum[?] free of charge to me. I did not think that I could accomplish it, but I have gotten together 25 of my better things, perhaps some among them are my best, for instance Dr. Knight's portrait, the "Ascension" and the "Offering to Eros." Have had 250 cards of admission combined with a catalogue printed & shall send them out probably tomorrow. . . . Of course it is not a large display, but I do really think it will be of some interest to the people as they do not often see such things & probably not more than one or two of them have ever seen any of my work. Personally, I do not believe they will sell *one* picture—not one. I feel it in my bones. Often people are more or less sanguine. Dr. Newton hopes to sell the Ascension to his guild, or rather to St. Stephen's Guild connected with his church. He is trying to sell it in shares for $500. May he succeed!

The purchase of the same picture has also been broached through Mrs. Cresson & Mr. Rudderow to the Misses Drexel of Philadelphia for the new

---

* *Eve's Giving Fruit to Eros*, later called *An Offering to Eros* (mahogany panel, 15½ × 27 inches), signed September 6, 1886: "3 naked figures: not a piece of drapery to be seen. Eros at the left accepting an apple from the centre figure—a female, while the female figure at the right with her back towards the spectator plucks another from the tree. Distance, the sea & a head land. The pale moon is rising under the wings of Eros. It is my most finished work I think, thus far. The tone is ivory." "Opera" Book, p. 59. It was sold to Mrs. Cresson in May 1887.

chapel they are erecting to the memory of their parents. It would indeed be strange if I worked the picture off so soon. . . .

. . . Charlotte has been painting & drawing lovely things on note paper for patterns Mrs. Cresson found her. Thereby she has gotten more orders and is working in a most cheerful and lively manner. . . . She is very very greatly better and seems fine almost. Yes, quite better than her old self, for she is more mature & gentle. I never saw her look better. . . .

Charlotte & I took a most charming row up the Seekonk River to Pawtuxet at the full moon. It was extremely lovely & mysterious. . . . She rowed home; over four miles in a little less than 50 minutes: which is capital. She was not tired.*. . .

Mother & father pretty well. I've been very well indeed. I am healthy beyond anything I've been before. I begin to take life more quietly and reasonable. My lute strings are not so tightly pulled! . . .

Mr. Smythe was in today & admired my "Blindman's Buff" extremely. He said that the N. Y. artists talked very savagely and somewhat contemptuously of Bannister, Whitaker, & Stetson, especially Stetson. Ha ha! give 'em time. They'll come, heaven help me! yet with open arms. It only is necessary to make a Metropolitan success. If I am recognized in London— well! I rather think they won't sneer so often. We shall see.

Have had pleasant chats with Miss Chapin.† Have been to delightful Sakonnet to work on Dr. Gardner's house. Art Workers Guild decorated 3 rooms.‡ I made a pine tree frieze and modelled a mermaid. I also suggested the frieze for the dining room but Mr. Burleigh carried the suggestion into reality. He modelled the Genie in the hall & made the hall frieze.

---

*In Charlotte Gilman's later fiction, there are a number of heroines who not only enjoy rowing but enjoy doing so far faster and more effectively than men

†Mary Louise Chapin, one of the first Providence artists to live in the Fleur de Lys building, is mentioned repeatedly in these last sections of the diary. An active PAC member and portrait painter, she did a well-respected portrait of Governor Samuel Arnold, now belonging to the Providence Historial Society.

‡About this time, Stetson, Sydney Burleigh, and John G. Aldrich joined together to form the Art Workers Guild. In part because of the favorable publicity on the Fleur de Lys building, they got work commissions for furniture, for home decorations, for a decorative frieze around the gallery of the new Providence Art Club House. As Charles Eldredge puts it, "Their collaborative efforts coincide with a general revival of decorative design in the last quarter of the nineteenth century, exemplified by the New York Society of Decorative Art (founded in 1877), Louis Comfort Tiffany's Company of Associated Artists (1879), and the Rookwood Pottery in Cincinnati (1880). Recently, historians have credited the Providence group as among the movement's pioneers in the establishment of the English guild concept in America." Eldredge, *Charles Walter Stetson*, p. 42.

. . .

24TH SEPT. 2 P.M.

. . . Father not well—worried about rent. Landlord's agent says he must move unless he pays all by the 1st Oct. . . . I don't think I could even borrow, for I have borrowed of almost everyone that cares for me enough to loan. It is humiliating, but not shameful, for God knows I have worked faithfully and hard and have not the slightest disposition to live upon others.

28TH SEPT. 1886. 4:15 P.M.

. . . Father has been asked to leave the house decorously because he is behind with rent and others want the tenement. Therefore he is going to move by the 10th Oct. Nobody to blame. I'm very sorry I cannot help him. But, with the exception of 5.00 which Mr. Purinton paid me today on portrait account, and which must be paid to servant, I am penniless! I never was so poor for my debts are accumulating alarmingly. This afternoon have started a solemnly toned picture of amorous centaurs by a pool. It is promising. Have worked on the laughing fool too. Mr. Purinton was in. He is growing to like his portrait more. I fancy it is not quite so "spruce" and pretty as he would like it. But I know that it is a good likeness and decently painted. . . .

Am full of thoughts of "Aphrodite." Tewksbury thinks a picture 6 × 8 or 7 × 9 feet will not be too large. Great God! What a chance! And if I have any power and knowledge of beauty I should surely make a noble and lovely picture of it. God help me! It means a large expenditure for models, & I can't make it yet, so the picture must wait. I am surprised to find that I have more of a reputation as a painter than I had thought. It is not so comforting as it might be under some circumstances. . . .

. . .

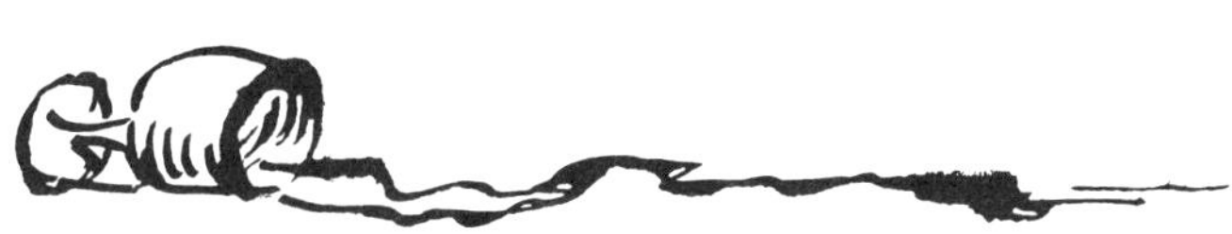

30TH SEPT. 1886. 1:30 P.M.

. . . Wonderfully beautiful sky this morning. Charlotte lovely also. Room very chilly. . . . I lighted my fireplace fire, soon had a big blaze and a warm room. Read while toasting my toes, in Ruskin's Modern Painters and with [Boccaccio's] the Decameron awaiting by my side.* Miss Chapin called soon to warm her toes. Talked of pictures and & Mr. Burleigh. . . .

2D OCT. 1886. 9:30 A.M.

. . . Letter from Rev. Dr. Newton in morning. Said exhibition attracted much attention, etc. He sent me papers with very "appreciative" notices. One that I value most by J[ames] H[enry] Moser, a southern fellow artist. I'm sure it was generous enough. The proper thing seems to be to compare my work to Watts! I'm sure it is pleasant. It is a comparison as far as possible from odious. Champney praised them highly.† Mr. Newton says that he said the coloring was equal to that of Watts and "This man is wonderful now; wait until he works out to his yet undeveloped self and the result will be genius." That's kind. But ah God! *is* it so? And all praise falls flat with notes due, grocer in want of money and early winter staring me in the face. But I will not be ungrateful. It is much to have one's reputation spreading and if it goes hand in hand with the name of Watts I can think of no other name of this day that I should prefer.‡. . .

5TH OCT. 1886 A.M.

Sunday afternoon a telegram came announcing the death of Julia—Charlotte's sister-in-law. It is sad, very sad, and most unexpected. Her poor husband! Heaven help him. . . .

· · ·

27TH OCT. 1886.

Week ago last Friday a message from the Hazards at Penns Dale to come down at once & stay overnight. Also one from Mrs. Cresson to come & stay till the next Wednesday. We went. Left Kate with Mrs. Perkins and Elise. Good time. . . .

New Journal soon I hope. *Vale.*

---

*On another occasion Stetson wrote, "Charlotte and I read Ruskin [*Modern Painters*] till bedtime: she finding a good deal of fault with his carping but in the end being conquered by his magnificent diction and nobleness of idea—all all must, it seems to me." Diaries, Nov. 26, 1886.

† Presumably James Wells Champney (1843–1903), American painter and illustrator.

‡ After this entry on Watts, Grace Channing wrote, "He changed *that* opinion, at least!" GEC to EBK, May 6, 1912, p. 34.

CHAPTER XV

. . . *spasms of horror*

November 18, 1886 – July 20, 1887

FOR THE NEXT SEVERAL MONTHS (November 1886–April 1887), Charlotte seemed happier. She was writing for *The Woman's Journal*, working at the gymnasium, reading widely, and selling watercolor greeting cards from time to time. She "is very lovely and loving," Walter wrote. "All the money she makes, the dear soul, she pays domestic bills with. She likes to do it." "She *is* so lovely, so tender, so true & strong" that even her "little eccentricities are very dear to me because they are hers."

There were, of course, some "little eccentricities" he found annoying: her tendency to "preach" about reform issues, or about "suffrage and other wrongs." Walter hardly could have known that Charlotte was starting to articulate theories that would later attract national and international attention. For the moment, he only knew they piqued his pride: "Charlotte of late has been so absorbed in the woman question . . . that she has tired me dreadfully with it." Her "schemes & theories for the betterment of the entire human race" may be "very noble & to an extent proper but to my rather Greek mind," they seem "a wee bit unhealthy, feverish."

For a time, Walter still seemed relatively hopeful, as though eccentricities and irritations were still relatively mild. But in April 1887, he wrote: "after making herself and me miserable for four or more years, [Charlotte] has found her real strength, which is weakness. My patience is about exhausted from sheer nervous strain. Not in any sense blaming her. But when one has had all his loving impulses checked, all his patience called carelessness, his home made next thing to hell a great part of the time, patience truly becomes a difficult virtue."

Thanks to the financial help and well-intentioned prodding of some friends and relatives, Walter and Charlotte decided to consult Philadelphia "nerve specialist" Dr. S. Weir Mitchell, who concluded that her case was "very serious" indeed. In fact she was doubtless "insane at times," he explained to Walter, and "cannot live at home—that is the long and short of it." Charlotte's solution was to ask for a divorce. "[She wants me to] take to myself some other who can make me happy—as if I could."

Characteristically, Walter used his journal to sort through his emotions. Her "spasms of horror" were "so terrible, so hard to minister to! . . . Some of her moods are so senseless that it calls for the very greatest forbearance. Sometimes it looks as if the actor side of her made her play a part, saturating her real nature with unnatural misery. And yet I dare not doubt that to her all the pains & heartache are terribly real. . . . Good God! how long must this last. I must *become* indifferent or lose all heart and hope. Nearly three years is a long time to bear to one of my temperament and God knows I have borne patiently and I *think* tenderly."

Meanwhile, scattered among descriptions of domestic crises are his professional reflections and reports. He had started doing portraits, and quite successfully. He received a commission from the State House to paint the Ex-Governor Henry Lippitt. He did portraits of Mayor Arthur Thomas Doyle, of Judge George Moulton Carpenter, of lawyer John C. Pegram, and also of several of his friends: Dr. Edward Knight, Courtland Dorrance, Mrs. Edward Allen. He wasn't very fond of doing portraits, or of thinking that his "mission" was to paint "uninteresting citizens in their Sunday coats." But with his capacity for seeing "fundamental" character, for viewing human beings "ideally," he was convinced he did them well. Still he kept hoping for some "larger" challenge. He wanted to paint his "patient and pathetic" mother, for instance, or the "weather beaten, life-worn face" of his "uncomplaining father." But far more important, he wanted to paint his dreams: the "lovely lines" and "palpitating pure flesh" of "my Aphrodite," the "very goddess of love." *

> The Journal that preceded this
> numbered 768 foolscap pages, and
> the last entry in it was 27th
> Oct. 1886.
>
> I changed to this note size be-
> cause the other was too inconvenient
> to handle.
>
> *Charles Walt. Stetson*

18th Nov. 1886
At the Fleur-de-Lys
On Thomas Street
Providence, R.I.

---

* The above quotations are from diary entries of the following dates: Nov. 18, Dec. 6, 1886; Feb. 9, Feb. 11, April 28, May 7, April 30, July 18, July 19, 1887; Dec. 22, Nov. 20, 1886.

[Second Journal]

18TH NOV. 1886. 4:06 P.M.

A new Journal! I like the look of it well. I had grown tired of the clumsy volume just closed, with its mechanical blue lines and commercial binding. It served its purpose, though, and saved many a reckless word and act by receiving the confessions of my heart.

If this does as well I can only be thankful. I am tired of wondering *why* I want to write my day's doings. I am conscious how pitiful a showing of self it makes, since the things that one records are by no means the best that one feels, and the best that one is, but something more earthy—the poor happenings of a really uneventful life. Montaigne would certainly laugh at so incomplete a revelation of one's intimate life, but, if I do not destroy these before I die, my child will have them, and I need not tell her the state of my bowels and whether or not I like the Truth. Possibly she can gather all those things from my words. If so, well. On the other hand, because this may be read by her I shall not conceal from day to day my real thoughts, on whatever subject I write but express them as clearly as may be. She will be wise enough to understand sometime.

Since I wrote I have been hard at work. Mr. Burleigh and I have made a frieze on Mr. Cornell's house and modelled four amorini, besides coloring and . . . doing a great deal of running about regarding the decorating of Mr. Comstock's house.*

Our new method of mural decorating seems capable of important development. I cannot truthfully say that after this trial I think it so well adapted for the ordinary rooms of a home as for large halls and the like; though Mr. Comstock's dining room is very beautiful we fancy.

We have other decorative work to think about and to soon do.

Mr. and Mrs. Tewksbury were here last week for two days, and he for not quite an hour a week ago today. . . .

We enjoyed their stay very much indeed. Mr. Tewksbury is 6 ft. 2 in., lank, loose-jointed and a trifle "slouchy" in his bearing. He is rather cross-eyed, has a thinnish black beard, a straight nose and delicate, sensuous mouth. The effect is of a very knowing tender, refined mind and a good heart. He entered our family as if he had known us all his life. When he came to our house first Charlotte entertained him for a while and gave him fruit; so when he went home with me he took to her a large basket of choice fruits

---

* Stetson's decorative work on Mr. Walter Comstock's home, and on the frieze of Mr. Cornell's house, was commissioned by the Art Workers Guild.

and nuts, for he said he *must* do it as he had not forgotten the delicious peaches she gave him from an amberina dish. They enjoyed my pictures and he bought *The Fool* (14 × 17) and a small upright panel of a woman in red with a lyre, and two water colors. Mrs. T. admired a nude figure that I had so much that I gave it her. . . .

Mrs. Tewksbury is tall, rather large, with a ridiculously small waist. She is extremely reticent but I liked her and think we should get fond of each other after a time. She is as eager for my pictures as he is. They have now nearly if not quite thirty. She says he is going to build a small gallery in the house for them.

Well, we got nearer together all of us. The friendship promises much. Charlotte says he is much like me in many small ways—in likes and dislikes. He wants the monthly payments to continue, much to Charlotte's and my pleasure, as it is a great comfort to feel that we have our house rent, no matter what else we have not. . . .

Charlotte has been working nobly painting cards etc. She seems very happy & is very lovely and loving. All the money she makes, the dear soul, she pays domestic bills with. She likes to do it. . . .

. . .

20TH NOV. 4:15 P.M.

. . . I wonder what the Venus I am to try to paint for Mr. Tewksbury will be like. Ah God! if I could but paint her as my dreams picture her. But what a dreary chilling material lies between my dream and the representation of it! How shall these poor hands trace the lovely lines and model the palpitating pure flesh aright! Well, if I cannot make her gloriously beautiful and the very goddess of love I will yet make her pure. Ah my Venus Milo! what grand thighs, and mighty chest for the casket of a great heart, and what breasts for the pillow and nourishment of all true lovers! And such a chin and eyes, and lips, fit for noblest kisses! Can *I* paint such a one! . . .

MONDAY 22D NOV. 1886 A.M.

Yesterday was a full day. In the morning Charlotte and I went walking. She thought I did not want to go but I did. She thought me rather cross. But I wasn't. I can scarcely tell why it is that the moment she feels as she did yesterday I involuntarily become taciturn and interior. I felt a few pangs in my digestion tract, but long before we reached Hunt's Mill I was quite myself again and she was frisking girlishly. We found some witch hazel blossoms, which neither of us had ever seen before: And we found some cranberry vines. Both were pleasant finds as we were out hunting for things to put on the Thanksgiving cards for the Hazards. . . .

23D NOV. 1886. II. A.M.

. . . All my Sonnets came back from the "English Illustrated Mag." this morning. They've been gone a long time. It makes me smile to see my poems come back with such persistency. I wonder if really they are good for nothing.

24TH NOV. . . . 4:05 P.M.

. . . Judge [George Moulton] Carpenter called. He was brisk & jovial. A keen, eccentric man, upon whose expression one should not build as it is readily changed with the mood or freaks of his digestive apparatus. He wanted me to paint the late Mayor Doyle for the Masons, & I agreed to paint a 20 × 24 in. canvas for $200–.* I am going at it at once and have ordered the canvas of [Eugene] Smyth. He said that he would have various photographs sent to me from which, with his written estimate of his character, I could make a resumé for my purpose.

While he was here Mr. Closson came.† I like him. He is mild pleasant, moderate, and evidently truthful and earnest. He said very charming things of my work, said that he saw my Boston show very hurriedly, but he saw enough to give him "a lift," as he expressed it, very much as [George] Fuller's pictures lifted him.‡ He looked at them all carefully, appreciatively. He thought my "Revery after the 'Purgatorio'" best suited to his purpose,

---

*Judge George Moulton Carpenter, an enthusiastic patron and collector, was later (1892–1893) President of the Providence Art Club.

The portrait of *Thos. Arthur Doyle, Mayor of Providence* (20 × 24 inches, canvas), signed December 1886. "This, with Mrs. Allen's portrait—& Dr. Knight's marks a turning point in my reputation here. People can understand a portrait—they feel that I have caught the character & they can admire the life-likeness. No one has condemned even in a modified way any of the 3 mentioned." "Opera" Book, p. 67.

†Stetson had heard from Art Club members that William B. Clossen, painter and wood engraver from Boston, was intrested in etching some Stetson paintings.

‡Stetson was pleased that his work was favorably compared to that of colorist and portrait painter George Fuller (1822–1884), but occasionally he found the parallel disturbing: "It is the hobby of modern critics to find an imitation of some master in a lesser man's works; as if two pictures may not be the same in motive without imitation." "Opera" Book, p. 17.

and the "Fountain"* next; not that he *liked* those pictures better than the "Centaur" etc. but that they seemed more suitable to his present need. He wanted me to have the "Revery" photographed at once. . . .

He said he would see that I lost nothing by any trouble I might take; that he would etch the "Revery" if he couldn't engrave it. I feel that knowing him is an acquisition. In some indefinable way I feel as if he would benefit me a good deal. He said we were quite old friends now—told Mr. Calder so.†

Now I must go buy some Malaga grapes and oranges to take home, for is not tomorrow Thanksgiving?

Charlotte was away a year ago. Now, thank God, she is here, in my very arms nightly, in my heart daily, well, happy, hopeful, good, true, loving beyond anything she ever was before. Ah how much can happen in one year! How miserable, how deeply unhappy we have been, and how glad and happy, in this twelve months! And the next—the next?—I will not think. But it seems to me it should contain a great deal of good work done, a great advance on every line of development. . . .

· · ·

25TH NOV. 1886. THANKSGIVING DAY A.M.

About 5 o'c. yesterday Dr. Allen . . . called to see Mrs. Allen's portrait.‡ The Dr. expressed himself very strongly in favor of it. He thought it beautiful, and the best portrait I have done. . . . They liked my *Mother and Child* very much also.§ . . .

· · ·

27TH NOV. 1886. 10:25 A.M.

. . . In the evening Doctor Mary Walker and Miss Oldfield called. Dr. Walker in her male attire was very funny, and her talk was bombastic and

---

* *The Fountain* (8 × 10 inches, canvas), signed June 2, 1885. "Girl nude, at the head of a stream. Silhouette against sky. Tone reddish brown." Sold to Dr. E. B. Knight for twenty dollars. "Opera" Book, p. 64.

† Albert L. Calder, active member of the Providence Art Club and for a time its Treasurer.

‡ *Portrait of Mrs. E. S. Allen* (20 × 24 inches, canvas), signed November 1886. "An excellent likeness; more than pleasing to her family. Given to Dr. E. S. Allen as a wedding present—though long delayed. No word but of praise for this." "Opera" Book, p. 65.

§ *A Mother and Child* (panel, 12 × 15 inches), signed February 5, 1887. "Lamp-light effect, from a sketch made from Charlotte & Katharine in '85." Sold to Mrs. G. V. Cresson in 1888; given to Katharine B. Stetson in 1909. "Opera" Book, p. 67. A painting entitled *Mother Nursing Child* (1887) was included in the 1913 Memorial Exhibit.

curious. The whole evening was devoted to dress reform. She surely has some excellent ideas, and there is a strange sweetness in some expression of her eyes; but on the other hand there is a weak look that suggests to me an unsound mind. She looked ridiculously puny beside Miss Oldfield, who has a fine presence, and seems to be a powerful woman. Had she lived in Mediaeval times she would have been a power in the land. It was altogether a unique evening. Elise, the good merry soul, did not dare to go through the dining room lest she laugh and offend the worthy Dr. After they had gone we sat by the fire awhile, ate Malagas and oranges and rehearsed some of the more farcical episodes of the non-sexual Doctor's visit.* . . .

. . .

FRIDAY, 3D DEC. 1886. 2 P.M.

Last evening, which was very cold, I put on my great beaver trimmed coat & went to Miss Sarah Doyle to see the photographs of the late Mayor. . . . They had prepared the table with a profusion of photographs. I found but one that would seem to help me. That I bore away in my capacious pocket. From there I went to the meeting of the A. Ex. at [Hugo] Breul's studio. Studio was picturesque and inviting, & I was warmly welcomed. Fell to some molasses candy that was at hand & examined his newly painted portrait of S. Brownell.† It was fair, but by no means extraordinary or commanding. He had also a certain sort of *genre* picture: One girl thrummed the guitar & another gazed dreamily out the window into a garden full of sunlight. The values were nicely rendered and the color was agreeable. . . .

The fellows came after awhile and they fell to the music which was the programme of the evening. But in due season the beer, pretzels and cheese were opened and we were duly inspired. They sang college songs, the older members going with a zest born of memories and the genial beer. Even Dr. Bogman,‡ the stiff and beefy marched the studio a bottle of beer in either hand singing "When I was a student at Cadiz" etc. And the guitar accom-

---

* Dr. Mary Walker—feminist lecturer, dress reformer, and Civil War medical worker—frequently antagonized contemporaries with her "masculine garb": "not only trousers but masculine jacket, shirt, stiff wing collar, bow tie, and top hat." Edward T. James, Janet Wilson James, and Paul S. Boyer, eds., *Notable American Women* (Cambridge: Harvard University Press, 1971), vol. 3, p. 533.

The Stetsons' contact with Dr. Walker may have resulted from Charlotte's recent article, "Why Women Do Not Reform Their Dress?" *Woman's Journal* 17 (Oct. 23, 1886), p. 338.

† S. Brownell, unidentified.

‡ Dr. Bogman, unidentified.

paniment and the bell chorus was admirably rendered by all with glasses and [illegible]. After awhile I proposed a game of ten pins with bottles and apples. It was begun but brought to a summary close by Mr. Hamilton, the too new and exuberant, who threw a bottle instead of an apple, shattering several. Although the evening could scarcely be called a devotion to higher aesthetics it was very pleasing, and I'm sure the freedom from restraint & the elasticity of recreation will bear fruit. I'm sure I feel better for it. There was very little beer drunken.

I got to bed a few minutes after twelve. It was a very cold night, but my love & my baby and I slept warm. . . .

. . .

MON. 6TH DEC. 1886. 10:20 A.M.

It snowed tremendously yesterday, but my Love, my baby and I were very comfortable at home, playing, reading, writing, drawing, talking! . . .

5:15 P.M.

Went to Comstocks. Dined at Caroline's. . . . Now I'm going home. Ah God, how good it is to have a home to go to, and so sweet a Love, so lovely a child! Charlotte certainly shines more dearly daily. She *is* so lovely, so tender, so true & strong. Her little eccentricities are very dear to me because they are hers. God keep her and help me to be worthy. . . .

. . .

9TH DEC. THUS. 1886

. . . I began the portrait [of Mayor Thomas Doyle] about 3 P. M. & worked with various interruptions until 6 o'c. from 4 o'c. by gas light. I think I have made a capital start. I have a likeness & a forcible character. I have modeled the face pretty well,—unusually well for the first painting. I believe I shall get a strong portrait of it. . . .

. . .

22D DEC. 1886. WED. . . . 4:40 P.M.

. . . Judge Carpenter called. He was still perfectly satisfied with Mr. Doyle. While he was here Mr. Bannister came—a rarity. Pleasant chat. I showed Bannister the things I've been doing lately. He does not seem in sympathy with my more fanciful & ideal work—that is with my compositions generally. But he expressed himself very strongly and favorably regarding my portraits. He said "You struck the right thing *this* time!" As if I'd been groping about and had turned out at last not a painter of dreams but of the realities of my contemporaries. I confess to a curious sort of a pang—an aching forecast; a sad questioning as to whether after all I can ever paint my dreams. In my heart of hearts I believe that I can. No one thinks higher of portrait painting than I. I know it is the means of expressing great things; that a great man can paint greatly even the smug tradespeople and speculators. Indeed I'd much rather be a *great* portrait painter than a tenth rate painter of other sorts. But I feel that with the gift of portraiture goes the power to express strongly character: And to one with my fertile invention and the power to portray character I can see no great obstacle to painter of a larger sort. In other & better words: whatever qualities as a portrait painter I may have are due to my study of other things—especially to the way in which I have considered human beings ideally. I believe that whatever merit the few portraits I have already painted may have it is due to the fact that I have sought persistently for the fundamental, the type. Well, may Almighty God do with me which is best. If it be true that my mission is to paint our rather uninteresting citizens in their Sunday coats—so be it: I will do it with my might. Truly there are maidens and matrons that one could make poems of. May they fall to my lot. And I have not yet painted my fascinating & lovely wife and child—that beautiful child whose equal we know not of in these parts—to speak without extravagance. I have not painted the patient and pathetic face of my mother nor the weather beaten, life-worn face of my uncomplaining father. Surely into such faces & forms one could put heart ache and long-suffering and love. I have not painted them! May God spare till I have.

Surely I shall be glad to paint many portraits. I like to do it. It is educational in a capital sense, if not remunerative also.

I don't feel very strong this afternoon. This evening Sydney & I are coming here to decorate some plates for Comstock's dining room. . . .

· · ·

II A.M. 27TH DEC. 1886.
Well, Christmas is past, in safety, with a certain amount of pleasure, a good deal of fun for our little folk, and some weariness for some of us elder ones. Ah, to feel as young as some seem to do!

All the family met at our house Xmas night, except Guss & Susie &

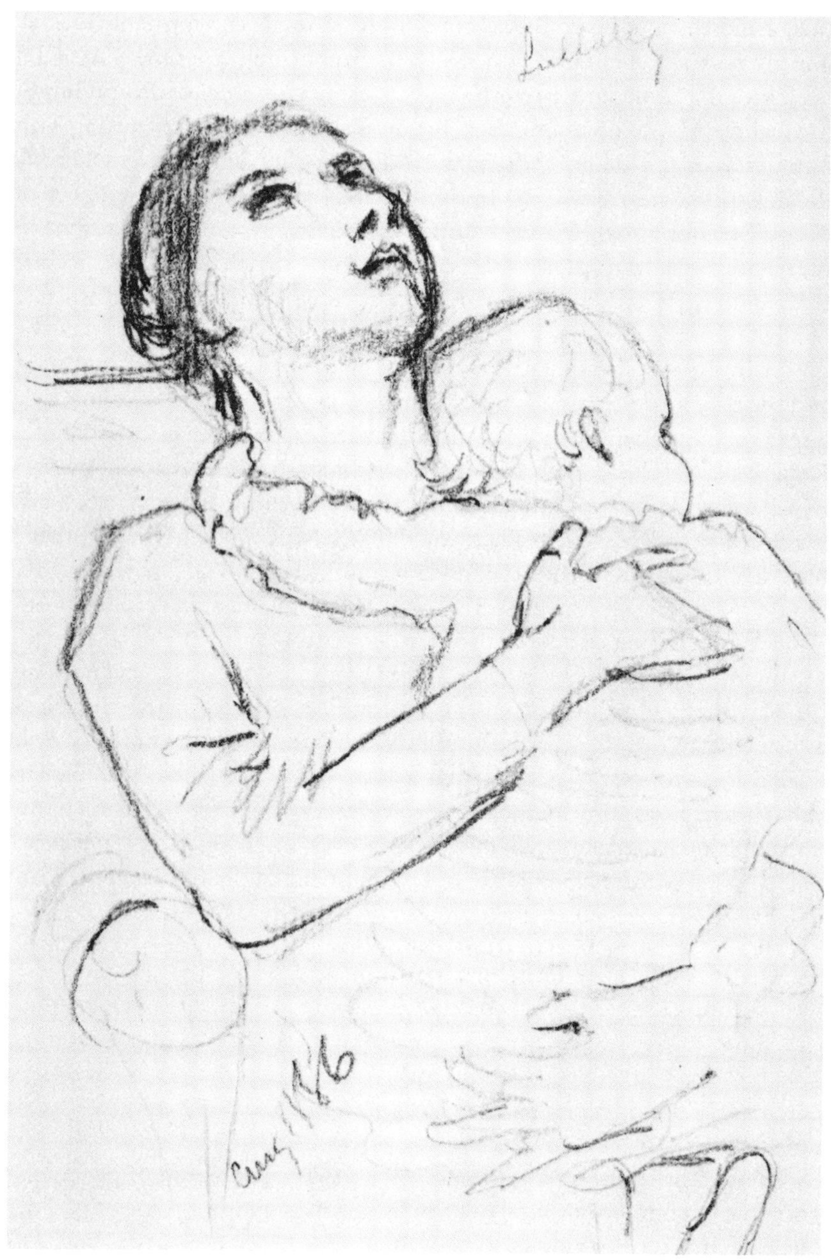

Lullaby. From Sketchbooks.

their children, who were sick.* There were about twenty of us. Charlotte had pre(pared) a fine supper for us. As good a supper of the size as I ever ate. We had a pleasant time, not too merry, God knows, but cheerful enough. Mother was not very well, that was the only draw back to our mirth—or *my* mirth, I do not know if anyone else thought of it.

The tree was beautifully gaudy & delighted the youngsters if no one else. Our sweet Kate was heavenly & had lots of quiet fun, and such a host of presents! We got to bed in good season, Charlotte feeling that her first attempt at having a party had been a complete success. I am inclined to a list of all the presents but I do not feel in the mood, somehow. In fact I'm rather tired & feel a reaction from the Doyle portrait, which though it was painted in about three sittings took some vitality. . . .

They say there was a good notice of the Doyle portrait in the Journal yesterday. . . .

. . .

4TH JAN. 1887. . . . 7:10 P.M.

I am waiting for the Misses Doyle to come & see their brother's portrait. The studio is very picturesque with lights properly arranged.

I dined with mother & father. On my return here I looked over some of my old drawings from the model and felt the pangs of impatience, for heaven knows how I long to be at work on something more imaginative than post mortem portraits. Before going to mother's I called on Bannister a few minutes. He seemed as regards art more serious than he has been for a few months, more as he used to be when I first knew him. He showed me some of his work. A deal of it showed hurry and commerce more than the higher qualities one learns to hope for, but he is so thoroughly the artist in instinct that even pot boilers have a tinge that is unmistakable. There was one of them that was thoroughly earnest & good. He also showed me two scriptural pieces that he has sketched on the canvas: one, Christ inviting humanity—I should call it, just drawn on the canvas in charcoal, a dignified promise surely, the other, Jesus & the daughter of Jairius himself & wife. The latter is in color & promises much. About 3:30 Dr. Knight came. He is always soothing. And he said some very comforting & encouraging things about the Doyle portrait. . . .

---

* Guss and Susie Stetson were Walter's brother and sister-in-law.

THURSDAY A.M. 6TH JAN. 1887.

Last evening brought a comparatively small bunch of people to see the [Doyle] portrait. Most of those came from the Art Club meeting which was held for the first time in the new Club House. I stopped there a few minutes before coming here. The comments on the portrait were very favorable. I got home about half past 10. Charlotte glad to see me. Dreamed all night, curious dreams some of the[m] very lonely and lonesome too. . . .

7TH JAN. ''87. 11 A.M.

Here again last evening [at the portrait exhibition]. Only about a dozen people came & few of those were such as I most cared to have see my work. I'm afraid that the love of Mr. Doyle is not so lively as was thought. The idea that some had of my having several thousand people to see it was based upon a fictitious assumption of our importance in their eyes. But the picture evidently pleased all who have seen it. . . .

8TH JAN. 2 P.M.

Worked yesterday afternoon on a small nude figure—back view. . . . Last evening was the final exhibition of the Doyle portrait. A fair sized crowd. Father & Guss among them. . . . But at no time has the number of persons reached that which was anticipated because of Mr. Doyle's prominence and character, which shows clearly I think how little Americans care for the memory of their eminent men. I believe that to most of us Washington has little significance and no sacredness. But woe, I say, is to come to any nation that forgets her great men. . . .

. . .

14TH JAN. 1887 A.M.

But little has happened since I wrote, except that I have begun a picture conceived two years ago, Eve & Cain. . . .

Letters from Tewksbury. He has bought "At the Terminus."* My, but

---

The Terminus (10 × 14¾ inches, cherry panel), signed September 6, 1886. "In foreground a stream which comes from an arched fountain head. Two trees something like stone pines. A woman leans against the left hand one. Also a terminus, before which lie two girls, one naked, on her back piping. The other in brilliant red. On the hillside, crowned with trees & a Temple, are a bevy of bright colored girls. Distance, purple mt. Sky blue & white. Tone, bright gold (copal medium). Sold to G. E. Tewksbury in 1887." "Opera" Book, p. 61.

he'll have a collection of Stetson's if he keeps on at this rate—heaven knows I hope he may. . . .

19TH JAN. 1887 2:30 P.M.

. . . Charlotte & I have just finished "Tale of Two Cities." I had never read it before. It is a noble book, & I think a poem too. I am impressed that Dickens was fully as much a poet as a novelist; his method seems to me to be that of a poet. To my mind this is as strong and in every way as satisfactory a story, as he wrote. We purpose reading now Carlyle's "French Revolution."

Charlotte seems very well & happy. She recommenced exercise at the gymnasium, & is pleased as a child about it. May the good God grant that her health & spirits may last—for our child's sake and for my sake as well as her own. Her happiness is very much indeed to me. I feel that I could bear almost any privation or pain if she were always happy; & I feel that I can do very much better work. . . .

. . .

SAT. 22D JAN. 1887. 1:30 P.M.

. . . Last night dined at Mr. Pegram's.* It was the finest dinner I ever took part in. Ten courses I think, with eight or nine kinds of drink. Misters Bates, Burleigh, Apollonj, Howard Hoffire, Geo. Whitaker, & Nickerson were there. Left about quarter of eleven. The plain truth is I ate just a mouthful too much & I did not get comfortably to sleep till something like 3 this morning. . . .

. . .

FRIDAY 11:30 A.M. 28TH JAN. 1887

. . . [Stopped on the way home from the Art Club] to make an appointment with Miss [Imogene] Smith for Monday afternoon.† [He is to paint her portrait.] She was just going out to a dance & was arrayed in yellow silk with lace net over it & really looked charming, though I couldn't help thinking that she was put out so on sale, as it were. For I fancy that

---

* Earlier Stetson wrote, "I dine Friday evening at [John C.] Pegram's. I don't want to. I'm afraid it is to be a formal affair and I hate them. Still I shall go." Diaries, Jan. 19, 1887. Several persons not previously mentioned include: Harvend Hoffire, architect; Edward Nickerson, Treasurer of PAC; and Aldolf Enrico Apollonj, sculptor and Art Club member. Later Apollonj did a bronze bust of James Sullivan Lincoln, the first PAC President.

† *"Portrait of Miss Imogene Smith* playing a guitar: seated before a yellow centaur on a rose colored cushion. . . . Began it the 1st of Feb. '87." "Opera" Book, pp. 69–71.

Mama & Papa are anxious to have her married. Insane supposition on my part, but one can suppose, I suppose. They greet me there with a good deal of warmth. Miss Imogene especially seems to think well of me. I have to say *funny* things to them, I don't know why, and they think me witty! Ye Gods!

But I do hope my wit will help me make a fine portrait of her for selfish as well as artistic reasons. She has a beautiful face & a nice neck but her arms I shall have to flatter a bit. . . .

. . .

2D FEB. ''87 . . . WED.

. . . If I can but paint Miss Smith just as she is I would ask no more— for the present. Her color is superb—lovely. I have posed her very simply facing the spectator & with shoulders nearly square too. She has just struck a cord [on the guitar], & is listening to it. I felt that so simple & uncoquet- tish a pose was more in keeping with her frankness than one more graceful in line perhaps. Still, of course, I intend to make it as beautiful as I possibly can. . . .

4TH FEB. FRI. 1887

. . . I took some color & palette & went to the Art Club where we made silhouettes of the Artists & committee of the Club for a frieze in the manager's room. Since I left them they added details that were funny: but Burleigh put under mine—they would have me in my fur cap—"Florentine of the 14th Cent." Not far from right that, I fancy. . . .

5TH FEB. 1887 A.M.

. . . After it grew too dark I thrummed on the guitar. I longed God knows how much, to make music, but only succeeded in skattering from the mystery a few chords and an air. That, even that paltry achievement did me much good. No one would guess how I hunger and thirst after music; how I have longed to be able to make it and have not been able to do so. I fear it is too late to educate my fingers & my ear, yet if I had money for lessons I would brave ridicule and fortune and all for the sake of the joy the right playing of one sweet melody would give me. It is sad to have one's life as devoid of music as mine is—no music in the house, no song, no money to buy the feast of concerts & operas with. My voice is cracked, I cannot sing even to myself for the vocal chords will not respond to the inward melody. I know that if in my youth I had been trained to it I could have made a singer and a musician, a player on some sympathetic instrument like the violin cello or harp. But alas, I lacked training of all sorts. I grew like a wayside weed. Perhaps my little Kate will be for music and I thus shall have it in my later years—if the late years are to be mine. I hope she may, God knows; not alone for the selfish joy of music but because music is so heavenly, and so divine a consolation in joy or sorrow.

Charlotte went to the gymnasium last evening and came back happy. . . .

7TH FEB. ''87—11:25 A.M.

. . . Read [Frances] Wright's "Womankind" yesterday.

8TH FEB. 87. A.M.

For some unexplained reason Miss Smith did not come yesterday. It upset my whole afternoon although towards night I began a 14 × 17 landscape which promises considerable. Mr. Hazeltine called a few minutes. Stopped at the Art Club on my way home. Charlotte was just going to gymnasium. I spent the evening till her return looking at Rembrandt's etchings. After she came we had a cup of chocolate & went to bed. This morning she feels rather unhappy. Secretly I think the gymnasium a little too much for her with what else she has to do. Was greeted here after coming through the rain—nasty day—by a stunning letter from the gas company & a letter from Mrs. Kilvert crying that I neglect her shamefully that I should write, heaven alone knows how often, and that I am very mean because I do not come to call on her. I record it after a long combat with the idea that women *are* very very "curious" creatures. I used to contend that they were just as reasonable, no more whimsical than men: but I must now believe that they are. . . .

WED. 9TH FEB. 87 A.M.

. . . Last evening I felt so dismal, & I saw so clearly that Charlotte felt dismal too & ready to discuss ad infinitum the woman question that I basely proposed, rainy as it was, to go to call on her mother. It was a proposition so novel that it seemed to startle her. She deemed it a duty at last, & we went. The evening was not unpleasant. . . . Home about 10. Charlotte of late has been so absorbed in the woman question—suffrage, other wrongs, that she has tired me dreadfully with it. I have tried to conceal from her how tiresome it is because she means so very well. But it *is* tiresome—nevertheless, especially when I go home from an unsatisfactory day's work haunted by unpaid bills and trouble. But she is a dear sweet loving girl! *

10TH FEB. 87—2 P.M.

. . . Charlotte not very cheerful, but she read all the evening, too steadily *I* think, for she had a heavy feeling in her head before going to bed. . . .

I feel great embarrassment on the streets now for I expect to meet at every step some creditor. It is hard to bear oneself calmly under such circumstances for I know that they think that I might pay if I would. Possibly they do not think as gravely of it as I do. Debt is intolerably heavy.

11TH FEB. 1887. 11 A.M.

. . . Charlotte went to call on the Hinckleys & had a decent time apparently.† She went to talk about "Reform" with them. I had heard so much "Reform" that, being fretty & worried, I spoke rather harshly to her. Surely it does get tiresome though I try to interest myself in her schemes & theories for the betterment of the entire human race. It is very noble & to an

---

*In later years Stetson was more sympathetic on the women's issue. He had learned not only from Charlotte but from Grace Channing as well, an active suffragist in her own right. In the midst of her letters to Dr. Knight describing and commenting on her late husband's diaries, she offered a detailed account of her reactions to the 1912 New York suffrage demonstration:

On Saturday we are going to offer up ourselves a living sacrifice,—and let us hope an acceptable one—in the cause of Suffrage. We march with the parade, from East 9th to 57th St., Carnegie Hall, where I am also asked to adorn the platform. . . .
. . . We expect to show up several thousand strong, and with flying banners and white costumes ought to make a very "moving" picture. . . . I have enjoyed a long immunity—living in Europe, but it wouldn't be possible for my parents' child to keep out of the Suffrage line here. I was born in it—so to speak. (GEC to EBK, April 30, 1912, pp. 20–21.)

Some days later she added:

The parade was really superb; it was a great pleasure to march up Fifth Avenue, so wide and magnificent, with rank upon rank of spectators the entire way. Not one inch of vacant space, and again and again the police had hard work to keep the avenue open for the lines. The estimates range all the way from 8000 to 20,000. . . . Roofs, windows, steps, sidewalks—and much of the street was solid humanity. . . . It was a surprise to everyone, I think—in its magnitude and dignity. . . . Charlotte was just ahead of me among the writers. . . . [She] looked remarkably beautiful—in white. (GEC to EBK, May 5, 1912, pp. 22–23.)
†Hinckleys, unidentified.

extent proper but to my rather Greek mind it seems a wee bit unhealthy, feverish. . . .

. . .

WED. 16TH FEB. 1887 4:30 P.M.

. . . This is the toughest phase financially I have been in yet as things are coming together so. I have written a note to Whitaker to ask him if he will lend me $15.00 and some notes to others to see if they will not buy pictures they have spoken of. The gas *must not* be turned off, for we have no oil lamps whatever & could buy none now; but how to get the money!— Ah God!

17TH FEB. 2:30 P.M. (1887) THURSDAY

Well, strange things happen. Yesterday afternoon after I had written Judge Carpenter came in. He talked about Eve [and Cain] very agreeably and at length lighted a cigar. Then he said that . . . he wanted to make me a loan of $50.00 and wanted me to say nothing about it, give him no receipt or anything of the sort; not worry myself about the payment of it a bit; and if he should die suddenly I must consider the loan paid. I was very much surprised & could only thank him heartily. This morning he sent the money over. It can be imagined that I was greatly relieved for I could go & pay my gas bill, pay Elise & some other things. . . .

. . .

TUES. 22D FEB. 1887 A.M.

Sunday Mr. & Mrs. Smyth dined at our house. Mrs. Smyth is a very sick woman. Mr. S. didn't seem to realize it. He talked rather dogmatically about color and art in general, but his ideas in the main seem to me good.*. . .

. . .

WED. 2D MARCH 1887 A.M.

Monday afternoon Miss Smith came. She had so bad a cold, her eyes troubled her so that it was useless for her to sit, so I made a fire in the fire-

---

*Charlotte wrote in her diary at about this time that she had a "good talk" with Mrs. Smyth, who was "another victim" with a "sickly child" and an ignorant husband who was "using his 'marital rights' at her vital expense." CPS, Diary, Feb. 20, 1887, AESL.

place; she stretched out on the rocker, and we talked. I found her very interesting and possessed of an ambition for self-improvement. She seems tender and affectionate. In short, I am fond of her—I like to have her here very much. . . . I sometimes think, indeed I still think that the unmarried who still love and yearn for a mate, have a keener invention, a loftier imagination than the wedded.

. . . I do not yet feel sufficient afflatus to warrant further work on Eve & Cain. Had some talk with Miss Chapin who is blue & cast down. She surely would be happier with some man to deeply love her. I feel that to be the truth strongly. Indeed she almost says it often. She has so tender & gentle a way & a so repressed and haunting look that there surely must have been some love-cross in her life. She cannot have lived without lovers she is so winning. Tuesday morning Sydney & I with Scott A. Smith went to the Church of the Epiphany which, of charity, we are to decorate as far as superintendance can accomplish it. . . .

28TH APRIL 1887 A.M.

How long it is since I wrote! And now I can only summarize. I have worked on Miss Smith's portrait every day, Sundays excepted, and today call it all done but glazing the left hand. Her family have not yet seen it. I feel certain it will not satisfy them, and I doubt largely if they buy it. . . .

Well, . . . I hope . . . to get her [mother's] permission to show it as a picture in the coming Art Club show. I consider it one of my most successful pictures. It is a problem in color solved satisfactorily I believe.

I have also painted my friend Burleigh. It is a characteristic and strong likeness, very simply—perhaps too simply—painted.*

I have put off as long as I can writing of Charlotte. She grew weaker. She was frightened; fancied her brain was sadly diseased; went to Dr. Knight who gave her medicine that helped her, and advised her to go into the country for a while.

Privately he told me that she was simply hypochrondriacal, and to his mind better than she was a year ago. About the same time Mrs. Diman had her on her mind, as she expressed it, and pressed Charlotte to take a gift of $100.00 which she could spare and go away with it. She rather wanted her

---

* *Portrait of S. R. Burleigh, Artist* (33 × 40 inches, canvas). "A strong and characteristic likeness." "Opera" Book, p. 73.

to see Weir Mitchell.* So Charlotte wrote to Mrs. Cresson, & Weir Mitchell was heard from. Charlotte left for Philadelphia Monday night to consult him and stay a week with Mrs. Cresson. I have not heard from her since. And so we see the result of a mistake as to one's strength and the truth of life!

Charlotte, dear girl, strove for self culture, and carried it mentally, physically for five years or more to a perilous extreme. But the end came with Katharine. At last, after making herself and me miserable for four or more years, she has found her real strength, which is weakness. My patience is about exhausted from sheer nervous strain. Not in any sense blaming her. But when one has had all his loving impulses checked, all his patience called carelessness, his home made next thing to hell a great part of the time, patience truly becomes a difficult virtue.

So we are broken up a second time. This time the baby and Elise are with Mrs. Perkins. I get my own breakfast and supper and make my own bed and pass much of the time in solitude. My art and my heart have suffered for it. And yet no one is to be blamed unless it be the grandparents of Charlotte. To be frank, I find myself too often sorry that I married; and too often my heart yearns for the fulfillment of the love it hoped for. But one must be true to one's wife even if she does not care for him and loves him little and wants him not at all. Whether one should use up one's life that way is a question I have not settled. I only know that my mind and heart are very rebellious for a few minutes at times. I love her. Ah God, if I had not loved her would I have stood it all for these years? Scarcely. I have said very few impatient words to her—very few. I have done all that I knew how to do. And how long is she to be away this time? I know not; I dare not think. It is a terrible trial to the bodily "virtue" of one of my temperament to be so bereft of wife and close love, and amid warm living beings who could love me I think. May I be able to bear it! It is not good for me. My mind is feverish and my body without peace. But who cares!

And I am without money. Debts pile up. Pictures do not sell. But outside the soft rain is falling, the meadows and lawns are green and gay with crocuses, tulips and daffodils. What is it all to me! Only a reminder of the spring when love was for me and I did not dream of what I am. I am tired, so very tired, and want help: but who will give it?

---

*Dr. S. Weir Mitchell, a nineteenth-century "nerve specialist," also treated Charlotte Stetson's great aunt, Catherine Beecher.

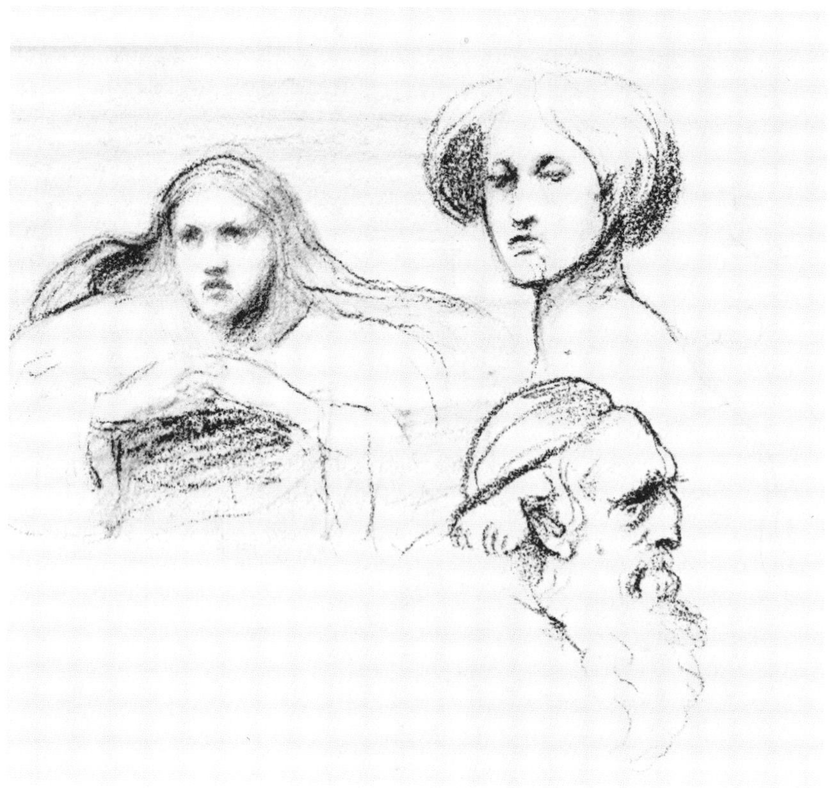

Drawing of unidentified faces. From Sketchbooks.

[29]TH APRIL ''87 A.M.

. . . I felt so lonely and dreary late yesterday afternoon that I went to the Club; found Dorrance there. I suggested that we come down in the evening and sit by the fire. He agreed and said he'd bring cider if I'd bring something to eat. I got my rubbers went to see the loveliest of little girls, my own sweet Kate, then to the Club. Mr. Grimshaw, by good luck, was there too, so we three sat about the fireplace and talked till about 11 o'c. Dorrance could not get cider so he brought a quart or so of lager. It was a very much better way than sitting about a solitary house would have been. Slept soundly but with vivid amorous dreams that made the world seem drearier on waking.

30TH APRIL ''87 11:30 A.M.

At last a letter from my wife. The tidings are very sad for me—very sad. Dr. Mitchell seems to think her case very serious, and says that separation from home for at least a year is very desirable. He also wants her to go to his sanitarium for a month. I think she will go. He says that she cannot live at home—that is the long and short of it, has a most unfortunate temperament with a graft of hysterical disorder of the mind. Her letter is very touching. She prays me to divorce her and take to myself some other who can make me happy—as if I could: as if I could ever be happy now knowing the great and terrible cloud that has come upon us. I feel perhaps worst for our dear child. Somehow it comes upon me like a benumbing wave. I do not feel the fierce pang I should have done once. The truth is it is but one more pain to all those that I have borne. God alone knows how many they have been. It is not her fault. It is not my fault. It is an instance of the terrific working out of the destiny of lives and the laws of heredity. And it has come. God help us!

I am heart sick. I dare not think how heartsick. And my body is only dragged about. I have no spirit. I am the abode from whence has gone a soul. Will it ever come back? Oh will it—will it? . . .

7TH MAY, 1887 2:10 P.M.

Letters from my Love. She seems hopeful but can neither read nor write. The nurse is her amanuensis, she says, and Mrs. Cresson, from whom a letter yesterday, says that she is very pleasantly placed. She can read but two letters a week and those must be of the most cheerful kind. Mrs. Cresson's letter made my heart cold—a kind of deathly chilliness in it, for she did not seem so hopeful as did Charlotte. She called it a doubtful experiment, and said that Dr. Mitchell said that Charlotte was doubtless really insane at times, and that he never had had but one other such case, and that of a lady with the same blood in her veins. I judge from her hints that he thinks her the victim of a kind of periodic insanity, and that it will always trouble her more or less. God knows that is exactly what I have most feared. But something unwritten but felt in Mrs. Cresson's letter took all strength away. I was faint and dizzy and numb. I lay back on the lounge and gazed at nothing. It seemed to me my own brain would give way. Miss Smith came at half past two to make a call however: that forced me from my condition for a while. I left here somewhat early, and called to see the dear baby. She is growing hearty and fat. My apprehensive mind however looked ahead and I could but shudder at the thought of the same trait, the same unfortunate temperament being reproduced in her combined with my own sensitiveness. Ah how I must watch her! How all excitants must be kept from her! I could not keep the tears back as I took her in my arms and felt that I must be mother as well as father to her. Then after a frolic which *she* at least enjoyed I crept away to my dark cold house, unwelcomed, with my own supper to get and to eat in the dismal place where everything told of my darling. Oh she was so loving so pure and good! When I went in and nothing but the chill greeted me I—cried and sobbed and fell upon the floor with the bursting of a long pent up grief. I prayed and begged God to cure her and to make her feel his power *then*. It seemed to me that I should myself go mad, for my brain whizzed and throbbed and I could not for some time control myself. But at last by thinking that I must be brave and endure for Katharine's sake I managed to overcome my passionate grief and got some hot chocolate & bread and milk. *It was a very teary meal.* Then I went upstairs to make the bed—our bed. It all came back. I fell upon it and like a great child, as I am God knows, I cried as if my heart would break. I think it did almost. I'm sure it would have done so if the baby's crib had not recalled me and I swore to be strong for her sake. I presented a sorry face I think when I went to the Art Club, but I masked it and tried to let no one know my grief. I even smiled and made a poor jest or two. Oh our hearts were not made for grief alone. The sight of bodies moving about recalls us from our interim anguish to a great extent. The evening did me good—that is it helped me bridge a deadly abyss of grief. I tried to sell some pictures for the other painters, and sold two of my own by not trying. They had coffee and sandwiches and at the end of the evening some of the young ladies and men danced. I purposely stayed here until I was very tired, dragged myself home and got to bed before the pang came on again.

But oh how empty is house and room and bed without her! But I feel that she is cared for there and happier than she would be with me. May God cure her!

Miss Smith's portrait is a complete success. The whole family enjoy it and praise it and want it. It is now in the Art Club Show. If I could bring myself to do it I would preserve some amusing things that happened in connection with it. I think they will buy it.

Miss Smith comes in rather often to see me. I think she is fond of me: not desperately of course, but evidently I am not disagreeable to her. She is very restful. . . .

*　　*　　*

10TH MAY 1887. 2 P.M.

No letter from my Darling. Ah it is dreary very dreary without her. I do not get used to the empty house, the empty bed, the empty clothing in the closets. I wonder how long it takes to get accustomed to such emptiness. Very very long I fear.

Why does she not dictate another letter? Is she worse? Don't she care? What a multitude of reasons flock to my mind. . . .

11TH MAY ''87 2 P.M.

A letter from Dr. Mitchell this morning. He says it is much too soon for him to offer any valuable judgment as to Charlotte and that the case is one of "profound interest" to him. And to me—!

In desperation—as I could not work—I went to the Club yesterday afternoon. I helped Miss Pegram with her sketches in sketch class. Mrs. Mackinney was in the gallery.* She wants me to paint a portrait picture of her daughter, as she is greatly pleased with Miss Smith's. . . .

I am reading [Ernest] Chesneau's "English School of Painting" [1885]. It interests me rather.

SAT. 15TH MAY 1887 10 A.M.

. . . Yesterday after a growling interview—growling on the part of Mr. Lippitt—I received the commission to paint his portrait for the State House.† It will be 40 × 48 in size. If I have time and remember to do so I must record his conversation with his deaf daughter and me. It is a good commission from an uninteresting and impatient subject. . . .

An interview with my lovely Kate last night. Such a dear child. At the Art Club till twelve. I felt quite in the mood of talking and did truly humor the mood. This morning to a sail maker to get a temporary sign made for the Club. Then here.

I had a very cheerful letter from Charlotte, her nurse, Wednesday. She said she felt much better even to the extent of wanting to come home in the

---

*Mrs. Hubert Mackinney was an Art Club member, a close friend of Sydney Burleigh and Edward Bannister, and exhibited at the Providence Art Club.

† *Portrait of Ex. Gov. Henry Lippitt* (40 × 48 inches, canvas), signed July 9, 1887. "Painted for the State House. He holds in his right hand a sketch of a portion of the R. I. headquarters at the Centennial Ex. which he gave to the City of Phil. This is an excellent likeness and a thorough portrait of character. To date probably my best portrait." "Opera" Book, p. 75.

course of time: and she gave a touching account of what Dr. Mitchell said to the effect of my looking like his son and John Keats.

WED. 26TH MAY 1887 A.M.

I have had two letters from Charlotte, neither by her own dear hand. She seems stronger, but the Dr. has given his consent to her starting a gymnasium if she wishes to do so, but he thinks the best thing if we could do it would be to go to England for a year. He thinks the climate would do a great deal for her. Oh if we might! We *must* in some way. I feel strongly that I never shall reach the place that will belong to me if I stay here always. She is coming home on the 1st June. . . . After she gets back we must settle on some plan of living that shall give her whatever freedom she wants. I scarce know what it can be more than she had for she has had a bed to herself, has been free of the cares of the house and for the most part of the baby. Still there is time enough in which to settle that. Perhaps she knows now more clearly what she wants. At any rate she feels hungry for kisses.

I have had three sittings from Mr. Lippitt. The head is practically done and is a good likeness and probably quite as good a piece of work as I have done. He never has sat over ¾ of an hour & that only once. The other time only half an hour. . . .

His daughter had told me he was a very impatient man and that he would dislike to sit, if he would at all. I was in the Art Club the day she brought him in to look at my work there. After she introduced me he said gruffly: "My daughter has dragged me into this—have been thinking ever since I was governor I'd have my portrait painted for the State House.—Do you think you can do it?"

. . . Then he said something about a photograph that he had and that he would send it in. I mildly but firmly told him I did not want it. Where at he was surprised if not shocked! "Well" he said "I'll go up and look at your work." . . .

. . . So we came. "Have you been in the State House recently?" said he. Not very, I replied. "Well, I asked so as to give you some idea about the size of canvas I want. Go to the State House . . . measure the largest portrait there—*that's* the size I want mine." . . .

He is a man of tremendous will power who however seems to indulge himself as he pleases. A man of very great ability without doubt but, whether naturally or not, he seems to me cruel. He told just how he wanted to be painted—sitting by a table, face ¾ view—paper in his hands. Didn't want very dark shadows on the face. The more it looked like him the better he'd like it! Prof. Appleton wanted to give me this advice: "Say yes—yes to everything he says then do as you damn please, and he'll like it." I could write a few more pages about the sittings but I must go to work. . . .

. . .

TUESDAY 21ST JUNE, 1887. A.M.

Nearly a month since I wrote. Since then I went to N. Y. to meet my wife at the boat and to her great surprise. We spent a long delightful night in our state room & came here early the next morning, whence to Stone Lea where we stayed a little over two weeks. It was the very pleasantest time we have had there. Charlotte is indeed very much better; is loving and brave and trying to follow the directions of complete recovery.* I have never seen her so well. Truly the stay in Phil. paid for itself. . . .

THURSDAY 23D JUNE 1887 1:45 P.M.

. . . Dr. Knight called with very great kindness & told me that in talking with Mr. [George] Burnham of the committee for getting a portrait of the mayor he found that they were very favorably disposed towards me, and that Mr. Burnham & confreres were coming in to see me & the [portrait of] Lippitt this afternoon.† . . . The price seems to be the trouble. They do not want to pay over $300—as that's what others of the mayors have been done for. . . .

MONDAY MORNING, 27TH JUNE 1887

I have nearly finished Mr. Lippitt. Have had the last sitting. I confess I am very well pleased with the result. Whether he will be—ah, that's a question. But every one that has seen it & knows him pronounces it a capital likeness. I have more show of having the mayor than I thought. I believe all but one member of the Committee wanted me. The chances are that he will

---

* S. Weir Mitchell's "directions of complete recovery" were: "Live as domestic a life as possible. Have your child with you all the time. . . . Lie down an hour after each meal. Have but two hours' intellectual life a day. And never touch pen, brush or pencil as long as you live." Gilman later commented, "I went home, followed those directions rigidly for months, and came perilously near to losing my mind." CPG, *The Living of Charlotte Perkins Gilman: An Autobiography* (New York: Harper & Row, 1975), p. 96.

† George Burham, unidentified.

be overruled. Saturday morning it seemed almost a certainty that I should have it, but with politicians it takes but little to turn the current of their regard. They had a meeting to decide it Sat. afternoon. As yet I have not heard the result.

Charlotte in her enthusiastic way took it for granted and Sunday she was spending the money for it in anticipation, paying all my debts and having several hundred left.

Sunday passed pleasantly and quietly. . . .

Charlotte seemed a little weak this morning, but I fancy it was because we had nothing for breakfast that she cared for, so she had not eaten.

We read "Dr. Jekyll & Mr. Hyde" Sat. eve. It is a masterly thing of the kind surely. Stevenson appears to me to be a master of style. There is a stimulus and freshness about his stories that are charming.

28TH JUNE, 1887. 2 P.M.

. . . Yesterday was full. Art Workers Guild business & callers, Dr. Knight among others. Charlotte came down in the afternoon looking very sad. She was feeling miserably. We went to the cafe and dined, then took a Camp St. car for a ride: walked around the reservoir, and saw a beautiful sunset. Home in the twilight through Arlington Ave. She felt more cheerful in the evening, went bravely to bed without crying; awoke after a fair sleep and seemed still braver this morning. She is such a dear sweet loving girl! . . .

30TH JUNE, 1887—A.M.

Yesterday was an exceeding disagreeable day as far as the weather went, and of course that had much to do with all the rest. . . .

2 P.M. . . . When I got home Charlotte was in the depths of melancholia again, with talk of pistols & chloroform. But I brought her around so far that she was comparatively cheerful before sleeping. She slept well; felt better this morning. . . .

14TH JULY 1887. 5 P.M.

Well, I got the Mayor after all for $500. He has not been to sit yet. . . .

Charlotte has been alternately cheerful and depressed. I left her this morning in a most doleful condition. Poor dear girl, how I ache for her. I hope to find her better tonight, but I doubt if I do. . . .

[Mary Channing] wants me to make a design for a Walt Whitman calendar which they hope to publish Xmas. Have been rereading "Leaves of Grass."

Whitman suggests a satyr to me—a very knowing one too. . . .

Now I'll go home early & hope to cheer Charlotte a little. Dear girl, she *is* so lovely and, so hard to live with!

*   *   *

18TH JULY. 4 P.M.

. . . Yesterday was the best Sunday I have passed for some time with Charlotte. . . . Charlotte had only two or three spells of morbidity. But I left her this morning in a bad condition. It is so terrible, so hard to minister to! I find it less & less easy to bear yet God knows I try and try persistently. Some of her moods are so senseless that it calls for the very greatest forebearance. Sometimes it looks as if the actor side of her made her play a part, saturating her real nature with unnatural misery. And yet I dare not doubt that to her all her pains & heartache are terribly real. . . .

TUES. 19TH JULY 1887. 10:10 A.M.

No, his Hon. the Mayor did not come yesterday. . . .

When I got home I found that Charlotte had taken Katharine to my mother's to spend the day. She was home in time for dinner, and she had had a hard time of it. I thought I saw that she was going to have a "spasm of horrors" so when the baby slept, despite the rain, I dragged her out and walked with her doing a little love making. She came home in a much better condition. I made her an eggnog, & we got to bed. Slept pretty well. Love this morning & then with a flow of the tide of her distemper she had a good deal to say about insanity. I got a little impatient and took the name of God—not quite in vain I hope. That seemed to have a salutary effect upon her, and I left her, after some talk about her poems, in a seemingly cheerful condition. She does not yet believe that I really am pained by her condition: she thinks me indifferent!

Good God! how long must this last. I must *become* indifferent or lose all heart and hope. Nearly three years is a long time to bear to one of my temperament and God knows I have borne patiently and I *think* tenderly.

The Mayor [Thomas Doyle] right here. He is decidedly pleasant and sensible. I confess there is more to his face than I saw at the City Hall. I almost think I can make an interesting thing of it. He sits tomorrow for the 1st time. . . .

20TH JULY 1887. 2 P.M.

Yesterday afternoon Mr. Pegram came to invite Burleigh & me to dine with him at 6 o'c. He said he was keeping bachelor's hall & we mustn't expect anything but roast duck. It was a very pleasant affair with an accompaniment of champagne, claret, & sherry. I stayed till half past eight. . . .

I plead guilty to having done nothing but read a little this morning, save to get ready for the coming Mayor. He will be here at 3. As usual before [I] commence a new picture I feel trembling in my vision, *real* trembling of a nervous nature, and have pathetic doubts of the success of my attempt. I doubt if I shall get over it. Like a mere beginner I wonder where I shall begin and how [to] get the subject properly on the canvas. . . .

CHAPTER XVI

. . . *to her I say God speed*

August 4, 1887–June 15, 1888

BY AUGUST 1887, Charlotte and Walter had decided temporarily to separate. "Seven years was the term of waiting in patriarchal days," Stetson reflected; "in these more rapid ones should not three be sufficient?" Sadly he explained the situation:

I have loved her, I do love her, God knows. . . . I have made sacrifices for her—not worth mentioning, to be sure—I have been patient with her, and offered her all I have. All I hoped for in return was companionship, a mind to share my thoughts, to interest itself in my work, my success or my failure. I looked for a kind of rest, a deep peace that should come of mutual love and thought. Instead I have had very little but unrest.

Although at first, Walter had assumed that Charlotte's "illness" was the major reason for their marriage problems, she had been so much better lately, he wrote, that "I need hope no longer that health will make her care more for home and my work and such love as I can give her." In fact, she has been "gladder to be away from me than with me," first travelling to California, then vacationing with Grace Channing in Rhode Island in the summer of '88. As long as Charlotte kept her distance, apparently, she could keep her health and happiness as well:

I'm not homesick a bit, don't think of missing you and am getting well so fast. I am astonished at myself. I haven't felt *unhappy* once since I left. The fogs and mists are rolling away; I begin to feel alive and self-respecting. Oh the difference! You are very dear to me my love; but there is no disguising the fact that my health and work lie not with you but away from you.

As Charlotte viewed it, as Walter viewed it, and as most people of the nineteenth century would have naturally assumed, Charlotte was selfishly placing her career ahead of family. But she would also recognize that she was forced to make a tragic choice. As she put it in a later fiction piece, a woman could "have love—and lose life"; or she could "have life—and lose love"; but never could she have them both. That was "the woman's problem," * and indirectly, that was a reason also for the failure of the Stetson marriage. In any case, as Walter confronted Charlotte's traumas, his summary was far too simple: "what I give her is insufficient. . . . All my love to her ambition is as the dried husks of corn to the hungry who craves the fatted calf. No, I do not, perhaps never can, supply what she needs."

Neither Walter nor Charlotte fully realized how much they shared: each yearned for creative work as well as satisfying marriage, each felt cramped by the "housewife" role. (Walter called himself the "house-band"). "Oh how I long to do my work," he wrote. "How hard it is when . . . one's hands are bound by the cords woven of care for others." "[My] craving" for art "gnaws and no dike could withstand forever the gnawing of the smallest of God's creatures: the waters at last must break through and ruin will lie in the path of the flood."

The last sections of the diary show the agonies and disappointments of the marriage break-up, but they also show Stetson's continuing commitment: to portraiture, to decorative work, to painting dreams. "I feel deep strong things working in my life. I feel a fixed certainty that unless an untimely death seize me I shall do some desirable noble work. God speed the day!" †

4TH AUG. "87 10:30 A.M.

Well, Mr. Lippitt seemed well satisfied with his portrait and after a futile attempt to reduce my price, $600–, to $500– paid for it and had it sent to his home for the summer. In the fall it will be shown at the Art Club & go to the State House. The money was quickly spent in paying bills. . . . That is very gratifying. I have done little but paint on the Mayor [Arthur Thomas Doyle]. The head is practically done. It is a good likeness & perhaps considering the difficulty, the most successful thing I've done.

SAT. 6TH (?) AUGUST "87 A.M.

. . . Have been down the River some, bathing etc. with Charlotte & Kate. . . .

---

* Charlotte Perkins Gilman, "Three Women," *Forerunner*, II (May 11), 134.

† With the exception noted, the above quotations are from diary entries (including quotations from Charlotte Perkins' letters) of the following dates: June 15, 1888; Aug. 6, Oct. 3, Aug. 6, Sept. 3, 1887.

Charlotte has been better but she thinks she is so not from any change in her but because she has a new plan for her and my salvation! She thinks she has a scheme by which she can dispose of the much-talked-of-amusingly Hartford property.* With the proceeds, $2000–, she is to take Kate & Elise, her mother and brother Thomas, emigrate to Pasadena & lead a happy life. I meantime am to get money enough to take me to Europe where I am to live nobly and regain lost enthusiasm and paint great things under the influence of the masterpieces. I may keep a mistress there, if she be clean so my generous wife says! I may do whatsoever seemeth to me good. And when we have grown stronger we are to meet again on Pasadena's happy shore and live joyfully ever after.

It is by no means an impossible scheme. Only supply the two requisites—the sale of the Hartford property and money for me and I see nothing to prevent except perhaps the lack of consent on her brother's part. I confess it is, as our relations are at present not an undesirable consummation. A heroic measure is needed. It would not be so hard for me, because one by one the fair ideals I had have been withheld and blown about like dead leaves that rustle a little but signify nothing but that summer is dead. . . . I love her, dearly, truly, always. But I know she is unhappy, that what I give her is insufficient for her, that all my love to her ambition is as the dried husks of corn to the hungry who craves the fatted calf. No, I do not, perhaps never can, supply what she needs. Gladly for her sake I will say her God speed. My heart would ache. She could not take the burden with her. There would be a relief at first I doubt not but I know what a weight and ache of longing I should carry about with me. I fear, and that is worst of all, that I should turn to some other woman not because I should love her as well if at all, but because my soul needs the feminine to complete its work. The full stream that began to flow so strongly was suddenly checked and I feel it working in volcanic ways down below the outer calm. I fear me. But I should try to do right.†

Yesterday came to Charlotte a letter from the Channings. It was kind in

---

* Charlotte had inherited some property in Hartford, and later sold it to the Hazards for $2,000 to help pay for moving expenses to California.

† Although it may not seem so surprising to find such comments in a private diary, Stetson's public statements on the subject do not easily accord with popular notions of Victorian propriety. In a lecture to the A. E. Club he argued:

> The mistake made is in trying to crush out the desire for sexual pleasure. We are so blind about it. Why not be men and grant the truth, that the desire is right and good? Why not insist that instead of being wicked and to be done in the dark it must be made the joyous attendant of manly love, its deeds to be done in the sunshine among such fair sights, sounds

the extreme. Grace knows our affairs, with little knowledge which proverb saith truly is so dangerous. She advised me, and now advises Charlotte, to insist on an immediate separation—not a divorce of a legal final sort, but truly a separation. She invites her with ardor, and pictures glowingly the sweets of it, to come to Pasadena and be their guest: tells her to leave Kate with her mother and me. It was kind very daring to admiration. I thank her. But I am the sufferer chiefly as in all this. It has added fuel to Charlotte's discontent. What chafed before bites the quick now. . . .

And I—I am a sorry wreck. I try to keep strong. I try to be philosophic. I am to an extent. I am calm with my fellows. Restrained in my house. But within is a cruel gnawing that nothing stills; there is a seething of the repressed hopes, desires, loves that is torture. Four years, three years ago my mind was full of pictures which I did not hesitate to try to paint. But now if ideas come as they will at times, I say—How can I? Every cent I get now has to pay bills and must be spent to distract Charlotte from her brooding. I cannot hire models. I cannot buy any of the accessories that I need. I am become in duty bound a mere supporter of a family. It is far from an ignoble calling. Done well it is noble truly. I shall continue to do it as long as need be. But no amount of nobleness satisfies the artist-craving of my nature. It may not be so high a calling as that of house-band but it gnaws and no dike could withstand forever the gnawing of the smallest of God's crea-

---

and odors as may be. It is the height of folly to think to destroy it. It is wisdom to do all in one's power to place it in the light of a gift of God, a solace for many world-pains, the beautifying spirit that attends procreation; an emanation from the will of God, not a foul effusion of the devil.

We are pitifully great children with our cry of Let's make believe we don't like this! Let's talk piously to our neighbor and deny what God has made; otherwise he may think us wicked. Out upon it! Let us be men, and own that we like it, and have faith, notwithstanding all the misery and crime of the world, in the strong, earnest, enduring love of man for woman and woman for man. . . .

Do not misunderstand me, I pray. I lament licentiousness, I do not believe in promiscuous intercourse and false passion: but I do believe that Love is the central truth of the universe; the love of sister and brother, father and mother, and children, the deep passionately immortal love of mistress, wife and God. Such love has been the inspiration of the greatest work the world has known, the profoundest most enduring poems, pictures and sculptures." (CWS, "The Nude in Art," A. E. Club Lectures, Feb. 19, 1886, Club Papers, no. 19, pp. 15–17, RIHS.)

In another lecture Stetson argued that because of the close connection between Art and Love, painters were "more sensitive" than many other men and had greater need for "wine and women and various Bohemian pleasures." "I may not be believed, but it is true: it is a *necessity*. It relieves a tension at once destructive to their work and dangerous to themselves." CWS, "The Price of a Picture," A. E. Club Lectures, June 19, 1890, Club Papers, no. 18, pp. 2–4, RIHS.

tures: the waters at last must break through and ruin will lie in the path of the flood. . . .

SAT. 13TH AUG. 1887 11 A.M.

After some negotiation through Mr. Burleigh rooms were secured for Charlotte, Katharine, and Emma Vaughn and our maid-servant Elise at Sakonnet, and yesterday morning they started by the "Queen City." Charlotte seemed to love me so much and want me with her so much that after a cursory examination of time tables I decided to go as far as Tiverton with them and then take a train home to arrive in time for the Mayor's sitting. But the boat was a quarter of an hour late and I could not return till about six. Kismet? I made a very pleasant virtue of necessity by going to Sakonnet with them. The sail was delightful. Charlotte was very glad indeed to have me with her. . . . Then with a loving parting came back at four o'c. It was a dreamy sort of journey home. The city lay like an amethyst vision in the twilight.

I reached our house about 8 o'c. I was strangely tired and slept soundly. This is a lovely September like morning.

The worst of keeping house as a solitary is doubtless dish-washing and—being alone. . . .

*   *   *

5:40 P.M.   . . . Good sitting [with the Hon. Mayor Doyle]. He pronounces that he *likes* it. He has but just left. He hopes his wife can be persuaded to sit for her portrait: so do I. Dick Aldrich to look at the Mayor so that he could write of it for tomorrow's *Journal*.*. . .

.   .   .

20TH AUG. '87 10:30 A.M.

A letter late yesterday afternoon from Charlotte praying me to spend Sunday with her at Sakonnet. She says she's lonesome and wants to be loved. So I'm going at 3:15 this afternoon. . . .

The Mayor yesterday afternoon finished the left hand. One more sitting, Monday I hope, and he will be finished. It is doubtless a success. I even flatter myself that it is a somewhat remarkable success considering the difficulty and my inexperience.

---

* Richard Aldrich, painter and PAC member, wrote occasionally for the Providence *Journal*, and later became music critic for the New York *Times*.

I have been making some more tentative drawings of my Venus dei Tewksbury.* I think I have settled upon a pose at last. Just emerged from the womb of the sea she will stand about unconscious of her power but with a dawning sense of her loveliness. (That sounds well. Let's see how 'twill *look* which is more to the purpose.) In her hands she will hold her wonderful hair as if almost surprised at it. She will look calmly with rather questioning eyes at the spectator. Above her two amorini with a lovely load of roses to personify the land. In the water will be tritons and nymphs feeling the joyous thrill of new birth and love. In the air at her right the south and west winds to personify the air, showing that Earth, sea, and air lay her tribute, wonder at her, love her. Figure ⅔ life canvas 7 × 8 feet. Pretty scheme! What delight 'twould be to search this town and others for a model for Venus. As it is I must make her a new sort of Minerva sprung from the head of a sort of Jove.

3RD SEPT. 1887. 3:15 P.M.

Judging by the infrequency of the entries here I am getting lazy. Since I wrote I have been to Sakonnet to come home with the people of my tribe. . . .

I have also had no end of exasperation from the Mayor's family and the Committee and of the portrait, what with delays and stupid criticism. . . . I am certain that if they do not like it it is because of ignorance. Indeed I feel especially bold and conceited today and would be quite willing to hang it beside either of the $2500– portraits that Herkomer did here. . . .

I feel deep strong things working in my life. I feel a fixed certainty that unless an untimely death seize me I shall do some desirable noble work. God speed the day!

Charlotte, dear girl, is so much better and so much more a help and inspiration that hope rises again. Hope surely is the bud of the flower of fair deeds.

5TH SEPT. 1887. 3 P.M.

Saturday afternoon was harrowing. The honorable Mayor brought in a goodly number of his friends and they criticised the portrait in an exasperat-

---

* Although Stetson did finally complete his Venus painting—"poor incomplete gal that she is!"—Tewksbury nonetheless discontinued his monthly drafts shortly thereafter. Diaries, Sept. 3, 1888.

ing, childish way. There was little to reply because the remarks *were* so childish. I tried to keep my temper & believe I succeeded tho' I went home with the sensation of having nourished leeches all day. The resume of their judgments was that the portrait was not satisfactory owing to its "seriousness." Ye gods! . . .

TUES. 5:30 P.M. 6TH SEPT. ''87

. . . Dr. Knight called about noon. I was heartily glad to see him. I think I am fonder of him than of almost any other of the men that come here. He looked so very well, browned by the sea air that it did me good to look at him. Besides he praised the portrait handsomely, intelligently. . . .

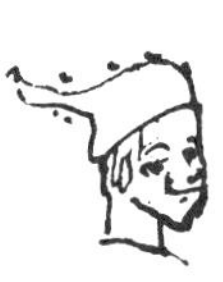 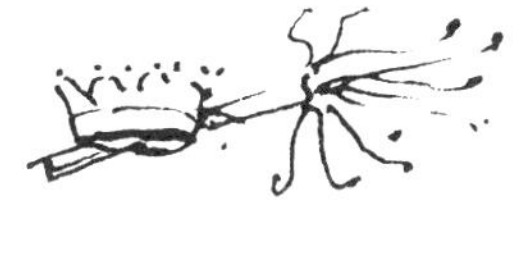

7TH SEPT. 1887. 4:40 P.M.

At last 'tis settled. The portrait is accepted. But what a time I've had with the ignorance and prejudice of the mayor's wife & sisters and the attachés he has brought in. The Committee stood up for me manfully, especially the chairman, Mr. Geo. Burnham. This afternoon they have been here, and am very nearly exhausted. I took 10 grains of quinine for the prevalent distemper by Dr. Allen's advice and my ears buzz and I am sweating hugely.

Now we can go to Nova Scotia—if they send the money in time which I think they will. . . .

10TH SEPT. 1887. 5:15

. . . Charlotte did not feel quite so well this morning. She thinks she is going to have another child. I do not. If so, tho! I had rather it had waited a year or so more, he or she shall be welcomed and cared for. But God save the dear mother! . . .

14TH SEPT. 1887, 2:30 P.M.

I have been sick since I wrote. . . . I got paid for the Mayor Monday, and Monday afternoon Charlotte & I went shopping. It did me good to have her able to buy some better garments for herself. She seems almost happy & quite well. Today she has gone to Hartford to try to sell the "Hartford Property." I fear she will not find it so easy and be disappointed. . . .

Monday we sail for the Provinces. . . . I purpose making sketches, and I hope to be able to make and sell enough (on my return) to pay the expense of the trip. . . .

Charlotte is lovely. I could not ask for her to be more agreeable and loving, and while I was sick she was tenderness itself. Poor girl, she never had before a chance to nurse me. I have just written a few directions and benedictions for those that are left in woe [if] I should die on my journey: I have no notion of dying as long as I can move, but steamships and railways are not too safe.

SAT. 17TH SEPT. 1887

Well, we start Monday for Nova Scotia. May God speed us. I have had a deal of running about to do.

Charlotte came from Hartford Thursday night. She was moderately successful in her quest. . . .

So I shall write no more in this till my return. I purpose keeping an account of our miniature travels for various reasons.

A letter from Grand Pre yesterday said that Sept. & Oct. were usually the best months there.

Well, to you invisible friends and visible pictures, Goodbye!

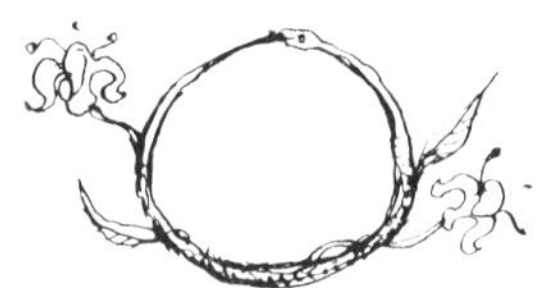

MONDAY 3RD OCT. 1887. P.M.

Home again. In fact we have been home since Thursday last. We only went as far as Eastport. I saw that Charlotte was tired and homesick; that it would be unprofitable and cruel to drag her farther, so I gave up Grand Pre and beyond and we took the State of Maine for Boston Wednesday morning. On the whole I can say that the journey was interesting and profitable. I cannot say that I enjoyed much of it, for Charlotte was uninterested and melancholy most of the way. She shall not be blamed: she was not well. . . .

Things here look very much as they did when I left. Have been working up some of my sketches, attending to some business for Art Workers Guild & Art Club. . . .

Oh how I long to do my work, and how heavy a burden I bear that gnaws so that I cannot do it! How hard it is when one is in the toils to do noble things! When one's hands are bound by the cords woven of care for others, of hesitancy in the face of two opinions. Ah God, what hope is there for him unless you come to his aid? . . .

It is almost time to go home. I yearn to go, yet almost dread to go, for I shall have to struggle with my wife, and with my own impatience—which is much the harder.

Ah God! it is so hard, so very hard to bear! Canst thou not cure her? And if so, wherefore dost thou not?

4TH OCT. 1887. 4:30 P.M.

Charlotte seemed more cheerful this morning. She seems trying to be strong and bear unmurmuringly. Katharine is better. . . .

There can be no doubt that I am suffering some change. I cannot fix my attention closely on my work. I do not seem able to make execution follow immediately on con*ception* as I used. My pictures fairly emerged like the moon from the sea of conception in those old days. Now I think perhaps too seriously of the way and the means. I do not see that my work is much, if any better for my pains. I suppose *I* cannot see. I am too near to it. I think too that portrait painting has a little disturbed me for ideal work. After one has had a reality to translate and refer to, the figment of a dream is a very unsubstantial model. And yet I may come back to it—indeed I *must* come back to it or perish as an artist. . . .

. . .

MONDAY, P.M. 10TH OCT. 1887

. . . This morning I came down rather late. . . . Saw Sydney. He wanted some money so I let him have $15– that I had saved for a model. (So it has always worked!) . . .

13TH OCT. 1887. 11 A.M.

I took the 6:40 train for Peace Dale this morning as I wished to correct the measurements for the Hazard panel. It was a beautiful ride, the whole way sparkling and gleaming with a heavy frost. How wonderful were the dull colors and fresh greens beneath and among the crystalization! . . .

Charlotte felt better and last night electrified my somewhat calloused heart by saying she had decided to go into Society. She began then & there by proposing that we go to the [Robert] Brown's, which we did and had a jolly time. The ladies talked a good deal about champagne, which topic was born of conversations regarding Mrs. Cresson's whist party and champagne frappe which was had then by a friend of the Brown's. One of them said that she would like champagne at that very moment. I amazed them by saying they should have some in a few minutes. So off I went to the studio & got one of the bottles that I have jealously kept here. Robt. Brown came with me charged by Miss Lizzie to get ice and macaroons. We had to go clear to the Cape St. George. Robt. carried the ice home on a wooden plate. It was a very Bacchic looking procession, I with a very evident bottle, he with the ice, and both with a somewhat immoral smile and laugh.

However the champagne unloosed the [illegible] tight corks and there was much medicinal & unhoped for merriment, especially on the part of the old girls of the house.

Charlotte seemed to enjoy it very much. In fact I think she needs more than anything else a little periodical self-forgetful dissipation. We all need it—all but sweet dear Katharine. . . .

. . .

22D OCT. 1887. SAT. A.M.

. . . Mrs. Perkins doleful in the extreme, and will, owing to lack of money, give up her house, store her goods with us and take our front chamber. Mercy knows how sorry I am to have her in the house again because she is so vexing and has so depressing an effect on Charlotte.

Yesterday I worked very closely on what Judge Carpenter calls Lady Macbeth—not a bad title either.* It pleases me to see that I have not lost my old power of coloring, & the effort in that direction has called up a host of pictures new & old that I want, yea long to paint. Well—

Home a trifle late as I stopped to make a sketch of a subject that came to me—a faun making love to a nymph. To the Art Club in the eve. . . .

30TH JAN. 1888 11:30 A.M.

How long you have been laid away, imprisoned in my strong box, my confidential book! It is 3 months since I wrote here. I dare not try to recall what has happened. On the whole things have gone in the family more peacefully and hopefully, and in my work much in the usual way except that

---

* *Lady Macbeth* (20 × 24 inches, canvas), signed November 3, 1887. "Red & white drapery. Gold hair, emerald necklace. Out o' doors. Tone warm & golden. I think the color equal to my best & the textures quite as good as anything I have done." Sold August 21, 1888, to G. E. Tewksbury, Topeka, Kansas, "Opera" Book, p. 77.

I have gained a good deal in technique, I think & perhaps have a better knowledge of what is best in Art. Burleigh and I have been busy with the decoration of Mr. [Lyman] Klapp's house, and do not expect to be through with it before March. I have completed Judge Carpenter's portrait.*. . . Charlotte is still expecting me to sail for Europe in May, but as far as I see now I do not see the slightest prospect of it. The dear girl is still deeply enthusiastic about her Pasadena scheme and Miss Grace Channing & she expect to spend the summer in the country after I sail. I'm afraid she has been laying up for herself a violent disappointment. I do indeed think it an admirable scheme, but it is asking too much of a man that he get ready for a sale of work unpainted & depart for Europe inside of four months. In the first place I have but few pictures, and they are not such as would sell for much. In the next place the Klapp work will take most of my time till the 1st of March. That will leave but two months for me to paint pictures enough in to raise a thousand dollars or more clear of my expenses.†

The Charlotte's Hartford property must be sold before she can go anywhere for I certainly shall not have money enough to work her scheme for her. Yet that dear girl who prides herself on being the pattern of reasonableness has made almost every plan—even that of a house to be immediately builded in Pasadena—and says that it will kill her if they are not carried out. It is, if all my needs were known, asking too much of me, and I cannot hold myself responsible for the result. I shall *try* That is the best I can do.

Her health has been better and she has been tender and loving in a way. . . .

---

* *Portrait of Hon. Geo. M. Carpenter* (33 × 40 inches, canvas), signed February 9, 1888. "Judge seated at table squarely in front, looking over his glasses at spectator, writing with quill interrupted. Wears gown and purple scarf. Brass ink stand. Law books at left. One open. Background, olive gold. Table cloth russet. Rich in tone. Very simply painted, carefully studied. No glazing. Excellent likeness other people say." "Opera" Book, pp. 79–81.

† Later Stetson wrote that Grace and Charlotte were "hot again" about their California plans: "Miss Channing divulged a scheme for having me go to Pasadena & see Charlotte settled & then go on to Europe via Japan! Fancy! Those Channing girls! [Grace and Florence Channing.] They are so dreadfully absentminded as regards funds & means at my disposal. They seek to move me about like a pawn on the chess board! But they can't move me very far. No one would object to going via Japan if he could and was sane, surely." Diaries, July 13, 1888.

5:10 P.M. 30TH JAN. 88.

. . . Sometime ago [Charlotte] instituted a whist club which meets at our house every Tuesday evening, and also the [George] Buffums come to our house one Saturday eve and we go there the next so that between the two I am becoming adept. . . .

These meetings have done a good deal for Charlotte. She finds that she has not lost as much as she had thought and the gentle excitement takes her out of herself very beneficially. Her mother is still with us, and has not yet made herself very obnoxious. She seems to be quite reconciled to me, and even, very funnily, takes my part frequently. . . .

Dr. Knight is still as delightful to me as ever and I feel that I am surrounded by fast friends who like me better all the time. I may flatter myself, it is true. The only trouble outside of Charlotte's sickness has been to overtake my debts—alas, to pay them, I should say. I have done pretty well, earned $2172—last year, & that is doing better than most artists in towns like this and the Klapp work will square up all I believe. . . .

.   .   .

9TH FEB. 1888. 2 P.M.

Yesterday was horribly wet and foggy but about 11 o'c. Tewksbury came. I was glad to see him. He had a bad headache and was out of humor but I treated him as if he were not & we got along finely. We lunched down town and came back to studio. I took him to the Art Club. The building interested him greatly. He did not seem to be in the mood for pictures or anything else in fact. We went to the house early so that he might see Charlotte for he found that he should have to take the 6 o'c. train for Boston—a ridiculously short call. It would take at least a week to get used to him, he is so peculiar. I did not even show him the Aphrodite!* I knew it would be useless in its present state and the humor he was in. He seemed to like best the Judge Carpenter. The most spiritual of us are fascinated by such reality of presentment. I was sorry to have him leave, for I feel that after the novelty wore off we could be a good deal to each other. There is a deep fund of tenderness in his nature that attracted me greatly and there is an element of mystery, a feeling of latency that is seductive. . . .

----

* Stetson's problem with the Aphrodite painting was his lack of models. Miss Jeffrey, the one he had used for the *Sleeping Girl*, was "married now, alas! She had so complete a *feeling* for posture that she was better than any model I had had before or have had since. She was grace itself. I need just such a one for this Venus, who by the way, is progressing. I think I have posed her rightly. I think the pose expresses dawning consciousness; and I think I shall get a correct expression in the face." Diaries, July 19, 1888.

I went in first thing to the Klapp house. They are moving in. Mr. &
Miss Klapp were there. Mr. K in a charming mood & insisted that we send
in our bill for completed work and services at once. He is more than pleased
with everything and is ready to pay anything we may charge. . . . When I
remember that Mr. Lincoln* did not command at most but $300 for a ¾
length even with his 78 years, and that I can at 30 get $600. for a much
smaller canvas I feel that there is hope for my financial future. . . .

17TH FEB. 1888 11:15 A.M.

Mr. [William B.] Closson, the engraver, was in for a half hour and left
but a few minutes ago. Mr. A. L. Calder came with him. He came to show
me the proof of my "Revery after the 'Purgatorio'" which he has etched. It
makes a very beautiful etching and I feel greatly pleased that he cared to do it
and that he has done it so well. He had other things that were capital. He is
altogether a charming man and I am proud to know him and have him like
my work.

Since I wrote I have been very busy with the Lincoln Show, which has
been got together through great tribulation as the people who loaned pictures were very stupid about giving us information. The catalog as far as
accuracy goes is the very worst the Art Club ever issued and I am almost
ashamed to have my name on it. But we really could do no better; we had so
little time and were bothered so.

Sydney and I are hard at work on Mr. Klapp's tapestry.

Charlotte has given several whist parties with great success of late. And
she has a more extensive one planning now; also lots of dressmaking. She is
very inconstant in her affection for me, but I do not doubt that she really
loves me. She has been up too late nights for a week or so, and that combined, if I think correctly, with too much talk with Mr. James Simmons
about "Christian Science" has not been good for her.

Mother-in-law is in excellent humor towards me, and is doubtless growing fond of me. Katharine is quite too good to last and mother and father
are not sick. After I got the first payment from Mr. Klapp & had settled
most of my bills I felt a great wave of hope, but the very next night Charlotte
quite undid it by being very—I can only call it disagreeable—so that it

---

* Distinguished portrait painter James Sullivan Lincoln (1811–1888) was the first President
of the Providence Art Club. Stetson chaired the committee that planned the Lincoln Memorial
Exhibit, February 16–March 2, 1888.

would seem that as soon as there is a ray of hope for me it is to be at once cut off. Still I am not discouraged for long at a time.

23D FEB. 1888. 2:20 P.M.

We have been steadily at work on the tapestry. It is practically all the painting I have done for sometime, but I think we shall be well through it in a week more, and then I purpose painting pictures.

I have had an interview with Mrs. Fairchild—a woman who claims to have been rich once, but whose husband has failed & is now in a comparatively humble position. She wants to be an artist's model. Indeed she claims to have posed a great deal for a woman artist in N. Y. and the way she poses bears out her statement. She has promised to come & take off all her clothes for me this afternoon so that I may see if she has a figure such as I want. I fancy that her legs are too short & heavy. Still he were a clairvoyant who could divine accurately what a woman's dress covers. She made a great deal of talk about it—as to how she *couldn't* pose nude, how she should be so very embarrassed, & the rest; but it showed only too clearly that she was aching to do it—and perhaps more if one should ask it.

Ah God! Shall I never have a model that shall be pure and good & lovely to look upon—a model that is thoroughly honest and yet one that loves art enough to pose well? I hope for it, long for it all the time. I so hate to paint from a woman that is frivolous or bad—not because I am pure myself, but because I know that it against my will affects my pictures. . . .

SAT. 25TH FEB. 1888. 10:15 A.M.

. . . Thurs. Mrs. F[airchild] came to undress for me as promised. She went through a great deal of mock delicacy and coquetry to which I paid no attention but sat down till she was ready to take off her clothes. First she came out in her chemise and stockings and asked if that wouldn't do. To which I replied something to the effect that we were wasting time for she came for the express purpose of taking them all off. But she said, she didn't want to, she should be *so* embarrassed; she *never* had for a "gentleman" and she shouldn't know how to act. I told her I thought she was *acting* very well. Then couldn't she have a piece of *gauze* over her, anything no matter how thin to disguise herself. I got her a very very thin gauze dress I have and she went behind the screen & came out with it half on. It was so thin that even the tiniest wrinkles could be seen through it, and I could but smile rather contemptuously at the peculiar "modesty" that asked for such a covering. The truth is she wanted it to seduce me with. I have no doubt of it she is crafty; she knows that flesh just hidden is much more attractive in a sensual way than the pure sensuousness of flesh perfectly naked. Well in time of course the gauze came off, for a few minutes only. I tried to pose her to see what I could do with her. She certainly has a very supple & well proportioned figure. In some respects better than any I have yet seen—still I think that statement would need qualifying. Her breasts are very fine, and it is almost incredible that she has borne a child.

Well, she lay around for an hour or more and practiced arts of seduction in the most bare-faced way. There can be no doubt that she is unusually amorous and very anxious to have men in her arms. Strange to say she did not get me there, although I confess it looked as if she might make embracing very pleasant. Had I been unmarried I should probably have enjoyed her. Being married and not in the business of whore master I refrained; and she did not even know, I am sure, that her wiles had the smallest effect on me. She probably will not repeat them. . . .

Charlotte has been unusually loving since yesterday morning. Ah it is so sweet & helpful to have her loving. I confess that when she is not so for such long times it almost drives me to seek pleasure and comfort in other women. It is a terrible temptation, for I feel too often that there is quite nothing gained by being the way I am. A man of my temperament at thirty is in the heyday of love, the very time when his strength & wishes incline him to get children and enjoy woman. If he may not in order it is well nigh certain that he will want to out of order. Still, if she were loving and appreciative I could very well content myself with only her affection. . . .

* * *

7TH APRIL, 1888 9:30 A.M.

[Stetson had mentioned earlier that his teeth bothered him, but that he felt "too nervous and weak to go to the dentist" (April 5, 1888).] Said I to myself last night: What a miserable coward you are become! Why don't you go and have your offending tooth out. The trouble will be nothing compared to that which you suffer daily, although the ache is not great. So this morning I got up early, shaved, broke fast, and rushed off to Dr. Church. He did not want to take it out except under the influence of nitrous oxide, as it was an ugly job. So I said, Give us the gas. He gave it. The sensation—the passing from bodily consciousness to bodily unconsciousness is very wonderful, but I am quite positive that I did not lose a real consciousness. . . .

[Four pages of the diary have been removed. The following was probably a continuation of the 7th April entry.] . . . I fancy this very very personal selfish chat would tickle Montaigne, who would probably make a very charming essay upon it called "Why men consider their own teeth of so much greater importance than those of other people." . . .

I am going to Boston Monday with Charlotte & Kate. I expect to stay Monday night at Rev. E[dward] E[verett] Hale's and come home some time Tuesday.

4TH MAY, 1888 3 P.M.

. . . I see that I have not written for a month, that I was about to go with Charlotte to Boston. I did go indeed and to my surprise much enjoyed staying at the Hale's.

The Hales are a queer lot. Only Miss Ellen, Bertie and Mrs. Hale were at home, with my daughter's great grandmother Perkins*—an aristocratic pink and white capped old lady who took at once to sweet Kate, & to whom Kate as quickly made much of. Bertie is the homeliest boy I ever saw—a face as coarse as a wild Irishman's and almost repulsive. I believe he is six feet two in his boots. But so brilliant is he that one utterly forgets his ugliness as soon as he speaks. I do not know but that his ugliness helps his brilliance somewhat. At any rate he is fascinating. Mrs. Hale is very sweet & comfortable looking. I should judge her to be an adept in all the arts of sensuous delight and to have gotten a great deal of pleasure of life. Miss Ellen is one of the most winning women I have met. She wins by her great frankness and simplicity of manner. She is much in earnest, and as an artist has very evident talent.† I stayed the night there and met Dr. Knight the next morning. . . . We went to see [Michael Von] Munkacsy's large theatrical "Christ on Calvary," which certainly showed his great and very enviable technical skill, but lacked utterly any quality that would rouse pity, awe, or worship. . . . From there to Chane's gallery to see [John] La Farge's water color sketches, which were very peculiarly interesting. Then home. It was a great day for the Dr. He said he felt like a school boy out on a lark. He is a most lovable man. Unquestionably I am more fond of him than of any other male person.

---

*Mary Foote Beecher Perkins was sister of Harriet Beecher Stowe and Catherine Beecher.

†Ellen Day Hale's portrait of Charlotte Perkins Gilman was recently purchased by the National Portrait Gallery, Smithsonian.

Katharine, bless her sweet heart, behaved in Boston like a Duchess. There is an aristocratic air about her that I scarcely know the origin of. Alas, she does not get it from me. I'm common enough.

I organized the Art Club Show—which is the best we have had,—finished such pictures as I could:—The "Neobule," "Golden Afternoon," "The Spell" and "Imaginary Landscape with Figures" * and began to make studies from Miss G. for the figure in the picture unnamed which represents a philosopher disturbed by a female figure representing the Joyousness of Life alluring him from his ascetic pursuits.

I could not bring myself to paint from the rather whorish Mrs. F[air-child] so I sent for Miss G. and asked her if she would pose for me in very very thin costume. She said, after a moment's hesitation that she would, *for me*, because she liked me and had heard a good deal of good of me which was very charming I'm sure. So she put on a very thin dress—so thin that she was practically nude. A most delightful form; I never saw such breasts. The truth is they are simply perfect—in shape, in texture, in color. The evident virginity of the nipples, the lovely pink aureole are captivating. And as for legs and thighs one would go very far to find better. To make it short; she is willing to pose for me now in any way—quite nude if I wish. The only condition being that no one shall know, as it would pain her mother, and bring her into disrepute among her associates. But it is very sure that she is a good & modest woman without an atom of affectation in her composition. If I get money enough I purpose drawing & painting all summer from her. It would profit me greatly. . . .

IITH JUNE, 1888, A.M.

Miss [Grace] Channing having come as expected, Charlotte & she & Kate & Elise went to Bristol last Friday to stay until the 1st of Sept. So I am

---

Neobule (18 × 24 inches, canvas), signed March 3, 1888. "A study of pink and green." Sold to Mrs. G. V. Cresson, 1888. "Opera" Book, p. 81. *Golden Afternoon* (12 × 20 inches, canvas), signed March 30, 1888. "Sea water in foreground; brown point of land, cliff facing sea (sea unseen) beyond. . . . Two figures, one in blue, one in red in foreground." "Opera" Book, pp. 81–83. The *Spell* (9½ × 8½ inches, panel), signed April 1888. "Against a blue & white sky on the top of a knoll of greenish brown a young woman in white lying against the knees of a man in red. She holds a mandolin in her right hand. Her left toys with his beard. She is bewitching him: he knows it: looks away and wonders how long he can withstand. Her yellow hair flies in the wind. His beard ruddy brown." "Opera" Book, pp. 83–85. *Imaginary Landscape with Figures* (18 × 24 inches, canvas), signed April 1888; description mostly illegible. "Opera" Book, p. 85.

left practically alone. Mother-in-law will stay with me until the 20th when she goes to Cambridge to stay at Dr. Hedge's for a week or so.

12TH JUNE 1888 A.M.

I can't pretend to tell all that has happened in a month. I have painted, but during June not steadily, for I have been well nigh sick. . . .

My money having given out I had to postpone sittings from Miss G. But fortunately I had nearly completed the woman asleep. I had her yesterday to do something more to the arms, but do not see how I can have her soon again. The truth is I am very hard up. . . .

When I read [William Powell] Frith's biography and see what an easy time he had with money matters it makes me groan. I confess I am envious. He had all his time, apparently to think of subjects and to paint them. Could wait for models & pay for them when he got them, could have costumes & accessories made at will: had the esteem & patronage of the wealthiest most influential people in England and the friendship of the best artists. It is little wonder that he is so successful a painter. I doubt if he is a great poet; in fact I know he is not. I envy his chances. It might be said that I have not made the most of my opportunities. Possibly not. I do not know. I only know that I feel as if I were dragging about a ball and chain; and sometimes it seems as if I could not bear it another day.*. . .

13TH JUNE 1888

. . . Yesterday was not a very profitable day. I got desperate about 3 o'c. and besought Miss Chapin to come and sit for me. I felt that if I did not paint something very real I should perish. I had hardly begun when Judge Carpenter called and Mr. Dorrance soon after. But I went on painting. The sketch is a good deal like her but by no means satisfactory. Having finished with her & seated myself to talk with my callers a moment Mr. Davis called

---

*Stetson also commented at length on Joseph Knight's *Life of Dante Gabriel Rossetti* (1887): "Rossetti is surely the most interesting man that I know: so supremely human and so very mysterious. But when one really understands the advantages of his birth, his ancestors, and his surroundings one cannot wonder that his genius so readily blossomed. When I remember that all my life I have not known as many people who cared for art & poetry as he could summon to his side in an hour I do not so much wonder that I have done so little. . . . I think Mrs. Cresson understands my poetry better than anyone else. I'm not sure but that she understands me better as a whole than does any one else" (July 26, 1888).

bringing with him Mr. Yewell,* the artist of N. Y. I liked Mr. Yewell. He was serious, discriminating & very much a man. We all went to the Art Club for I wanted him to see some of my work there. He seemed to like them; and said that they reminded him of Schiavone's work at Venice.† Yewell lived & studied in Italy for eleven years & is very familiar with the work of the Italians. He spoke very seriously of my work, and, I confess, encouraged me. . . .

Will the time ever come that I can be quite myself and do work that I know I might do? ‡

15TH JUNE 1888. 10:30 A.M.

I have just read a letter from Charlotte. [She is spending the summer with Grace Channing in Bristol, Rhode Island.] It seems to have laid a heavy hand on my heart, half suffocating me, and making a lump in my throat. I have loved her, I do love her, God knows. If either way I love her too well. I have made sacrifices for her—not worth mentioning, to be sure—I have been patient with her, and offered her all I have. All I hoped for in return was companionship, a mind to share my thoughts, to interest itself in my work, my success or my failure. I looked for a kind of rest, a deep peace that should come of mutual love and thought. Instead I have had very little but unrest. Daily the veil has fallen and I can but see myself as naked of such a love as ever I was. She has, it seems, always been gladder to be away from me than with me. God knows I have not urged her to stay, that I have given her any liberty she chose to take. Illness was a large excuse, but she has been so much better of late that I see I need hope no longer that health will make her care more for home and my work and such love as I can give her. The letter of this morning, written in the very presence of our child, but in the presence of friends also, who foster her feelings tenderly, says:

I'm not homesick a bit, don't think of missing you and am getting well so fast. I am astonished at myself. I haven't felt *unhappy* once since I left. The fogs and mists

---

*Portrait painter George Henry Yewell (1830–1923) studied under Thomas Couture in Paris, and later lived and worked in Rome.

†Andrea Schiavone (1522?–1582), Venetian artist and engraver.

‡The last sections of the diary show Stetson's continuing fluctuations about his art work. At times he complained that he was too "unsettled by Charlotte's going & the breaking up of our housekeeping and all the pressing debts." Diaries, Sept. 3, 1888. Yet at other times he was optimistic: "I really feel important things working within me." Diaries, July 16, 1888. It is interesting to note, however, that between April and October 1888, he lists no paintings in his "Opera" Book.

are rolling away; I begin to feel alive and self-respecting. Oh the difference! You are very dear to me my love; but there is no disguising the fact that my health and work lie not with you but away from you.

Oh the miserable fool that I am, to *try* to have her love me enough to want to live with me! For three years I've heard nothing else except now and then in some extraordinarily loving moment she would say "I *may* be—*may* be—I shall find I can live with you after all." That would encourage me, and, poor fool, I would try again. But it is of no use. I may as well give it up. She simply does not love me in the way an earnest man deserves to be loved. Or if she does she does not know it herself and disguises it from both of us.

God knows I have tried—tried—tried. I have done all that I knew how to do—and I might as well give it all up. It is only another of youth's, nay, manhood's ideals broken. What if it does leave an aching heart? It has made such love as I longed for impossible to me. I can never love again; should never trust love again. My standard of right, of morality is lower and more shifty than it was. I can see nothing better today than to leave her: to take a mistress when I am rich enough to supply the creative bodily desire; and give my *love* to man and to art. Pitiful fool! I still *hope* when I have no right to hope. I still hope with faintness at the heart that she may change, and I shall have the "reward" I deserve. Seven years was the term of waiting in patriarchal days: in these more rapid ones should not three be sufficient? It is strange: Whatever uprising of courage regarding art I feel there always comes with it something from her which turns courage to ashes. . . .

AFTERWORD

Except for occasional entries which have been incorporated into foot-notes, the remaining sections of the diary (June 19 through Oct. 8, 1888) have been omitted. Throughout the summer of 1888, Charlotte was vacationing with Grace Channing in Rhode Island. Walter visited them occasionally, and by September, they had decided on a short-term plan. Charlotte would take Kate to Pasadena to stay with the Channings and try to earn a living. Walter meanwhile would stay in Providence to continue painting, pay off debts, and some months later come to California to try again to work things out.

Understandably, Walter was discouraged by the prospect. He found himself "unsettled," for one thing, and "not in painting trim." In June, 1888, he wrote:

Well, I didn't sleep much Friday night. My senses went skylarking so to speak. I never was made to be a "continent" man. I should be healthier, happier and more useful if my creative instincts could have fuller play! I'm young yet. There is a fullness of life in my sexual nature that is now cramped, thwarted and made contemptible. If I lived in the 14th or 15th century I should keep mistresses. As I live in this and have inherited the moral nature, to some extent, of my Puritan forefathers combined with an extreme nervous sensitiveness, and a quick sympathy with the female sex, I am in a state far from blessed. I confess—and I am so blind that I do not feel shame for it—that I think it would be quite right for me, with my temperament and the circumstances of my married life to keep a mistress. Yet I shrink from it because of the respect in which I hold Charlotte, my love of her. But it is certain that I need more of that sort of thing than there is any way of my getting. All I fear is that at some time all the hunger of this side of my nature may break out and that I shall revel in some demoralizing nauseous excess. Let no one judge. There is no love of obscenity, no viciousness in my heart. A right instinct with conscience, gnawed by association but thwarted by environment. Ah if the private lives of many were known, I'm sure judgments of conduct would be less cruel. It has cost me many sleepless nights; it has cost me many inefficient days because of the disquiet and unsatisfied longings. If I had not the will of my dear mother—a will that has borne her through many a terrible place I should have succumbed long ago (June 19, 1888).

Another of Stetson's major worries during these final months of trial separation was of course lack of money: "I have positively one cent of cash and owe something like $700–!" (Sept. 17, 1888); and even more importantly his parents' grief:

I confess that I dread going there [to see his parents] since Charlotte decided to live in Pasadena. Very little had been said until today, but I found that father was what the country folk call "techy" because he was ill. . . . Very naturally we drifted into a conversation about Charlotte & Pasadena. Father rather indignantly exclaimed "What kind of a way is that to live—you here & she at the other side of the continent!" I explained mildly that I could not see but that it was all right if we were agreed about it. Then he asked if she was trying to get "a separation" from me, which of course meant a divorce. I had to smile, but I meekly said that I saw no signs of it & if she did she really need not take so much trouble & go to so much expense to do it. Then he had a good deal more to say which really made my heart ache, among other things he said "Mother & I are growing old you know and—." The stop made my heart leap to my mouth & choke me. None knows better than I how much that pause covered. . . . They have grown old with me in the house and are now leaning on me. They feel that while I am in California they may die—that I shall grow away from them—cease to care for them. I dare not write all the bitterness that I know it will be to them if I go far away for so long. As it is now if I fail to go to the house for a few days their world seems to be about ready to collapse and they imagine me dead or very ill. Oh, God I am afraid!

Would it kill them to have me go? Shall I have courage to leave them? Is it my duty to stay? Or is it my duty to go for Katharine's sake. I feel that I should be better able to care for Kate if I went. I feel that it would be better for Charlotte if I went. But—my mother's eyes call to me; the repressed quaver of her voice when she speaks of it calls me. Have I the courage—or heartlessness to go? God knows; I do not.

My visit this noon was a very very sad one. It would seem that I never can have the chance that others have. But I must endure (August 27, 1888).

Despite all of Walter's fears and disappointments, however, there was one unexpected pleasure in his life: his growing attraction for Grace Channing, the woman who would later be his second wife. To be sure, there are not many diary entries that talk about her, but each has a certain poignancy: "Had a pleasant talk with Miss Grace about various social & economic questions, and Art. She is certainly a most good, liberal minded & extraordinary person" (July 16, 1888). Or again in August: "Miss Channing says that she quite loves me, which means a good deal from her" (Aug. 27, 1888).

In September Charlotte finally sold her Hartford property to Rowland Hazard, so that one month later their plan was finally underway. "She has always had capital luck with the exception of when she married me," Stetson quipped (Oct. 8, 1888). The same day he wrote:

My darling and my dear Kate left for Pasadena this morning at ten o'clock. I am alone. I'm going to sleep at the studio for the first time tonight. I cannot deny that my throat aches with—I do not know what to call it.

INDEX

A. E. (Ann Eliza) Club, xvi, 80n, 191n,
  205n, 212n, 236n, 347n
Aaron Gallery, Providence, 80n
After the Bath, xiv, 299n
Aged Pan, 18n
Agresti, Olive Rossetti, 56n
Aldrich, John, 288, 295, 295n, 313n
Aldrich, Richard, 349, 349n
Allegro, 214, 226n, 227
Allen, Dr. Edward S., 65, 65n, 90, 186, 191,
  191n, 210, 223, 234, 239, 251–252, 322,
  322n, 351
Allen, Mrs. Edward, 318; portrait of, 321n,
  322, 322n
Allston, Washington, 51, 101n
American Art Association, xxiii, 267
Angell, Anne (?), 3, 14, 14n, 27, 41, 45, 67,
  77, 126, 128
Antigna, Jean Pierre, 236n, 269, 286
Antwerp Gallery, 193n
Aphrodite. See *Venus Aphrodite*
Apollonj, Aldolf Enrico, 329
Appian, Adolphe, 254, 254n
Appleton, John Howard, 176, 176n, 234, 341
Approach of a Centaur, 280, 280n, 283, 297,
  322
Arnold, Governor Samuel, 313n
Art Students' League, New York, 66n
Art Workers Guild, xxiv, 288, 295n, 313,
  313n, 319n, 342, 352
Arthur and Elizabeth Schlesinger Library
  on the History of Women in America
  (AESL), xvi
Ascension, 295, 300, 300n, 301, 305, 309, 312
At the Terminus. See *Terminus, The*
Autumnal Sacrifice, 70, 70n

Babcock, William P., 305, 306n
Bannister, Edward, xxiv, xxivn, 7–8, 8n, 11,
  11n, 15–16, 19, 47, 57, 228, 231, 238, 313,
  324–327, 339n
Barbizon painters, xxiv, xxxi–xxxii, 306n
Bartlett, T. H., 300, 300n
Batcheller, Frederick, 7, 141, 141n, 228
Bates, Isaac, xxiii, 7–8, 9n, 17–18, 83, 83n,
  90, 98, 141, 143n, 191, 192, 196, 263, 263n,
  280n, 295, 300, 304, 309, 329
Bathing Nymphs, 299, 299n
Beecher, Catharine, xxv, 335n, 360n
Beggar in a Pleasure Garden, 14–15, 15n, 48,
  48n, 51
Berkshire Athenaeum, 300n, 312
Blackwell, Alice Stone, 311
Blake, Ada, xxvi
Blake, Eli Whitney, xxvi
Blake, William, 191
Blomidon, 214
*Blomidon from Near the Shad Fishery, Grand
  Pre*, 79n, 80n
*Blomidon Seen Across the Great Meadow at
  Grand Pre*, 81, 83, 83n
Böcklin, Arnold, xxxi, 273n
Bogman, Dr., 323, 323n
Boston Art Club, xxiii, 15, 15n, 51, 134, 191n,
  274
Boston Museum of Fine Arts, xxiii, xxiiin,
  196, 230n, 236, 239, 254
Boston Museum School, 10
Bowater, Marian, xiii–xiv, xix
Bowater Art Gallery, xiii–xiv, xix
Boy Reading, 141
Boy with a Balloon, 163, 163n, 164
Bradley, Judge Charles H., 305
Brechs, Mr., 240

Breuil, Hugo, 181, 323
Brook, The, 50
Brooks, Dr. John P., 59
Brown, Robert, 353–354
Brown, Walter Francis, 48, 48n
Brownell, S., 323, 323n
Bucklin, Kate, 146
Buffums, George, 356
Burial of a Suicide, 21n, 140
Burleigh, Sydney, xvii, xxiv, 7, 9, 9n, 112, 133, 196, 230–231, 237–238, 285n, 288, 293, 295, 295n, 307, 313, 313n, 315, 325, 329–330, 334, 339n, 349, 353, 355, 357; portrait of, 334, 334n
Burne-Jones, Edward Coley, 182, 182n
Burnham, George, 341, 341n, 351
Burroughs, Reverend, 86
Burt, Annie T., 194, 194n

Calder, Albert L., 222, 322n, 338, 357
Cape Breton Girl, 101
Carlyle, Thomas, 329
Carpenter, Judge George Moulton, 307n, 318, 321, 321n, 324, 333, 354–356, 362; portrait of, 354–355, 355n, 356, 362
Carpenter, Miss, 232–234, 243
Carpenter, William B., 220, 220n
Carter, Elizabeth, 191, 191n
Catt, Carrie Chapman, xviii
Cazeaux, Pierre, 262
Chamberlin, Dorothy, xvi, xviii, 79n
Chamberlin, Katharine. *See* Stetson, Katharine Beecher
Chamberlin, Walter, xvi, 79n
Champney, James Wells, 315, 315n
Chane Gallery, 360
Channing, Florence, 355n
Channing (GEC), Grace Ellery, xiii, xvi, xxx, xxxii, xxxvii–xxxix, xxxixn, xl–xliii, 8n, 11n, 12n, 18n, 20n, 25n, 39n, 47n, 56n, 79n, 93, 99, 99n, 106, 106n, 119n, 135n, 136n, 188n, 191n, 193n, 196, 196n, 208n, 209n, 213n, 214n, 245, 252n, 263n, 287–288, 297, 300, 305n, 311, 315n, 345, 348, 355, 355n, 361, 363, 365–366
Channing, Mary, 99, 106, 106n, 343
Channing, William Ellery, xxvi, 11n
Channing, William Henry, 11n

Channing family, 347
Chapin, Mary Louise, 313, 313n, 315, 334, 362
Chesneau, Ernest, 339
Chopin, Frédérick, 100
Church, Dr., 359
Clark, Retta, 179, 179n, 271
Clarke, Thomas B., 21n
Closson, William B., 321, 321n, 357
Coggeshall, James H., 186
Coleman, Anna, 191, 191n
Comstock, Walter, 319, 319n, 324, 325
Corcoran Art Gallery, 66n
Corn, Wanda, xxxii
Cornell, Mr., 319, 319n
Corot, Jean Baptiste Camille, xxiii, xxxii, 218, 226, 235, 236n, 250, 252, 260, 271, 289, 299n
Correggio, Antonio Allegri, 226
Courbet, Gustave, 191n, 226n
Couture, Thomas, xxiii, 218, 236n, 252, 260, 274, 306n, 363n
Cresson, George V., xxiii, 18, 18n, 20–21, 24n, 26, 28, 57n, 61, 78–79, 90, 101, 101n, 115, 119, 140, 205–209, 222, 224, 230, 233, 236, 248, 268, 287
Cresson, Mrs. George V., xxiiin, 18, 20–21, 24, 24n, 26–28, 56, 57n, 61, 77–79, 101, 101n, 110, 115, 119–120, 139–140, 159, 168, 172, 188–189, 200, 205–209, 214, 219–220, 222, 224, 226–227, 230, 232, 236, 246, 248, 250–251, 254, 268, 271, 285, 287, 308, 311–312, 312n, 313, 315, 322n, 335, 337, 354, 361n, 362n

Da Vinci, Leonardo, 143n, 237
Dalton, John, 220, 220n
Dancing Girls, 103n. See also *May Dance*
Daubigny, Charles François, xxiii, xxxii, 218, 235, 236n, 252, 260, 271, 274
Davis, Mr., 362
De Kay, Charles, xxxi, 50, 50n, 52, 118, 168, 168n, 169, 175, 187, 188n, 227, 282–283
Decamps, Alexandre Gabriel, xxiii, 236n, 250, 252–253
Dewing, Thomas, xxxi
Dickens, Charles, 283, 329; *Tale of Two Cities*, 329
Diman, J. Lewis, 231n
Diman, May, 231n, 232n

Diman, Mrs. J. Lewis, 231, 232n, 334

Doll & Richards, 98–99, 102, 107, 118, 122–123, 126, 139–140, 170, 173, 176, 176n, 226, 237, 254

Doré, Gustave, 306

Dorrance, Courtland B., 25, 25n, 48, 70, 86, 196, 207, 220–221, 234, 318, 336, 362; portrait of, 25n, 65

Dowden, Edward, 203

Doyle, Mayor Arthur Thomas, 318, 321, 321n, 323, 324, 342–343, 346, 349, 350–351; portrait of, 327–328

Doyle, Sarah, 323, 327

Drexel, Miss, 312

Duner, 226

Early Millet. See Memento Mori

Early Morning after Rain, 169

Eddy, Miss Sarah J., 239, 239n

Eldredge, Charles, xiii, xix, xxxi, xxxiv, xxxviii, 19n, 80n, 101n, 273n, 285n, 299n, 305n, 313n

Eliot, George, 249

Elliott, Maud Howe, 48n

Ely, Dr., 249

Errand to the Sick, 20n, 21

Eve and Cain, 328, 333–334

Eve's Giving Fruit to Eros, 312, 312n

Fading Light, 103, 104n, 107

Fairchild, Mrs., 358, 361

Faneuil Hall, Boston, 254

Feuerbach, Anselm, xxxi

Field, Henry, 7

First Caress, The, 21n, 65

First Kiss, The, 21, 21n

Flagroot Gatherer, 50, 50n

Fleur de Lys studio building, xxiv, 9n, 285n, 288, 295, 295n, 296, 313n, 318

Fog Coming at Sunset, Baddeck, Cape Breton, xiv, 79n, 101, 101n, 226n

Fog Gathering about Red Head at Twilight: Baddeck, C.B., 101n

Fog Gathering at Twilight; Baddeck, Cape Breton, 101n

Fontainebleau, xxiv, xxxii

Fool, The, 320

Fool's Sermon on Death, 239n, 262, 264–265, 274, 281, 281n, 292

Forster, Maud, 142–143

Fountain, The, 322n

French, Daniel Chester, xxiiin

Frith, William Powell, 362

Fromentin, Eugène, 236n, 251–252, 254–255

Fruit and a Maiden, 241, 241n

Fuller, George, xxxi, 321, 321n

Game at Sunset, 297, 297n

Gardener, Dr., 197, 313

Garrard, Mary, xxxiv

Gärtner, Elise, 291, 303, 315, 323, 333, 335, 347, 361

Géricault, Jean André Théodore, 58

Gilman, Houghton, xxxviii, 118n

Girl Plucking Fruit. See Fruit and a Maiden

Girls at Play, 141n, 196, 207, 211, 214, 214n, 226n, 227

Girls, Hills, and the Sea, 231. See also Girls, Trees, and the Sea

Girls Jumping Rope. See Girls at Play

Girls Skipping Rope. See Girls at Play

Girls, Trees, and the Sea, 231n

Gladding, Augusta, 100, 100n, 112

Going to the Shad Nets after Leaving the Cart, 249

Golden Afternoon, 361, 361n

Goodale, David, xiii, xv, xvi, xviii, xli, 18n, 265n

Goodale, Julia, xiv, xvi

Goodard, Mrs., 305

Gosse, Edmund, 89

Greek Girl, 143n, 146, 163, 176, 176n, 181–182, 191, 193, 195, 205, 205n, 217, 225, 269

Gregory, Mr., 220, 284

Grieving Girl. See In Grief

Grimshaw, Mr., 336

Grosvenor, Dr., 305

Hale, Edward Everett, 117, 117n; family of, 117–118, 360

Hale, Ellen Day, 360, 360n

Hale, Emily Baldwin Perkins, 117n

Hamerton, Philip Gilbert, 250

Harland, Marion, 281, 281n

Hartford property, 117, 244, 301, 347, 347n,
  352, 355, 366
Hatfield, Mr., 102, 104, 118, 226
Hazard, Caroline, 53n
Hazard, Mrs. Rowland, 53, 53n, 353
Hazard family, 53, 53n, 54, 243, 315, 321, 347n
Hazard, II, Rowland, 53n, 366
Hazeltine, Charles, 77, 77n, 163–164, 193,
  196, 223, 331
Hedge, Charlotte, 59n
Hedge, Dr., 362
Herkomer, Hubert, 304, 304n, 350
Herrick, Robert, 89
Hinckleys, 332, 332n
Hoffire, Harvend, 329, 329n
Hoffman, E. T. A., 281
Honey moon, 57. See also *Saturnian
  Honeymoon*
Hooker, Isabella Beecher, xxv
Houghton, Lord, 271
Howard, Bronson, 234
Hudson River School, xxxiii
Hunt, Leigh, 284, 284n
Hurd photographers, 272

Imaginary Landscape with Figures, 361, 361n
Impressionists, xxxi, xxxiii, 226n, 231
In Grief, xiv, 281n, 284, 284n
Inness, George, xxiii, xxxi

Jackson family, 192, 210–211, 225, 229, 231
Jarves, James Jackson, 226, 266n, 288, 305,
  305n, 306, 307n
Jeffrey, Annie, 217, 237, 238, 240–244, 250,
  301, 303, 310, 356n
Johnson, Col. A. S., 281, 281n, 283–284
Johnson, Mrs. A. S., 283
Jongkind, Johann Barthold, 236n, 254, 254n
Joyous Place, 266n, 267

Katharine with Pomegranates, xiv
Kaufmann, Jr., Edgar, 285n, 295n
Keats, John, 58, 271–272, 340
Keller, Dr., 194, 211, 262, 279–280, 310
Kilvert, E. M., 265, 266n, 267, 305–306, 331
Kingman, Dr., 186
Klapp, Dr. Lyman, 251, 355, 356–357

Knight (EBK), Dr. Edward Balch, xvi,
  xxxix, xli, 252, 252n, 279, 293, 306–307,
  318, 322n, 327, 332n, 334, 341–342, 351, 356,
  360; portrait of, 305–307, 307n, 312, 321n
Knight, Joseph, 362n
Knight and Girl, 312

La Farge, John, 265n, 360
Lady Macbeth, 354, 354n
Lalanne, Maxime, 254, 254n
Lane, Charles A., xxvii, 49–50
Lane, Martha Luther. *See* Luther, Martha
Leavitt, Edward C., 7, 17, 19
Lincoln, James Sullivan, 329n, 357, 357n
Lindenschmidt, Wilhelm, 181
Linsey, Henry, 247
Lippitt, Governor Henry, 318, 340, 346;
  portrait of, 339, 339n, 341
Luminais, E. V., 236n, 271
Luther, Martha, xiv, xxvi–xxvii, xxviin,
  29n, 49–50, 63, 70–71, 75, 75n, 97–98,
  105–106, 117, 127, 151, 167, 207
Luther, Mrs., 70

Macbeth, William, 77n
McCauley, Lena, xvii, xxxii
MacDougall, Hamilton, 12, 12n, 13, 18, 91,
  93–94, 225, 302, 324
Mackinney, Mrs. Hubert, 339, 339n
Malloch, David, xxix, 75
Manchester, Mr., 236
Manet, Édouard, 226n
Marées, Hans von, xxxi
Marilhat, Prosper, 218, 236, 236n, 239, 245,
  249
Mason, John H., 138, 138n, 170, 173, 176n,
  182, 196, 223, 227, 234, 241, 271n, 274, 289,
  295, 297–298, 300, 309, 321
Massys, Quentin, 193n
Maud, 143n, 146
May Dance, xiv, 101, 103, 103n, 107, 126, 269
May Measure, 101
Medici, Lorenzo de, xxi
Memento Mori, 271, 271n
Menard, René, 267–268
Mendelssohn, Moses, 100
Metropolitan Museum of Fine Art, New
  York, 66n, 273, 306, 313

Millet, Jean François, xxxii, 226, 306n
Milton, John, xxi, 89
Mitchell, Dr. S. Weir, 318, 335, 335n, 337,
　339–341, 341n
Monk with a Candle, 18, 18n, 19–20
Montaigne, Michel Eyquem de, 319, 360
Monticelli, Adolphe, 58, 226
Morning Measure, 280, 280n, 281n, 283–284,
　292
Morris, William, 96, 235, 238
Morse, Miss, 250
Moser, James Henry, 315
Mother and Child, A, 322, 322n
Mother Nursing Child, 322n
Munkácsy, Michael Von, 360
Muntz, Eugene, 240
Museum of Anatomy, Providence, xxx, 202
Music, 47n
Mystic Rite, 103, 104n, 116

National Endowment for the Arts, xix
National Gallery, Washington, D.C., 66n
National Museum of American Art, the
　Smithsonian, xiii–xiv, xix, xxivn, 8n
Neobule, 361, 361n
New York Art Club, 66n
New York Society of Decorative Art,
　313n
Newton, Rev. W. W., 312, 315
Nickerson, Edward, 329, 329n
Noyes, Edward, 255, 255n, 257, 267, 274
Noyes and Blakeslee Art Gallery, 226, 254,
　255n, 257, 265, 266n, 267, 295
Nye, Mrs., 57, 57n

O'Reilly, James Boyle, 260
Offering to Eros. See *Eve's Giving Fruit to
　Eros*
Oldfield, Miss, 322–323
Ott, Joseph K., xiv
Ott, Mr. and Mrs. Joseph K., 101n
Over the Dorrent Meadow, 214

Pagan's Procession, A, 18n
Path of Duty, 306–307, 307n
Pearce, Mr., 47
Pegram, John Combe, 301, 301n, 304, 306,

318, 329, 329n; portrait of, 301, 301n,
　305, 309
Pegram, Miss, 339
Pennsylvania Academy of the Fine Arts,
　xxiii, 104n, 114, 231, 231n, 237, 244
Perkins, Frederick Beecher, xxv, xxvn, xxvi,
　80, 83, 117n, 145
Perkins, Julia, 300, 300n, 304, 306, 310, 315
Perkins, Julia de Wolf, xxvn
Perkins, Mary Foote Beecher, 360, 360n
Perkins, Mary Westcott, 26, 39, 54, 54n, 59,
　66–67, 67n, 68, 80, 83, 88, 94–95, 106–
　107, 110–113, 124, 124n, 125, 127, 133–135,
　137–139, 146, 177, 180, 196, 234, 258, 264,
　264n, 277–279, 297–298, 303, 309, 315,
　335, 347–348, 354, 356–357, 362
Perkins, Thomas Adie, xxvn, 134, 264n, 287,
　297, 300n, 347
Perkins, Thomas Henry, xxvn
Perry, A. J., 17
Phelon, Mr. and Mrs. Ray, 258, 258n
Philadelphia Centennial of 1876, 8n
Philadelphia Society of Artists, xxiii, 244
Place of Sighs, A, 271, 271n
Portrait of Ed. B. Knight, M.D., 307n
Portrait of Ex. Gov. Henry Lippitt, 339n
Portrait of John C. Pegram, Esquire, 301n
Portrait of Miss Imogene Smith, 329n
Portrait of Mrs. E. S. Allen, 322n
Portrait of S. R. Burleigh, Artist, 334n
Prang, Louis, 255, 255n
Procession to a Temple, 297, 297n
Prodigal Son—"And he arose," 18, 19n
Providence Art Club (PAC), xiv, xvi, xxiii–
　xxiv, 7–8, 8n, 13–15, 18, 18n, 20, 24, 25n, 26,
　47, 48n, 64, 66–67, 70n, 80n, 81n, 101n,
　126–127, 140, 176n, 231–232, 234, 240–241,
　244, 252n, 254, 271, 293n, 295n, 300n, 301n,
　304, 304n, 305n, 313n, 321n, 322n, 328–329,
　329n, 330–331, 334, 336, 338–339, 339n, 340,
　346, 349n, 352, 354, 356, 357, 357n, 361, 363
Providence Historical Society, 313n
Purinton, Mr. Frank, 81–82, 82n, 89–90,
　272, 314; portrait of, 312
Putnam, Sidney, 5, 5n, 17n, 25–26, 85,
　90–92, 206, 221–222

Raphael, xxi, 240
Read, Isa, 15

Regnault, Alexandre Georges Henri, 13, 13n, 58
Rembrandt (van Rijn), 226, 273, 331
Remorse, 292–293, 293n, 299, 306
Renoir, Pierre-Auguste, 226n
Revery after the "Purgatorio," 321–322, 357
Rhode Island Historical Society (RIHS), xiii–xiv
Rhode Island School of Design, xxiv, xxvi, 8n, 124n, 191n
Richmond, Sir William Blake, 182, 182n
Richter, 236
Rider, Frederick, 290
Robbins, Caroline, 26, 66–67, 67n, 68, 113, 138, 155, 177, 258
Robinson, Edwin, 230, 230n, 231, 254
Robinson, Frank T., 285n, 307n
Robinson, Thomas Harris, 191, 191n, 249
Rope Skipping Girls. See *Girls at Play*
Rosa, Salvator, 226
Rossetti, Dante Gabriel, xxi, xxiii, 56, 56n, 57, 85, 89, 102, 165, 182, 182n, 209, 228, 272, 273n
Rubens, Peter Paul, 192–193, 193n
Rudderow, Mr., 312
Ruskin, John, xxiii, 314, 315n
Ryder, Albert Pinkham, 51, 168, 168n

Sacrifice, 65
Sacrifice in the Afterglow, 101
Sanford, Nellie, 27n
Sanneman, Dr. and Mrs. Rodney E., xiv, 103n
Sartain, William, 66, 66n
Saturnian Honeymoon, 57n, 65
Schiavone, Andrea, 363, 363n
Schiller, Friedrich von, 210, 212, 212n
Schreiner, Olive, 200n
Scott, Sir Walter, 283
Selinger, John, 48, 192
Selinger, Mrs. John, 195
Servant of Royal Peacocks, 20n
Seurat, George, 299n
Shad Nets, 169
Shadowed Path, 239
Shakespeare, William, xxi, 86, 251; *Othello*, 121–122; *Two Gentlemen of Verona*, 77
Shelley, Percy Bysshe, 86, 89
Simmons, James, 238, 238n, 357

Simmons, Samuel, 238, 238n
Sketch at Baddeck, Cape Breton, 79n
Sketch of a Loafer, 163, 163n, 164
Slave, 20, 20n
Sleeping Girl. See *Greek Girl*
Slicer, Rev. Thomas, 112, 112n, 122
Smith, Imogene, 329–331, 333–334, 337–339; portrait of, 329n, 333–334, 337–339
Smith, Mrs., 159
Smith, Scott A., 17, 17n, 18n, 20, 28, 221, 334
Smith-Rosenberg, Carroll, xxvii
Smyth, Eugene, 304, 313, 321, 333, 333n
Society of American Artists, 66n
Spell, 361, 361n
Spencer Museum of Art, xix
Stetson, Caroline (Lindsey), 107, 206, 232, 272, 295, 309, 324
Stetson, Grace Channing. *See* Channing, Grace Ellery
Stetson, Guss, 325, 327n, 328
Stetson, Joshua, xx, xxn, 7–8, 13, 18, 65, 70, 73, 81, 83n, 86, 90, 100–101, 111, 113–114, 119, 125, 132, 134–138, 140, 163, 177–178, 217, 223, 249, 258, 260, 272, 274, 282–283, 287, 297, 313–314, 318, 327–328, 357, 365–366
Stetson, Katharine Beecher, xvi, xviii, xxx, xxxvii–xxxix, xli, 18n, 257, 261, 264n, 277–284, 293–294, 297–298, 303, 307, 309, 311, 315, 322n, 324, 327, 331, 335, 336–339, 343, 346–349, 353–354, 357, 360–361, 365–366
Stetson, Rebecca Steere, xix–xx, xxn, 7–8, 12–13, 58, 65, 81, 87, 100–101, 111, 113–114, 119, 125, 132, 134–138, 140, 163, 217, 235, 250–251, 253, 261, 272, 274, 282–283, 287, 292, 295, 297, 313, 318, 325, 327, 343, 365–366
Stetson, Susie, 325, 327n
Stevenson, Robert Louis, 342
Stone Picker, 81
Stowe, Harriet Beecher, xxv, 360n
Strauss, Richard, 47
Study of a Page in Red, 230
Sunset in Fog at Baddeck, 101, 101n
Sunset: Motive at Narragansett Pier, 249
Susanna and the Elders, xiv, xxxivn
Swamp of Pocassett, 230
Swedenborg, Emanuel, 69
Swinburne, Algernon Charles, 265n

Symbolist painters, xxxi, xxxii–xxxiii, 47n
Symonds, John Addington, 212, 224

Terminus, The, 328, 328n
Tewksbury, George, 103n, 143n, 264–265,
    267–271, 279, 281n, 283, 285, 292, 301,
    307–308, 314, 319–320, 328, 328n, 350,
    350n, 354n, 356
Tewksbury, Mrs. George, 239n, 283–284,
    292, 297, 320
Thos. Arthur Doyle, Mayor of Providence, 321n
Tiffany, Louis Comfort, 313n
Tiffany-Latage, 104
Tilden, Jr., Henry, 240, 263
Tintoretto, Jacopo Robusti, 226
Titian, Tiziano Vecellio, 193, 193n, 226, 306n
Tonalist painters, xxxi–xxxiii, 47n
Topeka Public Library Gallery of Fine Arts,
    xiv, 284n
Troyan, Constant, xxxii, 236n, 271
Twain, Mark (*A Tramp Abroad*), 48n
Twilight, 101

University of Kansas, xix

Vaughn, Emma, 349
Vedder, Elihu, xxxix, 265n, 305, 305n
Venus Aphrodite, 289, 307–310, 314, 318, 320,
    350, 350n, 356, 356n
Vose Gallery, Providence, 191n

Wagner, Wilhelm, 47
Walker, Dr. Mary, 322–323, 323n

Wall, Beriah, xxiii, xxiiin, 25, 217, 235–236,
    236n, 245, 248–249, 251–255, 260, 269,
    271–272, 285n, 286–287
Wall, George, 235–237, 245, 248, 251–255
Wanamaker, John, 140
Ward, Lydia Avery Coonley, xvii
Water Play, 299n
Waterman, Marcus, 81, 81n, 114, 260
Watts, George F., 273, 273n, 274, 315, 315n
Weeden, William B., xxiii, 7–11, 14, 20, 24,
    178, 243, 245, 247, 255, 260
Wellesley College, 53n, 230, 230n
Wells, Mr., 100
Wheeler, Mary C., 304, 304n, 305
Wheeler Art School, Providence, 304n
Whistler, James MacNeill, xxxi, 254
Whitaker, George, xviin, xxiii–xxiv, 7–8,
    8n, 18, 18n, 25, 47, 70, 79, 80n, 98–99,
    101n, 102, 104, 136, 141, 141n, 143n, 163–
    164, 180, 180n, 196, 205, 205n, 226, 228–
    229, 236n, 254, 262, 263n, 267, 273, 280–
    281, 292, 300, 304, 313, 329, 333
Whitman, Walt, xviii, xxx, 199, 201, 201n,
    202, 343
Wilkes, Mrs., 207
Woman Digging Flagroot, 50n
Women and Economics, xviii
Wright, Frances, 331
Wyant, Alexander, 66, 66n

Yellow Wall-paper, The, xviii, xviiin, xxxvi,
    xli, 289
Yewell, George Henry, 363, 363n

Ziem, Felix, 51